Ethics and Aesthetics of Translation

Literature and Translation

Literature and Translation is a series for books that address literary translation and for books of literary translation. Its emphasis is on diversity of genre, culture, period and approach. The series uses an open access publishing model to disseminate widely developments in the theory and practice of translation, as well as translations into English of literature from around the world.

Series editor: Timothy Mathews is Emeritus Professor of French and Comparative Criticism, UCL.

Ethics and Aesthetics of Translation

Exploring the Work of Atxaga, Kundera and Semprún

Harriet Hulme

UCLPRESS

First published in 2018 by
UCL Press
University College London
Gower Street
London WC1E 6BT

Available to download free: www.ucl.ac.uk/ucl-press

A CIP catalogue record for this book is available from The British Library.

ISBN: 978-1-78735-209-4 (Hbk.)
ISBN: 978-1-78735-208-7 (Pbk.)
ISBN: 978-1-78735-207-0 (PDF)
ISBN: 978-1-78735-210-0 (epub)
ISBN: 978-1-78735-211-7 (mobi)
ISBN: 978-1-78735-212-4 (html)
DOI: https://doi.org/10.14324/111.9781787352070

To my parents, Alice and Brian Hulme

Acknowledgements

This book could not have been written without the encouragement, enthusiasm and inspiration of several people. My thanks firstly to Timothy Mathews, for his assistance in the development of my ideas, his advice during setbacks, and his absolute dedication to helping me extend my critical understanding. His support during this process has been exceptional, and I am incredibly grateful to him for his hard work, his faith in me and his friendship throughout. Lucia Boldrini and Theo Hermans read my work with a rigour which pushed me to sharpen and develop my critical approaches to the question of translation. At UCL, Stephen Hart, Florian Mussgnug, and Jane Fenoulhet provided excellent advice during the early stages of the project. I am grateful to Moira Fradinger for advising me during my semester at Yale.

The first chapter of this book draws on two previously published articles: I am grateful to Clare Finburgh for her excellent editorial advice on my article, 'Creating Anew, Again: Deserted Islands and Textual Inhabitations in Bernardo Atxaga's *Obabakoak*' in *Comparative Critical Studies*, 11.2–3, October 2014; and to Olga Castro, Sergi Mainer and Svetlana Page for editing my chapter 'Self Translating Between Minor and Major Languages: A Hospitable Approach in Bernardo Atxaga's *Obabakoak*' in *Self-Translation and Power: Negotiating Identities in Multilingual European Contexts* (Basingstoke: Palgrave Macmillan, 2017). Many thanks also to Margaret Jull Costa for her help with my research on Bernardo Atxaga.

My friends and family have encouraged my work in numerous ways. I am particularly grateful to Francesca Barrie, Joanne Brueton, Alexandra Hills and Alice Podkolinski for numerous inspirational conversations about literature; and to Hugh Michell for his help and for introducing me to the work of Bernardo Atxaga. To my family – the Hulmes (both sets), the Hugheses and the Hingleys – for their support. Particular thanks to my mother, Alice Hulme, for her unending faith in me, and to my sister, Cressida Hughes, for her constant encouragement and her Spanish expertise.

Finally, to my husband, Jonathan Scrutton, who has shared in this book from start to finish, reading my work, discussing ideas and always helping me keep things in perspective. This book would not have been completed without his unwavering and invaluable support.

Contents

Introduction
Translation: perspectives on language and on life

> You can choose your philosophy of translation just as you choose how to live: the free adaptation that sacrifices detail to meaning, the strict crib that sacrifices meaning to exactitude. The poet moves from life to language, the translator moves from language to life; both, like the immigrant, try to identify the invisible, what's between the lines, the mysterious implications.– Anne Michaels.[1]

In *Fugitive Pieces,* Anne Michaels relates translation to questions of forgetting and remembrance, belonging and exclusion, understanding and confusion. For her protagonist, Jakob, life becomes a matter of translation: having escaped the Nazis as a Jewish child living in Poland, he makes a new life for himself in Greece, and learns to speak Greek and English. This linguistic gain enables him to survive the traumas of his past, but only by erasing his memories of that past: the experience of moving from one language to another, Michaels implies, involves an escape that is also, always, an erasure. In the extract quoted above, Michaels suggests that every moment of translation forces us to choose between freedom and constraint, significance and precision, past and present. These choices apply to the ways in which we interact with texts, but also to the ways in which we interact with the world. Do we live freely but lose our attachment to the past that shaped and formed us? Or do we cling to that attachment, at the expense of giving our life meaning in its present incarnation? In *Fugitive Pieces*, these questions have no easy answers: language and memory intersect, troubling Jakob's attempts to move forward, hindering his efforts to go back. But Michaels also suggests that translation offers us a unique perspective: operating from 'between the lines', translation enables us to explore what is unclear or uncertain, even as it sometimes obscures what we seek to understand, helping us to bridge the very differences which we create as we move across and between languages, cultures, identities, past and present.

As Michaels reveals, translation is about how we approach language, but it is also about how we approach life. When we translate a literary text across linguistic and cultural borders, we negotiate a series of aesthetic questions regarding the interaction of form and content, the location of textual meaning, and the challenge of transmitting that meaning interlingually while preserving the artistic shape of the text. But we also confront a set of ethical questions about our interlinguistic, interpersonal and intercultural relations. As Sandra Bermann suggests, 'the translator's task is inevitably an ethical one. In attempts to translate, we become most aware of linguistic and cultural differences, of the historical "hauntings," and of experiential responsibilities that make our languages what they are and that directly affect our attitudes towards the world.'[2] In the movement it creates between languages and cultures, translation offers us a model through which we can explore the losses and gains involved in all our communications with another. Can we recognize the diversity of our linguistic and cultural perspectives? Or are we trapped in monolingual and monocultural frames of reference, blind and deaf to alterity? Translation also highlights issues of memory and forgetting. When translating, we confront the spectres of the past – the original text, language, author and moment of publication. How should we negotiate those spectres: on their terms, or on our own? Can those two perspectives ever be aligned without annexation or erasure?

Translation helps us think about ethical questions because it foregrounds the appropriations and forgettings we enact even as we attempt to recognize and remember. My conception of the role translation can play in these ethical debates has been formed particularly by the work of Walter Benjamin, Jacques Derrida, Gilles Deleuze and Paul Ricœur. In this book, I draw upon these thinkers to develop a critical vocabulary of translation which explores not only interlingual but also intercultural, interrelational and interdisciplinary issues in the work of three bilingual authors. Bernardo Atxaga writes in both Basque and Spanish; Milan Kundera has written in Czech and French; Jorge Semprún wrote in Spanish and French.[3] Focusing particularly, although not exclusively, on one text by each author, I argue that, in each, translation – integrated into both form and content – works to raise and negotiate ethical questions surrounding some of the major political moments of twentieth-century history. But in each text translation also highlights a broader set of ethical questions, focused upon the limitations of the monolingual and the democratic possibilities of linguistic plurality; upon our innate desire to translate difference into similarity; and upon the ways in which translation responds to the challenges of individual and collective remembrance. Through these texts, I read translation as offering a potent, often violent, but always illuminating, vision of the possibilities of differentiation and connection, generation and memory, in temporal, linguistic, cultural and political terms.

What is a good translation?

Translation is always a dialogue: between two languages – source and target; two people – author and translator; and two different, but connected texts – the 'original' and the 'copy'. This dialogue foregrounds questions which are at the heart of our understanding of textual forms. Where does the meaning of a literary text reside – in its form or in its content? Can these ever be separated and, if not, what is the relation of one to the other? In the shift from the author's words to the translator's interpretation of those words, can textual meaning ever be transmitted intact? And who creates that meaning: the author, writing the original text, or the translator, creating a new text through his or her interpretation? For Italo Calvino, as the title of his 1982 essay 'Tradurre è il vero modo di leggere un testo' attests, translating is the true way to read a text; for Harry Mathews 'Translation is the paradigm, the exemplar of all writing'.[4] In fact, translation operates at the intersection of both reading and writing: the translator negotiates the challenges of interpretation and of creation in two languages. In this regard, translation responds to Roland Barthes's suggestion that we try 'd'abolir (ou tout au moins de diminuer) la distance entre l'écriture et la lecture [...] en les liant tous deux dans une même pratique signifiante'/'to abolish (or at the very least to diminish) the distance between writing and reading [...] by joining them in a single signifying practice'.[5] The translator occupies the space of this signifying practice, interrogating our understanding of writing and reading, the values we assign to originality and imitation, the location of textual authority and the possibility of its disruption.

The questions translation raises about the nature of textual production and interpretation are frequently channelled into a single question focused upon the purpose of translation itself: what type of translation would best respond to the challenges of transferring meaning from one language to another? Attempts to respond to this question have led to the description of translation through a series of binary oppositions: the word-for-word versus sense-for-sense approach, first articulated by Jerome in the fourth century; the split between a beautiful translation and a faithful one, attributed to Nicolas D'Ablancourt's translation process; the 'foreignizing' and 'domesticating' options proposed by Friedrich Schleiermacher; the 'visibility' versus 'invisibility' binary discussed by Lawrence Venuti.[6] These dichotomies highlight the challenges involved in translation: the need for a translated text to remain faithful both to the meaning and the aesthetic shape of an original; the importance of negotiating the claims of both source and target culture; and the difficulties of managing the hierarchical relations between original and copy, author and translator. Ultimately, however, each binary is a variation on a single question: what is a good translation? This question is one of both aesthetics *and* ethics. What type of translation can transmit meaning without distortion? And how can it do so without inflicting forms of violent appropriation or erasure upon texts, authors, languages, cultures, and the status of translation itself?

But how do the aesthetic questions raised by translation help us think ethically? Plato claims that artistic forms cannot help us understand the essence of morality or the absolute Truth of our experiences. Art is a 'false' discipline, a weak form of representation, 'at third remove from the throne of truth', which absorbs its audience into a fantasy world.[7] In *Phaedrus*, Socrates opposes writing to 'the living word of knowledge': words, once written down, can be distorted from their original meaning, opened to multiple interpretations which the author can no longer defend or correct.[8] Socrates elucidates this division of writing from knowledge through the story of the Egyptian god of writing, Theuth (Thoth). Theuth tells King Thamus that writing is a *pharmakon*, a remedy to prevent forgetting. But Socrates notes that *pharmakon* also translates as poison: writing, he posits, is thus not a remedy but a drug which allows forgetfulness by preventing the author and reader from striving to remember on their own. Translation, which is not only a copy of reality, a written inscription of lived knowledge, but a copy of that artistic inscription, would be at yet another remove from the understanding Socrates seeks. When we translate, we remove a text even further from the guidance of its author, inevitably distorting the knowledge that text originally contained. In Platonic terms, then, translation itself would be a *pharmakon*: a forgetting of a forgetting, an imitation of an imitation of reality, which separates us from the Truth.

And yet it is translation which Derrida deploys to interrogate, and ultimately destabilize, this Platonic critique of writing. In 'La Pharmacie de Platon', translation operates as revelation, challenging and unpicking what is masked within Plato's use of the word *pharmakon*: the accepted polysemy which enables this single word to be translated multiply – as 'remedy' and 'poison', 'recipe' and 'drug'. As Derrida demonstrates,

Plato relies on the polysemy within *pharmakon* to explain the damaging nature of writing. Writing, originally described by Theuth as a remedy, is revealed by Socrates's alternative translation of the term to be a drug. And yet this revelation collapses precisely because of this translation. By translating the word *pharmakon* only as 'drug' and not also as 'remedy', Socrates erases the innate polysemy of the word, ignoring the very contradiction within the meaning of *pharmakon* which initially enabled him to reverse Theuth's formulation and dispute the remedial powers of writing. In so doing, Socrates translates 'a nonphilosopheme', a word with multiple meanings, into 'a philosopheme', a philosophical formulation or principle which, in order to establish the Truth of an action or a concept, can only have one true meaning. For Derrida,

> [l]'unité plastique de ce concept, sa règle plutôt et l'étrange logique qui le lie à son signifiant, ont été dispersées, masquées, oblitérées, frappées d'une relative illisibilité [...] par la redoutable et irréductible difficulté de la traduction [...] d'un non-philosophème dans un philosophème. Avec ce problème de traduction nous n'aurons affaire à rien de moins qu'au problème du passage à la philosophie.
>
> The malleable unity of this concept, or rather its rules and the strange logic that links it with its signifier, has been dispersed, masked, obliterated, and rendered almost unreadable [...] by the redoubtable, irreducible difficulty of translation [...] of a nonphilosopheme into a philosopheme. With this problem of translation we will thus be dealing with nothing less than the problem of the very passage into philosophy.[9]

This 'passage into philosophy' is exposed, troubled and undermined by translation. For even when employed as a philosopheme, *pharmakon* still retains its dual meaning as remedy *and* drug. Plato's repression of this duality, his prioritization of one meaning over another, allows him to explain definitively the Truth of writing. But the definitive nature of this Truth is destabilized by the continued instability of the language he uses for that explanation. Through translation, Derrida thus addresses the impossibility of succeeding in an attempt to uncover a solid structure *outside* language through an enquiry which, inevitably, is pursued *through* language. As Kathleen Davis suggests, translation is central to Derrida's enterprise because it elucidates his concept of *différance*: the temporal and semantic deferrals and differences which occur every time we use language.[10] In every moment of translation, we negotiate the slipperiness of meaning, attempt to stabilize it, and find it again eluding our grasp. Derrida employs translation as exploration, as a violent and explosive force of insight into the nature of textual relations, but also into the centrality of these textual relations to our lived knowledge and our philosophical attempts to formulate that knowledge.

Derrida highlights the ways in which translation can offer us an insight into reality precisely *through* and not *despite* its textual distance from the reality being described. Similarly, in *Alberto Giacometti: The Art of Relation*, Timothy Mathews suggests that the copying of reality which takes place in artistic forms offers us a unique opportunity to recognize our perceptions of that reality: 'Lived reality is full, to copy it is to understand our capacity for exploration and self-exploration, vitality and humanity: for what can be copied other than the ability to see our own seeing and to account for it?'[11] Translation – a copy of a copy, a reproduction of an aesthetic form – illuminates our perceptions of our experiences. In translating from life to text, and then from one version of that text to another, channelled through the perspective and language of another, what do we see that we did not see before? As Adorno and Horkheimer suggest in *Dialectic of Enlightenment*, forms of copying and mimesis are always concerned with the relation between sameness and otherness: how this relation is developed and understood depends on the regulation of the mimetic action.[12] So too, translation is always implicated in questions of relation – between one text and language and another, but also between individuals, nations, and belief systems. In this sense, the illuminations offered by translation confront but also go further than an analysis of the ethical implications of translating novels. They touch upon the broader relationship between content and form, between ethics and aesthetics, between politics and literature. They are bound up with the violent nature of translation itself, a violence which contains the potential to alchemize the textual worlds which translation touches, and, through this alchemy, to shed light on the forms of our lived experience.

The ethical turn in translation

Translation is never a neutral activity: forms of linguistic, textual and cultural violence are an inevitable effect of the movement between languages, texts and sites of authorship. As Bassnett and Lefevere suggest, translation is a process of rewriting, and rewriting 'is manipulation undertaken in the service of power [which] in its positive aspect can help in the evolution of a literature and a society. [...] But rewriting can also repress innovation, distort and contain'.[13] While Bassnett and Lefevere see translation as simultaneously generative and reductive, Lawrence Venuti suggests that, conventionally, translation operates to bolster dominant discourses: 'Violence [...] resides in the very purpose and activity of translation: the reconstitution of the foreign text in accordance with values, beliefs and representations that pre-exist it in the target language, always configured in hierarchies of dominance and marginality, always determining the production, circulation, and reception of texts'.[14] For Venuti, this textual violence arises because translation is an activity which normalizes the alterations it effects, transforming a text without acknowledging the assumptions underpinning that transformation.

For Barbara Godard, responses to this violence are at the heart of an 'ethical turn' in translation, initiated by Antoine Berman in his 1984 text *L'Épreuve de l'étranger*, and pursued by Venuti in texts such as *The Scandals of Translation: Towards an Ethics of Difference*. This ethical turn hinges upon perceiving the oscillating, and often aggressive, dynamic between self and other, foreign and domestic, which occurs in translation. Godard explains:

> Cette logique des relations où le propre est fécondé par la médiation de l'autre se heurte à des résistances profondes dans la structure ethnocentrique de toute culture qui cherche à conserver son autosuffisance dans un retour au même. La traduction occupe alors une place ambiguë, à la fois ouverture et appropriation violente.
>
> This logic of relation, where the self is fertilized by the mediation of the other, collides with the profound resistance within the ethnocentric structure of every culture, which seeks to conserve its self-sufficiency through a return to the same. Translation thus occupies an ambiguous place, at once an opening and a violent appropriation.[15]

Situated between connection and annexation, translation reveals our engagement with alterity to be one of simultaneous expansion and annexation.

In responding to this oscillation, both Berman and Venuti draw upon Friedrich Schleiermacher's dichotomy of translation, which posits that a translation must either shift an author towards the reader or the reader towards the author, either foreignize a text or domesticate it.[16]

Berman suggests that the ethical potential of translation resides in foreignization: translations must 'féconder le Propre par la médiation de l'Étranger'/'fertilize what is one's Own through the mediation of what is Foreign' – essentially, transform and expand the domestic language through its interaction with the foreign one. This foreignization is ethical because it confronts 'la structure ethnocentrique de toute culture, ou cette espèce de narcissisme qui fait que toute société voudrait être un Tout pur et non mélangé'/'the ethnocentric structure of every culture, that species of narcissism by which every society wants to be a pure and unadulterated Whole'.[17] For Godard, however, Berman's articulation of the ethics of translation is limited by his focus upon 'le Propre' at the expense of 'l'Étranger': he recognizes the 'test' of the foreign enacted by translation, but reads the value of this test primarily in relation to the changes the foreign can create within the domestic.

In her exploration of the ethical turn of translation, Godard moves from Berman to Venuti, suggesting that Venuti converts Berman's 'test of the foreign' into a call for an ethics of translation situated in a recognition of the foreign on its own terms.[18] Venuti splits the violence of translation into oppositional terms: ethnocentric and ethical; domesticating and foreignizing; fluent and resistant; invisible and visible. Invisible translators domesticate the cultural and linguistic differences of the source text in order to create a fluent translation that attempts to repress the fact that the text has been translated at all.[19] To combat this invisible violence, Venuti proposes that translators make themselves visible through a process of resistant 'foreignization', rendering the linguistic and cultural differences between source and target text apparent in order 'to force translators and their readers to reflect on the ethnocentric violence of translation'.[20] In so doing, translation offers an ethical response to its own inherent violence.

As Godard suggests, the dichotomies Venuti offers provide useful entry points to discuss the ways in which we can engage ethically with the cultural and linguistic violence of translation.[21] But Venuti's argument also elides some of the nuances I read as integral to understanding the ethical vision which translation can offer us. Venuti's acknowledgement that violence 'resides in the very activity of translation' is undermined by his attempt to suggest that, if it is made visible, this violence can be tamed, whether by theorist or practitioner. For the violence of translation is not one which can be employed at will, either in the service of hegemonic or excluded discourses: rather, as Derrida reveals in 'La Pharmacie de Platon', it is a violence inherent within language and within texts, which translation reveals rather than counters. Moreover, Venuti's call for an ethics of foreignization involves a question integral to translation: can we ever recognize the foreign, other than on our own terms? By categorizing the violence of translation through the binaries of visibility/invisibility, domestic/foreign and fluent/resistant, Venuti creates an either/or approach which fails to account for the reality of translation: the complex and shifting negotiations it enacts between foreign and domestic, self and other, author and translator.

The narratives of two fictional translator figures, who initially appear to epitomize Venuti's binaries, reveal the ethical insights which are released when we shift from reading translation as an *either/or* to reading it as a *between*. Jake, the translator-protagonist in Iris Murdoch's *Under the Net* (1954), is the epitome of an invisible translator, a disenfranchized, disengaged 'hack-writer', defined by his reliance upon the words of others, both literally and figuratively, in order to survive: 'I am a parasite', he says, 'I just enjoy translating, it's like opening one's mouth and hearing someone else's voice come out'.[22] Jake's desire for invisibility leads him from translating texts to translating those around him. He engages in aggressive appropriations of their words, ideologies and experiences, seeking within their existence his sense of self, and failing to realize he has distorted their words in the process. Ermes Marana, the translator-protagonist of Italo Calvino's *If on a Winter's Night a Traveller* (1979) is, by contrast, a highly visible translator, 'a serpent who injects his malice into the paradise of reading' and who ensures his textual visibility by creating textual confusion.[23] In so doing, Marana makes the losses in the translation process only too apparent to the protagonist of the text, known only as the Reader, who finds that Marana's textual manipulations prevent him finishing any of the ten novels he begins: once touched by the 'interfering swindler', each novel terminates unexpectedly after its opening chapter.[24]

Jake and Marana reveal opposing approaches to translation: an invisible approach, which sees the translator fail to acknowledge the distortions of translation; and a visible approach, through which the translator profits from these distortions, rendering the Reader only too aware that he is reading a translation. And yet, as both texts progress, this opposition collapses, for each translator ultimately comes to offer a powerful insight into the nature of our textual and interpersonal relations. Marana's textual machinations reveal the impact translation can have upon textual creativity. Believing the translator's increasing invisibility will enable 'the spell of interrupted readings [to be] broken', the Reader-protagonist visits the library to request each of the ten novels he has begun. But for a variety of reasons, each one is unavailable.[25] As the Reader waits, he describes the books he has lost to another reader who, hearing their titles, constructs from them a new text:

> "May I see?" the sixth reader asks, taking the list of titles. [...] "*If on a winter's night a traveler, outside the town of Malbork, leaning from a steep slope without fear of wind or vertigo, looks down in the gathering shadow in a network of lines that enlace, in a network of lines that intersect, on the carpet of leaves illuminated by the moon around an empty grave – What story down there awaits its end? – he asks, anxious to hear the story.*" He pushes his eyeglasses up on his brow. "Yes, a novel that begins like that [...] I could swear I've read it..." [...]. "But, look here, there's a misunderstanding," you try to warn him. "This isn't a book...these are only titles [...] this isn't the story whose continuation I want to know....".[26]

Through Marana's actions, a text originating in translated fragments offers the possibility of another textual beginning, beyond the remit of the author. The 'serpent' in the 'paradise of reading' is, like the serpent in the garden of Eden, one who brings knowledge and change, as well as confusion, initiating a textual growth born from the fragmentary relation between the texts he touches.

In *Under the Net*, Jake's actions as a translator ultimately offer him an insight into the nature of interpersonal understanding. As the novel progresses, Jake begins to realize the distortions he has enacted as he translates the words of others into his language, their ideologies into his philosophy of life. Jake resolves to speak for himself. But he also comes to realize that translation is at the heart of all human interaction. A desire to translate the words, thoughts and beliefs of another into our own words, thoughts and beliefs is inevitable. And to do this without distortion is impossible. In that failure, however, lies the vision of translation, its ability to make us reflect upon the annexations we enact within all our relationships. At the end of the text Jake asks:

> When does one ever know a human being? Perhaps only after one has realized the impossibility of knowledge and renounced the desire for it and finally ceased to feel even the need of it. But then what one achieves is no longer knowledge, it is simply a kind of co-existence; and this too is one of the guises of love.[27]

Jake, the parasitic translator, thus moves from an understanding based upon appropriation to one based upon an understanding *of* that appropriation; a gesture of love towards difference which recognizes the desire to annex that difference: the type of understanding we might assign to translation itself.

Both *If on a Winter's Night a Traveller* and *Under the Net* reveal the insights that are available if we move away from locating an ethics of translation on one side of a binary divide. As Anthony Pym suggests, to read translation through dichotomies such as those used by Venuti is to 'silence the middle term of translation': the reality of translation as experienced by those who attempt to translate.[28] This reality is interstitial. As a process of crossing and transfer, translation must always negotiate the between: *between* languages, *between* voices, *between* individuals, *between* form and content. As Susan Bassnett discusses, translation is a 'threshold', a liminal space 'filled with mysterious power'.[29] Engaging with translation means inhabiting this threshold, exploring the liminal spaces *between* binary poles, rather than selecting one over another.

Translation: between the binaries

My understanding of translation in this book is indebted to a set of texts which themselves approach translation from between the elements in binary oppositions. In each, translation is revealed to be a propagative and connective action, as well as a disruptive one. In 'The Task of the Translator' (1923), Benjamin reads translation as a generative act, capable of challenging the chronicity of historical momentum. In 'Des tours de Babel' (1985) and 'Qu'est-ce qu'une traduction "relevante"?' (1998), Derrida draws upon Benjamin's thinking to emphasize the ways in which translation highlights our debt to the memory and body of the original text. In texts such as 'Causes et raisons des îles désertes' (1953) and *Mille plateaux* (1980), Deleuze develops a cartography of repetition with difference that, read tangentially, reveals ways in which translation can interrogate the linguistic, cultural, political and literary territories which impact upon us. And in *Sur la traduction* (2004), Ricœur suggests that translation allows us to think through forms of linguistic, cultural and social untranslatability and hospitality. In the work of each of these theorists, the binaries of translation are subjected to an interrogation. Defining a translation as good or bad, relevant or irrelevant; a text as translatable or untranslatable; a translation method as faithful or unfaithful; a language as major or minor, is, as Benjamin, Derrida, Ricœur and Deleuze emphasize repeatedly and diversely, never the end of a discussion of translation, but only its beginning.

More recent work in Translation Studies has continued to illuminate this space between the binaries, in linguistic but also historical, cultural and political terms. In her seminal text, 'The Politics of Translation' (1993), Gayatri Chakravorty Spivak explores the ways in which translation engages in forms of interpersonal 'fraying'. She suggests that translation allows us to imagine alterity even as we inevitably appropriate it into our own perspective.[30] In *The Location of Culture* (1994) Homi Bhabha offers his conception of 'cultural translation', arguing that cultural meaning is located, not in oppositional terms, but in the 'inter': 'For it is by living on the borderline of history and language, on the limits of race and gender, that we are in a position to translate the differences between them into a kind of solidarity', he suggests.[31] And in *The Translation Zone* (2006), Emily Apter argues that translation confronts the stability of our collective and individual identities, forcing us to confront, and transgress, the boundaries through which we constitute our sense of self. Texts such as these develop translation as a powerful and productive model with which to approach the critical questions of affective experience and of our relations one to another, to the communities we inhabit and the communications we attempt across those borders. This book follows their approach in engaging with translation as a paradigm for these interactions, on an interlinguistic but also an intercultural and interpersonal level.

Blendlinge and bilingualism: the liminal identities of Atxaga, Kundera and Semprún

In his 2012 book *On Translator Ethics*, Anthony Pym creates his own challenge to the binary oppositions which have conditioned discussions of an ethics of translation, from Schleiermacher to Berman to Venuti. Pym is interested in Schleiermacher's use of the term *Blendlinge* to describe the results of a foreignizing method of translation: Pym unpicks the etymology of the term, variously translated as 'bastards' (Lefevere), '*sang-mêlé*'/'mixed-bloods' (Berman) and '*half-breeds*' by Pym himself.[32] In Pym's reading, the singular form of *Blendlinge*, *Blendling*, connotes something or someone exotic but also false, perhaps, or shifty; exciting but inherently unnatural – the epitome of a translator-figure such as Ermes Marana, perhaps. In fact, Schleiermacher associates the term not with the figure of the translator, but with language itself, a language which has been forced to contort itself into unnatural forms to follow the phrasing and rhythm of a foreign source text as closely as possible. For Schleiermacher, this contortion is troubling, even dangerous, but it is also necessary as a means for the German language to grow, adapt and strengthen itself.

Yet for Pym, this connection of *Blendling* with a linguistic rather than an ontological state – with translation rather than the translator – undermines Schleiermacher's approach to translation, for it reveals Schleiermacher's failure to engage with the inevitable interculturality of the translator's identity. In fact, Schleiermacher rejects the possibility of *Blendlinge* as subjects: as Hokenson and Munson note, he suggests that bilingual identity is 'a flat impossibility', 'in defiance of nature and morality'.[33] In Schleiermacher's reading, the translator, necessarily able to understand both languages in question, remains unaltered by the transformative process of translation, always identifying only with the language and culture into which s/he translates: 'One must be loyal to *one* language or another, as to *one* nation'.[34] As Pym notes, Schleiermacher's emphasis upon the *one* – unsurprising, given the rhetoric of nineteenth-century nation-building within his text – links language and nation in essentializing and totalizing ways, positioning translation as a means of separation rather than connection: if you are *this*, it says, you cannot be *that*; if you are with *them*, then you cannot be with *us*.

What happens then, Pym asks, if you reject such essentialism? If you feel your identity to be dual, triple, plural? If you live not in one language but in two, three, four? For Schleiermacher, you are cursed to remain in the 'un-lovely in-between': at home in neither language; homeless in both.[35] This condemnation of the -inter reflects an understanding of the liminal space as threatening to the status quo: anyone who cannot be placed on one side or the other of a border – national, social, cultural, linguistic, political, literary – becomes unknowable and potentially dangerous. Yet the liminal – in anthropological terms – has also been associated with forms of insight and understanding which are not available in more conventional identities. Existing outside the laws and structures of social convention, the liminal individual within a ritual experience is not beholden either to what has come before – the pre-liminal – or to what will come later – the post-liminal. Rather s/he exists – temporarily at least – in a spatial and temporal moment which, precisely because it is between two states, can shed light on both.[36] Pym's reading of the *Blendlinge* positions multilingual individuals as similarly liminal, caught between linguistic and national identities, and, as such, able to illuminate the shape of this intercultural space. This space, like the liminal in ritual, is always temporary: anybody who operates between linguistic identities is always in motion between these – sometimes pulled in one direction by the claims of one tongue, sometimes pushed in another direction by the demands of the other tongue. But this push–pull makes the intercultural space one of continual and productive questioning about the status and stasis of the linguistic, national, political and cultural identities which surround it. For Pym, the existence of the *Blendlinge* opens onto an ethics of mediation, communication, and negotiation, 'issuing from a mix of cultures [...] roaming along the borders, traveling between the territorial powers'.[37] From this borderland, the *Blendlinge* are uniquely placed to understand translation, not as an *either/or*, but as a *between*, an endlessly liminal activity which they inhabit, shift and explore through their own experience.

It is the ethics contained within and revealed by this *between* that I approach in this book through the work of Bernardo Atxaga, Milan Kundera and Jorge Semprún. Why these authors in particular? The bilingualism of these three European authors reflects the violence of the twentieth century: their biographies and bibliographies are marked by the impact of Fascism and of Communism; by wars which have raged around national and linguistic borders; by tyranny and totalitarianism, exile and domination. Their texts approach these experiences in varying ways, but always with a concern for the role which aesthetic forms, and particularly narrative, can play in the exploration of socio-political questions. Their bilingual identities are implicated in this investigation of the relationship between the aesthetic and the political: in the work of all three authors, the possibility or impossibility of translation emerges as a way to explore the power of the *between* – understood in linguistic, political, cultural and national terms –, an exploration which positions identities which are liminal or in flux as potentially democratic and pluralist alternatives to the authoritarian and essentializing systems which all three authors critique in their texts.

On one level, then, the work of these three authors can be explored in relation to an aesthetics of the twentieth-century European bilingual novelist. Like the works of Michel de Castillo or Ágota Kristóf, their texts reflect the traumas of the post-war experience, deploying a multilingual aesthetics to shape their exploration of these traumas. And as with Eva Hoffman and Vassilis Alexakis, this approach becomes part of a broader focus upon the connection between language and identity. Yet, as Pym suggests in *On Translator Ethics*, attempts to universalize the experiences of those who work between languages elide the inevitable differences within those experiences. We must, he posits, always ask 'Why translate?', and acknowledge that the answer to this question will be situational rather than general.[38] In the same way, we must acknowledge that the ways in which bilingual authors experience the relationship between their two languages is always governed by the particular vibrations – economic, political, social and cultural – which surround those languages. To uncover these vibrations we need to ask 'Why translate?', as Pym suggests, but also a series of other linked questions: 'Why do you *not* translate?'; 'Why write in this language rather than the other?'; 'Why write in two languages rather than one?; 'Why write in one language rather than two?'

For Atxaga, Kundera and Semprún, responses to these questions have fluctuated across their careers, from one text to another, and between their fictional work and their discussions of these fictions in interviews and essays. The diversity of these responses, a diversity which emerges in relation to each author but also in their relations to one another, opens onto a complex territory of bilingualism, in which loss and gain, creativity and stultification, repression and liberation, the claims of the individual and those of the community, are repeatedly brought into focus. It is this territory which I map in their work, for these differences *within* a certain similarity have opened challenging and productive angles into my consideration of the ethical questions raised by and through translation. The impact of translation upon the work of these three authors – visible in the production, reception, content and form of their texts – has allowed me to take a multidimensional approach to understanding translation within their work, one which combines an understanding of translation as linguistic transfer with an approach which reads translation as a paradigm to express the experience of cultural appropriation, historical trauma and interpersonal relations.

While the work of these three authors can be read in two major European languages and situated within two major European literary systems – French and Spanish – their experiences as bilinguals open onto a diversity of linguistic, literary and political frameworks. Atxaga is a contemporary Basque author who first writes his texts in Basque before translating them into Castilian, either alone or in collaboration. Franco's repression of the Basque language and culture between 1936 and 1975 forced Atxaga to contend with questions about the role language and literature could play in relation to political calls for a Basque nation state. Basque is now a co-official language within the Basque Country in Spain, but the criticism Atxaga has received following his decision to self-translate his texts into Castilian reveals the asymmetrical power relations which continue to exist between the two languages. Milan Kundera began his career writing in Czech. When he was exiled from the Soviet-controlled Czechoslovakia in 1975 for the perceived dissidence of his texts, he began to publish in French translation, although he did not translate his texts himself. Kundera has sought to evade political readings of his texts, and believes that these early translations deliberately altered the form of his texts to emphasize their political, rather than novelistic, aspects: he subsequently authorized certain translations of his texts. Kundera now only writes in French. Jorge Semprún was born in Spain, but wrote the majority of his texts in his second language, French. His bilingualism reflects the series of political traumas which separated him from Spain: his family's move to France during the Spanish Civil War, his work for the French resistance and subsequent capture by the Gestapo, and his incarceration in Buchenwald concentration camp.

The experiences of each author reveal both the complexity of the bilingual experience and the complexity of European identity. Bilingualism can originate through forms of violence such as colonization and war. It can be created through exile and displacement, as in the movements of refugees, immigrants and the growth of diasporas. But it can also arise because of education and opportunity. It can occur as a form of resistance or collaboration, a choice or an imposition, a symbol of freedom or restriction. The disparity of experience revealed by Atxaga, Kundera and Semprún also troubles a generic understanding of European identity. All three authors invoke a sometimes-utopian conception of a multilingual Europe in their work, associating linguistic diversity with forms of resistance, whether implicit or explicit, to the challenges of nationalism and totalitarianism which they confront in their texts. On one level, this plurality is a reality: as bilinguals, all three authors reveal 'another' Europe, one traversed by the vibrations of more minor languages such as Basque and Czech, and by challenges to singular or stable national identities. Yet, as their texts reveal, this plurality is also subject to potential repression and violence: the borders of nation and language do not necessarily collapse when faced with transnational realities; sometimes they solidify by reifying, oppressing, or expelling difference. This tension between these two visions of Europe – heterogeneous and homogeneous; democratic and totalitarian; peaceful and violent; utopian and tyrannical – emerges within the texts of Atxaga, Kundera and Semprún, often in relation to questions of translation. Their work thus offers a challenging engagement with issues of European linguistic and national identity which remain as relevant now, in the twenty-first century, as they were when Atxaga, Kundera and Semprún began to write.

Writing and translating from the 'between'

The relative diversity within their identities as bilingual authors is replicated in the range of ways in which Atxaga, Kundera and Semprún respond to or reflect upon these identities in their writing. Hokenson and Munson describe the bilingual text as 'a self-translation, authored by a writer who can compose in different languages and who translates his or her texts from one language into another'.[39] This definition would ostensibly include Atxaga's novels, which appear in both Basque and Castilian, although his decision to move towards collaborative translations reframes his more recent texts as problematic examples of self-translations. But it would exclude Milan Kundera's work: both the Czech texts which appeared first in French translation, 'authorized' but not 'authored' by Kundera; and his more recent texts written in French. It would also exclude almost all of Jorge Semprún's texts, for while he composed texts in both his literary languages, he only self-translated one of these from French into Spanish.

The bilingual text, understood as the type of self-translation or parallel text described by Hokenson and Munson, offers one way in which a bilingual or multilingual author might choose to produce her or his texts. But texts produced by those who conceive of their identity as shared between different nations and languages can take myriad forms. There are authors who blend both languages within one text – Semprún, for example, or Chinese-English author Xiaolu Guo, whose novel *A Concise Chinese-english Dictionary for Lovers* mirrors its protagonist's attempts to learn English with a style built from misunderstood English words, Chinese characters and pinyin. There are those who are not fluent in another language, but whose work is nonetheless permeated with another linguistic identity (here one may think of Anita Desai's incorporation of German, Hindi and Urdu into her texts, or Atxaga's use of English words and phrases in *Obabakoak*). There are writers who begin their literary careers in one language and then later shift entirely to another. Kundera falls into this category, as does Nancy Huston, who began her career writing in her second language, French, before moving to English – her mother tongue – in later works. And there are authors, such as Joseph Conrad, or Tahar Ben Jelloun, who have always chosen to write in just one of their languages; or who, like Semprún, choose their language depending on the subject matter of the text in question.

None of these decisions renders a writer any less bilingual. But the decision as a bilingual to write a text in just one language – whether first or second – rather than in both, shifts that text from a linguistic *between* to a linguistic *either/or*. This *either/or* can enable critics to move away from intercultural and interlinguistic readings of writers of the 'in-between' towards a more monolingual approach. Kundera can be read as either a French author or a Czech one, depending upon which texts a critic chooses to consider, while the differences in subject matter and style between the texts produced in each language make it relatively easy to consider them as separate bodies of work. So too, Semprún's work can be categorized by a connection between language choice and subject matter that allows his French texts – which generally focus upon his experiences in Buchenwald – and his Spanish texts –which tend to explore his time as a member of the Spanish Communist Party – to be considered separately. In Atxaga's case, his decision to self-translate or to collaborate on the translations of his texts from Basque into Castilian does emphasize the liminality of his authorial identity. Yet the relatively small size of his Basque readership means that his Castilian self-translations often stand in for the Basque texts in an international literary market, thereby subtly erasing the duality of Atxaga's identity.

Reading Atxaga, Kundera and Semprún in translation

The potential for each of these bilingual authors to be situated within one linguistic and literary identity as opposed to two reveals the *between* they inhabit to be conditioned by the ways in which they are *read*, as much as by the ways in which they *write*. What does it mean, for example, to read Atxaga in Castilian rather than in Basque? Is such a reading an assimilation of Atxaga into a hegemonic discourse at the expense of a minor language? Or should both his texts be considered of equal value, each being a legitimate object of study? Are the authorized French translations of Kundera's texts more valid than unauthorized French, or indeed English, translations of his work? Or is the fact that Kundera now writes in French enough for all these translations to be accepted as part of his French œuvre? Should we consider Semprún a Spanish author who writes in French, or a French author who sometimes writes in Spanish? Given his dual literary and linguistic identity, are Spanish translations of Semprún's French texts part of his œuvre, despite the fact that he has had no input into them?

Questions such as these have arisen repeatedly as I have written this book, challenging me to justify my reading choices, my assumptions about language and authorship, and my understanding of the relationship between translation and originality. My experience of reading these authors has led to an awareness of the need for a continual and continuous negotiation with the question of why, how and under what circumstances we can, should and do read in translation. For this reason, I have focused predominantly upon the bilingual identity of these authors as it emerges within texts written in their second language. This focus has led me to those texts within their œuvre which I read as particularly liminal: either because of the ways they situate or reveal the relationship between the languages used by each author; or because of their destabilization or affirmation of an opposition between an original text and a translated one. Atxaga's *Obabakoak* was first published in Basque in 1988, but was republished in a Castilian translation created by Atxaga in 1989, with significant alterations. Kundera wrote *Le Livre du rire et de l'oubli* (henceforth *Le Livre*) in Czech in 1978; however, it was not published until its French translation by François Kérel in 1979. In 1985, Kundera revised the French text and offered a new authorized French version. *Quel beau dimanche!* was written in French in 1980, but it is also – as the narrator continually suggests – a rewriting of Semprún's first text, *Le Grand Voyage*, written in 1967. Semprún's 1994 text *L'Écriture ou la vie* offers another rewriting of several of the incidents which appear in *Quel beau dimanche!*, positioning this text on a spectrum between originality and repetition which exceeds interlingual questions.

Each of the texts upon which I focus in the chapters that follow is thus a rewriting, subject to a repetition between languages, between the voice of the author and the voice of a translator, and between different temporal and cultural locations. These texts are all positioned as unfinished projects, to be revisited in ways which integrate the ethical and aesthetic possibilities of translation into the ethical and aesthetic possibilities of the novel form. Individually, each text raises questions about the relationship of literary language to authorial identity; about the role of translation in disseminating the work of a bilingual author; and about the challenges of responding to such translations as an author who can work between source and target language. Brought together within this book, these questions also shed light on the often hierarchical relationship which exists between originality and repetition, and between author and translator. For these three texts are conditioned by their relative proximity to or distance from their author: Semprún's original text, Atxaga's self-translation and Kundera's authorized translation all appear to be positioned on a vertical axis descending from originality to replication. In fact, though, these three texts highlight, challenge, and sometimes upend the separation of original writing and translation, drawing our attention to the assumptions and reifications of authorial identity which lie behind our attempts to define a text as authentic or inauthentic, an original or a copy.

Yet despite the ways in which they problematize the relationship between a translation and an original text, all three books remain conditioned by their relation to their author, and are legitimized by the assumption of authorial control contained within the terms 'original', 'self' or 'authorized'. For this reason, I have also explored the English translations of the texts I discuss. In exploring these translations and including them as parallel quotations within the pages of this book, new issues emerged, both about the impact and role of translation within the work of Atxaga, Kundera and Semprún, and about the nature of translation itself. Margaret Jull Costa's 1992 English translation of *Obabakoak*, for example, contains additions to the Castilian text which is its model, raising questions about how and why a translation might be modified to connect with a new readership beyond those who can read in Atxaga's two languages. Kundera's decision to authorize Aaron Asher's 1996 English translation of *Le Livre* based upon Kerél's French translation, as opposed to Michael Henry Heim's 1980 English translation based upon Kundera's Czech text, gives added authority to the French version of *Le Livre*, and emphasizes Kundera's dominance over all his translations. And A. Sheridan's 1982 English translation of Semprún's *Quel beau dimanche!* was astounding for the sheer quantity of text which was not transmitted from the French book into the English one.

On occasion, then, and particularly in relation to Sheridan's text, I found myself modifying or adding to these translations according to errors or elisions I perceived within them. I have commented upon these modifications within this book, as and when they arise. But my decision to do so raises its own set of questions about reading in translation. To be able to modify a translation requires one to be able to read a text in both its original version and its existing translation: to be, to a greater or lesser extent, somewhere on the bilingual spectrum oneself. Bilingual readings of translated texts offer their own illuminations, revealing erasures, absences, mistranslations and additions between an original and a translation. But these bilingual readings also erase a key purpose of translation: if we were to answer Pym's question 'why translate?' as a reader rather than a translator, the response would probably be: 'because it is only through translation that I can gain access to this text'. In this regard, I have found myself continually confronting the losses and gains inherent within the experience of reading in translation. As a reader who does not understand Basque or Czech, I am indebted to the forms of cross-linguistic and cross-cultural connectivity which (self-)translation from these languages into Spanish and French respectively enables; at the same time, as a reader able to explore the English translations of these French and Spanish texts, I am only too aware of the ways in which that connectivity always entails a potential appropriation and/or erasure of the text it seeks to transmit interlingually.

This loss and gain inevitably raises the question of whether one should read and criticize a text in translation at all. Stanley Corngold asserts that '[d]oing comparative literature means studying works written in different languages without the benefit of translation. It means not needing to translate, on the claimed strength of being able to translate'.[40] Corngold's focus upon reading in an original language emphasizes the link between language and meaning, delegitimizing critical readings which take place in translation. Yet, whether we acknowledge it or not, some of what we do as comparatists does take place in translation, whether that be as a non-Russian speaker referencing the work of Bakhtin in English, or as a non-Japanese reader beginning a monograph with a translated quotation by Murakami. For none of us can read every text in its original language: we are all, to some extent, reading in translation if we wish to read beyond the borders of our linguistic abilities. If we refuse to do so, we risk shutting ourselves away, not necessarily in a monocultural world, but in one made narrower by the absence of translation: as George Steiner comments, 'Without translation we would inhabit parishes bordering on silence'.[41]

The alternative view, then, posits that reading in translation – the basis of World Literature – is essential if we are to avoid constructing canons which focus predominantly upon texts written in major languages. Yet, as Emily Apter suggests in *Against World Literature*, this approach often operates according to a 'translatability assumption' in which critics 'zoom over the speed bumps of untranslatability', creating a globalized canon in English which erases as much as it illuminates the diversity of global textual production'.[42] To conceive of reading in translation as a good thing in and of itself risks creating a homogenized literary culture which fails to recognize the value of learning languages other than our own. As Pym comments succinctly, 'Translations are for the person who stays home. Or are they *so that* the person stays home?'[43]

Reading in translation, then, like the process of translation itself, operates between domestic and foreign: between the desire, on the one hand, to read any text and attempt understanding beyond the limits of our linguistic abilities; and, on the other, to acknowledge the irreducibility of linguistic and cultural difference to homogeneous terms by approaching a text in its original language. These seemingly irreconcilable desires speak to the tension between the global and the local, but also between the translatable and the untranslatable. If we argue that all texts can be read in translation, we suggest, implicitly or explicitly, that meaning can be transmitted across linguistic borders – the translatability assumption. But if we refuse to read in translation, we insist that a text is so altered by translation as to render criticism of it in anything other than the original language illegitimate – the untranslatability assertion.

In fact, both these options – as opposed as they seem – delegitimize the partial, the incomplete and the between. By insisting either that the meaning of a text can be transferred perfectly into another language, or that, because the meaning and the language are so closely connected, reading in a language other than the original is illegitimate, we polarize translation and reject the very liminality which is characteristic of its process. For can any text ever be considered translatable, given the losses and distortions involved? Conversely, given that translation *does* occur, can any text really be defined as untranslatable? In *Le Monolinguisme de l'autre*, Derrida explores this paradox, claiming that 'Rien n'est intraduisible en un sens, mais en un autre sens tout est intraduisible, la traduction est un autre nom de l'impossible'./'In a sense, nothing is untranslatable; but in another sense, everything is untranslatable; translation is another name for the impossible'.[44] When we consider whether to read a text in translation we situate ourselves and our critical practice on this border between possibility and impossibility, understanding and confusion, the said and the unsaid, the read and the unread: approaching a text which we cannot read in its original language, we find ourselves again at the Tower of Babel, silenced and unable to comprehend the world which is presented to us without calling for help.

It is translation which answers this call. But in order to cross from silence to communication, we need to accept the partiality of that response. For only if we acknowledge what is lost *and* what is gained when we read in translation can we move away from the opposition between translatability and untranslatability. In *Against World Literature*, Emily Apter highlights the importance of this move, suggesting that both 'translation and untranslatability are constitutive of world forms of literature'.[45] Apter's response to this reality is to call for critics to take 'an approach to literary comparatism that recognizes the importance of non-translation, mistranslation, incomparability and untranslatability'.[46] In this book, I follow Apter by focusing upon moments of potential untranslatability or mistranslation in each of the texts I discuss, exploring these moments of resistance to linguistic transfer and the creative approaches this resistance enables each author to deploy. At the same time, however, I stake a claim for the possibility, the reality, the necessity, the creativity and the connectivity of translation by often reading in translation myself.[47] As Domínguez, Saussy and Villanueva suggest, a claim of untranslatability is in fact always a call for translation.[48] What appears to be a dead-end is in fact an 'arcade', to use Benjamin's term. Adapted to the context of translation, such an arcade might signify an opening onto other possible passageways that hold out the hope of enhancing understanding across linguistic and cultural borders. This understanding will always, inevitably, be incomplete: there are losses inherent in every reading, and particularly when reading in translation. Yet only in the failed attempt to understand can we grasp the limits of that comprehension.

In this regard, the work of bilingual authors offers a unique angle into the losses and gains inherent when reading in translation. When a bilingual author produces a text in two languages, s/he simultaneously expands and narrows the possibilities for reading and understanding: even as s/he increases the chance that a reader will be able to approach that text in an 'original' version, s/he also increases the chance that that reading will be partial, only one version of a text which is now doubled. This simultaneous expansion and narrowing is an inherent part of the impact which translation has upon a text. Through translation, the potential for a text to be encountered beyond its linguistic boundaries is amplified. But that encounter is also rendered incomplete, for the singular, definitive and original text has been fragmented and multiplied in ways which render every reading only one of many possible ones. In this regard, reading in translation both reveals the other languages, other worlds and other words that we fail, are unable, or choose not to hear, and emphasizes the ethical possibilities of seeking forms of cross-cultural and interlinguistic understanding.

Reading translation in Atxaga, Kundera and Semprún

This focus upon the possibility and limitations of understanding, illuminated by the experiences of translation, is an integral trope within the work of Atxaga, Kundera and Semprún. For if there is a link between these authors which has led me to engage with their work particularly within this book, it is in the ways in which their texts repeatedly raise questions about the miscommunications and misapprehensions which haunt all our attempts at understanding – intralingually as well as interlingually; as individuals and as communities; in both the public and the private sphere. The link resides also in the ways that translation – operating as linguistic transfer, as a textual motif, and as integral to the structure of the texts I discuss – offers partial but illuminating responses to these questions. In Atxaga's *Obabakoak*, translation highlights questions surrounding linguistic politics, interrogating the role the Basque language and literature have played in relation to the formation of the Basque nation state, and to the more hegemonic European literary and linguistic systems which surround it. In *Le Livre*, Kundera explores a series of individual and collective 'forgettings' in post-war Czechoslovakia under Soviet control, interrogating the ways in which aesthetic forms can operate to bolster forms of political and personal tyranny. And in Semprún's *Quel beau dimanche!*, forms of translation interrogate a double trauma: Semprún's lived experience of the Buchenwald concentration camp, and his textual understanding of the Soviet Gulag, an intersection of life and literature which also reveals the intersections between the Nazi and the Communist regimes.

In all three texts, questions about identity formation – on both an individual and a communal level – intersect with questions about the role aesthetic forms play within this formation. These questions return again and again to one crucial issue: how can we translate our experiences – past and present – into an aesthetic form without falling prey to essentialism or universalizing those experiences? In Atxaga, Kundera and Semprún's texts, possible answers to this question are offered through an aesthetics of translation: the inclusion of multilingual loans; the deployment of untranslated words; the glossing of challenging words or phrases; the inclusion of intertextual excerpts in translation. This aesthetics operates, on one level, to introduce and problematize the specific political enquiries at stake in each text. Atxaga's integration into *Obabakoak* of an intertextual network drawn from both Basque authors and from a global literary history reveals and challenges the insularity created when a literary and linguistic scene is defined by a nationalist struggle. Kundera's use of the 'untranslatable' Czech word *litost* within *Le Livre* draws attention to his exile, and highlights the forms of repression enacted by the Czech Communist Party. And Semprún's focus upon the German phrase *Jedem das Seine* is part of his enquiry into the parallels between the Nazi and the Stalinist regimes.

But this multilingual approach does more than highlight the specific political aspects of each text. To include multiple languages in a text is to emphasize the partiality of any single perspective, and thereby to reveal the dangerous illusions inherent in an attempt to support essentialist narratives of language, nationality and political belief through aesthetic forms which are inherently unstable, subject to misreadings, and subject to the dissonance between intention and interpretation. This dissonance is integral to the narratives of these three novels, which all suggest that we misread one another in the very ways in which we believe we understand. But it is also integrated into the form of each text through a series of textual 'mistakes' which only reveal themselves through close reading: in

Obabakoak, intertextual excerpts are falsely attributed or plagiarized; in *Quel beau dimanche!*, quotations are mistranslated or unreferenced; in *Le Livre*, a photograph is misdescribed or misremembered. Are such mistakes deliberate, or simply a reflection of the inevitable challenges of attributing meaning correctly in aesthetic forms? Whatever the case, their existence emphasizes the power of the illusion of understanding: we are all prey to the pull of authority, guilty of putting our faith in pre-digested meanings and accepting reality as it is presented to us without question.

Can we challenge this illusion? As I suggested earlier, forms of copying and translation offer us an opportunity to repeatedly consider our ways of being, our principles of action, and our forms of understanding. In each text, this opportunity is foregrounded through a narrative structure which we might characterize as 'writing-as-translation': a structure run through with forms of repetition which reflect the chronological challenges, multiple perspectives and connection between mimesis and originality inherent within translation. While all three texts have been described as novels, their fragmented, dialogic and elastic forms raise as many questions as they answer about the possibilities of the novel form. What is the correspondence between the different parts of each text? How do they speak to one another? And what do they illuminate about the relation between the aesthetic and the ethical in the novel form itself? Atxaga's connected stories, interlaced with intertextual excerpts, focus upon the creative power of repetition, promoting and employing plagiarism as a means to revive Basque literature. Kundera re-forms repetition as illumination, developing a novelistic structure based upon the repetition of key themes with variations, each one revealing a different way in which we might understand that theme and its permutations. And Semprún repeats words and phrases in different contexts in order to draw attention to the shifts in history and ideology that he is concerned with exploring, developing a text which fragments chronology and perspective to insist upon the illusions inherent in our understanding of the past. In this 'writing-as-translation', what do we see about the world which we could not see before? This question is posed again and again, repetitively itself, in the work of these three authors, as the ethical and aesthetic possibilities of translation are integrated into the ethical and aesthetic possibilities of the novel form.

A journey of translation

This is the first critical volume to bring these three authors together in one study.[49] In doing so, I seek to elaborate the connections between their approaches to translation, as both action and aesthetics, and through those connections to shine a light upon the ethics of translation itself. My argument in this book has been informed by several critical studies which have explored issues of translation and bilingualism in the work of each individual author. I discuss these critical responses at the start of each chapter, as part of a linguistic, historical, national, biographical and critical contextualization of each author. I then follow this overview by integrating the questions raised in this contextualization into a close reading of the ethical and aesthetic questions that these texts raise about translation.

Through the work of each of these authors, I thus follow a journey of translation, one which begins in the impact of translation upon their texts, continues into moments of linguistic translation, untranslatability and mistranslation within their texts, and ultimately becomes an exploration of social, political and affective (un)translatability. These journeys of translation often begin in the binaries of translation theory: in an opposition between major and minor languages; in the hierarchies of original and copy; in the categorization of certain words, texts or types of text as translatable or untranslatable; in a definition of a translation as good or bad, faithful or unfaithful. But these binaries are always interrogated, challenged and ultimately destabilized in the work of Atxaga, Kundera and Semprún: in each text, an engagement with questions of linguistic, cultural and political identity shifts from an *either/or* to a *between*, a liminal space that is constantly and consistently to be renegotiated in every instance of textual production, translation, reading or critical enquiry.

In the chapters which follow, I explore this *between* through *Obabakoak*, *Le Livre* and *Quel beau dimanche!* but also through a series of intersections between these texts and the theories of translation offered by Deleuze, Ricœur and Derrida, among others. These illuminating encounters, which I have framed primarily as a series of pairings – Atxaga and Deleuze; Kundera and Ricœur; Semprún and Derrida – offer new readings of the impact of translation upon and within the work of Atxaga, Kundera and Semprún. But these pairings also offer new readings of an ethics of translation, developed through an investigation of the practice of translation, its function as a textual motif, and its role as a theoretical paradigm for our interlinguistic, but also interpersonal and intercultural relations. These encounters have emerged through connections I perceived between the approaches to translation offered by each author within the pair; in bringing them together, however, these connections developed, shifted and extended, creating a dialogue between fiction and theory which offers both a reading *of* translation, and a reading *through* translation. We might, as Kenneth Reinhard suggests, consider these collisions of fiction and theory as *neighbourhoods* rather than *families* of thought or critical practice: 'a mode of reading logically and ethically prior to similitude, [...] determined by accidental contiguity, genealogical isolation and ethical encounter'.[50] In responding to these contiguities, I have chosen not to approach these texts chronologically, but rather to pursue 'constellations' of thinking, to use Benjamin's term, which emerge as three connected but also independent, complex and diverse stories of translation.

Chapter 1, 'Bernardo Atxaga's *Obabakoak*: towards a minor literature of translation', explores the ethical role translation can play with regard to the asymmetry between minor and major linguistic and literary systems. Bernardo Atxaga's translation of *Obabakoak* from Basque to Castilian reveals the violence of translation and its ability to alter texts for inclusion in hegemonic literary cultures. But Atxaga's representation of the Basque language through a spatial figuration, the desert island, emphasizes the role translation can play as a force of both connection and separation. Reading Atxaga alongside the geoliterary and geopolitical questions developed by Gilles Deleuze, I reframe the debate surrounding Atxaga's self-translations. I argue that, through translation, Atxaga creates his own form of 'minor' literature. I understand this term in the sense Deleuze and Guattari give to it: a literature which challenges the stasis of linguistic, national and literary identity.

Chapter 2, 'Milan Kundera's *Le Livre du rire et de l'oubli*: a hospitable translation', explores the spaces between translatability and untranslatability, fidelity and betrayal. Beginning with a discussion of Kundera's alleged attempts to write with a view to 'translatability', I argue that his attitude to translation reveals his awareness of the impossibility of absolute translatability. I then turn to Kundera's discussion of the 'untranslatable' Czech word *litost*, exploring the forms of linguistic, relational, political and aesthetic untranslatability which Kundera develops through his engagement with this word. Kundera's famous privileging of the novel form above the poetic hinges, I suggest, on a division between translatability and untranslatability which Kundera's texts repeatedly dissolve. Drawing on the work of Paul Ricœur, I argue that by dissolving this division ourselves, as readers, and exploring the spaces between fidelity and betrayal as an alternative way to understand translation, we can discover the hospitable reality of translation, and Kundera's embrace of this hospitality in his aesthetics of the novel.

Chapter 3, 'Jorge Semprún's *Quel beau dimanche!*: a "relevante" translation', explores the question of what might constitute a 'good' or 'relevant' translation. Beginning at the intersection of writing and politics which characterizes Semprún's work, I argue that translation is integral to his attempt to narrate the complex history of the twentieth century in which he was immersed. I focus on his multilingual interrogation of memory and survival, and particularly his analysis of the German language loan *Aufhebung*, the Hegelian dialectical term which the narrator of *Quel beau dimanche!* suggests both structures and dissolves the Stalinist understanding of Marxism. Reading this alongside Derrida's discussion of a 'relevante' translation, which itself draws a parallel between translation and dialectical thinking, I argue that translation interrogates the power of the dialectic. In Semprún's work this interrogation operates to reveal the traumas of the past and acknowledge the impossibility of transcending them.

Each chapter thus offers a vision *of* translation and a vision *through* translation, a vision concerned with exploring linguistic, affective, historical and relational forms of (mis)understanding in the texts discussed. This vision is always diverse: the perspectives offered by translation are never unitary, but always complex, shifting and plural. Yet, through this diversity, translation offers a powerful critical vocabulary with which to explore the ethical challenges involved in the communicative impulse, on both an individual and a community level, and to begin to negotiate and transform those challenges into productive forms of understanding.

Notes

1 Anne Michaels, *Fugitive Pieces* (London: Bloomsbury, 1998 [1996]), 109.
2 Sandra Bermann, 'Introduction', in *Nation, Language and the Ethics of Translation*, ed. Sandra Bermann and Michael Wood (Oxford and Princeton, NJ: Princeton University Press, 2005), 6.
3 Semprún's name is written with an accent in Spanish, and without one in French. I retain the Spanish spelling despite focusing upon Semprún's French texts, to emphasize the duality of his linguistic identity.
4 Italo Calvino, 'Tradurre è il vero modo di leggere un testo', in *Saggi 1945–85,* II (Milan: Mondadori, 1995), 1825–31; Harry Mathews, 'The Dialect of the Tribe', in *Country Cooking and Other Stories* (Providence, RI: Burning Deck, 1980), 40.
5 Roland Barthes, 'De l'oeuvre au texte', *Revue d'esthétique* 24 (1971): 30; 'From Work to Text', in *Image, Music, Text*, trans. Stephen Heath (London: Fontana Press, 1977), 162.
6 Jerome, 'Letter to Pammachius' (395 CE), trans. Kathleen Davis, in *The Translation Studies Reader,* 2nd edn, ed. Lawrence Venuti (London: Routledge, 2002), 21–30; Nicolas D'Ablancourt, 'Prefaces to Tacitus and Lucian' (1640 and 1654), trans. Lawrence Venuti, in *The Translation Studies Reader*, 31–7; Friedrich Schleiermacher, 'On the Different Methods of Translating' (1813), trans. Susan Bernofsky, in *The Translation Studies Reader*, 43–63; Lawrence Venuti, *The Translator's Invisibility. A History of Translation*, 2nd edn (London: Routledge, 2008).
7 Plato, *The Republic,* trans. Desmond Lee, 2nd edn (Harmondsworth: Penguin, 1974), 4.
8 Plato, 'Phaedrus', in *The Dialogues of Plato*, 4th edn, trans. B. Jowett (Oxford: Oxford University Press, 1953), 185.
9 Jacques Derrida, 'La Pharmacie de Platon', in *La Dissémination* (Paris: Seuil, 1972), 80.; Jacques Derrida, 'Plato's Pharmacy', in *Dissemination*, trans. Barbara Johnson (London: The Athlone Press, 1981), 71–2.
10 Kathleen Davis, *Deconstruction and Translation* (London and New York: Routledge, 2014 [2001]), 14–15.
11 Timothy Mathews, *Alberto Giacometti: The Art of Relation* (London: I. B. Tauris, 2013), 6.
12 Max Horkheimer and Theodor W. Adorno, *Dialectic of Enlightenment: Philosophical Fragments*, ed. Gunzelin Schmid Noerr, trans. Edmund Jephcott (Stanford, CA: Stanford University Press, 2002 [1969]), 148.
13 Susan Bassnett and André Lefevere, 'General Editors' Preface', in *Translation/History/Culture: A Sourcebook*, ed. André Lefevere (London: Routledge, 1992), xi.
14 Lawrence Venuti, *The Translator's Invisibility,* 18.
15 Barbara Godard, 'L'Éthique du traduire: Antoine Berman et le «virage éthique» en traduction', *TTR : traduction, terminologie, rédaction* 14.2 (2001): 55. All translations of this text are mine.
16 Schleiermacher, *On the Different Methods*, 49.
17 Antoine Berman, *L'Épreuve de l'étranger. Culture et traduction dans l'Allemagne romantique* (Paris: Gallimard, collection 'Tel', 1984), 16; Antoine Berman, *The Experience of the Foreign: Culture and Translation in Romantic Germany*, trans. S. Heyvaert (Albany: State University of New York Press, 1992), 4.
18 Godard, 'L'Éthique du traduire', 72.
19 Lawrence Venuti, 'Introduction', in *Rethinking Translation: Discourse, Subjectivity, Ideology*, ed. Lawrence Venuti (London: Routledge, 1992), 5.
20 Lawrence Venuti, *The Scandals of Translation: Towards an Ethics of Difference* (London: Routledge, 2002 [1998]), 11; Lawrence Venuti, *The Translator's Invisibility,* 41.
21 Godard, 'L'Éthique du traduire', 71–3.
22 Iris Murdoch, *Under the Net* (London: Penguin, 1960 [1954]), 21, 20.
23 Italo Calvino, *If on a Winter's Night a Traveller*, trans. William Weaver (London: Vintage, 1998 [1981]), 125.
24 Calvino, *If on a Winter's Night*, 238.
25 Calvino, *If on a Winter's Night*, 241.
26 Calvino, *If on a Winter's Night*, 258–9.
27 Murdoch, *Under the Net*, 238.
28 Anthony Pym, 'Schleiermacher and the Problem of Blendlinge', *Translation and Literature* 4.1 (1995): 5.

29 Susan Bassnett, 'Prologue', in *Tradition, Translation, Trauma: The Classic and the Modern*, ed. Jan Parker and Timothy Mathews (Oxford: Oxford University Press, 2011), 7.
30 Gayatri Chakravorty Spivak, 'The Politics of Translation', in *The Translation Studies Reader*, 370.
31 Homi Bhabha, *The Location of Culture* (New York: Routledge, 1994), 56, 244.
32 Anthony Pym, *On Translator Ethics: Principles for Mediation between Cultures*, trans. Heike Walker (Amsterdam: John Benjamins: 2012), 21–2. This English text is a version of Pym, *Pour une éthique du traducteur* (Arras, France: Artois Presses Université, 1997), which has been revised and updated by the author.
33 Jan Walsh Hokenson and Marcella Munson, *The Bilingual Text: History and Theory of Literary Self-Translation* (London: Routledge, 2014), 3; Schleiermacher, *On the Different Methods*, 58.
34 Schleiermacher, *On the Different Methods,* 58.
35 Schleiermacher, *On the Different Methods*, 58.
36 Victor W. Turner, *The Ritual Process: Structure and Anti-Structure* (Harmondsworth: Penguin, 1969), 88–118.
37 Pym, *On Translator Ethics*, 32.
38 Pym, *On Translator Ethics*, 6.
39 Hokenson and Munson, *The Bilingual Text*, 1.
40 Stanley Corngold, 'Comparative Literature: The Delay in Translation', in *Nation, Language and the Ethics of Translation* 14.
41 George Steiner, *ERRATA: An Examined Life* (New Haven, CT: Yale University Press, 1999 [1997]), 107.
42 Emily Apter, *Against World Literature: On the Politics of Untranslatability* (London: Verso, 2013), 3.
43 Pym, *On Translator Ethics*, 18.
44 Jacques Derrida, *Le Monolinguisme de l'autre ou la prothèse de l'origine* (Paris: Éditions Galilée, 1996), 100; *Monolingualism of the Other, or the Prosthesis of Origin*, trans. Patrick Mensah (Stanford, CA: Stanford University Press, 1998), 56–7.
45 Apter, *Against World Literature*, 16.
46 Apter, *Against World Literature*, 4.
47 I reflect this reality within this book by including all quotations, fictional and theoretical, in the language(s) in which I was able to access them: in translation into English when this was my only access point to a text; in French or Spanish when I read them in these languages. I also include English translations for all foreign language quotations.
48 César Domínguez, Haun Saussy and Darío Villanueva, *Introducing Comparative Literature: New Trends and Applications* (London and New York: Routledge, 2015), 85.
49 There is currently one critical text which offers a comparative study of Kundera and Semprún: Tijana Miletic's *European Literary Immigration into the French Language: Readings of Gary, Kristof, Kundera and Semprun* (2008). My chapter 'A Politics of Form: Fantasy and Storytelling as Modes of Resistance in the Work of Atxaga and Kundera', in *Fear and Fantasy in a Global World,* ed. Susana Araújo, Marta Pacheco Pinto, Sandra Bettencourt (Amsterdam: Rodopi, 2015) compares Atxaga's and Kundera's uses of fantasy.
50 Kenneth Reinhard, 'Kant with Sade, Lacan with Levinas', *Modern Language Notes* 110.4 (1995): 785.

Chapter 1
Bernardo Atxaga's *Obabakoak*: towards a minor literature of translation

Introduction: the territory of translation

> '[E]l cohete – *Translatio, Traductio, Tradutrice* – esta siempre cerca; a veces, dentro de la propia casa.'/'[T]he spaceship – *Translatio, Traductio, Tradutrice* – is always nearby; sometimes, inside the house itself.' – Bernardo Atxaga.[1]

In his essay 'Superficies de la literatura vasca', Bernardo Atxaga discusses the persistent line of questioning which accompanies his decision to write his texts primarily in the Basque language, also known as Euskera. Referencing the territorial asymmetry between a planet and an asteroid, Atxaga emphasizes a similar disparity which exists linguistically between those languages conceived as major – Spanish or French, for example – and those conceived as minor, such as Basque. Encircled by the more dominant linguistic territories of French and Spanish, Basque – a language with fewer than one million speakers worldwide – only developed as a unified language in the late 1960s, a delay reflected in the relatively small size of the Basque bibliography and the small readership for Basque texts. Why then, as a bilingual author, able to write in Castilian as well as Basque, does Atxaga choose to write in this minor language?

Atxaga suggests that it is precisely because he is a bilingual author that such divisions between major and minor languages lose their relevance: he is subject to two languages, and is an inhabitant of both literary systems. And the best response to the question of why he writes first in a minor language, he claims, is offered by translation: translation operates as 'un cohete especial' – a spaceship – which can travel with ease from asteroid to planet, minor language to major, in only a few months.[2] In Atxaga's case, translation from Basque to Castilian and beyond, into twenty-four other languages, has transformed his readership. Yet, as Michael Cronin notes, 'translation relationships between minority and majority languages are rarely divorced from issues of power and identity'.[3] This charged relationship holds true even for bilingual authors who choose, like Atxaga, to self-translate between minor and major languages. While Atxaga emphasizes the connective and liberating power of translation in 'Superficies de la literatura vasca', the question remains whether his choice to translate his texts in fact accentuates the minority status of the Basque language.

In this chapter I explore this question, focusing predominantly upon Atxaga's 1988 text, *Obabakoak*. I engage with both Atxaga's 1989 Castilian self-translation of *Obabakoak* and Margaret Jull Costa's 1992 English translation of this Castilian text. Both these translations add new paratexts to frame the text within its Basque context for a non-Basque readership. These paratexts focus particularly upon the unusual features of the Basque language and its literature, thereby exposing Atxaga to the criticism that he has exoticized his text for translation to meet the expectations of the new, more dominant, Castilian and English readerships. Yet while the changes Atxaga makes for his self-translation appear to affirm the minority status of the Basque literary, linguistic and cultural scene, in the narrative of *Obabakoak* Atxaga confronts and disturbs this conception. Throughout the text, Atxaga employs forms of literary recreation – plagiarism, translation, intertextuality – to create a textual territory traversed by the vibrations of multiple languages, literatures and voices. In so doing, Atxaga problematizes the relationship between the terms minor and major in relation to his texts. For in texts which blend languages and literary traditions from around the globe, and which are themselves translated, what precisely do these terms mean?

In this chapter I argue for a reconception of the ways in which *Obabakoak* can be conceived as a text from a minor literary and linguistic system. For Deleuze and Guattari, in *Kafka: Pour une littérature mineure*, 'becoming-minor' is not an exoticizing or limiting exercise, but rather a powerful reframing of the different power structures which surround and constrain us. Drawing upon their work, I explore the ways in which both the narrative of *Obabakoak* and Atxaga's translation of the text into Castilian involve forms of 'becoming-minor'. In the stories Atxaga tells, rigid hierarchies and stable identities often collapse: his characters are transformed physically and mentally by their connection to languages, worlds and experiences different from their own. Moreover, the creative adaptations Atxaga deploys in the translation of his text from Basque to Castilian involve a similar transformation, in which his text is altered and reframed by its connection to a new language. This connection impacts his text, but it also has an impact upon the two literary and linguistic systems – Basque and Castilian – within which *Obabakoak* is formed. As I suggested earlier, a translation from a minor to a major language is often understood to create a lopsided dynamic in favour of the dominant language. But could we, in fact, read such a translation as a form of minor literature itself, in the sense Deleuze and Guattari give the term: a literature which challenges the stasis of the linguistic and literary systems which surround it? In this chapter, I argue that, in relation to Atxaga's *Obabakoak*, translation operates as a potent and transgressive form of minor literature, reframing the relation between the minor and major in Atxaga's literary practice and, in so doing, shifting the ways in which we might approach and read his texts in translation.

Atxaga: writing between identities

The territory of Basque literature

Joseba Irazu Garmendia, who uses the pen name Bernardo Atxaga, was born in 1951 in the small village of Asteasu, in the province of Guipúzcoa in the Basque Country of Spain.[4] Atxaga grew up speaking Basque as his first language, and only learnt Castilian later, at school.[5] Nevertheless, Atxaga suggests that he considers both these linguistic identities to be mother tongues: Euskera he describes simply as the '*primus inter pares*' – the first among equals.[6] Given that one of these languages was learnt at home and one at school, Atxaga's definition of both as 'mother' tongues appears contradictory. In fact, his comment reflects the diglossia within the Basque Country, which means that the majority, if not the totality, of Basque speakers are bilingual.[7] In Atxaga's writing process, this diglossia gives his two languages equally crucial, if distinct, roles to play: Basque, the '*primus inter pares*', is the language in which Atxaga first creates his novels; Castilian, his second mother tongue, is the language into which these texts are subsequently (self-)translated, thereby expanding his readership beyond the Basque-speaking world.

Yet while Atxaga suggests that each of his languages has a crucial part to play in his literary process, his decision to write initially in Basque has implicated him in a '"national author" paradigm', and positioned his work as integral to a potential revitalization of the Basque language and literature.[8] Until the latter half of the twentieth century, Basque struggled to assert itself as a literary language, despite the presence of foundational Basque-language texts such as Etxepare's *Kontrapas* (1545) and Axular's

Gero (1643). When, in 1901, Miguel de Unamuno called for the death of the language, he was reflecting a prevailing understanding that Castilian Spanish was a superior literary language and Basque an 'outmoded' form of expression.[9] From Etxepare's onwards, texts written in Basque could not just be produced, but had to justify their mode of production in a minority language. As Lasagabaster notes, 'authors would inscribe in their works a defence of the language to prove its versatility and compare it to other, more developed languages capable of expressing complex universes, both real and ideological'.[10] The need to justify its existence meant that the Basque novel was subordinated to a linguistic purpose, and was circumscribed by perceptions of it as a tool for the promotion and teaching of the language, a conception that destroyed its autonomy beyond the language of its expression.[11]

The latter half of the twentieth century saw the Basque novel begin to loosen those constraints. In 1978, Basque was recognized as an official co-language for the Basque Autonomous Region of Spain. This political validation led to the inclusion of Basque in the school curriculum of the region, thereby relieving the Basque novel of its primary role as linguistic disseminator. Instrumental to this recognition was the development of a standardized form of Basque, Euskera *batua*, a language which also gave Basque literature a significant boost. Before the arrival of *batua* in the late 1960s, texts classed as Basque might have been written in one of a number of dialects, creating a fragmented system in which texts were comprehensible only to a tiny minority who spoke the same dialect. Standardization enabled Basque literature to develop a unified literary system, and created the foundations for Basque writers to prove that Euskera *batua* was as viable a literary language as Castilian. But, as Lasagabaster notes, 'writers [...] had a challenging job ahead of them: turning a somewhat "artificial" version of the language into a live, flexible [language] for the literary expression of the new realities'.[12] As the most prominent of the three hundred or so people currently writing in Basque, Atxaga has undoubtedly embraced this challenge: he has been described as the 'Shakespeare of his language'.[13] But Atxaga's eminence in this regard has also led to claims of erasure and appropriation: Gabilondo suggests that Atxaga's approach to turning Euskera *batua* into a literary language has inflected it with a syntax drawn from his own dialect, Gipuzkoan, a move which authors with backgrounds in other Basque dialects have read as an 'imperialist imposition'.[14] In this regard, Atxaga has also had to accept the responsibility and the criticism that come with pre-eminence in a minor literary field; his every move is scrutinized for its potential impact upon the Basque literary and linguistic scene.

Atxaga's impact on this scene has certainly been notable. Until the mid-twentieth century, the Basque novel focused predominantly on moral, religious or political issues.[15] Atxaga was part of a group of new writers who sought to shift this emphasis: his texts blend fantasy with realism, twentieth-century literary theory with nineteenth-century narrative techniques, the novel form with short stories and poetry, and a focus on the Basque community with a more global perspective. His 1988 novel *Obabakoak* was his first major international success, gaining Atxaga a new readership both within the Basque Country and beyond, and positioning Atxaga as a role model for a future generation of Basque writers. Yet the dominance of Atxaga's name inevitably has its drawbacks; like all canons, the Basque canon offers opportunities for imitation and disruption but also for exclusion. In the small field of Basque literature, where so few texts are known globally, the dominance of Atxaga's name means that his inclusion in a non-Basque academic text or debate can substitute for the entirety and diversity of the Basque literary scene.

Indeed, Atxaga's place at the forefront of the Basque canon means that, when discussed by non-Basque critics, his name is frequently considered synonymous with Basque literature.[16] Such a response is unsurprising, but for Atxaga, the ways in which it shapes readings of his work can be problematic. In 'Mi primera lengua', he describes several stereotypes which accompany the transmission of his texts beyond the borders of the Basque Country. In particular, he suggests, critics and interviewers tend to emphasize the importance of orality in Basque literature: '"Usted habrá escuchado muchos cuentos en el regazo de su abuela", le dirán, en un tono tal que dará la impresión de el resto de los escritores de este mundo carecen de abuelas con regazo'./'"You probably heard many stories at your grandmother's knee," they will say, in a tone of voice which gives the impression that other writers in the world do not have grandmothers with knees'.[17]

The light-hearted tone of Atxaga's comment here belies his frustration with the rhetoric of exoticism and isolation which infiltrates discussions of his work. In fact, Atxaga plays with this rhetoric in *Obabakoak*, subjecting a vision of the Basque literary scene as simultaneously insular and mysterious to a vehement, if tongue-in-cheek, critique. But there is, Atxaga notes, a more serious strand to the stereotype of the Basque author: 'Una palabra de más y el euskaldun se convierte en una nacionalista furibundo e incluso en un colaborador de los terroristas de ETA'./'One word too many and an *euskaldun* can become, in the eyes of others, a rabid nationalist and even an ETA collaborator'.[18] If Atxaga's decision to write in Basque has positioned him at the forefront of Basque literary development, it has also brought him firmly into the politico-linguistic debate which surrounds the language. Euskera is indelibly linked to the identity of the Basque people and the Basque land, a connection which has seen the language repeatedly made a pawn in the power struggles waged over the Basque Country. In 1894, when the founder of Basque nationalism, Sabino Arana, created the Basque Nationalist Party, the revitalization of Basque was at the heart of his project.[19] *Euzkadi,* the name Arana coined to represent the geopolitical entity that was to be the Basque nation state, means simply 'the place where *euskera* is spoken'.[20] During his dictatorship (1939–75), Franco turned this connection into a weapon: he attempted to annihilate Basque nationalism by repressing all elements of Basque culture and banning Euskera, in order to enforce his vision of Spain as a nation united culturally and linguistically.[21] Against this backdrop, speaking or writing in Basque became an act of linguistic rebellion, as powerful and dangerous as any act of violence or sabotage.[22] When the Basque armed separatist group ETA was formed in 1958, a key part of its campaign to create a Basque nation state involved the regeneration of this banned language.[23] In this politically charged context, texts written in Basque could be part of a linguistic rebellion, resistance or revitalization, but they struggled to be independent from the political context in which they were written.

Atxaga's decision to write in Basque involves him, inevitably, in this conflicted literary scene: when he began writing in the 1970s, Euskera was still banned, and Atxaga notes that his initial impetus for writing in Basque was political as much as literary.[24] The dynamics of the struggle for Basque nationalism have infiltrated several of his texts: *El hombre solo* (1993), *Esos cielos* (1995) and *El hijo del acordeonista* (2003) all explore the experiences of members of ETA. *El hijo del acordeonista* focuses particularly upon the relationship between Basque politics and the Basque language: the ETA group which the narrator eventually joins arrives in Obaba on the pretext that its members are developing a Basque-language version of a set of playing cards. Unlike the abovementioned texts, *Obabakoak* does not directly discuss politics, and is above all a playful exploration of literary theory, intertextuality and the power of storytelling. However, through its focus upon the importance of literature and writing, *Obabakoak* implicitly explores Atxaga's concern with the connection between the Basque political situation and the Basque literary scene.[25] Indeed, the text has been considered the embodiment of a nationalist allegory of Basque identity.[26]

Despite the political themes which dominate his early work, Atxaga continually asserts the importance of literary autonomy, even – or perhaps especially – in a literary arena as politically charged as the Basque one. Literature, he suggests, can engage powerfully with collective social issues, but only if it can resist being coerced into a tool for political consumption.[27] Atxaga was a founding member of the group Pott (Failure), which argued that literature should be engaged in the exploration of aesthetic form and literary creativity, rather than the dissemination of particular political viewpoints.[28] This fascination with the possibilities of aesthetic form is apparent in all Atxaga's texts, which, even when discussing the political context of the Basque Country, do so through a form which challenges and disturbs any simplistic vision of that context. Both *El hombre solo* and *Esos cielos*, for example, offer a nuanced exploration of the internal world of ETA, using interior monologues to explore the psychological and personal realities contained within the sometimes one-dimensional media depiction of ETA and the Basque troubles which existed at the time these texts were written.[29]

The desire among authors of Atxaga's generation to separate the political and the literary, coupled with the changing political situation in Spain after the death of Franco in 1975, led to an increasing liberation of the Basque literary scene from overtly political concerns in the latter part of the twentieth century.[30] Nowadays, Gabilondo suggests, Basque literature is concerned with defining itself within a post-nationalist context, as opposed to a nationalist one.[31] Atxaga's more recent texts seem to reflect this increased autonomy from the question of how to write, and write about, the Basque community: his 2009 novel *Siete casas en Francia* focuses on the early twentieth-century Belgian Congo, and is his first book set entirely outside the Basque Country. Within the text, Atxaga reveals a continued interest in political themes: *Siete casas en Francia* is a book about politics on a micro and a macro level, about social breakdown, individual arrogance, and the repression and abuse of an indigenous community. In setting his narrative completely outside the Basque Country for the first time, Atxaga shifts the 'national paradigm' surrounding his texts, insisting that the freedom to choose theme, content, setting and form exists for a Basque author as much as for any author. To expect otherwise, to believe that a Basque author will and can only address the political situation in the Basque Country, is to be guilty of the same constricted perception which believes that only Basque authors have 'grandmothers with knees'.[32]

This concern with shifting the 'national paradigm' continues in *Dias de Nevada* (2013), Atxaga's fictionalized account of his time as a writer-in-residence in Nevada. The events of the text – predominantly a series of encounters with the human, animal and inanimate inhabitants of Nevada – displace Atxaga's literary world beyond the borders of the Basque Country. Unlike the Congolese location of *Siete casas en Francia*, however, the location of *Dias de Nevada* is not as removed from the Basque Country as it might appear: Nevada is home to several thousand members of the Basque diaspora, who arrived there in search of wealth during the Gold Rush, or of refuge during the Spanish Civil War.[33] The Basque genealogy of the Nevadan landscape infiltrates the text itself, as the narrator finds his time in Nevada troubled by dreams and stories from his past in the Basque Country. In blending the foreign and the domestic in this way, Atxaga displaces and disturbs the location of Basque literature without losing his link to it, a textual engagement with the tension between connection and separation which he began in *Obabakoak* twenty-five years earlier.

Despite this shift of narrative location away from the Basque Country, however, critical responses to Atxaga's work remain conditioned by his place of birth. As Gabilondo notes, his work is never considered as 'literature' but always as 'Basque literature'.[34] In fact, Gabilondo has suggested that, despite being set outside the Basque Country, both *Siete casas en Francia* and *Dias de Nevada* reflect and enforce an 'othered' conception of a Basque identity: 'They guarantee a rural, idealic [sic] Basque Country from a global point of view: even Africa and California end up being more global versions of the Basque town of Obaba whose ultimate reader is still the Spanish state'.[35] Gabilondo's point here is part of a broader critique of Atxaga's texts as always caught up in the desire to write a national, and nationalist, allegory of Basque identity, one Gabilondo suggests is designed to fit Western expectations of Basque culture as rural, magical and 'other'.[36] As Gabilondo notes, Atxaga has often appeared exempt from negative reviews because of his status as the founder of a contemporary Basque canon.[37] Gabilondo's own critique of Atxaga's rural and idyllic vision of the Basque Country can then be seen as an attempt to interrogate rather than institutionalize Atxaga's cultural capital, an approach which is essential to the development of a Basque critical scene able to challenge as well as laud its literary figures. Yet by insisting upon the 'Basqueness' of even those of Atxaga's texts that are set outside the Basque Country, Gabilondo's particular criticism also affirms the geographic limitations placed upon Atxaga's writing experience. For, whether positive or negative, all critical approaches to Atxaga's work maintain their focus upon the link between Basque language, literature and national identity, as read from within his texts.

Translation and self-translation: between minor and major languages

As we have seen, then, despite his assertions of the importance of literary autonomy, the changing linguistic scene post-Franco, and his own decision to shift the location of his texts outside the Basque Country, Atxaga continues to face questions regarding the political and literary role of an author who writes in a minority language. Writing only in Castilian would undoubtedly allow Atxaga to evade at least some of these questions. Tijana Miletic notes that many bilingual authors choose to write in a second language because it 'provides them with the freedom from the conscious and unconscious heritage of their mother tongue'.[38] Miletic's comment is directed towards bilingual authors such as Kundera and Semprún, whose bilingualism was the result of exile from their country of birth. Yet in Atxaga's case, his bilingualism is the result of living in his country of birth: the diglossia in the Basque Country implicates both Castilian and Basque in a complex – and connected – political, cultural and social heritage, thereby limiting the freedom either language could provide alone.

With over one hundred million speakers, Castilian is classed as a 'supercentral' language, and is the only official language throughout the whole of Spain; Basque, like Galician, Catalan and Aranese, has co-official status, but only within one region of Spain, and therefore inevitably occupies a peripheral space within the Spanish linguistic system.[39] The status granted to Basque reveals the simultaneous recognition and exclusion at stake within Spanish linguistic policy: as Sally Perret notes, by officially conceding (some of) the diversity of languages and cultures within Spain, this policy acknowledges the multicultural and multilingual nature of the nation. At the same time, the ways in which this multilingualism is regulated contain and control this diversity by maintaining Basque's marginal position within the Spanish state.[40] For Gil-Oslé, the dynamic between Basque and the broader Spanish subsystem is characterized by a controlling and excluding impulse: 'En España, el escritor en vasco es un extraño, un ente colonizado'/'In Spain, the Basque writer is a foreigner, a colonized being', he suggests.[41] The linguistic duality which Atxaga describes as his inheritance is, then, always caught up in the historical reality of violence and cultural oppression wielded within and by the Spanish state upon the Basque community.[42] At the same time, it is connected to the broader political, cultural and economic dynamics which surround all relationships between minor and major languages.

In *El hijo del acordeonista*, Atxaga focuses upon some of these undercurrents, suggesting that for a Basque author, writing only in Castilian would merely replace one set of difficulties with another. At the start of the text we learn that David, a Basque rancher now living in California, has written a memoir about his experiences growing up in a Basque community struggling with the legacy of the Spanish Civil War. To the surprise of his American wife Mary Ann, who cannot understand his loyalty to a language with such a small readership, David decides to write this memoir in Basque. But, as David's friend Joseba explains, for a Basque writer, linguistic decisions are about much more than attaining maximum readership:

> ¿Desaparecería nuestra lengua? ¿Éramos, él y yo y todos nuestros paisanos, el equivalente al último mohicano? «Escribir en español o en inglés se le haría duro a David [...] Somos muy poco gente. Menos de un millón de personas. Cuando uno solo de nosotros abandona la lengua, da la impresión de que contribuye a su extinción».
>
> Would our language disappear? Were we, he and I and our fellow countrymen and women, the equivalent of the last Mohican? "Writing in Spanish or English would have been very hard for David. [...] There are so few Basque speakers, fewer than a million. And every time even one of us abandons the language, it feels as if we were contributing to its extinction".[43]

Disappearance, abandonment, extinction: the vocabulary of erasure Atxaga employs here emphasizes the sense of linguistic and emotional betrayal which would accompany a decision to write in any language but Basque. In the face of this potential loss, *El hijo del acordeonista* articulates the need for a linguistic revival. At the start of the novel, we discover that David has been burying Basque words in the land around the ranch in California for his children to dig up in order that they may, quite literally, uncover their linguistic heritage. While the burial of these words emphasizes the death of the language, Atxaga highlights the possibility of a resurrection through the actions and engagement of another generation of Basque speakers. David's decision to write his memoir in Basque is similarly situated as both a testament to linguistic forgetting and an attempt to halt its progression, a textual memorial offered to his children which will require them to engage with their linguistic heritage in order to discover their familial one.

While writing in Castilian might enable Atxaga to evade the paradigm of the national author, this decision would thus implicate him in another paradigm: that of the disloyal Basque author, abandoning a minority language while validating the hegemony of Castilian and, implicitly, the Spanish literary and political system. Such a critique has been levelled at other bilingual writers who have chosen to write in Castilian rather than a minority language: as Kirsty Hooper discusses, a number of Galician authors, including Alfredo Conde and Emilia Pardo Bazán, have found their commitment to Galicia questioned because of their decision not to write in Galician.[44] The link between nation and language – inherent in Schleiermacher's rejection of the possibility of bilingualism which I discussed in the Introduction – remains, in relation to minor languages, and particularly those languages without an accompanying independent nation state, a critical subject of enquiry. Indeed, as Giorgio Agamben suggests in *Means Without End*, a necessarily violent entangling of people, language and the state often arises when the existence of that state is in question.[45] The violence of this enmeshing of ontology and language does not diminish the importance of a connection between a people and its language, but it emphasizes the ways in which such a connection can force bilingual authors to choose their minority language over their other tongue or risk accusations of betrayal.

But writing only in a minority language also has its limitations, as Atxaga explores in *El hijo del acordeonista.* For while David's decision to write in Basque connects him to the preservation of his language, it simultaneously operates to exclude his non-Basque-speaking wife Mary Ann from the history of which she is a part. In the same way, were Atxaga to write only in Basque, he would exclude readers from his 'other' mother tongue, a language which also forms part of his linguistic and cultural identity. Given that our relations and our sense of self frequently exceed monolinguistic boundaries, there is a need for other forms and models of connectivity. In *El hijo del acordeonista* Atxaga promotes translation and rewriting as the best solution to this type of linguistic exclusion. The linguistic boundaries that prevent Mary Ann from reading David's story will be dissolved, Atxaga suggests, by two rewritings: firstly, an intralingual rewriting of David's text by Joseba, which will bring the text to the attention of a wider audience; secondly, an interlingual translation, based upon this rewriting, into a language Mary Ann can understand.[46]

Translation and self-translation offer Atxaga a similar pathway through the impasse surrounding his two languages, allowing him to replace a substitutive dynamic with a conjunctive one, and support Basque without being circumscribed – politically or creatively – by its minority status. Atxaga's international success is in fact predicated on translation: he is the most translated author in the Basque literary canon to date.[47] But Atxaga's decision to self-translate is not exempt from the complex and charged dynamic between his two mother tongues. Is this decision actually a choice? Or is it a compulsion? As Rainier Grutman discusses, 'a variety of political or market-related reasons' can explain why speakers of minority languages 'might feel compelled to translate their work into the dominant language'.[48] Atxaga's decision to translate *Obabakoak* into Castilian falls squarely in this camp. In 1989, *Obabakoak* was nominated for the Spanish Premio Nacional de Literatura (National Prize for Literature). While nominated texts can be written in Castilian, Catalan, Galician or Basque, they must be translated into Castilian before they will be considered by the jury, a reality which, as César Domínguez notes, somewhat ironically represses the very diversity of the literary system which the prize purports to represent.[49] Atxaga complied with this request, hiring three different translators to help him translate *Obabakoak* into Castilian in order to ensure that it was ready in time, and then proof-reading and creating a text from these different versions.[50] *Obabakoak* was named that year's winner. As Domínguez comments, 'award of the prize was, therefore, indissolubly linked to that (self-) translation to Castilian'.[51] Domínguez raises a crucial point: although Atxaga continues to be read predominantly as a Basque author, his authorial success is in fact predicated upon his ability to conform to the demands of the hegemonic Castilian literary subsystem through translation. Rather than the connective and liberating 'spaceship' Atxaga discusses in 'Superficies de la literatura vasca', translation here operates to further separate and reify the unequal dynamic between the literary and linguistic territories which it touches.

Atxaga subsequently decided to replace this collaborative translation with a self-translation; it is this self-translation which was published and which provides the basis for translation into other languages, including the English translation by Margaret Jull Costa.[52] As Elizabete Manterola notes, although Atxaga has himself drawn attention to the collaborative aspect of the original translation of *Obabakoak*, the names of the translators are not credited within the final published text.[53] The erasure of this collaborative element – part of *Obabakoak*'s textual journey from Basque to Castilian – emphasizes the higher status assigned to self-translations, a status confirmed by the decision to use the Castilian text as the source for subsequent translations. These two decisions affirm the hegemony of authorship within the subsystem of translated literature, a hegemony which emerges in similarly problematic forms in relation to Kundera's work. The use of Castilian as source text also reaffirms the dominance of Castilian, relegating the original Basque text to second-order status within the international literary market. On one level, this decision reflects the small number of Basque speakers, and therefore the potential challenges of finding a translator capable of working between Basque and Albanian, for example. Yet there is no such excuse for the use of the Castilian as a source text for the English and French translations, since there are several Basque–English and Basque–French translators. In 'Mesa Redonda', Atxaga suggests that the international preference for using the Castilian source text is connected to an editorial desire to use renowned translators, few of whom can translate from Basque, to maximize the 'name' associated with the text.[54] Atxaga's comments refract and nuance the invisibility which Venuti suggests is the preserve of the translator: certain translators are rendered invisible because of the minority status of the language from or into which they translate; others become visible by developing sufficient fame to attain a status not dissimilar to that of an author.

Atxaga's relationship to translation has shifted in recent years. As Manterola discusses, Atxaga now works with a professional translator – normally Asun Garikano – on the translations of his texts into Castilian, and her name is given precedence in the book credits.[55] And in a collapse of the separation of original and translation, author and translator, Atxaga's 2012 text *Borrokaria – El luchador – The Fighter*, appeared in a one-volume version including Atxaga's Basque text, Garikano's Spanish translation and an English translation of the Basque text by Amaia Gabantxo.

But the translation of *Obabakoak*, the text considered seminal to the creation of a twentieth-century Basque literary identity, remains caught up in the power asymmetry between Basque and Castilian, an asymmetry exacerbated by the ways Atxaga chose to alter the text as it moved from source to target language. Some of these alterations were dictated by the specific challenges of translating from Basque: Olaziregi notes that one story, written in a Basque dialect particular to the mountain region of the Basque Country, was removed because it proved too difficult to translate into Castilian.[56] The erasure of this particular story, which implicitly acknowledged the diversity of dialects within the Basque language, emphasizes the ways in which the difference *within* the Basque community, as opposed to the difference *of* it, can be repressed by the process of translation. Other changes to the text reveal the challenges inherent within all translations, regardless of the languages in question. As Olaziregi discusses, the original Basque text is split into two sections, and the second of these contains a series of short stories organized in alphabetical order.[57] This alphabetization adds another interpretative layer to the text, connecting the stories to one of the key themes of *Obabakoak*: the development of language itself. As Atxaga explains:

> el sonido "B" es el primero que emitimos como seres humanos. […].en Obabakoak se hablaba de unas gentes que […] pasaban del mutismo a decir algo. Decidí que el nombre de la geografía debería tener varias "B", y elegí "Obaba" por ser una palabra que figura en las canciones de cuna vascas.
>
> the sound "be" is the first that we make as human beings. [...] *Obabakoak* described a people […] who moved from silence to saying something. I decided that the name of the geographic space should contain several "B"s and chose "Obaba" since it is a word which appears in Basque lullabies.[58]

Atxaga's decision to create a sequence of alphabetized stories in the text mirrors this linguistic journey from babyhood to adulthood, from silence to speech. Yet the Castilian text does not – or rather cannot, if it wishes to remain faithful to the meaning of the stories' titles – reproduce this alphabetization. The loss of this structure in the Castilian undermines the connections between these stories and the linguistic journey Atxaga posits as a key theme of *Obabakoak*. In so doing, Atxaga's translation from a minor to a major language enacts a double erasure: as Euskera is literally erased from the text by translation, it is also erased thematically, and the importance Atxaga assigns to giving a voice to the Basque community is weakened by the loss of this structural emphasis in the text upon linguistic development.

In place of this formal focus upon the development of Basque, Atxaga supplies in the translated text a content-based discussion, adding a new section, 'A modo de autobiografía', to guide the non-Basque reader into the specifics of the Basque linguistic, literary and cultural scene. 'A modo de autobiografía' focuses upon the challenge of writing in Basque, and particularly the limited precedent for such a project:

> Nosotros, los que ahora empezamos a ser traducidos a otras lenguas, partimos con muy poco equipaje. Mirábamos nuestro hatillo y allí no encontrábamos más que cinco o diez libros escritos en la lengua en que pretendíamos escribir. […] Lo que nos faltaba era *el antecedente* […] nos faltaban libros donde aprender a escribir en nuestra propia lengua.

> Those of us who are just beginning to be translated into other languages, set off with very little baggage. We looked into our bundle and found only five, at most ten, books written in the language we were trying to write in. […] What we lacked was an antecedent […] we lacked books from which we could learn to write in our own language.[59]

The problem with such a lack of heritage, suggests Atxaga, is dual: writers who wish to express themselves in Basque must effectively construct their own language in order to do so; once they have done this, however, they still face the challenge of finding a readership, given the limited material and precedent for reading in Basque. Atxaga notes the progress that has been made in recent years, which 'permite que escritores como yo puedan vivir de los derechos de obras como […] *Obabakoak* (1988)'/'enables writers like myself to live off the royalties from such works as […] *Obabakoak* (1988)'.[60] In referring to *Obabakoak* metatextually here, Atxaga emphasizes that the text we are reading is a translation, positioning this autobiographical section as a paratextual addition to an already existing text.

Gérard Genette suggests that paratexts operate 'pour le *présenter* [le texte], au sens habituel de ce verbe, mais aussi en son sens le plus fort: pour le *rendre présent*, pour assurer sa présence au monde, sa «réception»'/'to present [the text] in the usual sense of this verb but also in the strongest sense: to make present, to ensure the text's presence in the world, its "reception"'.[61] 'A modo de autobiografía' presents *Obabakoak* as a Basque text, ensuring it is received as such within the more hegemonic literary system it is entering. In focusing upon the cultural specificity of the text, Atxaga appears, in Lawrence Venuti's terms, to 'foreignize' the Castilian version of *Obabakoak*, insisting upon its status as a translation, and upon the marginal elements of its source culture.[62] For César Domínguez, however, Atxaga's paratext evokes that specificity through a rhetoric of marginality and limitation which exoticizes the Basque linguistic and literary culture.[63] Unlike Venuti's conception of foreignization, which seeks to present the marginal on its own terms, the concept of exoticization invokes otherness as a product for consumption by a more dominant receiving culture, thereby affirming an asymmetrical relationship between the two.[64] In this regard, Domínguez addresses Atxaga's comment that 'a los veintitrés, ya había acabado de leer toda la literatura vasca que el dictador no había conseguido quemar'/'by the time I was twenty-three, I had read all the Basque literature that the dictator had not managed to burn'.[65] 'There is', writes Domínguez,

> no doubt of the desired impact – unnecessary in the case of the Basque audience – on the Spanish audience of the record of a literature that can be read in all its entirety in three years. Thus, we have the motif of a "small literature" thematized in a hermeneutic experience impossible for the audience of the "great" literatures.[66]

For Domínguez, the translation enacts a 'Castilian-ization' of *Obabakoak*, presenting the text through a rhetoric of smallness and marginality which accords with the pre-existing beliefs of the wider Spanish literary system. This focus upon the minor elements of the Basque language and culture is inevitably transferred into translations of *Obabakoak* based upon the Castilian version, such as Jull Costa's English text.[67]

In fact, this emphasis upon the minority status of Basque literature is extended in Jull Costa's translation of *Obabakoak* by the inclusion of another paratext, the poem 'Prologue'. This poem was written by Atxaga in Castilian, but specifically for the English edition of *Obabakoak*, in order to elucidate the literary and linguistic context of the text.[68] 'Prologue' is thus a poem written specifically for translation, and for a readership assumed to have a limited awareness of the source culture. And again, as in 'A modo de autobiografía', the entry of *Obabakoak* into a new literary and linguistic system is accompanied by an emphasis upon the unusual elements of the system in which the text originated:

> I write in a strange language. Its verbs
> the structure of its relative clauses,
> the words it uses to designate ancient things
> – rivers, plants, birds –
> have no sisters anywhere on Earth.
> [...]
> Born, they say, in the megalithic age,
> it survived, this stubborn language, by withdrawing,
> [...]
> The language of a tiny nation, so small
> you cannot even find it on the map,
> in four centuries it produced only a hundred books...[69]

In introducing the Basque language to an English audience, 'Prologue' emphasizes five key points about that language: its strangeness, its age, its isolation, the smallness of the geographical and political space in which it resides, and the limitations of its bibliography. Atxaga here highlights the parallels between language, literature and geography which Arana, and later ETA, developed into a rhetoric of linguistic and literary nationalism.

'Prologue' implicitly and explicitly explores the inadequacies of such rhetoric: the language Atxaga describes here is one which has survived for centuries by 'withdrawing' and resisting political and cultural attempts at erasure or appropriation. Atxaga also focuses upon the connections which exist between Euskera and other languages, playing, through issues of translation, with the very strangeness and isolation which his poem initially evokes:

> The sun of the long winters we call *eguzki* or *eki*;
> The sun of the sweet, rainy springs is also
> – as you'd expect –
> called *eguzki* or *eki*
> (it's a strange language but not that strange)
> [...]
> Yet its isolation could never have been absolute
> – cat is *katu*, pipe is *pipa*, logic is *lojika* – [70]

This emphasis upon the connections between the Basque language and the Romance languages which surround it highlights the inconsistency of Arana's linguistic policy, which sought to create linguistic purity by purging Basque of any words derived from Latin.[71] Atxaga also discusses the expansion of the Basque bibliography during the twentieth century. But despite Atxaga's references to connectivity and growth, 'Prologue' continues to underline the differences between the source and target cultures, contrasting the still small Basque bibliography with the extensive British one: the poem describes *Obabakoak* as 'this book published now in this city,/the city of Dickens, of Wilkie Collins and of so many others'.[72] In invoking the strength of the British canon, 'Prologue' maintains the asymmetry between the Basque literary scene and the hegemonic one which *Obabakoak* enters through translation.[73]

For Domínguez, paratextual additions such as 'A modo de autobiografía' and 'Prologue' reflect the dominance of motifs of geographical limitation within the literary field of translations from Basque: 'when they abandon the Basque language', he suggests, 'literary works and histories need to be presented, a presentation that is highly geographical and, in consequence, reveals Euskal Herria as the true terra incognita of the Peninsula'.[74] This geographical presentation, he argues, reframes the relationship between minor literatures and territories invoked by Deleuze and Guattari in *Kafka: Pour une littérature mineure*: 'Basque historiography made spatial limitation into a sign of identity for its literature, a conception of small literature that privileges territorialization, while Deleuze and Guattari denied it'.[75] Domínguez here refers to Deleuze and Guattari's reading, through Kafka, of minor literatures as forms of writing which operate to 'deterritorialize' the different territories they encounter. In Deleuze and Guattari's thinking, territories signify systems of thought – political, social, national, cultural, poetic, familial, bureaucratic, literary – which are static and implicated in existing assemblages. These territories are traversed by multiple lines: 'molar lines', which regiment and stratify; 'molecular lines', which travel and transmit beyond these territories, but adapt themselves to the new systems they encounter; and 'lines of flight', which create paths of mutation and change which can 'deterritorialize' these assemblages.[76] As Parr suggests,

> Deterritorialisation can best be understood as a movement producing change. In so far as it operates as a line of flight, deterritorialisation indicates the creative potential of an assemblage. So, to deterritorialise is to free up the fixed relations that contain a body all the while exposing it to new organisations.[77]

Deleuze and Guattari read Kafka's writing as an expression of a literary deterritorialization which transforms content and form, allowing the German language to 'disarticulate', and in the process to shift the relations between the text and the politicized linguistic systems which border it.[78] In so doing, Kafka's texts 'become-minor', entering a process of continual creativity and change which transforms not only their own form and content, but also their relation to the political, linguistic and literary territories which inform them.[79]

Deleuze and Guattari's conception of minor literature is, then, less about denying its territoriality than about suggesting forms of literature which work to repeatedly engage and disengage with the multiple literary, political and linguistic territories which surround them. Given this, we might rethink the opposition Domínguez reads between the territorialized vision of small literature described by Basque historiography and the deterritorialized one which Deleuze and Guattari invoke. As we have seen, for Deleuze and Guattari, territorialization and deterritorialization are not opposed; instead, all territories contain their own deterritorializing lines which traverse and transform the boundaries which enclose them, just as movements of deterritorialization often find their limits in other territories. Nonetheless, the paratexts Atxaga adds to his self-translations undoubtedly emphasize a highly geographic conception of Basque literature, and work to root *Obabakoak* within one, specifically Basque, territory. In Deleuze and Guattari's terms, his self-translation creates a 'molar line' which connects the text firmly to the existing literary, linguistic and political frameworks of the Basque Country. Simultaneously, however, it also creates a 'molecular line', which transforms the text but only to align it to the expectations of a new framework: that of the Castilian and English readerships. In this sense, the process of 'becoming-minor' which *Obabakoak* undergoes in translation appears less as the transformative process of rethinking territorial relations understood by Deleuze and Guattari, and more as a process which solidifies the asymmetrical relationship between the minor text and the major assemblages which surround it.

Obabakoak: a literary puzzle

If the translation of *Obabakoak* consolidates the asymmetry between minor and major languages and literary systems, the narrative of the text itself reveals Atxaga's exploration of the Basque territory to be more complex than a major/minor hierarchy allows. In the text, Atxaga plays with the semblance of geographical unity, exploring and disturbing the relations between inside and outside, foreign and domestic, connection and isolation. As Margaret Jull Costa suggests, *Obabakoak* is concerned with 'the power of language and literature to open [...] doors that show us other countries and cultures'.[80] In the thirty years since its publication in Castilian, *Obabakoak*'s unusual title, its fragmented yet connected form and its wide-ranging frame of reference have led editors and publishers to replace a literal translation of the title with a gloss or subtitle, each one highlighting a particular – and frequently different – element of this complex text. English-language titles have focused upon genre: Graywolf Press added 'Stories from a Village', while Pantheon Press opted to include the subtitle, 'a novel'. Such definitions only emphasize their limitations: *Obabakoak* is neither a novel nor an unconnected collection of short stories, but rather a series of interlinked and independent stories which hinge loosely upon the inhabitants of Obaba, a fictional town in the Basque Country. The Portuguese translation focused upon this spatial unity, adding 'Um Lugar Chamado Obaba' – 'A Place Called Obaba' – to the title. But if this addition gestures towards geographic cohesion, this too is undermined by the book itself, since the characters who inhabit Obaba also travel far from this space, to Barcelona, to Hamburg, to South

America, thereby fracturing and fragmenting the ostensible focus on Obaba. Moreover, the book's constituent stories are interspersed with others drawn from a global literary tradition reminiscent of *A Thousand and One Nights*, which transport the reader to China, to France, to Baghdad. Through these wide-ranging narratives, *Obabakoak* welcomes a myriad of diverse genres, from magical realism to metafiction, and draws on varied textual influences, from Dante to Gautier.

The range of intertextual elements within *Obabakoak*, some explicit, others masked, engages the reader in a game of 'spot the reference', and several translations of the title highlight this ludic element. The German translation adds, 'Ein literarisches Puzzle' – 'A Literary Puzzle' – positioning the text as a mystery to be decoded or uncovered. In many of the stories, characters undertake to solve such puzzles: in 'Esteban Werfell', the eponymous protagonist seeks to make sense of a mysterious and formative episode from his past, an exchange of letters with a beautiful German girl whom he met only once, in a dream; in 'Exposición de la carta del canónigo Lizardi', an unnamed narrator pieces together fragments of a series of letters, hoping to uncover the denouement of the tragic story of a young boy who metamorphosed into a wild boar; in the final set of stories, 'En busca de la última palabra', a Basque author investigates a mysteriously prophetic old wives' tale which he believes explains the deafness of one of his school friends. The Dutch translation picks up this playful motif, entitling the text *Obabakoak of het ganzenbord – Obabakoak or the Game of the Goose*. 'The Game of the Goose' is a board game with a combination of lucky and unlucky squares, which Atxaga references briefly in 'En busca de la última palabra'. In 'A modo de autobiografía', Atxaga returns to this motif, describing it as a metaphor for life itself, 'una viaje lleno de dificultades donde, a partes iguales, intervienen el Azar y nuestra Voluntad'/'a journey full of difficulties in which Chance and Free Will intervene in equal measure'.[81] These difficulties are an integral element of the text itself: 'Esteban Werfell' and 'Exposición de la carta del canónigo Lizardi' are among a series of stories in the first section of the Castilian text, entitled 'Infancias', each of which explores a challenging experience of childhood or adolescence.

But 'The Game of the Goose' can also be read as a description of another process of maturation: 'la vida de un escritor vasco'/'the life of a Basque writer'.[82] The importance of writing and reading is a theme which runs throughout *Obabakoak*: Atxaga's characters are themselves frequently storytellers – the text abounds with diary extracts and letters – each offering a different perspective on the community they inhabit and the communities which surround them. The importance of storytelling infiltrates Atxaga's translation of the name 'Obabakoak', which he provides for the English reader in 'Prologue':

> Obaba is just Obaba: a place, a setting;
> ko means 'of'; a is a determiner; k the plural.
> The literal translation: *The People* or *Things of Obaba*;
> a less literal translation: *Stories from Obaba*.[83]

The discrepancy between the literal and the less literal translation here dramatizes the central tension at the heart of *Obabakoak*, namely that between the people of Obaba whose experiences Atxaga narrates, and the international stories with which he frames these experiences. In this way Atxaga highlights the power of the storyteller to create imaginative connections which stretch beyond geographic or linguistic borders. In 'Método para plagiar', one of the stories from the final section of the text, the story told is that of Basque literature itself, as the narrator of the story explores the importance of looking beyond the boundaries of his own community for narrative inspiration.

A deserted island

'Método para plagiar' is the account of a dream which the narrator uses to explain a new theory he has uncovered regarding literary originality. The dream begins, in the narrator's description, 'en medio de una selva agreste, tupida e inhóspita'/'in the midst of a wild forest, dense and inhospitable'.[84] Attempting to explore the forest, he finds at first only 'completa oscuridad [...] los parajes de alrededor estaban sin vida, y ninguna planta crecía en aquella tierra estéril'/'utter darkness [...] no sign of life anywhere to be seen, not a single plant growing in that sterile soil'.[85] Suddenly, however, he is approached by a shadowy male form which he identifies as the Basque writer Axular, whose seventeenth-century text *Gero*, as I mentioned earlier, is one of the foundational works of Basque literature. Guided by Axular, the narrator climbs through the forest until he reaches a peak from which he looks down upon 'una isla, perdida en la inmensidad del mar. Era muy pequeña, y no había en ella señales de vida'/'an island, lost in the immensity of the seas. It was very small and there was no sign of life there'.[86] The limited size and empty terrain of the island, are however, figurations which exceed the cartographic. For, as the narrator comes to realize, 'aquella isla no era como la de Sardinia, o como la de Sicilia, sino que estaba hecha de otra materia; y que, por increíble que pareciera, aquel accidente geográfico que contemplaba no era otra cosa que mi propia lengua'/'the island was not like the islands of Sardinia or Sicily, but made of quite different material. Incredible though it may seem, the geographical feature I was looking at was none other than my own language'.[87] Atxaga's decision to imagine the Basque language as a desert island surrounded by an immense, empty ocean, maps geographically an isolation which exists linguistically. For Basque is a language isolate, a language which, having been compared with every other known Eurasian language, has demonstrated no discernible genealogical relationship with any of them. The sea surrounding the island is empty, then, because of the lack of linguistic correspondence between Basque and the Indo-European romance languages which surround it geographically.

For Domínguez, island motifs, such as the one Atxaga creates in *Obabakoak*, reflect a form of self-perception conditioned by insularity within Basque literary historiography:

> Islands are only those (literary) spaces whose inhabitants, but also whose visitors, perceive them as such. [...] One constant of the geo-symbol of the island is the minimal territoriality, the limitation, the claustrophobia of the border, which make the space in question a microcosm. "Large" islands cease to be islands and are lived as continents. A literature is (self-)defined as insular when it presents itself as "small".[88]

Domínguez's focus upon the island motif emphasizes its role as part of the minor–major rhetoric surrounding Basque literature. In this reading, dominated by invocations of exoticism and separation, the Basque island refuses to perceive itself as a continent, insisting upon its inability to sustain life and its difference from other national literatures. In choosing to depict Basque as an isolated, deserted island, Atxaga employs the same rhetoric of limitation which he uses paratextually in 'A modo de autobiografía' and 'Prologue'. This rhetoric, then, is an integral part of *Obabakoak* in all its versions. But Atxaga's construction here is highly self-aware: rather than represent Basque as an island in order to emphasize the insularity and limitation of the language, he develops this figuration in order to point out the limitations of such emphases themselves. In the narrative, Axular is keen to lay the blame for the isolation of the island firmly on the Basque community. A ship approaching the island carries some of those whom Atxaga's imagined Axular holds particularly responsible for this isolation: the hypocrites who talk at length about the importance of sustaining Basque culture but never act upon their words;

the politicians who come only to spread anger and enmity among the island's inhabitants; and 'los *tristes*' (author's italics) – the sad ones, who offer the island only grief and defeatism. There are also the banausians, whose name derives from the Greek word *banausos* and is etymologically connected to ideas of profit, vulgarity and commercialism. For Atxaga's Axular, this group is much to be feared because they seek to make money by playing upon the isolation and ostensible exoticism of the Basque language and culture.[89]

Atxaga's Axular is clear that responsibility for the aridity of the island lies precisely with the forms of insular self-perception which Domínguez describes in his exploration of the island motif – in projects which, whether actively or passively, isolate the language and literature. Such projects have had a knock-on effect upon the literary culture of the Basque country, inhibiting Basque writers from drawing upon other texts and other languages in order to develop their own literary practices. As this fictional Axular tells the narrator, 'Si se hubieran escrito en euskara tantos libros como se han escrito en francés o en cualquier otra lengua, también el euskara sería una lengua rica y perfecta como ellas, y si eso no es así, son los mismos euskaldunes los que tienen la culpa, y no esta isla'/'if as many books had been written in *euskera* as have been written in French or in any other language for that matter, it would be as rich and perfect as they are and if that is not the case it is the speakers of *euskera* themselves who are to blame, not the island'.[90]

This provocative quotation, which lays the blame for the limitations of Euskera at the feet of its speakers, is adapted from the actual Axular's prologue to *Gero*, in which Axular legitimizes his decision to write in Basque.[91] Atxaga's inclusion of this intertext in *Obabakoak* highlights the rhetoric of accusation and justification which has surrounded the Basque language question since Axular was writing. The contrast between the insularity of the island and the richness of the linguistic worlds which surround it emphasizes the continued tension at the heart of Basque literature with which Atxaga is concerned in *Obabakoak*. For without literary ancestors, Basque authors remain castaways, adrift in an empty sea, gazing longingly across the water at more habitable scenes. How, then, can life be returned to the island of Euskera? From which literary tradition can Basque writers draw inspiration?

In the narrator's dream, Axular commands him to turn to plagiarism – the rewriting of canonical stories from other, more dominant, languages into Basque – in order to restore creativity to the island. Initially, the narrator is resistant; plagiarism, he notes, has extremely negative connotations: 'Tan mal como el robar. Hoy en día, el trabajo de un escritor ha de dar la impresión de haber sido creado de la nada. Dicho de otro modo, el trabajo ha de ser original'/'It's considered as bad as stealing. Nowadays, the work of a writer has to give the impression of being created out of nothing. In other words the work has to be original'.[92] The narrator's perception of plagiarism here reflects a hierarchical binary of original/simulacrum which devalues forms of textual replication. But the imagined Axular responds to the narrator's perception of plagiarism by upending this hierarchy, suggesting that it is the desire for absolute originality, for an absolute separation from other languages and literatures, which has made the island barren and bare. 'De verdad te digo que esa consideración de latrocinio es prejudicial'/'The idea that it is theft is most unfortunate', he suggests, for in devaluing the work of the plagiarist, Basque authors have deprived themselves of the literary ancestry to be found beyond the boundaries of the island.[93] Atxaga's Axular suggests that plagiarism should be viewed not as theft, but as a valuable literary tool which builds connections with other languages and literatures and, while imitating these, seeks to create from them anew. Finally convinced, the narrator awakes, and goes on to develop his own 'método para plagiar'.

In 'Método para plagiar', Atxaga highlights a dichotomy at the heart of perceptions of plagiarism: is plagiarism a derivative form of literary theft? Or is it a creative adaptation of a global literary heritage? In *Pragmatic Plagiarism,* Marilyn Randall explores this question, suggesting that our assessment of what constitutes plagiarism is entirely subjective: plagiarism, she states, 'is in the eye of the beholder'.[94] Randall explores a 'discourse of repetition' surrounding textual production, which splits textual repetition into two, value-laden forms: plagiarism is its negative manifestation; intertextuality and allusion its positive expression. The difference between these forms hinges less upon any objective dissimilarity, and more upon our understanding and interpretation of the values of intellectual property and authenticity. In Randall's reading, textual repetition – or rather, how we think about textual repetition – takes on an ethical slant: the term 'plagiarism' is a judgement imposed upon a text, which reveals our own judgements about the type and strength of the authority systems which inform textual production and reception.[95]

As Randall's reading suggests, the value we assign to imitation is always in flux. In the Classical period, *imitatio* was considered an innately innovative exercise; the Romantics valorized originality – understood as authorial inspiration – above any other form of artistic production; in the twentieth century, intertextuality and quotation were perceived as inherently creative. In *Obabakoak*, Atxaga engages with this contemporary revalorization of copying, playing with the fine line between plagiarism and intertextuality in order to explore some of the ways in which textual authority is constituted. His narrator suggests that the potential plagiarist can evade accusations of plagiarism by manipulating his or her critics through a discussion of the importance of 'metaliterature':

> Tengo que decir que esos que andan buscándole el pelo al huevo para desacreditar a los demás están muy retrasados en lo que a teoría literaria se refiere. A lo mejor ni tan siquiera han oído una palabra acerca de metaliteratura. [...] No hay nada nuevo bajo el sol, ni tan siquiera en literatura. [...] Los escritores no creamos nada nuevo, que todos escribimos las mismas historias.
>
> I must say that these hairsplitters intent on discrediting others are very backward when it comes to literary theory. They've probably never even heard of metaliterature. [...] All the term means is that there's nothing new under the sun, not even in literature. [...] We writers don't create anything new, we're all continually writing the same stories.[96]

The hyperbole of the narrator's statement – that there are no new stories, but only variants of previous ones, literary myths which travel across time and space – highlights a shift away from a Romantic faith in originality as the preserve of authorship, towards a 'metaliterary' focus upon repetition as the innate property of all literature. From T. S. Eliot's description of mature poets stealing from their literary past, to Roland Barthes's comment that all writing repeats an anterior gesture, this preoccupation with the inevitability of repetition has revalued the status of plagiarism, positioning it as an inevitable, but also creative and inspirational, element of textual production.[97] Atxaga's comic gameplay with this critical preoccupation affirms that, as Randall proposes, plagiarism is indeed in the eye of the beholder. Atxaga's narrative suggests, however, that the definition of plagiarism is prey to the manipulations of those who use literary theories such as metaliterature to close down, rather than open up, debates surrounding the relationship between originality and repetition, between plagiarism and intertextuality.

A textual inhabitation

How might we read the dynamic between originality and repetition without imposing a critical framework which elides, as opposed to explores? Can plagiarism, as Atxaga's Axular suggests, bring creativity from other literary spheres into a fragile literary scene such as the Basque one? Or is it a reprehensible appropriation of the words of another, a parasitic form of textual production which erases originality and merely confirms the authority and superiority of the plagiarized text upon which the plagiarism depends for its own existence? Atxaga's suggestion, offered through the voice of Axular, that plagiarism could provide a solution to the aridity of the desert island seems caught in a double-bind, halfway between repetition and originality, between a connection to other literary worlds and an attempt at literary self-sufficiency. For Domínguez, it is precisely this conflict between insularity and connection which is at the heart of Basque literature, and which is evoked by the use of the desert island motif: 'a geo-symbol where closure (the island as a metaphor of self-sufficiency) and longing for communication (the island as the expression of a broader geographical reality) meet'.[98] In this sense, the potential plagiarist appears to reflect, without necessarily disrupting, the problematic tension at the heart of the Basque literary scene as evoked through Atxaga's own desert island figuration.

In fact, the similarity of the tensions involved in plagiarism and those evoked by the figuration of the desert island – one set articulated textually, the other geographically – elucidates possible ways in which forms of textual repetition could regenerate Basque literature. In his 1953 essay 'Causes et raisons des îles désertes', Deleuze suggests that the evolution of a desert island figures *geographically* a tension between repetition and originality, and connection and separation, which exists *imaginatively*:

> Rêver des îles, avec angoisse ou joie peu importe, c'est rêver qu'on se sépare, qu'on est déjà séparé, loin des continents, qu'on est seul et perdu – ou bien c'est rêver qu'on repart à zéro, qu'on recrée, qu'on recommence. Il y avait des îles dérivées, mais l'île, c'est aussi ce vers quoi l'on dérive, et il y avait des îles originaires, *mais l'île, c'est aussi l'origine*, l'origine radicale et absolue. [Author's italics]

> Dreaming of islands – whether with joy or in fear, it doesn't matter – is dreaming of pulling away, of being already separate, far from any continent, of being lost and alone – or it is dreaming of starting from scratch, recreating, beginning anew. Some islands drifted away from the continent, but the island is also that toward which one drifts; other islands originated in the ocean, *but the island is also the origin*, radical and absolute.[99]

In the form of their creation, desert islands are poised between connection and separation: 'des îles dérivées' are born of fragmentation, of a separation from the mainland to which they were once connected; 'des îles originaires' are born of eruption, the creation of land where once there was only sea. In the geological pressures producing these two sorts of island, Deleuze reads the structures of the human imagination as conditioned by desires for creation *and* replication, by dreams of self-sufficiency *and* communication. For Deleuze, our imaginative, critical and creative responses to the untouched space of the desert island both produce and reflect the form of these desires and dreams. Do we choose to remain alone, and in that way resist the pressures to conform? Do we seek to recreate a previous world on the island, replicating the systems to which we are accustomed? Or can we utilize the interplay in our desires for separation and connection, our need for repetition and originality, to re-draw the boundaries of creativity and its models?

Deleuze explores this choice through two texts which depict desert island re-beginnings: Daniel Defoe's *Robinson Crusoe* (1719) and Jean Giraudoux's *Suzanne et le Pacifique* (1921). Defoe's text, suggests Deleuze, responds to this creative possibility by seeking a return to 'the continent': for Robinson, the island offers a blank space on which he can recreate the values and systems of the world from which he came, a world built upon the desire to produce, to grow, to colonize what is other. In Giraudoux's text, however, the creative possibility within the island remains untapped. For Suzanne, the island is sufficient in and of itself; it already contains everything she desires, and as such it forecloses her potential to create anew. In Robinson's story, then, it is the connection to the old world, the continent, which is continually recreated, whereas in Suzanne's it is the independence of the new world, the desert island, which is constantly reaffirmed. While one imaginary island is built upon connection and one upon separation, Deleuze suggests that both are built upon a desire to maintain the status quo. Consequently, as Stewart Williams notes, 'As a repetition of the same, neither the island depicted in such tales, nor its potential for novelty and difference, is fully realized there or elsewhere'.[100] In this 'repetition of the same' lies the closure of the creative potential of the desert island as a space capable of helping us to rethink our relation to the cultural, ethical, political and aesthetic systems which structure our experiences.

In *Mille plateaux,* Deleuze and Guattari develop a relation between this 'repetition of the same' and forms of textual representation and interpretation which they define as 'tracings': 'Culturel, le livre est forcément un calque: calque de lui-même déjà, calque du livre précédent du même auteur, calque d'autres livres quelles qu'en soient les différences, décalque interminable de concepts et de mots en place, décalquage du monde présent, passé ou à venir.'/'The cultural book is necessarily a tracing: already a tracing of itself, a tracing of the previous book by the same author, a tracing of other books however different they may be, an endless tracing of established concepts and words, a tracing of the word present, past, and future.'[101] Tracing reaffirms the already-thought, already-created, or already-defined: if we seek to trace what we already understand, or what already exists, we can only maintain our textual and linguistic structures, imitating the imaginative territories we already inhabit. As Atxaga suggests in 'Método para plagiar', seeking to maintain the isolation of the Basque language obliges Basque authors to trace the existing path of Basque literature, forcing the language to repeat itself over and over, without the prospect of development. Like Suzanne, alone on her island, this self-sufficiency can sustain certain possibilities but never transform them.

Yet plagiarism, Axular's solution to this insularity, seems no less problematic; tracing other literary models from a European or global canon could simply reinforce those major literary and linguistic territories and their systems of thinking. As Even-Zohar discusses in *Polysystem Theory*, young literatures which have limited models within their own languages often draw on more dominant literary cultures, through translation, to develop these languages. Yet such a practice can lead to dependence upon the source culture, affirming rather than destabilizing the power structures surrounding source and target culture.[102] Like Crusoe colonizing his island, this focus upon the wider literary world can expand creativity, but it risks discounting the uniqueness of the island itself, or in this case the creative differences within Basque language and literature. The forms of erasure through translation which Venuti defines as 'domestications' can be read, in more elaborate forms, in Deleuze's account of tracing as a repetition which sublimates variance, whether linguistic, cultural, geographic or temporal, in order to affirm what already exists.[103]

For Deleuze and Guattari, an alternative form of textual interaction can be enabled by 'mapping'. Unlike tracing, mapping seeks to experiment with, explore and modify the textual assemblages and forms of thinking it encounters, drawing the contours it perceives without trying to flatten these into images: 'La carte est ouverte, elle est connectable dans toutes ses dimensions, démontable, renversable, susceptible de recevoir constamment des modifications. […] Une carte a des entrées multiples, contrairement au calque qui revient toujours «au même».'/'The map is open and connectable in all of its dimensions; it is detachable, reversible, susceptible to constant modification. [...] A map has multiple entryways as opposed to the tracing, which always comes back "to the same"'.[104] Deleuze's figuration of the desert island is itself a map: through the connections and experimentations he pursues in his reading of the desert island he generates a cartography of creativity, mapping the spaces of our imagination and their relation to ideas of sameness and difference.

Deleuze suggests that it is by mapping the island differently, by acknowledging its simultaneous movement away from and towards the old world and its structures, that the potential for novelty and difference can be unmasked from within its geological pressures. For within the desert island, Deleuze suggests, 'ne s'opère pas la création elle-même mais la re-création, non pas le commencement mais le re-commencement. Elle est l'origine, mais l'origine seconde. À partir d'elle tout recommence'/'it is not creation but re-creation, not the beginning but a re-beginning that takes place. The deserted island is the origin, but a second origin. From it everything begins anew'.[105] For Deleuze, the fact that the desert island offers a second beginning positions it as uniquely able to figure the difference, as opposed to similarity, within forms of repetition: 'La seconde origine est donc plus essentielle que la première', he writes, 'parce qu'elle nous donne [...] la loi de la répétition'/'This second origin is more essential than the first since it gives us [...] the law of repetition'.[106] Deleuze's thinking on repetition itself produces differences indefinitely, but broadly it can be understood as movement which creates difference even as it appears unchanged. As Adrian Parr writes, 'repetition is best understood in terms of discovery and experimentation; it allows new experiences, affects and expressions to emerge. To repeat is to begin again; to affirm the power of the new and the unforeseeable'.[107] A desert island offers the law of repetition precisely because it offers such discovery and variation. For even as the island gives us the chance to repeat our world, to begin it again, that 'again' is always being displaced temporally and spatially: where we begin again is never where we began originally, but neither is it totally separate from that original moment. In Deleuze's reading, this displacement becomes creative: as questions of connection and separation collapse into each other, the island becomes a space capable of generating life anew, *again*.

While Domínguez suggests that the dominance of the desert island motif in Basque literary historiography emphasizes the territoriality of the Basque literary scene, Deleuze invokes instead the innate deterritorialization which exists within figurations of the desert island.

Positioned between sea and continent, between old world and new, a desert island is always, endlessly, caught up in generating transformative and creative collisions between these different territories. The forms of creativity Deleuze develops in response to the desert island help us to think about the ways in which plagiarism might offer a reinvigoration of the Basque literary territory. If we see plagiarism as developing creativity through – as opposed to despite – the interplay of separation and connection, and of repetition and difference that defines it, plagiarism becomes a force of exploration and experimentation, rather than derivation and colonization. In *Obabakoak* Atxaga develops a method of plagiarism which incorporates this exploration and experimentation: he suggests that the desert island of Euskera will be brought to life, not by tracing the literary world it already contains or the literary world which exists beyond it, but by constructing collisions between those two worlds, mapping the relation between minor and major literary and linguistic systems in transformative ways.

In 'Método para plagiar', the narrator describes how such a textual form might function:

> Supongamos que lo que hay que plagiar es una historia que sucede en Arabia o en la Edad Media, y que sus dos protagonistas – que están enzarzados en una discusión a causa de un camello – son Ibu al Farsi y Ali Rayol. Pues bien, el plagiario debe tomar la historia en su conjunto, pero – pongamos por caso – situándola en la Inglaterra de hoy en día. De manera que los protagonistas se conviertan, por ejemplo, en Anthony Northmore y Philip Stevens y la causa de la discusión entablada entre ambos sea, en lugar de un camello, un coche. Esos cambios, come es fácil de suponer, traerán consigo otros mil, con lo que la historia quedará prácticamente irreconocible para cualquiera.
>
> Let's suppose that we have to plagiarise a story that takes place in Arabia or in the Middle Ages and that its two protagonists – who are embroiled in an argument over a camel – are Ibu al Farsi and Ali Rayol. Right, the plagiarist should take the story in its entirety and set it – let's say – in modern-day England. So the protagonists become, for example, Anthony Northmore and Philip Stevens and, instead of a camel, the cause of the argument between them can be a car. As you can easily imagine, these changes will bring in their train a thousand more so as to render the plot completely unrecognisable to anyone.[108]

Plagiarism here becomes a process which is simultaneously repetitive and original: as an author repeats the original myths and stories of one language and culture, he or she repeatedly and necessarily reinvents them, displacing them temporally and spatially so that they offer not creation but re-creation, not a beginning but the re-beginning. Just as Deleuze's desert island maps geographically an imagined re-beginning, so plagiarism here offers a textual 'second origin', recreating a text in another time, space, and language which are not the original ones and never can be.[109]

Throughout *Obabakoak,* Atxaga engages in plagiarisms, adaptations, translations and alterations of existing texts which follow the method the narrator proposes in 'Método para plagiar', creating collisions between the Basque territory and the other literary territories which surround it. We can read these creative collisions as integral to the ways in which Atxaga himself returns life to the island of Euskera, for *Obabakoak*, this foundational text within twentieth-century Basque literature, is formed in no small part by Atxaga's varied repetitions of other texts drawn from around the world, which contribute to the genre fluidity and expansive narrative focus of the text. As I explore in the next section of this chapter, mapping the contours of Atxaga's use of plagiarism and translation alongside Deleuze and Guattari's thinking on repetition with difference reframes the dynamic between the major and minor territories at stake in the production and reception of Atxaga's work, and simultaneously offers different perspectives upon the nature of repetition and its own varied textual forms.

Repetition with difference

Plagiarism

In 'Método para plagiar', the narrator discusses the types of stories most suitable for plagiarism. In an ironic reference to hierarchical perceptions of minor and major literary communities, he directs the potential plagiarist away from 'las culturas de ámbito reducido, donde, al haber poco espacio, las relaciones – en particular las literarias – suelen estar llenas de intrigas, malicia y odio'/'minority cultures where, since there is little space, relations – especially literary ones – tend to be rife with intrigue, malice and hatred', instructing them to head instead towards '*Boulevard Balzac* [...] *Hardy Gardens* [...] *Hoffman Strasse* [...] *Piazza Pirandello*': 'lo que, expresado de otra manera, quiere decir que ha de elegir sus modelos entre los autores que andan en boca de todo el mundo'/'in other words, he must choose his models from amongst writers who are household names'.[110] The humorous dichotomy the narrator creates between major and minor literatures becomes, in Atxaga's hands, an opportunity for a creative interrogation and transformation of this dichotomy: Atxaga conforms to the stereotype of the intriguing minor author by 'stealing' stories from major literatures and using these as the backbone for his stories from Obaba.[111]

The most obvious instance of this is 'Una grieta en la nieve helada', a supposed plagiarism of a story by Auguste Villiers de l'Isle-Adam, 'La Torture par espérance' (1888), which follows directly from 'Método para plagiar'. In Villiers de l'Isle-Adam's story, the protagonist, held by the Spanish Inquisition in Segovia, is allowed to believe he is about to escape before, in sight of the door, he is recaptured and sent for 'auto da fé'.[112] Atxaga's story maintains this narrative backbone but, as suggested by the narrator in 'Método para plagiar', transposes the narrative in time and space, resituating it in the Himalayas in the twentieth century. But Atxaga acknowledges that while the place and context have been altered, the basic plot is the same and 'Algunas frases [...] las había copiado palabra por palabra'/'Some sentences [...] I copied word for word'.[113] In fact, Atxaga bases much of the narrative of *Obabakoak* upon texts by other authors. 'En busca de la última palabra', for example, takes as its frame narrative Cortázar's 'Las babas del Diablo' (1959), converting the photo of an amorous French couple at the heart of Cortázar's text into a photo taken at a primary school in Obaba. 'Método para plagiar' begins with an excerpt adapted from Dante's *The Divine Comedy* (1320), and transforms Dante's journey to the underworld, guided by Virgil, into the narrator's journey to the island of Euskera, guided by Axular. 'Jóvenes y verdes' alludes to Dylan Thomas's poem 'Fern Hill' (1945), transposing the poetic lament for lost youth from Thomas's visits to his aunt's farm in Wales to the narrator's experience growing up in Obaba.

Are these plagiarisms, adaptations, intertextual excerpts or linguistic and temporal translations? The textual collisions Atxaga creates problematize these definitions again and again, foregrounding the critical assumptions we make when we perceive similarities and differences between forms of textual repetition. However we choose to define them, these inserts hinge upon a 'domestication' in which a text is pulled from its original context and rewritten according to the 'values, beliefs and representations' of another – precisely the type of alteration which enacts the dangerous erasure that potentially attends Atxaga's self-translations.[114] Atxaga's use of such domestications in *Obabakoak*, however, re-evaluates their potential: he suggests that a text becomes original precisely in, as opposed to despite, the ways that it appropriates, alters and adapts a pre-existing work. In this sense, Atxaga's work resonates with the literary approach which John Barth describes as a 'literature of replenishment'. Discussing Borges's story 'Pierre Menard', in which the French author Menard attempts to compose – rather than imitate or repeat – Cervantes's *Don Quixote,* Barth suggests that Borges 'writes a remarkable and original work of literature, the implicit theme of which is the difficulty, perhaps the unneccessity, of writing original works of literature [...] he confronts an intellectual dead end and employs it against itself to accomplish new human work'.[115] In Barth's reading, what is fascinating about Borges's story is not that it reveals the impossibility of originality, but rather that, through exploring that impossibility, it creates a new, inherently original text. Similarly, Atxaga's discussion of the limitations of the Basque literary scene in 'Método para plagiar' offers him the material to exceed those limitations, bringing the Basque literary scene into a state of replenishment, and positioning this foundational text of twentieth-century Basque literature as one formed through the different territories – linguistic, literary and political – which are implicated in the creation of his text.

By creating his Basque stories from canonical texts, Atxaga also flips the dynamic between minor and major literatures in relation to his work, incorporating these canonical texts from different eras into the creation of a text routed firmly in contemporary literary models. These intertextual insinuations are not immune to the challenging dynamic between the global and the local which is always at stake in Atxaga's project. Still and Worton have suggested that intertextual forms are 'an attempt to struggle against complicity and exclusion', to create a path between identity and difference which does not always construct one in opposition to the other.[116] Yet in seeking such a path, the particularity of the local is always at risk of erasure, of being subsumed by a more dominant literary scene. But while Atxaga's decision to draw upon these global texts invokes their power, his deployment of them in the service of a more peripheral literary system also destabilizes the locus of that power. In this sense, Atxaga returns to the Classical tradition of *imitatio,* which saw Roman authors imitate and translate texts from Greek literary culture. As Rita Copeland notes, this process simultaneously invoked a reverence for that culture and a desire to displace its hegemony – something Copeland describes as the 'paradox of difference through replication'.[117] In a similar way, by creating his Basque stories from canonical texts, Atxaga flips the dynamic between minor and major literatures: rather than a major culture imposing itself on a minor one, forcing the minor culture to conform to its cultural or linguistic systems, the minor culture here imposes itself on a major one, forcing major texts to conform to its dynamics.

At the same time, the inclusion of these canonical texts as the framework for elements of *Obabakoak* shifts our understanding of the shape and form of the Basque literary scene itself, revealing the transformative potential of infusing a minor literary scene with more established literary influences. The stories Atxaga tells exceed the boundaries of Obaba: drawing on influences from Borges to Michel Tournier, Atxaga narrates stories set far beyond the Basque Country, transposing the reader from Germany to China, Baghdad to Barcelona. Through this intertextual game, Atxaga re-maps and re-imagines the geographic focus for his 'stories from Obaba': whether written in Basque or Castilian, these stories outstrip their initial focus upon the Basque community to reveal Obaba, and Atxaga's own writing, to be plural, dynamic, and engaged in illuminating insinuations into the hegemonic literary, linguistic and cultural systems which threaten to enclose it.

Atxaga's creative collisions thus transform both the plagiarized text and the text created through this plagiarism, affecting both the major literary system from which the plagiarized text is drawn and the minor literary system into which it is incorporated. As Parvati Nair suggests, 'whilst Atxaga has undoubtedly put Basque literature on the world map, his narrative strategies reveal [this literature] to be a hybrid site of interconnections'.[118] But as much as it destabilizes an opposition between minor and major literary systems, Atxaga's hybridity also challenges conceptions of plagiarism as either theft or innovation, and literature as either inherently repetitive or innately original: instead, Atxaga creates a form which is both original and repetitive, formed through both theft and innovation. How might this hybridity affect our understanding of the creative nature of repetition itself? In *Mille plateaux,* Deleuze and Guattari describe a double process of 'deterritorialization' and 'reterritorialization' at stake within the collision of two different forms, and elucidate through this figuration the relationship between repetition, representation and imitation:

> L'orchidée se déterritorialise en formant une image, un calque de guêpe; mais la guêpe se reterritorialise sur cette image. La guêpe se déterritorialise pourtant, devenant elle-même une pièce dans l'appareil de reproduction de l'orchidée; mais elle reterritorialise l'orchidée, en en transportant le pollen. [...] On pourrait dire que

l'orchidée imite la guêpe dont elle reproduit l'image de manière signifiante (mimesis, mimétisme, leurre, etc.). [...] En même temps il s'agit de tout autre chose: plus du tout imitation, mais capture de code, plus-value de code, augmentation de valence, véritable devenir, devenir-guêpe de l'orchidée, devenir-orchidée de la guêpe [...] Il n'y a plus imitation ni ressemblance, mais explosion de deux séries hétérogènes dans la ligne de fuite.

The orchid deterritorializes by forming an image, a tracing of a wasp; but the wasp reterritorializes on that image. The wasp is nevertheless deterritorialized, becoming a piece in the orchid's reproductive apparatus. But it reterritorializes the orchid by transporting its pollen. [...] It could be said that the orchid imitates the wasp, reproducing its image in a signifying fashion (mimesis, mimicry, lure, etc.). [...] At the same time, something else entirely is going on: not imitation at all but a capture of code, surplus value of code, an increase in valence, a veritable becoming, a becoming-wasp of the orchid and a becoming-orchid of the wasp. [...] There is neither imitation nor resemblance, only an exploding of two heterogeneous series on a line of flight.[119]

The creativity of this figuration, which itself deterritorializes and reterritorializes a dynamic from the natural world into a philosophical exploration, positions difference as a productive force of development. The wasp and the orchid share points of contact, but their different anatomical structures, their different relations to one another and to the natural world around them, mean that each pushes the other beyond its own limits. In this continuous movement between deterritorialization and reterritorialization, mimesis is replaced by symbiosis, and the possibility of imitation mutates into capture, increase, becoming.[120] For, in their symbiotic relationship, neither wasp nor orchid can imitate the other without subjecting themselves to a transformation: as each captures, alters and takes on the attributes of the other, any attempt at replication is converted into a becoming – a becoming-wasp and becoming-orchid.

Deleuze and Guattari's discussion of the relations of life and production in the natural world in terms of the relationship between deterritorialization, reterritorialization, imitation and becoming offers a swerve of thought which elucidates, and is elucidated by, the forms of textual repetition in *Obabakoak*. In Atxaga's plagiaristic play, one text is caught up in another, bringing both the texts and the literature and language in which they originated into a symbiotic relationship.

Deterritorialized from its original context, the plagiarized text becomes part of a new assemblage, incorporated into *Obabakoak* in a way which transforms the plagiarized text's own shape, narrative and interpretative possibilities. Reterritorialized into this new context, the plagiarized text also enables *Obabakoak* to 'become', shaping and forming Atxaga's text and providing the backbone for Atxaga to engage in creative rewritings which extend the geographic and cultural scope of *Obabakoak* itself. In this capture, two a-parallel textual forms – developed from within two different literary systems, at very different moments in their creativity and development – collide, coincide and combine, but never replicate one another.

In *Dialogues*, Deleuze suggests that the forms of interaction and relation he describes as 'capture' and in terms of 'devenir' are opposed to those of plagiarism:

> Voler, c'est le contraire de plagier, de copier, d'imiter ou de faire comme. La capture est toujours une double-capture, le vol, un double-vol, et c'est cela qui fait, non pas quelque chose de mutuel, mais un bloc asymétrique, une évolution a-parallèle, des noces, toujours «hors» et «entre».
>
> Stealing is the opposite of plagiarizing, copying, imitating, or doing like. Capture is always a double-capture, theft a double-theft, and it is that which creates not something mutual, but an asymmetrical block, an a-parallel evolution, nuptials, always "outside" and "between".[121]

But Atxaga's approach to plagiarism in *Obabakoak* suggests that this textual practice can be a variation of stealing, in the meaning Deleuze gives to this term: a collision of two different entities engaged in a productive, transformative but not imitative interaction. In Atxaga, plagiarism is both theft and creative adaptation: it captures a text and is also captured by that text, thereby creating a space outside and between the traced models of our textual production.

Deleuze's figuration of the desert island, and Deleuze and Guattari's account of the wasp and the orchid, allow us to think differently about the problematic and shifting dynamic between repetition and originality, illuminating the ways in which two different texts can connect and separate, collide and transform in a-parallel formations. Creativity is born from this a-parallel evolution: it is the *lack* of similarity between two texts – the different modes of their production and reception – which incorporates difference into the textual evolution enacted by plagiarism, an evolution of alteration, then, rather than duplication. Could this figuration also help us think about translation, and particularly the relationship between the two different languages implicated in Atxaga's experience of self-translation?

Translation

As Barbara Godard emphasizes in 'Deleuze and Translation', '[t]ranslation [...] is not a question with which Deleuze was much concerned – explicitly, that is'. Nonetheless, she suggests, Deleuze's thinking contains 'an implicit theory of translation as creative swerve', which becomes decipherable when his texts are read 'transversally'.[122] Mapping, rather than tracing, the contours of Deleuze and Guattari's accounts of deterritorialization, reterritorialization, repetition and becoming allows me to explore new readings of the dynamics of translation, particularly in relation to Atxaga's work. As with the desert island, Atxaga's creative identity is torn between dreams of connection and dreams of separation; like the wasp and the orchid, Atxaga's two texts and his two languages are derived from two different power structures. This asymmetrical dynamic can position translation as a violent imposition: when a text is incorporated into a new linguistic, literary and political system, its original system is disrupted, domesticated or destroyed. An ethics of translation, in Venuti's terms, involves revealing this asymmetry, foreignizing a translated text so that this violence can be acknowledged and discharged. But, helped by the relation Deleuze and Guattari develop between the wasp and orchid, we can also read translation as a capture which replaces an either/or dynamic with a conjunctive one, as a theft which incorporates deterritorialization *and* reterritorialization into diverse movements of transformative and creative evolution.

Atxaga has described the relationship between his two languages and cultures as involving a 'leap'.[123] In an interview with *El Mundo* in 1989, he suggested that this asymmetry makes it 'prácticamente imposible traducir directamente del euskera al castellano. [...] Lo que hice fue plantearme la novela de un modo distinto'/'practically impossible to translate directly from Basque to Castilian. [...] What I did was think about the novel in a different way'.[124] Atxaga's comment positions translation as a re-beginning, an opportunity, like the one Deleuze reads in the geography of the desert island, to recreate in different forms upon an existing territory. The dynamics of this recreation hinge upon an interplay of difference and repetition: in translation, difference produces repetition; repetition, in turn, produces more difference. For without the linguistic and cultural dissimilarity between Basque and Castilian, or between these and English, there would be no need for Atxaga's text to be repeated through translation. At the same time, translation incorporates differences, both explicit and implicit, into every text with which it engages. Just as the wasp and orchid together produce an explosion of creativity through the interaction of their different forms, so translation – in its very attempt to bridge the gaps between cultural and linguistic differences – creates an evolution-as-hiatus, in which each impasse and divergence only pushes creativity and development further. In the temporal, spatial and linguistic displacement created by translation, Atxaga acknowledges the impossibility of imitation or replication, deploying this impossibility in order to generate a 'becoming' of his original text. This 'becoming', produced through the creative pressures between his two literary and linguistic territories, incorporates difference into the structure of *Obabakoak* itself. These structural changes reposition the text within its new literary system, but the form of the alterations Atxaga makes also illuminates the disruptive, but potentially connective and transformative, nature of translation itself.

As I discussed earlier, a desire to introduce the Basque literary scene to a foreign readership provides the impetus for Atxaga to shift *Obabakoak* into self-questioning narrative forms through the introduction of the paratext 'A modo de autobiografía'. On a structural level, this paratext enacts a literal 'becoming' of *Obabakoak*, deferring its ending by extending the text by another six pages. This extension is particularly notable because of the focus of the series of stories which it follows: 'En busca de la última palabra' explores the endings we seek, both in life and in literature. The title, 'In Search of the Last Word', reflects the desire of the narrator, a Basque author, both to 'have the last word' – to prove that he is right – and to 'find the last word' – to finish the text he is writing. Ironically, the first of these desires culminates in the narrator's inability to achieve the second. Convinced that an old wives' tale that warns children '[n]unca os quedéis dormidos sobre la hierba [...]. Si los hacéis, vendrá un lagarto y se os meterá en la cabeza'/'Never go to sleep on the grass [...]. If you do, a lizard will come along and climb inside your head' is not metaphorical but literal, the narrator ends up spending the night locked in a hut full of lizards.[125] Subsequently, he begins to lose his ability to create or comprehend any abstract use of language. As the text ends, we understand that the narrator has given up writing and will remain in Obaba, the boundaries of his experience limited by his inability to understand any non-functional use of language. In 'Preguntas desde

Japón' Atxaga suggests that *Obabakoak* is a text about the development of language; yet, the text – in its Basque version at least – culminates with the loss of language and creativity. For Gil-Oslé, Atxaga's focus upon this loss of language integrates humility and humour into his project to reinvigorate Basque literature, revealing that this project must always confront its limitations.[126] For Gabilondo, it converts the violent history of the Basque Country into a magical-realist narrative which cannot threaten the Spanish state.[127] But the forms of this loss of creativity also have particular relevance to Atxaga's exploration in 'Método para plagiar' of the aridity of the Basque literary scene. For the loss of the narrator's ability to use abstract language occurs because of his decision to assign a functional rather than an experimental role to the lizard story, to read it as fact rather than fiction. The suggestion here is that to assign language or literature a solely utilitarian purpose – be that purpose cultural or political – undermines the ability of that language to function as an instrument of relation with the world.[128]

But while the narrator's desire to have the last word proves creatively limiting, his failed search for the last word of his text proves creatively productive. For this search is subject to a continual postponement: every time the narrator seeks to tell us his story, a story destined to end in his own creative and, we understand, actual death, his words are delayed by the words of others, by the translations, variations and plagiarisms which run throughout *Obabakoak*: 'Una vez más, la última palabra tendrá que esperar. [...] Ha llegado, pues, el momento de hacer otro inciso, porque me resulta imposible continuar en busca de la última palabra sin antes transcribir este relato. He procurado traducirle lo mejor posible.'/'Once again, the last word will have to wait. [...] The time has come, then, to insert another parenthesis, because I find it impossible to continue my search for the last word without first transcribing this story. I did my best to make the translation a good one.'[129]

As in *A Thousand and One Nights*, in *Obabakoak* every story the narrator tells defers his existential and textual ending; and, just as the figure of Axular suggests in 'Método para plagiar' that plagiarism can bring life to the creatively desolate Basque language, so drawing upon the words of others replaces the creativity the narrator himself begins to lack. It is thus particularly apt that the last words of 'En busca de la última palabra' are themselves extended by translation, through the insertion of 'A modo de autobiografía' into the Castilian version. Even more aptly, the content of this paratext, while focused upon the limitations of the Basque language, ends with an emphatic refusal to allow such limitations to stultify the creativity of the Basque literary scene: 'Pero seguiremos intentándolo, seguiremos escribiendo. El tablero está ahí para que juguemos'/'But we will keep trying, we will keep writing. The reason the board is there is for us to continue playing'.[130] In the narrative of 'En busca de ultima palabra', translation enables a continuation of writing, offering the material for new forms of creativity; in the translation of *Obabakoak* into Castilian, this material becomes incorporated into a literal continuation of the text itself, and into a shift of focus which sees the text end, not with a loss of literary creativity, but with a call for its continued development.

In the Castilian translation of *Obabakoak*, Atxaga complements the extension created by 'A modo de autobiografía' with another structural modification: a shift in the order of the stories. The story which begins the Basque text, 'Exposición de la carta del canónigo Lizardi', becomes the second story, replaced by 'Esteban Werfell', the third story in the Basque text. The difference between these two stories is the focus and location of their action. 'Exposición de la carta del canónigo Lizardi' is the story of an insular Basque community, its rejection of an outsider and the devastating consequences of this rejection. Narrated through the fragmented letters of Canon Lizardi, the story focuses upon Javier, an illegitimate child abused and finally excluded because of the nature of his birth. This exclusion takes a dramatic turn when a beautiful white boar appears in the village, bearing an uncanny resemblance to Javier himself. Just as they sought to destroy Javier-the-boy through emotional brutality, so the Obaban community seeks to destroy Javier-the-boar through physical cruelty. Unable to accept what they cannot understand, the villagers taunt and threaten the boar, until he turns on those who have harmed him, killing some and injuring others, before he is finally destroyed himself.

While 'Exposición de la carta del canónigo Lizardi' focuses upon a somewhat parochial Basque community, 'Esteban Werfell' is a story about the pull of the world beyond that community. Esteban is a child torn between two cultures: the world of Obaba, where he lives and from where his mother came, and the world of Hamburg, where his father grew up. The battle between Esteban's two cultures is thematized through the experience of writing: Esteban's father, desperate to prevent him remaining enclosed in Obaba, writes letters to Esteban from an imaginary German girl. The experience of writing to someone beyond Obaba alters Esteban's life irrevocably: 'Yo [...] iba a convertirme, a partir de ese momento, en un complete extraño [...]. Comencé a sentirme superior a la gente de Obaba. [...] Yo prefería quedarme en casa, estudiando alemán'/'I realised that the letter marked the end of an era in my life. I [...] was about to become, from that moment on, a complete foreigner [...]. I began to feel superior to the people of Obaba. [...] I preferred to stay at home studying German'.[131] Having learnt another language and connected, through this, to a world beyond Obaba, Esteban finally leaves Obaba for university, never to return.

Atxaga's decision to begin his translated 'stories from Obaba' with a story focused on a departure from Obaba emphasizes connectivity (as opposed to isolation) as the dominant trope of his imagined Basque community. Gabilondo has criticized *Obabakoak* for its invocation of a magical, archaic and pastoral Basque identity which conforms to Western expectations of a minority culture.[132] But any expectation on the part of the Castilian, and later English readership, that *Obabakoak* will offer a stereotyped vision of a rural, isolated and somewhat archaic Basque world, such as the one explored in 'Exposición de la carta del canónigo Lizardi', is disrupted from the outset in the translated texts: in 'Esteban Werfell' Atxaga emphasizes that Obaba is part of a broader European reality as well as a specifically Basque one. Atxaga's alteration to the order of stories thus mirrors a shift enacted by the process of translation, in which a text is liberated from its foundations in a single culture and brought into connection and conjunction with another culture and language. In translation, *Obabakoak* undergoes a journey, similar to the one experienced by Esteban, from separation to connection through the process of being written in another language.[133]

While the narrative of 'Esteban Werfell' explores the power of such connections, though, it also reveals the potential losses they involve. For the relationship Esteban builds through his letters – an imaginary one, after all – is formed at the expense of his existing, and very real, Basque culture. The loss of this culture has a limiting effect upon Esteban: 'Nunca escribía o hablaba directamente, nunca se relacionaba francamente con la gente que le rodeaba. [...] En su vida, todo había sido silencio, pasividad, retiro'/'He never spoke or wrote directly, he never dealt frankly with the people around him. [...] His whole life had been one of silence, passivity, withdrawal'.[134] For Esteban, the triumph of the world beyond Obaba appears ironically to have limited his ability to connect in any meaningful way to the world around him. In 'Esteban Werfell', Atxaga suggests that the connections we form through writing, through translation into languages other than our own, are not only expansive, creative and generative: in the movement from one culture and language to another, something is lost as well as gained.

This loss and gain is something Atxaga recognizes as implicit within his own experience of translation. In the epilogue to his Castilian translation of his novel *Bi anai*, he suggests that this translation, *Dos Hermanos*, which appeared eleven years after the Basque text, equals '"Bi anai" más-menos once años de la vida de su autor'/'*Bi anai* plus-minus eleven years of the author's life'.[135] The expression 'más-menos' is a recognition that, in every moment of re-writing, a text becomes different, its creation, production and reception altered by the passage of time. Even when two texts appear exactly the same, they interiorize a temporal, but also experiential, difference which cannot be sublimated, a disjunction – like the one Deleuze reads in the geography of the desert island – between a first and a second beginning. In *Différence et répétition,* Deleuze invokes Borges's text 'Pierre Menard' to elucidate this interiorized difference. Menard's story, suggests Deleuze, reveals to us the transformative, illuminating power of repetition, by demonstrating that even 'la répétition la plus exacte, la plus stricte a pour corrélat le maximum de différence («Le texte de Cervantes et celui de Ménard sont verbalement identiques, mais le second est presque infiniment plus riche...»)'/'In this case, the most exact, the most strict repetition has as its correlate the maximum of difference ("The text of Cervantes and that of Menard are verbally identical, but the second is almost infinitely richer...")'.[136] Deleuze's discussion of Borges's text articulates the difference inherent within 'identical' texts, the contextual and historical transformations generated in the very moment of apparent replication.

But in that very difference lies the ability of translation to shift representation into transformation, imitation into becoming. I began this chapter by discussing Atxaga's figuration of translation as a spaceship travelling on a flight path between his two linguistic territories. In this figuration Atxaga extols the ability of translation to overcome asymmetries and distances between languages to enable connection and transmission. But translation is never simply connective: it is simultaneously transformative, challenging, and disruptive. In their figuration of the wasp and the orchid, Deleuze and Guattari suggest that the two create an 'explosion de deux séries hétérogènes dans la ligne de fuite'/'an exploding of two heterogeneous series on a line of flight', a force field of development and change operating at the intersection between different territories.[137] We might therefore position translation itself as a 'line of flight', as opposed to a flight path, between different linguistic, literary and cultural territories. For Deleuze and Guattari, lines of flight create points of departure from the systems of thought which grasp us in formations of identity or similitude. Lines of flight connect to translation as two varied but linked forms of modification, mutation and metamorphosis, both being elements in an account of the ways in which systems and assemblages interact, connect and transform one another.

Lines of flight are not simply modes of escape: they also return us to the systems we try to evade, reterritorializing us in new structures. As Deleuze and Guattari recognize, '[o]n fait une rupture, on trace une ligne de fuite, mais on risque toujours de retrouver sur elle des organisations qui restratifient l'ensemble, des formations qui redonnent le pouvoir à un signifiant.'/'You may make a rupture, draw a line of flight, yet there is still a danger that you will reencounter organizations that restratify everything, formations that restore power to a signifier'.[138] In 'Aesthetics of Encounter: Variations on Translation in Deleuze', Michael LeVan suggests that lines of flight help us think about translation precisely *because* of their potential for failure:

> A line of flight is given in the mode of risk – that a movement of deterritorialization can always turn into a line a death. In other words, translation has no guarantees, no pre-ordained telos, and often is susceptible to failure. In this sense, translation [...] is not an end in itself, but a risky and necessary mode for the possibility of the constitution of the new social arrangements.[139]

LeVan here emphasizes the immanent and temporary mode of translation: in every movement away from static forces of representation and understanding, we enter into dangerous territories which are not pre-formed but which may as easily lead us into new systems of limitation as free us from old ones.

In this risk, however, resides the force of translation: because of its ability to liberate and constrain, to deterritorialize a text and reterritorialize it elsewhere, to repress but also expand, to overwrite but also to renew, translation offers us a site through which to interrogate the assemblages surrounding textual production. Translation can operate as a 'molar line', designating, ordering and regimenting the literary field of any text. But it can also be a 'molecular line', transmitting and travelling across these designated territories, bringing information in and out, but seeking to adapt itself either to the culture from which it comes or to the culture into which it enters. Deleuze and Guattari's distinction is one we might, with Venuti, characterize as a double movement of 'domestication' and 'foreignization'.[140] But Venuti's characterization fails to account for the other lines and vibrations at play within translation. For, conceived as a process of repetition with difference, translation can also behave as a line of flight, travelling beyond these regiments, beholden to neither source nor target, pursuing its own process of mutation and change through which it transforms and transmutes the territories it encounters, while never evading the possibility of re-appropriation.

As I discussed at the beginning of this chapter, Atxaga's experience of writing has been conditioned by his bilingualism, and particularly by the minor–major dynamic which exists between his two languages. But does translation inevitably assert a hegemonic discourse at the expense of a minor one? Or can translation, operating as a line of flight, enable a different reading of the connection between translation and major/minor dynamics, particularly in relation to Atxaga's self-translation of *Obabakoak*? In the final part of this chapter, I turn to Deleuze and Guattari's discussion of minor literature in *Kafka: Pour une littérature mineure*, and explore the ways in which both the narrative of *Obabakoak* and Atxaga's translation of the text engage in forms of 'becoming-minor'.

Towards a minor literature of translation

From metaphor to metamorphosis

For Deleuze and Guattari, bilingual authors inhabit a unique position: existing between two languages, they belong simultaneously to both and to neither. This liminality makes these authors foreigners in their own tongue, an experience which Deleuze and Guattari suggest is the property of minorities, and minor literatures: 'Combien de gens aujourd'hui vivent dans une langue qui n'est pas la leur? Ou bien ne connaissent même plus la leur [...]? Problème des minorités. Problème d'une littérature mineure'/'How many people today live in a language that is not their own? Or no longer, or not yet, even know their own [...]? This is [...] the problem of minorities, the problem of a minor literature'.[141] In *El hijo del acordeonista*, Atxaga suggests, through the voice of Joseba, that it is precisely this sense of alienation which underlines the difference between the descendants of Basque speakers, who may not speak Basque themselves, and those of speakers of more major languages: 'Nunca se dará el caso de que un inglés o un español diga: "Las palabras que estuvieron en boca de mis padres me resultan extrañas"'/'You'd never hear a speaker of English or Spanish saying: "The words that were in my parents' mouths are strange to me"'.[142] As Atxaga discusses in 'A modo de autobiografía', authors who write in Basque, and readers who engage with their texts, repeatedly confront this sensation that their language is not their own:

> Cuando un lector lee, en castellano, una novela con mucho diálogo, es muy probable que no vea los continuos *dijo, respondió y replicó* del texto. [...] Que las ha leído tantas veces que ya no repara en

> ellas. Escribiendo en euskara, yo no tengo problemas con *dijo* (esan), o con *respondió* (erantzun); pero empiezo a tenerlos con *replicó* (arrapostu), debido a que esta palabra no le es familiar al lector [...]. Así las cosas, el escritor vasco sabe que su lector se detendrá en esa palabra, que supondrá una interferencia.
>
> When a reader reads a novel with a lot of dialogue, he probably doesn't even see the constant repetition in the text of 'he said', 'he replied' and 'he retorted'. [...] He has read the words so many times, he doesn't even notice them. Writing in *euskera*, I have no problems with 'he said' (*esan*) or with 'he replied' (*eratzun*) but I begin to have problems with 'he retorted' (*arrapostu*) because this word is not familiar to the reader [...]. So the Basque writer knows that his reader will stop at that word, that it will be a stumbling block.[143]

Atxaga suggests that this 'interference' is problematic because it renders a literary language too obviously artificial. But for Deleuze and Guattari, one of the ways in which a writer can become-minor is by becoming a stranger within his or her own language: to confront the artificiality of linguistic structures is also to confront their limits, to replace language as a site of representation and signification with language as disarticulation and experimentation, and to position writing as an impossible task, a continually unfulfilled pressure to inhabit new, challenging forms.[144]

Deleuze and Guattari map this impossibility through Kafka's experience as a Jew living in Prague, writing in German: 'Kafka définit en ce sens l'impasse qui barre aux juifs de Prague l'accès à l'écriture, et fait de leur littérature quelque chose d'impossible: impossibilité de ne pas écrire, impossibilité d'écrire en allemand, impossibilité d'écrire autrement'/'In this sense, Kafka marks the impasse that bars access to writing for the Jews of Prague, and turns their literature into something impossible – the impossibility of not writing, the impossibility of writing in German, the impossibility of writing otherwise'.[145] Deleuze and Guattari's reading presents Kafka's work as a literary machine, constituted of lines of flight and escape, of impasses and blockages, of desires and intensities, developed through space, object, character, event and expression.[146] Kafka's literary machine operates through experimentation, rather than interpretation, metaphor, allegory or symbolism, as a way of engaging with the political and social realities which surround it: 'Kafka tue délibérément toute métaphore, tout symbolisme, toute signification, non moins que toute désignation'/'Kafka deliberately kills all metaphor, all symbolism, all signification, no less than all designation'.[147] As Keith

Woodward and John Paul Jones III suggest, Deleuze and Guattari conceive metaphor as a 'major' form of expression, which, like tracing, operates to affirm an existing pattern of hierarchized relations: 'They maintain that metaphor belongs to an idealist realm of relation that, like the evolutionary natural sciences, uses strategies of 'series and structure' to produce degrees of resemblance and difference between a set of terms'.[148] Deleuze and Guattari argue that Kafka shifts metaphor – an imitative linguistic process which transfers properties from one system to another while suppressing their transformative relation – into metamorphosis – the mutual becoming of two forms conceived through the combinations created by their difference. The shift from metaphor to metamorphosis recalls the figuration of the wasp and the orchid in *Mille plateaux*, through which Deleuze and Guattari displace a conception of evolution as uninterrupted progression with a conception of evolution as becoming-through-hiatus: 'La métamorphose est le contraire de la métaphore. Il n'y a plus sens propre ni sens figuré, mais distribution d'états dans l'éventail du mot'/'Metamorphosis is the contrary of metaphor. There is no longer any proper sense or figurative sense, but only a distribution of states that is part of the range of the word'.[149]

Deleuze and Guattari argue that in Kafka's *The Metamorphosis* (1915), Gregor's conversion into an insect is not metaphorical but metamorphic, 'capture d'un fragment de code, et non pas reproduction d'une image'/'the capture of a fragment of the code, and not the reproduction of an image'.[150] In this metamorphic shift, the 'code' of Gregor and the 'code' of insect – their habits and conventions, the structures of their actions and thinking – fragment and are captured and exchanged, each code overwriting, developing and distorting the original nature of the other:[151]

> Il ne s'agit pas d'une ressemblance entre le comportement d'un animal et celui de l'homme, encore moins d'un jeu de mots. Il n'y a plus ni homme ni animal, puisque chacun déterritorialise l'autre [...]. Il s'agit d'un devenir qui comprend au contraire le maximum de différence comme différence d'intensité [...].
>
> It is no longer a question of a resemblance between the comportment of an animal and that of a man; it is even less a question of a simple wordplay. There is no longer man or animal, since each deterritorializes the other [...]. Instead, it is now a question of a becoming that includes the maximum of differences as a difference of intensity [...].[152]

In this reading, imitation and metaphor shift into becoming, subjecting the libidinal, bureaucratic and familial structures forming and constraining Gregor to a deterritorialization, and positioning him on a line of flight into a new territory, in which his marginality can – briefly – be recognized rather than suppressed.

This deterritorialization disrupts the binary oppositions between man and animal, Gregor and insect: Gregor-insect is neither one nor the other, but a molecular convergence of two different forms which interact in an endless process of becoming. In Deleuze's and Guattari's thought, becoming-animal, like becoming-woman and becoming-minor, involves a movement from opposition to interrelation: as in the figuration of the wasp and the orchid, two different entities engage in a dynamic transfer which transforms the oppositional systems which structure them. 'Becoming-animal' reframes the opposition human/animal; 'becoming-woman' unpicks the opposition man/woman'; 'becoming-minor' disturbs the opposition major/minor. This final opposition is connected to the others through extension and development: to become-animal or become-woman is also to engage in a politics of becoming-minor. Excluded from the majority discourse of possession, identity and being, such voices create and inhabit a space of difference through a process of endless metamorphosis, for only by undoing the oppositions which exclude it can the margin be incorporated into an interior, transforming that interior in the process.

Atxaga's experience of writing is conditioned by a similar set of linguistic impossibilities to those Deleuze and Guattari discuss in relation to Kafka's work: the impossibility of writing in Euskera, because of its limited genealogy; the impossibility of not writing in Euskera, and thereby betraying his identity as a Basque author, and, implicitly, the Basque language itself; and the impossibility of not writing in Castilian, because of the ways this would limit his readership. Moreover, there are also interesting parallels within the narrative of *Obabakoak* to Deleuze and Guattari's exploration of the connection between Kafka's 'killing' of metaphor and his development of metamorphosis and the transformative power of becoming, particularly in relation to the loss of language which Atxaga describes in 'En busca de la última palabra'. For the decay of the narrator's language within this story culminates, specifically, in an inability on his part to understand metaphor: when his uncle, attempting to make him comprehend what has happened, says 'tu cabeza era antes como una antorcha […] pero que esa antorcha se está apagando por momentos'/'before, your head was like a flaming torch. […] but that torch is burning lower by the minute', the narrator replies, 'No le dije nada, pero creo que mi tío se está volviendo loco. Mi cabeza siempre ha sido redonda, nunca ha sido como una antorcha'/'I didn't say anything at the time but I really think my uncle is going mad. My head has always been round, it's never been anything like a torch'.[153] As in Kafka's texts, the narrator's loss of metaphor is transformed into a material metamorphosis: following his failure to understand the relation of similarity which allows his uncle to progress from 'torch' to 'head', the narrator begins to undergo his own metamorphosis, incorporating the characteristics of the lizards he has been researching into his own identity, until his literary aspirations are replaced by a desire to do nothing more than catch flies. The last words the narrator utters announce that '[m]e aburro sentado aquí en la biblioteca. Menos mal que hay moscas. Quiero decir que luego iré [...] a pescar, y que entonces nos vendrán de perlas las moscas que ahora estoy cazando aquí'/'I get bored sitting here in the library. Just as well there are some flies here. I mean later on I can go fishing [...] and they'll come in really handy then, these flies I'm catching now'.[154]

The import of this 'becoming-lizard' can be read on multiple levels within Atxaga's work. On one level, it is part of a series of becomings which permeate *Obabakoak*, becomings which raise questions about the structures that delimit our sense of individual identity. In 'Exposición de la carta del canónigo Lizardi', Javier's metamorphosis into a white boar enables him to escape from and wreak a just revenge upon those who have tortured him. In 'Margarete y Heinrich, gemelos', a ship worker, unable to recover after the suicide of his twin sister, finds a new happiness after he inhabits her identity, gaining a connection to those around him in a way he found impossible as a man. As in Deleuze and Guattari's reading of *The Metamorphosis*, in *Obabakoak* these becomings offer the characters freedom from the restrictions – social, familial and literary – which bind them. But they are not simply metaphors of escape, for these transformations occur on a molecular level which renders the characters *neither* male *nor* female; *neither* man *nor* animal. Instead, they inhabit a space *between* both identities, a liminality emphasized by a narrative ambiguity that leaves us unable to adequately determine or define the nature of their identity.

The narrator of 'En busca de la última palabra' develops the characteristics of a lizard, his purpose defined by his need to catch flies. Yet Atxaga never reveals to the reader his narrator's physical shape. The narrator is effectively suspended between man and animal, the resolution of his identity dependent on the reader's interpretations. Neither does Atxaga offer any definitive answers regarding the nature of Javier's transformation. Indeed, the villagers who are so enraged by his presence fear him precisely because they are unable to quantify him: is he man, or animal? His physical shape is animal, yet his actions are motivated by his human loyalties, griefs and rancour: he only seeks revenge on those who hurt him as a boy, and protects those who protected him. The villagers' desire to destroy Javier reveals their inability to accept an identity which exists between the binary opposition of man *or* animal. Finally, Heinrich's appropriation of his sister's identity shifts his own identity into a peripheral space. His initial transformation is a superficial one: he puts on his sister's dress. But this surface transformation brings with it a fundamental alteration to the formation of his self: 'la transformación se produjo en cuanto el vestido tocó su piel [...]. – De ahora en adelante seremos la misma persona, Margarete–murmuró'/'the transformation was made as soon as the dress his touched his skin [...]. "From now on we will be one and the same person, Margarete," he murmured'.[155] Yet the ambiguity remains for the reader, in the Spanish text if not the English, through the lack of gender-specific pronouns to refer to Heinrich: throughout, his name remains masculine, and the only pronoun used to refer to him is the female 'ella', used only once, at the very end of the text.

The ambiguity of Spanish pronoun use, which does not require a subject pronoun, and conjugates the possessive pronoun according to the noun it precedes, is rendered problematic in the English translation, which requires the translator to select either male or female forms. Jull Costa maintains the use of 'him' and 'he' throughout, a shift which represses the liminality of Heinrich's gender identity in the text. But in both texts the identity of the character, and our understanding of that identity, remains caught between two poles – between man and animal, man and woman – foregrounding and challenging our understanding of those definitions themselves. While metaphor emphasizes a *resemblance* between the behaviour of man and animal, or man and woman, metamorphosis initiates a *becoming* in which each identity is deterritorialized within the other, challenging the stasis of the structures through which we define gender and species identities in the first place.

Becoming-minor does have its limits: as in translation, the lines of flight the characters pursue away from the systems which repress them can culminate in what Deleuze and Guattari term 'lines of death'. In *The Metamorphosis*, Gregor loses the will to live, and starves to death; the transformation of his relation to the systems constraining him collapses as those systems begin to regain their power. In *Obabakoak*, Javier is wounded by those who abused him as a boy, and ultimately dies at the hands of a friend who cannot bear his suffering; Heinrich finds that becoming his sister means absorbing her destiny, and at the end of the story we understand that he too will commit suicide; the narrator of 'En busca de la última palabra' undergoes a creative death which is the prelude to his imminent actual death.

Are becomings always destined to culminate in death? For Deleuze and Guattari, the possibility of failure is one of the principles of becoming: 'N'est-ce pas plutôt que les devenirs-animaux n'arrivent pas à remplir leur principe, gardent toujours une ambiguïté qui fait leur insuffisance et les condamne à l'échec?'/'Isn't it rather that the acts of becoming-animal cannot follow their principle all the way through – that they maintain a certain ambiguity that leads to their insufficiency and condemns them to defeat?'[156] This ambiguity, as I have suggested, is at the heart of Atxaga's narration of the metamorphoses in *Obabakoak*. But perhaps it is also what prevents metamorphosis from drifting back into metaphor, for if metamorphosis can never complete its transfer, can never shift one form into another without failing and leaving traces of that first self behind, it remains a transformative, as opposed to transcendent, mode of interaction. Metaphor requires a revelatory leap of interpretation which negates the difference between its originary terms, replacing and masking this difference with a semblance of similarity; metamorphosis, and the failure of absolute metamorphosis, insists that transfer can never be perfected, that no Ideal form can be attained through the interaction of two different terms.

The ethical potential Deleuze and Guattari find in this shift of metaphor into metamorphosis elucidates a second level on which we can read the forms of minor literature at play within Atxaga's work, namely the level of translation. In 'On the Border with Deleuze and Guattari', Woodward and Jones explore Deleuze and Guattari's conception of metaphor in terms which reveal its relation to translation. They speak of

> [t]he organization of a closed system that assembles terms and relations according to likenesses, imagining for itself a prior, transcendental Ideal form to which all other terms speak [...] a hierarchical model that uses the supposed unity of the first term in the series, the Ideal subject or object, as a grounds for producing the individual (individuated) unities of subsequent subjects/objects, each of which differ in varying degrees of perfection, but find their wholeness through a hierarchy of likenesses.[157]

This reading of metaphor bears a striking resemblance to Platonic conceptions of translation, which perceive translation as a likeness, in varying degrees, of a transcendental and Ideal original text. To read translation in this way is to insist upon a hierarchy of relations which positions an original – in Atxaga's case, a Basque original – as the Ideal 'to which all other terms speak'. But we can, with Deleuze and Guattari, read translation differently, as a form of becoming which shifts hierarchies between texts, languages and cultures into dynamic interrelation. Reading translation as part of a metamorphic, as opposed to metaphoric, interaction between languages allows me to explore the ways in which our understanding of translation itself illuminates and is illuminated by the form of minor literature. For, as I will explore below, there is a dynamic dialogue between translation and the three characteristics that Deleuze and Guattari ascribe to minor literature.

Translation as minor literature

Deleuze and Guattari invoke three characteristics of minor literature: 'la déterritorialisation de la langue, le branchement de l'individu sur l'immédiat-politique, l'agencement collectif d'énonciation'/'the deterritorialization of the language, the connection of the individual to a political immediacy, and the collective assemblage of enunciation.'[158] The first of these three characteristics is apparent in Atxaga's experience of writing in Basque: to write in Basque from within the broader Spanish sub-system is to trouble the hegemony of Castilian, and to insist upon the multilingualism of the Spanish state; equally, as I have discussed, in choosing to write in this minority language Atxaga inevitably connects his authorial identity to that of a collective, political, expression of Basque national identity. Yet for Deleuze and Guattari, minor literatures are not necessarily those written in the language of a small nation: the terms minor and major are more fluid than a simple separation between hegemonic and peripheral linguistic systems, determined by number of speakers, for example. For Deleuze and Guattari, '[u]ne littérature mineure n'est pas celle d'une langue mineure, plutôt celle qu'une minorité fait dans une langue majeure'/'A minor literature doesn't come from a minor language; it is rather that which a minority constructs within a major language'.[159] All languages have minor and major functions: a minor language is run through with lines of flight, with movements of deterritorialization which fragment and transform the possibilities it articulates; a major language is defined by the orthodoxy of its structures of thought and expression, and its attempt to create solid power structures.

In *Remnants of a Nation*, Gabilondo explores this link between *Obabakoak* and Deleuze and Guattari's conception of minor literature.

He argues that Deleuze and Guattari actually exclude texts written in small languages such as Basque from their discussion of minor literatures, because of their suggestion that it is only by writing in a major language that one can create a true minor literature.[160] Yet for Deleuze and Guattari, defining a language as minor or major is not about size but approach; crucially, even languages considered small can aspire to major uses. As they ask, '[c]ombien de styles, ou de genres, ou de mouvements littéraires, même tout petits, n'ont qu'un rêve: remplir une fonction majeure du langage, faire des offres de service comme langue d'Etat, langue officielle'?/[h]ow many styles, or genres, or literary movements, even very small ones, have only one single dream: to assume a major function in language, to offer themselves as a sort of state language, an official language'?[161] Deleuze and Guattari are here referring to a tendency of literary theories to seek to establish themselves as essential structural components of our understanding, but the point remains applicable to languages in general. Despite being a small language, Basque has historically been assigned a major function because of its conception as a building block within the struggle for Basque nationalism; for Arana, Euskera's role was that of state language, a role he sought to affirm by insisting that Euskera remain rigid and unchanging, and refusing its connections with other languages and literatures.[162] Given the political rhetoric surrounding Basque literature and its ability to revitalize the Basque language at the time his career began, Atxaga's decision to write *Obabakoak* in Basque would thus, in Deleuze and Guattari's terms, constitute not a minor use of the language but a major one.

For Deleuze and Guattari, resisting this major use of language requires a writer to 'faire le rêve contraire: savoir créer un devenir-mineure'/'[c]reate the opposite dream: know how to create a becoming-minor'.[163] Such a 'becoming-minor' would see an author '[s]e servir du polylinguisme dans sa propre langue, faire de celle-ci un usage mineure ou intensif'/'make use of the polylingualism of one's own language, to make a minor or intensive use of it'.[164] Could we read Atxaga's decision to self-translate his texts into Castilian as the locus of such a becoming-minor? Does his self-translation, which emphasizes the polylingualism of Atxaga and his text, put the stability of the major linguistic, political and literary territories which surround his work into flight?

As I discussed in the Introduction to this chapter, the development of Basque literature and the Basque language was for many years positioned as part of a political development, and the linguistic boundaries of the Basque Country were seen as a way to represent or stand in for its fluid, challenged or imagined national and geographic boundaries. In an interview, Atxaga explores this relation between language and politics, and suggests that it depends upon maintaining the dangerous illusion that language can directly represent or signify a national essence: 'Tampoco estoy de acuerdo con aquellos que defienden las lenguas como "una visión del mundo". Creo que esa concepción es sospechosa, y que no tiene otro objetivo que el dominio político. [...] Hay que ser más sensatos. Lo que muestra una lengua es la historia de la gente, cómo vivió y cómo vive'/'Nor do I agree with those who defend languages as a "world view". I think that view is suspect, and has no other objective than political domination. [...] We must be more sensible. A language is the story of a people, how they lived and how they live'.[165]

As Atxaga suggests, to equate a language with a particular world view is to both acknowledge and elide difference: a language is positioned as simultaneously unique – able only to represent the perspective of one particular community – and generic – able to represent the shared perspective of *all* the members of that community. In languages conceived as major – English, Spanish, German – such an idea appears spurious from the outset: speakers of these languages are culturally, politically and geographically diverse. But in the case of a language such as Basque, with fewer than a million speakers worldwide, and the majority of those located in a geographical space of only 20,000 km^2, this rhetoric of linguistic essentialism inevitably carries more weight. In *Means Without End*, Giorgio Agamben suggests that Basque is a language which lacks 'state dignity' – it is not fully attached to the structures of the state and therefore cannot be understood only in relation to these. Operating as a dialect or a jargon more than a grammar or a structure, Basque, like Catalan or Gaelic, loosens the relationship between language and state-formed identities in a way which Agamben reads as ethical in its ability to challenge these essentialist narratives.[166] Yet, precisely in the ways in which Basque is *not* a state language, it also offers itself to appropriation as such, to a rewriting into the discourses of nationalism, deployed as part of the 'nexus between the existence of language, grammar, people, and state' that Agamben suggests languages conceived as jargons could resist.[167]

In his own discussion of the dangers of linguistic essentialism, Atxaga emphasizes the interpretative leap required to equate language with ontology. A language, he notes, is a story of a people, and that story contains multiple narrative voices, plots and perspectives: to perceive a language as representative of a single political or cultural world view involves a metaphoric erasure of the empirical diversity of those perspectives. As Gabilondo notes, this diversity is integral to the Basque linguistic identity: there are numerous Basque speakers across Europe, America and Australia, and their experience of language is conditioned by a multilingualism which includes English as well as Spanish and French. Gabilondo is clear that this multilingualism remains caught up with questions of colonialism, exile, and historical and contemporary forms of repression.[168] But these entanglements reveal the reality of that multilingual experience. To associate just one language with the essence of what it is to be Basque is to be guilty of an essentialism which has no grounding in contemporary, bilingual, reality. And you cannot tell a story of a community – its repression and expansion, violence and peace, past and present – by ignoring that reality.

Atxaga is a Basque author. But he is also inscribed into and described by a literary and linguistic tradition which exceeds the borders of the Basque language, through a continual and constant process of translation. Translation, a process both created through and generative of difference between and within languages, inevitably reveals the limits of forms of linguistic essentialism. Translation shifts language from metaphor to metamorphosis, from representation to becoming, from a major use into a minor. In translation, language confronts its poverty as well as its richness, the limits as well as the possibilities of its structures, words and expressions, before finding meaning reconstituted in new forms and new voices, in a transformative process of switch and exchange. The very existence of translation reveals the impossibility of containing a national essence within language: as the translation of *Obabakoak* into twenty-five languages suggests, no single language can articulate the experience or essence of a community; equally, that experience and essence is never only articulable in a single language.

Indeed, as Deleuze and Guattari suggest, even single languages are always multiple: 'Même unique, une langue reste une bouillie, un mélange schizophrénique, un habit d'Arlequin à travers lequel s'exercent des fonctions de langage très différents et des centres de pouvoir distincts'/'Even when it is unique, a language remains a mixture, a schizophrenic mélange, a Harlequin costume in which very different functions of language and distinct centers of power played out'.[169] The concept of harlequinism emphasizes both the major and minor functions of a language: all languages can delimit and frame, but they can also experiment, liberate and transform. And translation, which foregrounds the failure of any single language to account for the diverse experiences of reality, forces the languages and the texts it touches to reveal their harlequinism: their minor and major vibrations, their plurality and their difference.

For Gabilondo, Atxaga's self-translation of *Obabakoak* is problematic precisely because of a relation he reads between it and Deleuze and Guattari's conception of minor literature. He suggests that the only way in which a minor literature, under this conception, could occur in Spain is through 'linguistic difference' – essentially by including literatures written in other languages, such as Basque, within the Spanish canon.[170] In this regard, the translation of *Obabakoak* into Spanish becomes key, not as a challenge to the hegemony of this canon, but as something to be appropriated by the Spanish state: 'The fact that it was originally written in Basque is simply a symbolic sign of its "genuine minority status," for ultimately the text that serves as the basis for translation is not the original, but its Spanish version'.[171] For Gabilondo, the decision to write the text initially in Basque symbolically insists upon the importance of the Basque language as the epitome of a minorized, exoticized difference; at the same time, however, Atxaga prevents this otherness becoming problematic for readers by offering a Castilian translation.

But this potential exoticization and appropriation, this incorporation of Atxaga into a Spanish narrative of difference and his ostensible resistance to this narrative, is the reality of Atxaga's writing process and his bilingualism. In 'Preguntas desde Japón', Atxaga describes his experience of translating *El hijo del acordeonista* from Basque to Castilian as one illuminating, and illuminated by, the plurality and difference within his own linguistic identity:

> desde el mismo momento en que entregué el original a mi editorial vasca, Pamiela, mi mujer y yo ya estábamos traduciendo el libro al español. [...] Esta es la única manera de ser un escritor bilingüe. El escritor tiene que desdoblarse. Más aún cuando las dos lenguas que maneja son muy distintas, tan distintas como el castellano y el Euskera.
>
> from the moment I gave the original to my Basque publisher, Pamiela, my wife and I were already translating the book into Spanish. [...] This is the only way to be a bilingual writer. The writer has to double/split themselves. Especially when they are handling two languages which are very different, as different as Castilian and Basque'.[172]

Atxaga's description of the task of the (self-)translator explores the exhausting temporal overlap within the writing of the two texts, and emphasizes the collaborative aspect of his translation process. The most interesting element of Atxaga's discussion, however, is his use of the reflexive verb *desdoblarse*, which connotes both splitting and doubling, to describe his experience of translation. The experience of self-translation, suggests Atxaga, is one of division and multiplication, of reduction and expansion. Self-translation positions Atxaga as a foreigner in both his languages: his authorial identity and the identity of his text are formed by his relationship to two languages, a relationship which prevents him and his text from inhabiting entirely any single linguistic or literary system. Indeed, from the moment of their conception, his texts are preparing to be doubled, to be pulled from one system into another, through the collision of his two languages.

By doubling, splitting and shifting his linguistic identity, Atxaga's self-translations disrupt a 'major' use of the Basque language and literature: language as the site of identity, of possession and of delimitation, is metamorphosed into language as the site of becoming-other. Manterola reveals that Atxaga has described his experience of working on *Siete casas en Francia* with Garikano as a 'continuous flow, from the translation to the original and from the original to the translation'.[173] In this flow, the text begins in Basque and is then translated into Castilian; this Spanish text re-informs the Basque version, which is thus modified; these modifications are then retranslated into Castilian.[174] This movement, between two texts, between two languages, between two people, emphasizes the collaborative aspects of Atxaga's particular translation practice, aspects which have in fact been implicit in all his translations from *Obabakoak* onwards. But Atxaga's discussion also speaks to a more general understanding of translation as a tangential connection between original and copy, a 'living-on', to use Benjamin's term, in which continuation is also, always, transformation.[175] In this transformative continuation, every new version modifies the versions which came before, by its very existence changing and expanding the shape of the 'text' – which, following Barthes's definition, we can understand as a proliferating and dynamic body of literature which spills over from the author's original 'work'.[176] As translation fragments the possibility of linguistic essentialism, it emphasizes in its place linguistic diversity and multiplicity, creating a textual identity run through with vibrations from other voices and other places. This is both a disparate and a collective identity, which reforms the spaces of Atxaga's literary practice with every reading, every translation, every text.

Deleuze and Guattari suggest that minor literatures are defined by their ability to offer a collective enunciation of a community, or a potential community. But if *Obabakoak* depicts a community of collective voices, loosely framed by the fictional space of Obaba, it is through translation that this enunciation becomes truly collective. As these stories from Obaba are transmitted in different voices around the world, they are opened up to different readings and potential vibrations. In her discussion of translating Atxaga's work in *Between the Lines*, Jull Costa emphasizes this collective encounter within translation: 'in a sense', she comments, 'it is a duet [...] it's my voice as well as [...] Atxaga's voice [...] and they can't be separated, that's the strange thing about it'.[177] Like the plagiarist whom Axular promotes, the translator operates between two literary assemblages, two voices, and between reader and writer, and thus becomes part of a collective enunciation which both absorbs and emits creativity. As Godard suggests, '[a] practice of the outside, translation affirms the expansion of creative possibilities in the scattering of tongues'.[178] These creative possibilities are an encounter, like that between wasp and orchid, a two-way interaction between reading and writing, creating and critiquing, but one defined by its a-parallel quality, which generates movement through the clash of difference.

In creating such an encounter, translation shifts the location of textual authority from singular to multiple, reframing in the process our understanding of textual truth. As LeVan suggests, translation 'falsifies' a text: the unique perspective it offers is not limited to its inevitable difference from the original, but instead derives from the uniquely new truth it offers, a truth that is fermented in its creation through a 'population of others', which operates 'outside the polar concerns of fidelity and freedom that are always accountable to an original'.[179] This dynamic is critically relevant to the political implications of Atxaga's work, for it positions translation as a medium through which the possible alliance of political truth and textual form can be challenged, falsified and transformed. Atxaga's work is always political, always traversed with the possibility of collectively enunciating 'what it means' to be Basque, and always subject to readings which emphasize the relationship between language, literature and the Basque political and geographical territory. In this regard, it is a text imbued with national meaning. But *Obabakoak* is also political in the sense Deleuze and Guattari perceive minor literature to be: it brings different voices together in a collective assertion of difference, putting to flight major systems which seek to promote a transcendent political or national ideal. More than other forms of writing, translation also has the ability to play with questions of political and national identity, to connect with and remain separate from multiple linguistic, cultural and national paradigms. In translation, Atxaga occupies and navigates different linguistic and literary territories, transforming his authorial identity and his text as he seeks to transform the creative and critical spaces informing the Basque literary scene.

Epilogue: on not reading Basque

Asserting the power of translation to reformulate, rather than reify, the rhetoric of minor/major which accompanies discussions of Atxaga's work raises questions about the ways in which we might read this work in its translations from Basque into Castilian and English. In 'On Visible and Invisible Languages: Bernardo Atxaga's *Soinujolearen semea* in Translation', Mario Santana suggests that 'the reader and scholar of translated texts is [...] bound by particular ethical demands – and that those demands are even higher on readers of minority literatures when translated into dominant, globalized languages'.[180] Santana expresses concern about a trend in US universities to approach Atxaga's work solely through the Castilian translations, without addressing the erasures and alterations created in the process of translation. In reaction to this, Santana invokes Venuti's call for visibility in translation to suggest that an ethical approach to reading translated texts must involve 'the study of the "reminder" [sic] – the textual and linguistic features that are added to a translated text and frustrate any attempt to domesticate the work within the target language'.[181] Santana engages in such a study of *El hijo del acordeonista,* comparing the Basque and Castilian versions of the text in order 'to make visible what the dominant languages of globalization would rather keep invisible under the pretense of universal transparency' – in this case, particular Basque words included within the Castilian version, which deterritorialize the text, preventing 'the reader from establishing a comfortable, monolingual relation' with it.[182] So too, in 'Historiography and the geo-literary imaginary', Domínguez calls for comparative readings of the Basque and Castilian versions of Atxaga's texts, suggesting that without these the alterations enacted by self-translation remain encoded and unseen: 'But seeing that a contrastive reading of the original and final texts is not a habitual practice', he notes, 'this Castilian-ization is not noticed by the average Spanish-speaking reader'.[183]

As both Santana and Domínguez suggest, comparative criticism is invaluable in helping us understand the powerful political, linguistic and cultural violence which can be wielded by translation, particularly between asymmetrical languages. Just as Pierre Menard's *Quixote* shines new light on Cervantes's text, so all comparison elucidates difference, and the variety between ostensibly similar texts. Yet at the same time, as Domínguez suggests above, translations – particularly those from minor to major languages – are rarely created to be compared. In this regard, comparative readings often rely upon bilingual critics who, by definition, have no need of the translation which is their object of study. Critical interpretation is often a form of translation, a textual interaction which requires others to decode those elements which evade our understanding. The process of such decoding adds a new voice and language to the multiple languages and voices which already constitute our critical vocabulary. But while we always depend upon these voices to guide, challenge, and extend our own readings, our dependence increases when we require help with interlinguistic as well as intralinguistic decoding. This engagement with the work of other critics does not discount the importance of comparative readings; indeed, it emphasizes the creative collisions and encounters which translation enables. At the same time, given that comparative readings are often only made possible by the participation of those who do not require the translations which they explore, it seems reasonable to ask whether comparison is the only ethical approach to reading in translation.

For Deleuze, a comparative search for resemblance or dissimilarity misses the fundamental element at play within all forms of repetition: the innate, interiorized difference which means that two events, two texts, two moments of thought or expression, can never be the same, but only part of a continuous process of becoming, transformation and change. Crucially, as Cliff Stagoll suggests, such becomings *cannot* be understood comparatively, for they are unique in and of themselves:

> For Deleuze [...] becoming is neither merely an attribute of, nor an intermediary between events, but a characteristic of the very production of events. It is not that the time of change exists between one event and another, but that every event is but a unique instant of production in a continual flow of changes evident in the cosmos.[184]

For Deleuze, thinking about repetition as becoming is not about comparison, nor about subtracting an end point from a start point, but rather about seeing the in-between, the intermediate, as the unique point in and of itself. When thinking about the relationship between an original and a translation, Deleuze's perception of becoming would mean replacing a rhetoric of comparison with a relation of difference, governed by the a-parallel and developing relation between two texts.

What would this move look like? A shift from comparison to difference would have a powerful effect, both on the ways in which we read translations, and on our understanding of the nature of translation itself. Reading translations through a narrative of resemblance, as similar to or different from an original text, maintains certain hierarchies between source and target, original and copy, foreign and domestic. In *The Bilingual Text,* Hokenson and Munson suggest that the act of self-translation inevitably disrupts such traditional binaries: 'Theoretical models of source and target languages [...] break down in the dual text by one hand, as do linguistic models of lexical equivalence, and foreign versus domestic culture. Literary critical models [...] of translation as diminution and loss, a falling away from the original, similarly cannot serve.'[185]

But if these models do not serve, they remain surprisingly dominant, particularly in relation to self-translations between minor and major languages and cultures. The strength of these hierarchies is apparent in the translations of Atxaga's work. As Santana describes, the Catalan and Galician translations of Atxaga's *El hijo del acordeonista* enact a subtle denigration of the Castilian text, by claiming 'to be translations of the original Basque' when 'they are in fact based on the Spanish version'.[186] Santana reads this erasure of the Spanish version as a form of resistance on the part of the Catalan and Galician translators and publishing houses to the dominance of Castilian within the Iberian Peninsula. But, he notes, this erasure also belittles the experience of second-hand translation, positioning it, as Gideon Toury suggests, as 'some kind of a disease to be shunned [...] an approach [which] only reflects a fallacious projection of a currently prevalent norm, ascribing uppermost value to the ultimate original, onto the plane of theoretical premises'.[187]

Margaret Jull Costa has revealed that a similar sense of shame dominates her experience of translating from Atxaga's Castilian text: 'I do feel embarrassed about it, not translating from the Basque', she suggests, describing 'that feeling that I'm translating from a translation, even though the translator of that translation is the author, and so I'm at another remove from the original'.[188] Jull Costa's comment, like Toury's, echoes the rhetoric of resemblance which, in *Rethinking Translation*, Lawrence Venuti suggests can condition perceptions of translation, ranking translation according to a Platonic distinction between authorized copy and deviant simulacrum.[189] By ranking the translation below the original, such cultural practices marginalize the translation, insisting that it can only be understood in relation to that original. While self-translations might be expected to be exempt from such marginalization –

they are, after all, a copy true to the author – their status as a translation, as a secondary repetition of a pre-existing text, means that the criteria of resemblance continues to apply. The implication that a self-translation might be *less authentic* than the original text has particular resonance in relation to my reading of *Obabakoak*. If the Castilian text is perceived as less valid, less authoritative and less original than the Basque one, does this reduce the validity and authority of any reading based upon that translation?

If our readings of translations are forged solely in relation to Platonic conceptions of originality, resemblance and representation, then the answer is probably yes. But if we open ourselves to other ways of thinking translation, then we also open up other ways of reading translated texts, other avenues of productive exploration. For Deleuze, readings which insist upon viewing simulacratic texts as an unsatisfactory imitation of an already failed copy of reality fail to grasp the disruptive and generative nature of those texts:

> Le simulacre est construit sur une disparité, sur une différence, il intériorise une dissimilitude. C'est pourquoi nous ne pouvons même plus le définir par rapport au modèle qui s'impose aux copies, modèle du Même dont dérive la ressemblance des copies. Si le simulacre a encore un modèle, c'est un autre modèle, un modèle de l'Autre dont découle une dissemblance intériorisée.
>
> The simulacrum is constructed around a disparity, a difference; it interiorizes a dissimilitude. That is why we can no longer even define it with regard to the model at work in copies – the model of the Same from which the resemblance of the copy derives. If the simulacrum still has a model, it is another one, a model of the Other from which it follows an interiorized dissimilarity.[190]

Deleuze's distinction positions the simulacrum as difference *in* and *of* itself, rather than in relation to an external comparative, as a becoming of an event, a text, an experience. This becoming is innately creative in its ability to destabilize the value of terms such as *original* and *copy*, *model* and *reproduction*. Deleuze's conception of the simulacrum sees it as a uniquely chaotic, disruptive, but inherently joyful force for celebrating difference, one which leads to the collapse of overarching authorities, and the birth of a repetitive, but illimitably different world – a world in which resemblance is not sought, in which hierarchies can be dissolved, and the power of the unique affirmed: 'Il n'y a pas de hiérarchie possible:

ni second, ni troisième... [...] C'est la ressemblance qui se dit de la différence intériorisée, et l'identité, du Différent comme puissance première.'/'There is no possible hierarchy: neither second, nor third [...] It is resemblance that speaks of interiorized difference and identity, of Difference as a primary power.'[191] In Deleuze's reading, when unleashed from a rhetoric of *same as* or *different from*, the simulacrum is freed to release its own powerfully charged originality and difference.

To read not only Atxaga's self-translations, but all the translations of his work as a simulacrum in Deleuze's sense would transform the power differential between Basque and Castilian, or English, French, Russian or Vietnamese; between original and translation; and between author and translator. Originality and difference would be inserted *into* those translations, forms of writing-as-becoming which are different in and of themselves, rather than only in relation to another text. Such a project might be utopian, for how can we understand difference without thinking about similarity? But it sparks debate around the ethical frameworks through which we can approach our own relations – political, personal, and textual. As Heidegger commented, 'Tell me what you think about translation and I will tell you who you are': how we think about translation and about reading in translation reveals a great deal about our own critical practice.[192] If we read translations *only* in their relation to another text we diminish them, whether intentionally or not, and in so doing diminish the potential translation offers us as a mode of thinking, reading, and writing.

To read a translated text as simulacratic in a Deleuzian rather than a Platonic sense would be to perceive its differences as inevitable, as the heart of a liberating exploration of the structures of textual authority and linguistic power. To read in this way acknowledges our own limitations as critics, for it forces us to accept the difference within every textual event which renders our own interpretations transitory, unfinished and unfinishable. Translation is, inevitably, an encounter with another: as Brodzki suggests, 'translation is the mode by which various discourses read each other, locate their commonalities, and name their differences'.[193] But perceiving these differences and commonalities need not be exclusively conceived as an attempt to map the violence and erasures of translation: it can also be part of an acceptance of those differences, an acknowledgement that without them our own experience would be a little less rich, an awareness that these differences are the very heart of translating, of writing, of reading, of critiquing, of thinking.

Notes

1 Bernardo Atxaga, 'Superficies de la literatura vasca', in *Um lugar llamado Obaba* (Madrid: Alfaguera, 2013), 34. My translation. Parts of this chapter are drawn from two previously published essays: Harriet Hulme, 'Creating Anew, Again: Deserted Islands and Textual Inhabitations in Bernardo Atxaga's *Obabakoak', Comparative Critical Studies* 11.2–3 (2014); Harriet Hulme, 'Self-Translating Between Minor and Major Languages: A Hospitable Approach in Bernardo Atxaga's *Obabakoak*', in *Self-Translation and Power: Negotiating Identities in Multilingual European Contexts*, ed. Olga Castro, Sergi Mainer and Svetlana Page (Basingstoke: Palgrave Macmillan, 2017).

2 Atxaga, 'Superficies de la literatura vasca', 33.

3 Michael Cronin, *Translating Ireland* (Cork: Cork University Press, 1996), 4.

4 In using the term 'Basque Country' here I refer to the Basque Autonomous Community, *Euskadi*, a legal autonomous community in Spain, as opposed to the culturally wider Basque Country, *Euskal Herria*, which also includes four provinces in South-West France.

5 Bernardo Atxaga in Hasier Etxeberria, *Cinco escritores vascos*, trans. Koldo Biguri (Irun: Alberdania, 2002), 314.

6 Bernardo Atxaga, 'Preguntas desde Japón' (2004). https://www.atxaga.eus/es/testuak-textos/preguntas-desde-japon [Accessed 29 December 2017]. (No page references for this text.)

7 Elizabete Manterola Agirrezabalaga, 'La tradductión de la literatura vasca a otras lenguas', *mTm: minor Translating major – major Translating minor – minor Translating minor* 3 (2011): 60.

8 Annabel Martín, 'Modulations of the Basque Voice: An Interview with Bernardo Atxaga', *Journal of Spanish Cultural Studies* 1.2 (2000): 193.

9 For further discussion of Unamuno's distinction between Euskera and Castilian, see Mari Jose Olaziregi, 'Worlds of Fiction: An Introduction to Basque Narrative', in *Basque Literary History*, ed. Mari Jose Olaziregi, trans. Amaia Gabantxo (Reno: University of Nevada Press, 2013).

10 Jesús María Lasagabaster, 'Introduction: Basque Literary History', in *Basque Literary History*, 14–15.

11 Lasagabaster, 'Introduccíon a la narrativa vasca actual', in *Antología de la narrative vasca actual*, ed. Jesús María Lasagabaster (Barcelona: Edicions de Mall, 1986), 14.

12 Lasagabaster, 'Introduction: Basque Literary History', 14.

13 Mark Kurlansky, *The Basque History of the World* (London: Vintage, 1999), 329.

14 Joseba Gabilondo, *Remnants of the Nation: Prolegomena to a Postnational History of Contemporary Basque Literature* (Bilbao: University of the Basque Country Press, 2006) (in Basque). Translation in English under contract with Tamesis. Introduction and first chapter available at: https://www.academia.edu/5129880/Remnants_of_the_Nation_Prolegomena_to_a_Postnational_History_of_Contemporary_Basque_Literature._Bilbao_University_of_the_Basque_Country_Press_2006._in_Basque_._Translation_in_English_under_contract_with_Tamesis._Introduction_and_first_chapter_available_here [Accessed 29 December 2017], 32.

15 See Olaziregi, 'Worlds of Fiction: An Introduction to Basque Narrative', 139–52.

16 Mari Jose Olaziregi, *Waking the Hedgehog: The Literary Universe of Bernardo Atxaga*, trans. Amaia Gabantxo (Reno, NV: University of Nevada Press, 2005), 59.

17 Bernardo Atxaga, 'Mi primera lengua', in *Um lugar llamado Obaba*, 23. All translations of this text come from 'My First Language', *The Threepenny Review* 108 (2007), trans. Margaret Jull Costa, no page references. http://www.threepennyreview.com/samples/atxaga_w07.html [Accessed 29 December 2017].

18 Atxaga, 'Mi primera lengua', 23–4.

19 Kurlansky, *The Basque History of the World*, 165.

20 Robert P. Clark, *The Basques, the Franco Years and Beyond* (Reno, NV: University of Nevada Press, 1979), 421.

21 John Hooper, *The New Spaniards*, 3rd edn (Harmondsworth: Penguin, 1995), 383.

22 Kurlansky, *The Basque History of the World*, 195.

23 See Teresa Whitfield, *Endgame for ETA: Elusive Peace in the Basque Country* (London: Hurst, 2014) for an extended discussion of ETA's formation, aims, and actions.

24 Atxaga in Etxeberria, *Cinco escritores vascos*, 320.

25 Juan Pablo Gil-Oslé, 'Bernardo Atxaga: canon, plagio y euskera literario', *Bulletin of Spanish Studies* XCI.6 (2014): 871.

26 Gabilondo, *Remnants*, 30.
27 Atxaga in *Cincos escritores vascos*, 334.
28 Olaziregi, *Waking the Hedgehog*, 48.
29 Olaziregi, *Waking the Hedgehog*, 214, 164–5.
30 Ur Apalategui, *La Naissance de l'écrivain Basque: l'Évolution de la problématique littéraire de Bernardo Atxaga* (Paris: L'Harmattan, 2000), 64–5 .
31 Gabilondo, *Remnants*, 34–5.
32 Atxaga, 'Mi primera lengua', 23.
33 Gloria Pilar Totoricaguena, *Basque Diaspora: Migration and Transnational Identity* (Reno: University of Nevada Press, 2005), 94–7.
34 Joseba Gabilondo, 'Indifference as Terror: On State Politics and Basque Literature in Globalization', *Oihenart* 25 (2010): 230.
35 Gabilondo, 'Indifference', 231.
36 Gabilondo, *Remnants*, 31.
37 Gabilondo, *Remnants*, 12.
38 Tijana Miletic, *European Literary Immigration into the French Language: Readings of Gary, Kristof, Kundera and Semprun* (Amsterdam: Rodopi, 2008), 29.
39 Abram De Swaan, *Words of the World: The Global Language System* (Cambridge: Polity Press, 2002), 4–5.
40 Sally Perret, 'In the Name of the Nation? The National Award in Narrative Literature, and the Democratization of Art in Spain (1977–2013)', *Journal of Spanish Cultural Studies* 16:1 (2015): 80.
41 Gil-Oslé, 'Bernardo Atxaga: canon, plagio y euskera literario', 884. All translations are mine
42 Gabilondo, *Remnants*, 6.
43 Bernardo Atxaga, *El hijo del acordeonisata*, trans. Asun Garikano and Bernardo Atxaga (Madrid: Punto de lectura, 2006 [2003]), 21. *The Accordionist's Son*, trans. Margaret Jull Costa (London: Vintage, 2008 [2007]), 10. All translations of the Spanish text come from this English translation. Page numbers in subsequent references refer to: Spanish text; English text.
44 Kirsty Hooper, *Writing Galicia Into the World: New Cartographies, New Poetics* (Liverpool: Liverpool University Press, 2011), 22.
45 Giorgio Agamben, *Means Without End: Notes on Politics*, trans. Cesare Casarino and Vincenzo Binetti (Minneapolis: University of Minnesota Press, 2000), 67.
46 Atxaga, *El hijo del acordeonista*, 24; 13.
47 Manterola, 'La traducción de la literatura vasca a otras lenguas', 66–7.
48 Rainier Grutman, 'Self-translation' in *The Routledge Encyclopedia of Translation Studies*, ed. Mona Baker and Gabriela Saldanha, 2nd edn (London: Routledge, 2009), 258.
49 César Domínguez, 'Historiography and the geo-literary imaginary', in *A Comparative nguez* (Amsterdam: John Benjamins, 2010), 102–3.
50 Bernardo Atxaga, 'Mesa redonda', *Vasos comunicantes* 4 (1994): 61–2. See also Elizabete Manterola Agirrezabalaga, 'Paratextual Analysis of the Work by Bernardo Atxaga', in *Translation Peripheries: Paratextual Elements in Translation*, ed. Anna Gil-Bardají, Pilar Orero and Sara Rovira-Esteva (Bern: Peter Lang, 2012), 97.
51 Domínguez, 'Historiography', 103.
52 See also Manterola, 'Paratextual Analysis of the Work by Bernardo Atxaga', 89.
53 Elizabete Manterola Agirrezabalaga, 'Collaborative Self-Translation in a Minority Language: Power Implications in the Process, the Actors and the Literary Systems Involved', in *Self-Translation and Power: Negotiating Identities in Multilingual European Contexts*, ed. Olga Castro, Svetlana Page and Sergi Mainer (London: Palgrave, 2017), 202.
54 Atxaga, 'Mesa Redonda', 63.
55 Manterola, 'Collaborative Self-Translation', 202–3.
56 Olaziregi, *Waking the Hedgehog*, 150.
57 Olaziregi, *Waking the Hedgehog*, 98.
58 Atxaga, 'Preguntas desde Japón'.
59 Bernardo Atxaga, *Obabakoak*, trans. Bernardo Atxaga (Madrid: Punto de Lectura, 2008 [1989]), 438–9. *Obabakoak*, trans. Margaret Jull Costa (London: Vintage, 2007 [1992]), 324–5. All translations of the Spanish text come from this English translation. Page numbers in subsequent references refer to: Spanish text; English text.
60 Atxaga, *Obabakoak*, 441; 326.
61 Gérard Genette, *Seuils* (Paris: Éditions du Seuil, 1987), 7; *Paratexts: Thresholds of Interpretation*, trans. Jane E. Lewin (Cambridge: Cambridge University Press, 1997), 1.

62 Lawrence Venuti, *The Scandals of Translation: Towards an Ethics of Difference* (London: Routledge, 2002 [1998]), 11.
63 Domínguez, 'Historiography', 104.
64 Edward Said, *Orientalism* (New York: Pantheon, 1978), 7.
65 Atxaga, *Obabakoak*, 438; 324.
66 Domínguez, 'Historiography', 104.
67 Domínguez, 'Historiography', 103.
68 Margaret Jull Costa, unpublished email to Harriet Hulme, 9 March 2014.
69 Atxaga, *Obabakoak* (English text), ix–x.
70 Atxaga, *Obabakoak* (English text), ix.
71 John Hooper, *The New Spaniards*, 396.
72 Atxaga, *Obabakoak* (English text), xii.
73 'Prologue' appears in Castilian in Atxaga's series of poems, *Nueva Etiopia*, but minus this final paragraph which locates the poem's reception within a particular country. Bernardo Atxaga, 'Escribo en una lengua extraña', in *Nueva Etiopía: Canciones, conversaciones y poemas* (Madrid: El Europeo, 1996), 17–18.
74 Domínguez, 'Historiography', 105.
75 Domínguez, 'Historiography', 109.
76 Gilles Deleuze and Félix Guattari, *Mille plateaux* (Paris: Les Éditions de Minuit, 1980), 629–32.
77 Adrian Parr, 'Deterritorialisation/Reterritorialisation', in *The Deleuze Dictionary*, ed. Adrian Parr, rev. edn (Edinburgh: Edinburgh University Press, 2010), 69.
78 Parr, 'Deterritorialisation/Reterritorialisation', 69.
79 Gilles Deleuze and Félix Guattari, *Kafka: Pour une littérature mineure* (Paris: Les Éditions de Minuit, 1975), 34–50.
80 Margaret Jull Costa, 'Translating Bernardo Atxaga's *Obabakoak*', *Salzburg Studies in English Literature, Poetic Drama and Poetic Theory* 204 (1998): 279.
81 Atxaga, *Obabakoak*, 438; 323.
82 Atxaga, *Obabakoak*, 438; 324
83 Atxaga, *Obabakoak* (English text), x.
84 Atxaga, *Obabakoak*, 351; 259.
85 Atxaga, *Obabakoak*, 351–2; 259.
86 Atxaga, *Obabakoak*, 353; 260.
87 Atxaga, Obabakoak, 353; 261.
88 Domínguez, 'Historiography', 116.
89 Atxaga, *Obabakoak*, 355–7; 261–2.
90 Atxaga, *Obabakoak*, 354; 261.
91 Axular, *Despues, Gero* (bilingual text), trans. Luis Villasante (Oñati Jakin, 1976), 16.
92 Atxaga, *Obabakoak*, 358; 264.
93 Atxaga, *Obabakoak*, 358; 264.
94 Marilyn Randall, *Pragmatic Plagiarism: Authorship, Profit, and Power* (Toronto: University of Toronto Press, 2001), xii.
95 Randall, *Pragmatic Plagiarism*, 3.
96 Atxaga, *Obabakoak*, 366–7; 270–1.
97 T. S. Eliot, *The Sacred Wood: Essays On Poetry and Criticism* (London : Methuen & Company Ltd, 1921), 114; Roland Barthes, 'La Mort de l'auteur' in *Le Bruissement de la langue* (Paris: Seuil, 1984 [1968]), 65.
98 Domínguez, 'Historiography', 116.
99 Gilles Deleuze, 'Causes et raisons des îles désertes', in *L'Île déserte et autres textes (1953–1974)*, ed. David Lapoujade (Paris: Éditions de Minuit, 2002), 12. 'Desert Islands', in *Desert Islands and Other Texts 1953–1974*, trans. Michael Taormina (Paris: Semiotext(e), 2004), 10. All translations of the French text come from this English translation. Page numbers in subsequent references refer to: French text; English text.
100 Stewart Williams, 'Virtually Impossible: Deleuze and Derrida on the Political Problem of Islands (and Island Studies)', *Island Studies Journal* 7.2 (2012): 219.
101 Deleuze and Guattari, *Mille plateaux*, 35. *A Thousand Plateaus: Capitalism and Schizophrenia*, trans. Brian Massumi (London and New York: Continuum, 2004 [1987]), 26. All translations of the French text come from this English translation. Page numbers in subsequent references refer to: French text; English text.
102 Itamar Even-Zohar, 'Interference in Dependent Literary Polysystems', *Poetics Today* 11.1 (1990): 80.

103 Lawrence Venuti, *The Translator's Invisibility: A History of Translation*, 2nd edn (London: Routledge, 2008), 19.
104 Deleuze and Guattari, *Mille plateaux*, 20; 13–14.
105 Deleuze, 'Causes et raisons des îles désertes', 16; 13.
106 Deleuze, 'Causes et raisons des îles désertes', 17; 13.
107 Adrian Parr, 'Repetition', in *The Deleuze Dictionary*, 225.
108 Atxaga, *Obabakoak*, 363–4; 268.
109 Deleuze, 'Causes et raisons des îles désertes', 16; 13.
110 Atxaga, *Obabakoak*, 364, 362; 269, 267.
111 See Olaziregi, *Waking the Hedgehog*, 139, for a comprehensive list of the intertextual sources included in *Obabakoak*.
112 Auguste Villiers de l'Isle-Adam, *La Torture par espérance* (Bayonne: les Germes, 1994).
113 Bernardo Atxaga, *Lista de locos et otros alfabetos* (Madrid: Ediciones Siruela, 1998), 130. My translation.
114 Lawrence Venuti, *The Translator's Invisibility*, 18–19.
115 John Barth, *Literature of Exhaustion: Literature of Replenishment* (Lord John Press, 1982), 8.
116 Judith Still and Michael Worton, *Intertextuality: Theories and Practices* (Manchester: Manchester University Press, 1991), 33.
117 Rita Copeland, *Rhetoric, Hermeneutics, and Translation in the Middle Ages* (Cambridge: Cambridge University Press, 1991), 30.
118 Parvati Nair, *Configuring Community: Theories, Narratives, and Practices of Community Identities in Contemporary Spain* (London: MHRA, 2004), 62.
119 Deleuze and Guattari, *Mille plateaux*, 17; 11.
120 Alberto Toscano, 'Capture', in *The Deleuze Dictionary*, 45.
121 Gilles Deleuze and Claire Parnet, *Dialogues* (Paris: Flammarion, 1977), 13; '*Dialogues II*, trans. Hugh Tomlinson and Barbara Habberjam (1987; repr. New York: Columbia University Press, 2007), 7.
122 Barbara Godard, 'Deleuze and Translation', *Parallax* 6.1 (2000): 56.
123 Margaret Jull Costa, email to Harriet Hulme, 9 March 2014.
124 Enma Rodríguez, 'Bernardo Atxaga: me gusta la sobriedad', in *El Mundo*, 26 November 1989, 1. Quoted in José Angel Ascunce Arrieta, *Bernardo Atxaga: Los demonios personales de un escritor* (San Sebastián: Saturrarán, 2000), 25. My translation.
125 Atxaga, *Obabakoak*, 206; 155.
126 Gil-Oslé, 'Bernardo Atxaga: canon, plagio y euskera literario', 887.
127 Gabilondo, 'Indifference', 231.
128 Harriet Hulme, 'A Politics of Form: Fantasy and Storytelling as Modes of Resistance in the Work of Atxaga and Kundera', in *Fear and Fantasy in a Global World*, ed. Susana Araújo, Marta Pacheco Pinto, Sandra Bettencourt (Amsterdam: Rodopi, 2015), 223–4.
129 Atxaga, *Obabakoak*, 290, 397; 214, 294.
130 Atxaga, *Obabakoak*, 442; 326.
131 Atxaga, *Obabakoak*, 38, 40–1, 42; 25, 27, 28.
132 Gabilondo, *Remnants*, 30.
133 See Ascunce, *Bernardo Atxaga: Los demonios personales de un escritor* , 27–9.
134 Atxaga, *Obabakoak*, 15; 7.
135 Bernardo Atxaga, *Dos hermanos: El cuarto canto* (Madrid: Ollero & Ramos, 1995), 156–7. *Two Brothers*, trans. Margaret Jull Costa (London: Harvill Press, 2001), 118.
136 Gilles Deleuze, *Différence et répétition*, (Paris: Presses Universitaires de France, 1993 [1968]), 5; *Difference and Repetition* trans. Paul Patton (London and New York: Continuum, 2001 [1994]), xxii. For the quotation, see Jorge Luis Borges, 'Pierre Menard, autor del Quijote', in *Ficciones* (Madrid: Alianza Editorial, 1997 [1974]), 52.
137 Deleuze and Guattari, *Mille plateaux*, 17; 11.
138 Deleuze and Guattari, *Mille plateaux*, 16; 10.
139 Michael LeVan, 'Aesthetics of Encounter: Variations on Translation in Deleuze', *International Journal of Translation* 19.2 (2007): 60.
140 Lawrence Venuti, *The Translator's Invisibility*, 18–19.
141 Deleuze and Guattari, *Kafka*, 35. *Kafka: Toward a Minor Literature*, trans. Dana Polan (Minneapolis: University of Minnesota Press, 1986), 19. All translations of the French text come from this English translation. Page numbers in subsequent references refer to: French text; English text.

142 Atxaga, *El hijo del acordeonista*, 21; 11.
143 Atxaga, *Obabakoak*, 440; 325.
144 Deleuze and Guattari, *Kafka*, 35; 19.
145 Deleuze and Guattari, *Kafka*, 29; 16.
146 See John Marks, 'Franz Kafka', in *The Deleuze Dictionary*, 137–9.
147 Deleuze and Guattari, *Kafka*, 40; 22.
148 Keith Woodward and John Paul Jones III, 'On the border with Deleuze and Guattari', in *B/ordering Space*, ed. Henk van Houtum, Olivier Kramsch and Wolfgang Zierhofer (Aldershot: Ashgate, 2005), 238.
149 Deleuze and Guattari, *Kafka*, 40; 22.
150 Deleuze and Guattari, *Kafka*, 26; 14. See Franz Kafka, *The Metamorphosis*, trans. David Wyllie (Classix Press, 2009).
151 Philip Goodchild, *Deleuze and Guattari: An Introduction to the Politics of Desire* (London: SAGE, 1996), 38.
152 Deleuze and Guattari, *Kafka*, 40; 22.
153 Atxaga, *Obabakoak*, 435; 322.
154 Atxaga, *Obabakoak*, 435; 322.
155 Atxaga, *Obabakoak*, 337; 249.
156 Deleuze and Guattari, *Kafka*, 27–8; 15.
157 Woodward and Jones, 'On the Border with Deleuze and Guattari', 238.
158 Deleuze and Guattari, *Kafka*, 33; 18.
159 Deleuze and Guattari, *Kafka*, 29; 16.
160 Gabilondo, *Remnants*, 22.
161 Deleuze and Guattari, *Kafka*, 50; 27.
162 See John Hooper, *The New Spaniards*, 396.
163 Deleuze and Guattari, *Kafka*, 50; 27.
164 Deleuze and Guattari, *Kafka*, 49; 26–7.
165 Bernardo Atxaga, 'Interview-Howl'. https://www.atxaga.eus/testuak-textos/interview-howl. [Accessed 3 January 2018]. My translation.
166 Agamben, *Means Without End*, 68. See also Emily Apter, *The Translation Zone: A New Comparative Literature* (Princeton, NJ and Oxford: Princeton University Press, 2006), 244.
167 Agamben, *Means Without End*, 69.
168 Gabilondo, *Remnants*, 6.
169 Deleuze and Guattari, *Kafka*, 48; 26.
170 Gabilondo, *Remnants*, 31.
171 Gabilondo, *Remnants*, 31.
172 Atxaga, 'Preguntas desde Japón'.
173 Atxaga, from an Unpublished Interview with Elizabete Manterola, 24 November 2008. As quoted in Manterola, 'Collaborative Self-Translation', 203.
174 Manterola, 'Collaborative Self-Translation', 204.
175 Walter Benjamin, 'The Task of the Translator', in *One-way Street and Other Writings*, trans. J. A. Underwood (London: Penguin, 2009), 31.
176 Roland Barthes, 'De l'oeuvre au texte', *Revue d'esthétique* 24 (1971).
177 Margaret Jull Costa, 'Translation and Reading', in *Between the Lines*, conversation with Timothy Mathews, 11 September 2013. http://www.ucl.ac.uk/multidisciplinary-and-intercultural-inquiry/between-the-lines/between-the-lines-podcasts-publication/margaret-jull-costa-translation [Accessed 3 January 2018].
178 Godard, 'Deleuze and Translation', 61.
179 LeVan, 'Aesthetics of Encounter', 54.
180 Mario Santana, 'On Visible and Invisible Languages: Bernardo Atxaga's *Soinujolearen semea* in Translation', in *Writers in Between Languages: Minority Literatures in the Global Scene*, ed. Mari Jose Olaziregi (Reno: Center for Basque Studies, University of Nevada, 2009), 213.
181 Santana, 'On Visible and Invisible Languages', 215.
182 Santana, 'On Visible and Invisible Languages', 216.
183 Domínguez, 'Historiography', 103.
184 Cliff Stagoll, 'Becoming', in *The Deleuze Dictionary*, 26.
185 Jan Walsh Hokenson and Marcella Munson, *The Bilingual Text: History and Theory of Literary Self-Translation* (London: Routledge, 2014), 3.
186 Santana, 'On Visible and Invisible Languages', 221.

187 Gideon Toury, *Descriptive Translation Studies and Beyond* (Amsterdam and Philadelphia, PA: John Benjamins, 1995), 130. As quoted in Santana, 223.

188 Jull Costa, *Between the Lines*, and in an email to Harriet Hulme.

189 Lawrence Venuti, 'Introduction', in *Rethinking Translation: Discourse, Subjectivity, Ideology*, ed. Lawrence Venuti (London: Routledge, 1992), 3.

190 Deleuze, 'Platon et le simulacre', in *Logique du sens* (Les Éditions de Minuit, Paris: 1969), 297. 'Plato and the Simulacrum', trans. Rosalind Krauss, *The MIT Press* 27 (1983): 48–9. All translations of the French text come from this English translation. Page numbers in subsequent references refer to: French text; English text.

191 Deleuze, 'Platon et le simulacre', 302–3; 53.

192 Martin Heidegger, *Hölderlin's Hymn "The Ister"*, trans. William McNeill and Julia Davis (Bloomington and Indianapolis: Indiana University Press, 1996 [1984]), 63.

193 Bella Brodzki, *Can These Bones Live?: Translation, Survival and Cultural Memory* (Stanford, CA: Stanford University Press, 2007), 3.

Chapter 2
Milan Kundera's *Le Livre du rire et de l'oubli:* a hospitable translation

Introduction: the paradox of translation

> 'les traductions représentent tout'/'translation is everything'. – Milan Kundera[1]
>
> 'translation is my nightmare' – Milan Kundera[2]

As his somewhat contradictory definitions of translation quoted above suggest, Milan Kundera has a complicated relationship with translation. Kundera's 'authorization' of the French translations of the texts he produced before he began writing only in French in 1993 suggests an approach to translation concerned with translatability and absolute fidelity to an original text. But in his texts themselves, Kundera is fascinated by issues of semantic instability and miscommunication, exploring the inevitable betrayals of meaning which arise as we seek to understand one another and ourselves. How can we interpret this paradox between Kundera's approach to the translation of his texts and the issues with which he is concerned within those texts? In this chapter, I explore this question, focusing predominantly upon *Le Livre du rire et de l'oubli* (henceforth *Le Livre*), a text which, while originally written in Czech, was first published in 1979 in its French translation by François Kérel. *Le Livre* consequently occupies the fascinating position of having been *originally* published in translation, *originally* read by the majority of its readers in translation, but *originally* written in another language. In French translation it is thus simultaneously original and copy, a text which, in its very existence, queries the hierarchy of that ostensible binary.

Within the text of *Le Livre*, Kundera highlights one particular instance of linguistic 'untranslatability': the Czech word *litost*. *Litost*, for Kundera, defines a contradictory emotion which arises when our need to make perfect sense of our experience – our desire for translatability – confronts our inability to do so – the inevitability of untranslatability. This contradiction is an unavoidable element of our experiences, personal and political, but it is potentially dangerous: as Kundera explores, dreams of unity and consistency are often contingent upon repressing difference, both in our own identities and in our relations to those around us; upon forgetting the material reality of our individual and collective histories; and upon rejecting anything or anyone we deem to be untranslatable in the framework of our thought or action. In *Le Livre* Kundera explores such forgettings through the link he creates between lyric poetry and a certain type of totalitarian thinking, embodied in the Communist regime which came to power in Czechoslovakia in 1948. Both lyric poetry and totalitarian thinking, he suggests, share a desire to remove ambiguity in order to embrace absolutism, whether in art, life or politics. Kundera's criticism of lyric poetry in *Le Livre* is not unique to this novel: in several of his texts, Kundera creates a heuristic opposition between the perfect translation of experience into aesthetics offered by the poetic form and a more ambiguous translation offered by the novel form. But as always in Kundera's work, such an opposition contains a paradox: as Kundera's use of the novel form attests, the novel has its own poetry, which we can read in the polyphony, the repetition, the structural and thematic variations through which Kundera explores and challenges the forgettings he suggests are enacted by lyrical constructions.

Translation is crucial to the particular poetics which Kundera develops in *Le Livre*, and to his ability to articulate the dangers as well as the attractions of seeking perfection aesthetically, textually, personally or politically. In the novel we follow a journey of translation, one which begins, with *litost,* in linguistic untranslatability, but which ultimately becomes an exploration of social, political and affective untranslatability: a movement from the *praxis* of translation to an *ethics* of translation. This ethics, I suggest, can be explored through an engagement with two different dichotomies within translation theory: untranslatable versus translatable, and betrayal versus fidelity. In *Sur la traduction* (2004), Paul Ricœur explores the limitations of these dichotomies, and, from the spaces between the two, negotiates his ethical paradigm of *linguistic hospitality*. In this hospitality, what is foreign and untranslatable is incorporated into the desire for perfection, while that desire for perfection continues to expand and stretch the limits of what we believe we can transmit between self and other, home and abroad, domestic and foreign. In this chapter I argue that Kundera's novelistic process is concerned with a similar hospitality, one which is embodied within his exploration of *litost,* the untranslatable word which always, endlessly, demands translation.

Kundera: writing between identities

Translatability and untranslatability

It was the impact of the political situation in Czechoslovakia which pushed issues of translation to the forefront of Kundera's literary career. Kundera joined the Communist Party of Czechoslovakia (KSČ) in 1948, and, apart from a six-year spell between 1950 and 1956 when he was expelled from the Party, remained a member until after the collapse of the liberal ideals of the 1968 Prague Spring. While some of Kundera's early writing reflected Communist ideals, he subsequently became vocal about the importance of literary autonomy. In a speech given at the Fourth Congress of the Czechoslovak Writers in 1967, he spoke out for the importance of artistic and intellectual independence, commenting that any restrictions upon this were 'a chain entangling the limbs of our national literature as it tries to bound forward'.[3] Any possibility of intellectual freedom was dramatically reduced by the Russian invasion of Czechoslovakia in August 1968 and the subsequent clampdown by the KSČ: following this, Kundera's experiences as a writer and an intellectual altered irreversibly. In 1970 he was expelled from the Party, his teaching post was withdrawn, and all his books were banned. Kundera moved to France in 1975, and in 1979, following the publication of *Le Livre*, his Czech citizenship was revoked.

Like Bernardo Atxaga, Kundera highlights the reductive political readings and forms of censorship which dominate when an author writes in a minor language such as Czech.[4] Unlike Atxaga, however, Kundera has shifted his writing entirely into a major language: since 1993 he has written only in French. In her book *Kundera: The Ambiguity of Authorship*, Christine Angela Knoop explains Kundera's decision to write in French as part of an attempt to evade what he perceives to be reductive interpretations based only upon his national identity and biography.[5] Kundera has certainly revealed a mistrust of responses which focus heavily upon his personal and political biography, insisting somewhat polemically that critics who read a novel by an Eastern European writer according to 'some wretched political code' are 'murder[ing] it, no less brutally than the work of the Stalinist dogmatists'.[6] Tijana Miletic's comment, discussed in Chapter 1, that writing in a second language provides bilingual authors 'with the freedom from the conscious and unconscious heritage of their mother tongue' carries more weight in relation to Kundera than to Atxaga, for the relationship between Kundera's two languages is not caught up in a complex political, cultural or economic diglossia.[7] In this sense, French offers Kundera a form of expression through which he can attempt to elude the specific political 'code' which he suggests surrounds his work when produced in Czech.

Kundera's choice of French is not, however, an attempt to position his work within an exclusively French tradition. As he comments in *Une rencontre* (2009) in relation to the work of the Franco-Czech author Vera Linhartova: 'Quand Linhartova écrit en français, est-elle encore un écrivain tchèque? Non. Devient-elle un écrivain français? Non plus. Elle est ailleurs'/'When Linhartova writes in French, is she still a Czech writer? No. Does she become a French writer? No, not that either. She is elsewhere'.[8] This 'ailleurs' is a textual as well as a biographical space, concerned with the political and the national but not delimited by these. While ostensibly motivated by necessity, Kundera's decision to write in French can also be read as an attempt to inhabit and mirror such a space within his texts and own authorial identity. In fact, Kundera's 'ailleurs' does have a geographical and cultural location. In his 1983 essay 'Un occident kidnappé ou la tragédie de l'Europe Centrale', Kundera suggests that Central European literature has been betrayed by critical readings which insist upon emphasizing its connections to the East as opposed to the West.[9] In this sense, the 'ailleurs' Kundera occupies through his decision to write in French – an elsewhere which is nonetheless situated within a very specific Western European tradition – enables Kundera to reframe his texts within this cultural heritage.

As Michelle Woods notes, however, Kundera's decision to write in French has been seen as a 'betrayal' of his language and a 'snub' to his Czech heritage.[10] In fact, accusations of linguistic betrayal had been levelled at Kundera even before this decision, with several critics suggesting that Kundera had created a deliberately 'translatable' style in his Czech texts to render them easier to transmit to a non-Czech literary market, and that he removed their culturally specific elements when authorizing their French versions. In this regard, Allison Stanger suggests that Kundera erased specific elements of Czech history in the English and French versions of *La Plaisanterie* in order to make it more accessible to a foreign readership.[11] Stanisław Barańczak believes that Kundera wrote in Czech 'in a deliberately translatable, clear and unequivocal style, so that the translator would not be prodded into too many deviations from the intended meaning'.[12] For Søren Frank, Kundera attempted to neutralize the linguistic and cultural specificity of his Czech texts in his revised translations of them into French. Frank notes that even when Kundera includes Czech words in his French texts, he removes the Czech diacritics – *lítost* appears as *litost*, for example. Moreover, according to

Frank, Kundera adds explanatory passages for certain parts of his texts which might be too culturally specific for a Western reader.[13]

These accusations of enhanced translatability position Kundera as on a quest to attain the holy grail of translation practice: a translation which could be achieved without any distortion of the original text – which also implies a faith in the existence of a translatable style which could obviate or diminish such distortions. Such a style, as Florence Uniacke suggests, would be designed to enhance the commercial viability of a text:

> It is often heard that to be truly great you must achieve international success. Combine this view with a competitive market and it's easy to envisage a writer sidestepping lexical gaps. This trend has been termed 'Literary Starbucks', where publishers are seeing writers adopting more 'neutral' language and avoiding cultural idioms in order to appeal to foreign readers and editors.[14]

In the idea that lexical gaps *can* be sidestepped, and the differences of language neutralized, there resides a utopian faith in the possibility of a truly translatable form, style or language. But what is an unequivocal, translatable style? Could such a style, if it exists, really neutralize linguistic difference and so prevent deviations of meaning? Given the complexities of interlingual translation, even if we were to specify the elements of an absolutely translatable style it is unlikely that we would be able to realize such a style in practice.

But, whether or not it is actually possible, the *desire* for full translatability reveals a problematic conception of translation, tasking it with the absolute elimination of linguistic and cultural difference. In his essay *Sur la traduction,* Paul Ricœur explores the concept of the 'perfect translation' which, he suggests, stems from just such a desire. Ricœur argues that 'Le rêve de la traduction parfaite équivaut au souhait d'un gain pour la traduction, d'un gain qui serait sans perte'/'The dream of the perfect translation amounts to the wish that translation would gain, gain without losing.'[15] This gain would enable translation to transcend its own limitations and offer access to a linguistic universal. Ricœur offers two examples of the form such a task of perfect translation could take: either a Borgesian 'Library of Babel' (which would encompass every possible text and thereby erase the idea of untranslatability), or a Benjaminian universal language capable of transcending the very need for translation.[16] Both of these models reveal the desire to erase from a language what is untranslatable within it, that which simultaneously calls for translation and makes translation so challenging: 'la différence indépassable du propre et de l'étranger'/'the impassable difference of the peculiar and the foreign'.[17] The perfect translation is, then, constructed from a wish to neutralize the possibility of linguistic, textual and cultural misunderstanding, and to erase specificity in the name of universal comprehension.

The criticism levelled at Kundera implicates him in this search for neutrality, shifting the emancipatory value of the *elsewhere* he seeks to inhabit through his bilingual writing into a rootless *anywhere* or *nowhere*. This shift, as Emily Apter discusses in *Against World Literature*, endorses cultural equivalence, replacing an ethical acknowledgement of forms of linguistic or cultural untranslatability with an insistence upon universal understanding.[18] Yet, as Frank points out, any attempt to attain translatability for the novel form via cultural neutrality is fundamentally at odds with both the theories Kundera espouses within his novels themselves and the form through which he articulates those theories.[19] Kundera's texts are frequently formed through a polyphonic technique which disrupts any generalized or universal narrative viewpoint. In *Le Rideau* (2005), he writes of the power of novels to fragment the dominance of single narratorial perspectives, 'casser ce pouvoir, [...] détrôner le narrateur, [...] éclairer une seule «story» sous des angles multiples et faire [du] roman un carnaval des vérités individuelles et de leur irréductible relativité'/'to break that power, to dethrone the narrator [...] throw light on a single "story" from several angles and [make the] novel a carnival of separate truths and their irreducible relativity'.[20] This fragmentation infiltrates all Kundera's novels, which through a combination of personal and political stories explore the endless mistranslations and misinterpretations involved in attempts to communalize meaning. But are such textual assertions about the relativity of our individual truths not fundamentally contradicted by Kundera's desire to make these assertions universally understood through translation? How are we to understand the tensions which exist between form and content, theory and practice, in Kundera's work? What is the nature of the dissonance between them that he seems to manufacture?

Authority and ambiguity

Kundera's desire for translatability should be understood within two different contexts: his experience of political exile, and the nature of his theoretical assertions. Firstly, Kundera's exile to France, combined with the repression of his books in Czechoslovakia, meant that translation was crucial to the dissemination of his work. He claims that 'my books lived their lives as translations; as translations they were read, criticised, judged, accepted or rejected'.[21] Translation became a necessity, but more than this, it became 'everything'. For if Kundera's original language could no longer be his literary language, then the alternatives before him were inevitably conditioned by the experience of translation. Kundera could write his texts in Czech but publish them first in French translation, positioning the Czech text as a blueprint for the translation, rather than the translation as a copy of the original – the approach he took in *Le Livre*. He could write them in Czech and then self-translate them, creating two versions of the same text himself. (Kundera has ostensibly never taken this approach, although there is a critical consensus that *L'Immortalité* (1993) is a self-translation which Kundera published under the pseudonym Eva Bloch).[22] Or he could write only in French, thereby replacing Czech with his second language and inevitably bringing an element of translation into his writing process. This third option is the one Kundera has followed since 1993. On one level, these linguistic decisions can be read as a journey from translation to original writing, from the Czech of the exiled and censored writer to the French of the naturalized citizen. At the same time, each of these literary practices reveals the impossibility of separating Kundera's writing from issues of translation: in each of these options, forms of linguistic transference, doubling or substitution are implicit in the original instance of textual creation. Indeed, Kundera acknowledges that, before he began writing only in French, he created his texts in Czech with Kérel in mind. This admission, rather than confirming Kundera's quest for 'translatability', merely reflects the reality of a situation in which Kérel was his first, his only, and his most essential reader.[23] To indict Kundera for writing with an eye to translation is thus to address a fact rather than formulate a plausible accusation.

The second context within which Kundera's desire for translatability should be understood is the broader framework of his affirmations – taken as a whole – on the nature of textual work, affirmations which help to clarify the apparent dissonance between his theories and his practice. The main accusation Kundera levels at the idea of universality, whether on a personal, political or textual level, is that it operates by rejecting ambiguity, seeking to create perfect alliances between thought and word, word and action, action and theory, theory and existence. Throughout his work, Kundera repeatedly highlights the ethical power of ambiguity, suggesting that the ability to understand the contingency of our experience requires an act of heroism: 'Comprendre avec Cervantes le monde comme ambiguïté, avoir à affronter, au lieu d'une seule vérité absolue, un tas de vérités relatives qui se contredisent [...] posséder donc comme seule certitude la *sagesse de l'incertitude,* cela exige une force non moins grande.'/'To take, with Cervantes, the world as ambiguity, to be obliged to face not a single absolute truth but a welter of contradictory truths [...], to have as one's only certainty the *wisdom of uncertainty*, requires no less courage.'[24]

The value Kundera assigns to ambiguity here, and throughout his work, elucidates somewhat the contradictions between his apparent desire for translatability and the general philosophical approach he espouses. For this contradiction reasserts, in Knoop's phrase, the ambiguity of Kundera's authorship, an ambiguity founded precisely on a continually reframed dissonance between theory and practice. The courage Kundera associates with accepting uncertainty resides in the difficulty of suppressing our human desire to convert relativity into certainty: 'L'homme souhaite un monde où le bien et le mal soient nettement discernables car est en lui le désir, inné et indomptable, de juger avant de comprendre. Sur ce désir sont fondées les religions et les idéologies. [...] Elles exigent que quelqu'un ait raison'/'Man desires a world where good and evil can be clearly distinguished, for he has an innate and irrepressible desire to judge before he understands. Religions and ideologies are founded on this desire. [...] They require that someone be right', he writes in *L'Art du roman.*[25] As Kundera's somewhat dogmatic tone in this statement attests, a desire to attain certainty is present in all our pronouncements, interpretations and judgements, including Kundera's own. Indeed, as Liisa Steinby notes, the forcefulness of Kundera's textual pronouncements makes him a difficult author to approach critically: he writes, Steinby suggests, 'in a manner that saves scholars from their usual task of grasping the thematic content and formal features', so that critics often find his interpretation of a text included within its pages.[26] But, as I go on to discuss, it is *through* as opposed to *despite* this conflict in Kundera's work – between the ambiguity he promotes as the language of the novel and the attractions of certainty – that we can see the ethical charge of Kundera's approach.

Acknowledging this ambiguity and its accompanying desire for certainty is crucial when interrogating Kundera's relationship to translation. If there is a dissonance between Kundera's attempts to universalize elements of his writing and his sense of the relativity of all such pronouncements, there is an even greater one between these pronouncements and his engagement with the translation of his texts themselves. Kundera plays an active role in the translations of his texts, particularly the French translations, which he revised between 1985 and 1987, and which he now describes as 'authentic' versions of his work, equivalent to the Czech originals. This contentious description, with its implicit destabilization of the very concept of originality, gives credence to Kundera's reputation as an exponent of absolute authorial control, and in fact, Kundera's decision to revise the French translations of his texts did stem from his growing and vocal dismay at the alterations which the first French translator of his books, Marcel Aymonin, had made to *La Plaisanterie* when it was translated in 1968. Realizing that these translations, rather than the Czech originals, were serving as the source texts for translators of his work who could not read Czech, Kundera sought to rectify the flaws he perceived in them.[27] As Woods discusses, subsequent translations of Kundera's work into English have been taken from these authorized French versions, thereby giving Kundera 'ultimate authority over the English translations', as well as the Czech originals and their French counterparts. Woods suggests that Kundera has in fact 'effectively translated' both the definitive French and the definitive English versions of *La Plaisanterie* through the extensive additions and alterations he has made to the translations of both texts.[28]

As Woods notes, Kundera's interest in the translation process has led him to engage in extensive debates and disagreements with both publishers and translators of his work.[29] These debates have given Kundera a certain notoriety among critics, who 'castigate Kundera [...] for a quixotic and irrelevant game of textual changes', designed purely to assert his authorial power.[30] Knoop suggests that Kundera's insistence upon controlling the translations of his work stems from an unswerving dedication to the hegemony of authorship which he perceives translation fatally to distort:

> in a rather conservative way, he believes in 'faithful' translations of texts and is very involved in their creation. This seemingly unsophisticated position is connected to an understanding of art as containing a certain, fixed essence that can be maintained irrespective of the language used to express, and is closely related to his refusal to allow for the semiotic complexity of the issue of non-mother tongue writing, the problematic of which must be very present to him.[31]

For Knoop, Kundera's attitude to translation reveals an essentialist vision of texts which rejects the impact of language upon meaning. Knoop is by no means alone in her assessment of Kundera's relationship with translation: in *The Scandals of Translation*, Lawrence Venuti uses Kundera as an example of an author with a distinctly unethical approach to translation, one that is 'remarkably naïve'. 'He assumes that the meaning of a foreign text can avoid change in translation, that the foreign writer's intention can travel unadulterated across a linguistic and cultural divide', claims Venuti. 'Kundera doesn't want to recognize the linguistic and cultural differences that translation must negotiate'.[32] More recently, in 2013, Liisa Steinby commented that Kundera 'considers his own language to be clear and explicit' and, because of this, insists 'that the translator find exact equivalents', suggesting that Kundera maintains a faith in the possibility of absolute semantic identification between different languages.[33]

A Sisyphean task

Readings such as those offered by Steinby, Venuti and Knoop position Kundera as an author who believes in absolute translatability, in the possibility of a semantic essence which can be transferred from language to language intact, provided the translator has the capability and understanding to do so. Kundera has certainly acknowledged his great interest in translation, and his desire to control how his work is produced in other languages. He writes that '[j]usqu'alors je n'avais pas l'habitude de lire et de contrôler mes traductions; aujourd'hui, hélas, je consacre à cette activité sisyphesque presque plus de temps qu'à l'écriture elle-même'/'until then, I was not in the habit of reading and controlling my translations; nowadays, alas, I dedicate almost more time to that Sisyphean task than I do to writing itself'.[34] Yet in Kundera's description of the monitoring of the translation of his works as a Sisyphean task, a never-ending attempt to direct what is disseminated, resides the implication that he is only too aware that there is *no* fixed essence to his texts, no stable element which can survive intact the semantic transfer of translation. In Greek mythology, Sisyphus was condemned for eternity to haul a stone up a mountain in Hades, only to watch it roll down again as soon as he reached the top. Kundera's efforts to control the translation of his work reflect a similar attempt to find a resting place for the weighty stone of textual ambiguity. But, like Sisyphus, Kundera is only too aware that this desire can never be realized.

In her excellent *Milan Kundera and Translation*, Michelle Woods suggests that the central connection between Kundera's attitude to translation and his novelistic poetics is his focus upon the inevitability of *untranslatability* between various forms of communication, and therefore the *impossibility* of achieving the type of translatability that he is frequently accused of pursuing in his writing practice. 'Kundera does not believe a translation can be absolutely faithful to the original', Woods claims. 'The untranslatability of language because of cultural differences inherent in it is a paradox that Kundera focuses on again and again'.[35] Woods argues cogently for re-envisioning Kundera's perceived relationship to translation, precisely because she believes Kundera to be an author who reveals an almost hyper-awareness of the impact of language upon the meaning of texts and, therefore, the potential pitfalls involved in any attempt to transfer meaning interlinguistically and intralinguistically. This hyper-awareness, which is integral to both Kundera's novels and his theoretical texts, leads Woods to conclude that Kundera's attitude to translation is neither naive nor mistrustful, but instead one informed by 'insight into misunderstanding rather than communication as the human norm of language'.[36]

This insight is apparent throughout several of Kundera's texts: *L'Insoutenable légèreté de l'être*, *L'Immortalité* and *Le Livre* all include extended explorations of the forms we use to convey ideas, emotions and experiences – words, texts, gestures, expressions – and their ability to be endlessly translated into different modes and models of understanding and communication. In *L'Insoutenable légèreté de l'être*, Kundera creates an entire section, entitled 'Les Mots incompris' – words misunderstood – in order to reveal, through the mutual incomprehension of two lovers, Sabina and Franz, the multiplicity of perspectives which the same situation can engender. Franz, a professor, lives his life according to the idea of *faithfulness*: he has faith in absolute love, in grand ideals and in the beauty of a total sacrifice for those ideals. Sabina, an artist, is the mistress of *betrayal*; she refuses to weaken herself in love, evades idealism and seeks absolute freedom rather than absolute loyalty. In Sabina and Franz's attempts at communication, the differences implicit in their respective attitudes cause every word the one utters to become fundamentally incomprehensible to the other: '[i]ls comprenaient exactement le sens logique des mots qu'ils se disaient, mais sans entendre le murmure du fleuve sémantique qui coulait à travers ces mots'/'although they had a clear understanding of the logical meaning of the words they exchanged, they failed to hear the semantic susurrus of the river flowing through them'.[37] This 'semantic susurrus' is the result of the life they have lived, which causes the same words to have entirely different meanings for each of them. Interestingly, the split between Sabina and Franz mirrors one of the crucial binaries in translation theory: in Ricœur's terms 'fidelité *versus* trahison' /'faithfulness *versus* betrayal'.[38] While Kundera's pronouncements on translation suggest a desire for fidelity to the original text, his exploration of Franz and Sabina's different attitudes to existence reframes the value assigned to this fidelity: while Sabina's attitude of *betrayal* prevents her from engaging with another in an individual sense, Franz's *faith* in grand ideals is revealed as both absurd and destructive on a much larger scale. Kundera's refusal to prioritize one attitude over the other is symptomatic of his sense of their proximity, a proximity which, as I will discuss later in this chapter, is integral to understanding his discussion of the betrayals of translation.

It is not only the endless mutability of people's words which Kundera explores in his fiction, but also the mutability of people's movement. In *L'Immortalité* he focuses upon the semiotic translation of a single gesture, and its changing affective meaning as it is performed by three different women in three different temporal and spatial moments. As a teenager, Agnès watches her father's secretary wave goodbye to him, with a gesture 'si inattendu, si beau, qu'il resta dans la mémoire d'Agnès comme la trace d'un éclair'/'so unexpected and beautiful that it remained in Agnès's memory like the imprint of a lightning bolt'.[39] Agnès begins to use the gesture herself when she says goodbye to her boyfriends, mimicking it so that she too may access the desires and depths which she equates with adulthood. But one day she sees her eleven-year-old sister, Laura, making the same gesture, and realizes that 'ce geste fût à la disposition de tout le monde et nullement sa propriété; comme si, en l'accomplissant, elle se rendait coupable d'un vol ou d'une contrefaçon'/'the gesture was available to all and thus did not really belong to her: when she waved her arm, she was actually committing theft or forgery'.[40] In Kundera's exploration here, we see the same gesture translated in time, place and relation, its status as original masked by the possibility that it may always be appropriated by another, its affective stability belied.[41]

Both *L'Immortalité* and *L'Insoutenable légèreté de l'être* thus foreground the impossibility of any 'certain, fixed essence that can be maintained irrespective of the language used to express it'.[42] The interaction between Kundera's novelistic discussions of the fluidity of language, on the one hand, and his interference in the translations of his texts, on the other, draws attention to the inherent tensions running through his work: the tension between writing in Czech and writing in French; between the role of the translator and the role of the author; between interpreting a text and appropriating it; between seeking translation and valorizing its impossibility. In these tensions, however, and particularly in the dissonant connection which exists between his words and his actions, lies the productive charge of Kundera's work. This charge is best articulated through an exploration of a text which itself sits between French and Czech; between theory and fiction; between Kundera's voice and the voice of his critics, readers and translators, namely the paratext which appears at the end of the Gallimard editions of Kundera's work. This reads: 'Entre 1985 et 1987 les traductions françaises des ouvrages écrits en tchèque ont été entièrement revues par l'auteur, et dès lors, ont la même valeur d'authenticité que le texte tchèque'/'Between 1985 and 1987 the French translations of works written in Czech were entirely reviewed by the author and now have the same authentic value as the Czech text'.[43] This comment appears to return us to the idea of Kundera as ultimate authoritarian, seeking to control his texts and their authenticity. And yet, as with so many of the comments connected to Kundera, this statement elides as much as it reveals. For 'the same authentic value' can only be assigned if we can fully understand and control the original, authentic value of an utterance, a gesture, or a text. And this understanding is one which, throughout his texts, Kundera reveals to be a Sisyphean activity. The quest to understand the nature of authentic value, though it is both impossible and endless, is also seemingly inescapable, being intimately connected to our sense of our own lives and our relations with others. The value of Kundera's texts thus lies in their acknowledgement of their own uncertainty, inauthenticity and instability, an acknowledgement implicit in Kundera's continual rewriting and revision of his texts through translation.

Form and architecture

Kundera's acknowledgement of his texts' instability is tempered, however, by his faith in the illuminating power of form. If content can never resist the impact of context, it is form alone which can give shape and purpose to our interpretations, enabling us to engage productively with issues of semantic and affective mobility. Kundera's texts are based around certain formal principles that often reflect Bakhtin's theories of the novel: a musical approach, which includes shifts in tempo and polyphonic variations upon different themes; an emphasis upon dialogism as opposed to monologism; the use of ellipsis, repetition and a structure based around the number seven.[44] The connection Kundera creates between this architecture and the affective impact of his texts helps to explain his mistrust of any translation which he believes domesticates his style to ensure it corresponds with the stylistic norms of the target language. This mistrust is apparent in Kundera's 'Note de l'auteur' in the revised 1985 edition of *La Plaisanterie*, in which he comments that 'le traducteur [...] n'a pas traduit le roman; il l'a réécrit'/'the translator did not translate the novel; he rewrote it'.[45] Kundera's distinction between translating and rewriting suggests that he does not see rewriting as necessarily accompanying the changes which occur in the shift from one language to another. Rather it is the choices the translator makes in dealing with that shift, her or his ability to maintain or ignore the symbiosis between textual architecture and affective content, which either uphold or distort the emotional impact of the text.

Kundera suggests that it is just such a distortion which occurred in *La Plaisanterie,* when Aymonin took the opportunity to rewrite the form of the text, converting a deliberately clear and repetitive structure into something 'fleuri et baroque'/'flowery and baroque'.[46] While Kundera dislikes this formal rewriting in and of itself, he vehemently condemns what he perceives as its impact upon the critical reception of this text: following alterations to its form the text was, he suggests, 'lu d'une façon unilatéralement politique'/'read in a unilaterally political way'.[47] *La Plaisanterie* does engage with political themes: its protagonist, Ludvik, is a Communist activist excluded from the Party for sending a satirical postcard. But Kundera suggests that this political content should not elicit a unilaterally political reading. Ludvik's experiences are grounded, interrogated and fragmented through a prismatic form which Kundera perceives as ethical precisely in its refusal to offer any single political viewpoint. Kundera believes, however, that the multiple angles and perspectives of the text depend upon the spare and repetitive form through which he narrates events, emotions and experiences. For Kundera, Aymonin's shift of stylistic emphasis elides this plurality in favour of a flowery rhetoric vulnerable to a dominant political message. [48] For Kundera, then, Aymonin's betrayal resided not in the translation *per se*, but rather in the conversion, through translation, of an intentionally ambiguous text into one which was universally read as political.

By suggesting that alterations to the form of a text can create immutably political interpretations, Kundera highlights the powerful influence he perceives translation to exert upon the relation between the political and the aesthetic. In fact, Aymonin's selection as the translator for *La Plaisanterie* raises wider questions surrounding this relation: as Jan Rubeš discusses, Aymonin gained a monopoly over the translation of Czech authors into French because he was the only French translator trusted by the Czech Communist Party. His political past thus sets him at odds with the satirical content of *La Plaisanterie*, a fact which partially explains the vehemence of Kundera's reaction to his translation. At the same time, Kundera's connection to Aymonin through translation inevitably drew attention to Kundera's own Communist past, and particularly the state-approved poetry which he wrote in the 1950s. For Rubeš, erasing Aymonin's translation and replacing it with Kérel's is part of an attempt by Kundera to erase this former political and aesthetic commitment to Communism, and replace it with more autonomous and ambiguous forms.[49]

Kundera's resistance to Aymonin's translation is thus caught up in the relation between the political and the aesthetic which runs throughout his work and his experiences as a writer. In *Understanding Milan Kundera,* Fred Misurella suggests that Kundera's authorial resistance to translation is always a form of attempted resistance to coercion, one which links Kundera's refusal to allow Western editors and translators to change his text for the purposes of fluency to his former refusal to allow Czechoslovak state censors to alter his texts so that they would conform to Stalinist diktat.[50] In both these instances, Kundera's rejection of attempts to change the structure of his texts reveals the potent connection he perceives between form and content, and the integral role played by both in the impact of his work. Within his texts, Kundera's concern with the ways in which significance is created and transmitted hinges upon the relation of the political and the aesthetic: political movements, he suggests, have their own aesthetics, just as aesthetic forms have their own politics and ethics. Kundera's attitude to translation, and the approaches to translation which appear throughout his texts, express and interrogate the shape of this dynamic between politics and aesthetics. My exploration, below, of Kundera's use of an aesthetics of translation within *Le Livre* seeks to reveal the form and potential of this interrogation.

Le Livre du rire et de l'oubli: variations on laughter and forgetting

Le Livre is a novel in seven parts, which segues between the comic and the tragic, the factual and the fantastic, the individual and the collective. The text also spans the political and the personal, for Kundera believes that these two spheres are not mutually exclusive, but rather mutually illuminating: '[p]olitics unmasks the metaphysics of private life', he claims, 'private life unmasks the metaphysics of politics'.[51] Kundera's comment elucidates his own position within the rather nebulous genre of the political novel: the rationales and impulses which motivate political actions, he suggests, are not exclusive to the political arena; rather, these are innately human instincts which emerge in both public and private spheres. Because of this, Kundera has emphatically argued that *Le Livre* is not a political allegory and is not using personal stories to outline a political thesis.[52] Instead, personal and political strands mirror and illuminate each other, intersecting through thematic explorations of the two phenomena contained in the title: laughter and forgetting.

Laughter, Kundera initially suggests, is a binary phenomenon, split between the laughter of the Devil, which 'désignait l'absurdité des choses'/'denoted the absurdity of things', and the laughter of the angels who 'au contraire se réjouit que tout fût ici-bas bien ordonné, sagement conçu, bon et plein de sens'/'on the contrary meant to rejoice over how well ordered, wisely conceived, good, and meaningful everything here below was'.[53] Through this dual laughter Kundera introduces an opposition between sense and nonsense which is fundamental to each of the stories in *Le Livre*. Yet this opposition is heuristic, for Kundera's vision is kaleidoscopic as opposed to split-lens, and the theme of laughter explodes beyond binary constraints and fragments into a multitude of different stories. Through vignettes focusing upon individual and collective relationships – sexual, marital, familial, pedagogical – Kundera explores the bathos, the poignancy, the possibilities and the dangers of our attempts to assign significance to our personal and political experiences. Questions of memory dominate these explorations: do we, Kundera asks, build the narratives of our personal lives and of our political communities by eradicating, rewriting and even forgetting history? Can we ascribe coherence and sense to our actions only by overlooking or denying the past?

Translation is integral to the form and content through which Kundera explores these questions. Formally, *Le Livre* is constructed around a series of 'variations' on key words, through which Kundera translates a single theme into multiple contexts. These key words, he explains, are crucial to *Le Livre* not only linguistically, but also on a structural and a thematic level:

> Le roman est fondé tout d'abord sur quelques mots fondamentaux. […] Dans *Le Livre du rire et de l'oubli,* la « série » est la suivante: l'oubli, le rire, les anges, la « litost », la frontière. Ces cinq mots principaux sont, dans le cours du roman, analysés, étudiés, définis, redéfinis, et ainsi transformés en catégories de l'existence. Le roman est bâti sur ces quelques catégories comme une maison sur des piliers.

> A novel is based primarily on certain fundamental words. [...] In *The Book of Laughter and Forgetting*, the "row" goes: forgetting, laughter, angels, *litost*, border. Over the course of the novel, those five principal words are analyzed, studied, defined, redefined, and thus transformed into categories of existence. The novel is built on those few categories the way a house is built on its pillars.[54]

In this chapter I engage with each of these five different but interconnected 'categories of existence', beginning with the Czech language loan *litost*. While Kundera does not directly explore *litost* until the fourth chapter of the text, the themes which it introduces – the desire for absolute interpersonal or intrapersonal identification, and the impossibility of attaining either – are at the heart both of *Le Livre* and of my exploration of the relevance of translation to understanding Kundera's particular ethics and aesthetics of the novel.

What is *litost*?

In the fourth section of *Le Livre*, Kundera dedicates an entire chapter to an exploration of *litost*, 'un mot tchèque intraduisible en d'autres langues'/'an untranslatable Czech word'.[55] The narrator's plaintive remark that '[p]our le sens de ce mot je cherche vainement un équivalent dans d'autres langues, bien que j'aie peine à imaginer qu'on puisse comprendre l'âme humaine sans lui'/'I have looked in vain in other languages for an equivalent, though I find it difficult to imagine how anyone can understand the human soul without it', provides the impetus for a textual search for the meaning of *litost*.[56] This is a search which proves simultaneously fruitless and fruitful: fruitless, because what is untranslatable within *litost* remains untranslatable, refusing to unveil itself from within its multiple folds of meaning; fruitful because, in its attempted translation, *litost* provides Kundera with the springboard for a thematic as well as a formal enquiry into the nuances and contradictions of the human soul, both personal and political.

Kundera's narrator suggests that the closest translation for *litost* into French renders it as 'un état tourmentant né du spectacle de notre propre misère soudainement découverte'/'a state of torment created by the sudden sight of one's own misery'.[57] Yet even this expanded translation elides the subtleties of *litost*: given that the word remains in Czech throughout the French text it is, we understand, only by translating *litost* into lived or, rather, fictionalized experience, by glossing it rather than translating it interlingually, that we can grasp the multiple complexities contained within this single word. 'Je vais donner un exemple'/'Let me give an example', states the narrator, before relating the comic story of a student who attempts and fails to consummate his relationship with Christine, the young wife of a butcher.[58] This is a story which hinges upon linguistic and semantic misunderstandings, as the student repeatedly seeks, and fails, to grasp the reason for Christine's sexual reluctance:

> Mais quoi? Christine résiste! [...] Il aurait voulu lui demander pourquoi elle lui résistait, mais il ne pouvait pas parler. Mme Christine était si timide, si délicate qu'en sa présence les choses de l'amour perdaient leurs noms. Il n'osait parler que Le Langage du souffle et du toucher. Qu'avaient-ils à faire de la pesanteur des mots? Est-ce qu'il ne brûlait pas en elle? Ils flambaient tous deux de la même flamme!
>
> But what's this? Kristyna is resisting! [...] He wanted to ask her why she was resisting him, but he could not speak. Kristyna was so shy, so delicate, that love's functions lost their names in her presence. He dared use only the language of breathing and touching. Weren't they beyond the heaviness of words? Wasn't he burning within her? They were both burning with the same flame![59]

The difference between the English and French renderings of the name Christine/Kristyna highlights a discrepancy between these two versions that I will return to later. In both versions, however, Kundera constructs an image of romantic love based upon a yearning for an absolute affective connection with another person. 'L'absolu de l'amour est en réalité un désir d'identité absolue'/'Love's absolute is actually a desire for absolute identity', the narrator claims, and the student's every interaction with Christine, whether spoken or silent, emotional or physical, is motivated either by his faith that he can identify absolutely with her or by his desire to achieve such an identification.[60]

The student's refusal to speak to Christine in spite of his inability to understand why she will not consummate their relationship suggests that he believes such an identification to be attainable without the need for the concrete weight of words. In desiring a world in which the language of touch is sufficient in and of itself, the student is seeking a space in which the inevitable slippage which occurs in spoken or written language between signified and signifier – which is further testified to by the slippage of translation – is taken out of the romantic equation. But the student's faith in his ability to identify absolutely with Christine continues even when they do begin to speak:

> «J'en mourrais. C'est vrai. J'en mourrais» répéta Mme Christine [...]. L'étudiant éprouvait un désespoir teinté de béatitude. [...] Elle l'aimait à en mourir, elle l'aimait au point d'avoir peur de faire l'amour avec lui parce que, si elle faisait l'amour avec lui, elle ne pourrait plus jamais vivre sans lui et elle mourrait de chagrin et de désir. [...] «Je te comprends ! Je mourrai avec toi !»
>
> "It would kill me. It's true. It would kill me," Kristyna repeated. [...] The student felt despair tinged with bliss. [...] She loved him as no one had before. She loved him so much it would kill her, she loved him to the point of being afraid to make love with him because if she were to make love with him, she would never be able to live without him and she would die of grief and desire. [...] "I understand you! I'll die with you!"[61]

The student's exclamation 'Je te comprends' is as spurious as his earlier faith that 'la même flamme' burnt in their silence: whether in silence or in speech, the student has repeatedly misunderstood Christine by imposing his own vision and version of events upon her gestures and speech. The following morning, Christine reveals the reality behind her words: '«Tu sais, il ne faut pas m'en vouloir, c'est vrai que je pourrais en mourir. Le docteur m'a dit après mon premier accouchement qu'il ne fallait plus jamais que je sois enceinte.»'/'"You know, you shouldn't [hold it against me], it really could kill me. The doctor told me after I had my baby I should never get pregnant again."'[62] The student's failure to consummate his relationship with Christine is here revealed to be a failure of understanding but also of translation: in his exchange of silences, gestures and finally words with Christine, the student has repeatedly translated the pragmatic roots of Christine's sexual reluctance into an utterly misguided vision of absolute romantic identification.

In his seminal text *After Babel,* George Steiner describes 'translation as understanding': 'To hear significance is to translate', he writes, suggesting that all our communication, interlingual or intralingual, involves a translation between another's idiom and our own, between their 'fleuve sémantique' and ours.[63] By creating an analogy between understanding and translation, Steiner's aphorism allows the ethical dilemmas and the potential involved in the act of interlingual translation to illuminate similar dilemmas and a similar potential within our attempts at interpersonal understanding. To acknowledge the veracity of such an analogy is to acknowledge that the inevitable distortions, miscommunications, losses and elisions present in every attempt to understand another individual are also present in translation. It is to acknowledge, too, the subjectivity of relation, the alterity present in our intralingual as well as interlingual communications, the hierarchical frameworks we impose and affectively enact. Steiner's analogy allows us to perceive the task of understanding another person as one precisely of translation, undertaken in the knowledge that it can never be completed fully or perfectly. This recognition requires us to understand translation as a task without end, as a process which can never achieve an absolute identification between a source and a target text. The student in *Le Livre* fails to achieve this recognition, for his desire to attain a perfect understanding of Christine hinges upon his belief that he can attain a perfect translation between her language, experience and individuality, and his own.

In *Sur la traduction,* Paul Ricœur suggests that the utopian idea of the perfect translation hinges upon precisely this desire to achieve an absolute identification between source text and target text. To return to the quotation I offered earlier, Ricœur suggests that '[l]e rêve de la traduction parfaite équivaut au souhait d'un gain pour la traduction, d'un gain qui serait sans perte [...] adéquation totale [...] une *identité* de sens démontrable'/'The dream of the perfect translation amounts to the wish that translation would gain, gain without losing. [...] total adequacy [...] a demonstrable *identity* of meaning'.[64] Ricœur's comment emphasizes the affective power within our desire for this harmony of sense across languages: we dream of attaining the perfect translation, even as we acknowledge its impossibility. As Richard Kearney notes, Ricœur's paradigm of translation is twofold. There is, first, 'the *linguistic paradigm* which refers to how words relate to meanings within language or between languages. And, second, the *ontological paradigm* which refers to how translation occurs between one human self and another'.[65] Ricœur then, like Steiner in *After Babel*, interweaves translation and understanding to suggest that translation embodies, on the linguistic level, the dynamics of our exchanges on the level of the ontological. Linguistically, the desire for the perfect translation is born of the desire for an absolute identity of copy and original, of source and target language: the desire to eliminate the untranslatability of a word such as *litost*, for example. Ontologically, in our relations with one another this desire becomes the affective desire for the absolute identity of self and other, of another's language and our own. Such is the desire of the student in *Le Livre*.

Thus, through his construction of the student's story, Kundera develops his own narrative of the desire for a perfect translation. And in the student's failure to achieve unity between himself and Christine we see the failure of this desire mapped both linguistically and relationally. For, paradoxically, it is through this failure of *relational* translation that we come to understand how *litost* itself might be *linguistically* translated. 'Mais dès que l'illusion de l'identité absolue est brisée [...] l'amour devient une source permanente du grand tourment que nous appelons *litost*'/'But when the illusion of absolute identity vanishes [...] love becomes a permanent source of the great torment we call *litost*', writes Kundera.[66] *Litost*, 'un mot tchèque intraduisible', here exceeds its interlingual untranslatability to become representative of the untranslatability of relation. This untranslatability exists in both an interpersonal and an intrapersonal sense, for while the *litost* the student experiences arises from the failure of his desire to identify absolutely with another, it is ultimately symbolic of his inability to identify absolutely with *himself*, to correlate the lyricism of his vision with the actual banality of his experience.

What then is *litost*? His failure to consummate his relationship with Christine forces the student to confront the discrepancy between his vision of love as absolute and its provisional and contingent reality, between his perception of the world and his experience of it, between his desire for a perfect translation and his inability to attain one. It is this confrontation which terminates in the experience of his 'propre misère'/'own misery', his *litost*.[67] In this sense, *litost* can be understood as a state which arises from untranslatability, from a sudden awareness of the impossibility of a matching communication and a matching understanding, whether with oneself or with another. In *Sur la traduction*, Ricœur suggests that the perfect translation reveals a desire for a space from which 'les intraductibilités auraient toutes été effacées'/'the untranslatabilities would all have been erased'.[68] Through Kundera's return to *litost*, the student is made to confront the impossibility of such an effacement, for just as what is foreign within *litost* itself cannot be absorbed into the French translation of *Le Livre*, so too what is foreign in the student's experience with Christine cannot be absorbed into his vision of what has happened.

Variations on *litost*

In the seven stories of *Le Livre*, Kundera constructs multiple variations upon this 'désir d'identité absolue', whether in a sexual, romantic, pedagogical or political context. In 'Litost', Kundera mirrors the personal narrative of the student in a more explicitly political one. For the narrator, the untranslatability of *litost* hints at the possibility that it is an emotion more innate to the Czech soul than that of other nations, and therefore one integrally connected to the political and historical experiences of the Czech nation: he suggests that 'l'histoire des Tchèques [...] est l'histoire de la *litost*'/'The story of the Czechs [...] is a story of *litost*'.[69] Kundera's connection between a national emotion and an apparently untranslatable word returns us to the intertwining of nation and language which I discussed in Chapter 1. The question of untranslatability is always caught up in this intersection; as Apter discusses, by approaching those words within a text which appear to be untranslatable, we can acknowledge forms of cultural and linguistic specificity which cannot be homogenized in a global context.[70] But to read the Untranslatable as the epitome of an absolute difference which can never be understood beyond its cultural and linguistic specificity is a move which always leads towards an essentialized understanding of that difference. Kundera's deployment of this link in *Le Livre* seeks to position it as a form of insight rather than essentialism, exploring *litost* as integral to understanding the thread of revolution and defeat running through Czech history. His narrator suggests that a desire on the part of the Czech people to identify themselves as strong and independent led them to revolt again and again against various invading forces. But these continual revolts against those stronger than themselves ended in 'cette succession de glorieuses défaites qui mettaient en branle le cours de l'Histoire et conduisaient à sa perte le people'/'a succession of glorious defeats that launched their history and led [the people] to ruin'.[71] Obliged to submit to external powers stronger than itself, the Czech nation entered into a collective emotional encounter with *litost*, brought about by the discrepancy between a national conception of its political strength and the reality of its relative weakness.

Elsewhere in the text of *Le Livre*, Kundera narrates several stories, personal and political, which focus upon characters who attempt and fail to create coherent versions of their identities. In the first chapter, Mirek, an ex-Communist, struggles with what is untranslatable within his romantic history: his love affair with a woman he now considers to be ugly, an experience as shattering to his sense of self as the student's failure to consummate his relationship with Christine. In the fourth and sixth chapters, Tamina, a Czech émigré living in an unnamed town in the West of Europe, seeks to reunite, and re-identify with, the fractured strands of her past through the recovery of her lost diaries. When she fails to do so, her sense of identity disintegrates until, in a dream-like episode, she allows herself to be transported to an island populated only by children who have no past. In the third chapter, 'Les Anges', the angelically named Mme Raphaël attempts, somewhat comically, to identify with a diverse range of different ideological systems:

> Elle a toute sa vie cherché un cercle d'hommes et de femmes auxquels elle pourrait donner la main pour danser une ronde, elle l'a d'abord cherché [...] dans le parti communiste, puis dans le parti trotskiste, puis dans le parti trotskiste dissident, puis dans le mouvement contre l'avortement (l'enfant a droit à la vie!), puis dans le mouvement pour la légalisation de l'avortement (la femme a droit à son corps!), elle l'a cherché chez les marxistes, chez les psychanalystes, puis chez les structuralistes.
>
> All her life she had looked for a circle of men and women with whom she could hold hands in a ring dance, first [...] in the Communist Party, then in the Trotskyist Party, then in a Trotskyist splinter party, then in the movement against abortion (a child has a right to life!), then in the movement to legalize abortion (a woman has a right to her body!), then she looked for it in Marxists, in psychoanalysts, in structuralists.[72]

Like the 'major' uses of language I discussed in Chapter 1 through the work of Deleuze and Atxaga, the different 'circles' described here seek to prove themselves dominant by ignoring the possibility of an alternative point of view, a ploy Kundera renders comically inadequate by emphasizing the almost endless series of groups to which Mme Raphaël seeks to belong. Through the diversity of the systems within which Mme Raphaël attempts to define her sense of self, Kundera positions this desire for perfect harmony as an intransitive urge, one which requires no object to come into being, and which seeks out any object through which to fulfil its needs.

Through these variations, Kundera emphasizes the inescapability of *litost* in both our individual and our collective experiences: our desire to identify with something, or someone, beyond our present selves confronts the limitations of this desire, impacting affectively upon the relationships we form and the decisions we make. In the inevitability of this desire lies its danger. Kundera explores the example of a political movement which, he suggests, built its power precisely by manipulating our innate wish to belong. In the first chapter of *Le Livre*, 'Les Lettres perdues', Kundera interrogates the KSČ's 1948 rise to power, which the narrator suggests was based partially upon the Party's ability to tap into a collective desire for communal understanding and perfect harmony: 'cette idylle de justice pour tous [...] où le monde ne se dresse pas en étranger contre l'homme et l'homme contre les autres hommes, mais où le monde et tous les hommes sont au contraire pétris dans une seule et même matière'/'that idyll of justice for all, [...] where the world does not rise up as a stranger against man and man against other men, but rather where the world and all men are shaped from one and the same matter'.[73] In Kundera's construction of it, the Communist idyll can only function when content and form ally *absolutely*, when individuals are united both by what they believe and the ways in which they believe it. If Kundera's depiction of *litost* shows the untranslatability of elements in amorous relation, his depiction of the idyll shows a political desire for absolute translatability, an absolute unity of understanding and relation between individual and individual, and individual and world.

In Ricœur's *Sur la traduction*, the latent desire for a perfect translation can only be sustained by the repression of the foreign, which threatens to reveal the impossibility of a linguistic universal. 'L'universalité recouvrée voudrait supprimer la mémoire de l'étranger [...] Pareille universalité effaçant sa propre histoire ferait de tous des étrangers à soi-même, des apatrides du langage, des exilés'/'Recaptured universality would try to abolish the memory of the foreign. [...] Erasing its own history, the same universality would turn all who are foreign to it into language's stateless persons, exiles'.[74] In this statement we can read echoes of Kundera's desire for an 'ailleurs', to be achieved through a writing capable of transcending its original linguistic, national and cultural borders. But for Ricœur, such a universality can only exceed these borders by erasing what is foreign, by suppressing those elements which threaten to challenge the perfection of its unanimity. In this reading, it is Kundera himself, rejected by Czechoslovakia for contravening the ideals of its Communist idyll, who embodies one of Ricœur's 'apatrides du langage', his political untranslatability resulting in his linguistic and national exile.

A similar erasure of the 'foreign', of individuals who cannot be gathered within the idyllic vision of universal understanding, occurs in Kundera's representation of the idyll. In the idyll, he suggests 'chacun est une note d'une sublime fugue de Bach, et celui qui ne veut pas en être une reste un point noir inutile et privé de sens qu'il suffit de saisir et d'écraser sous l'ongle comme une puce'/'everyone is a note in a sublime Bach fugue, and anyone who refuses to be one is a mere useless and meaningless black dot that need only be caught and crushed between thumb and finger like a flea'.[75] Kundera's representation of the idyll hinges upon a division between meaning and non-meaning: within the inner sanctum of the idyll, meaning is unified, universal, total: outside the inner circle one is 'privé de sens', meaningless, translated out of context and beyond understanding. In Kundera's vision of the idyll in *Le Livre* we can read the dangers of Ricœur's perfect translation transposed into a political context. Like the perfect translation, the Communist idyll can only sustain itself through the erasure of any element which threatens its vision of harmony and coherence.

Erasing the untranslatable

Throughout *Le Livre*. Kundera is interested in exploring our desire to embrace absolutely something other than our present selves, whether that be another individual, a political group, a literary theory or our own past identity. But he is equally invested in exploring what happens when this desire collapses, bringing *litost* in its wake. How do we deal with the consequences of that collapse? How do we cope with *litost*? Kundera's answer, articulated repeatedly and diversely through the various strands and narratives in *Le Livre*, is that we seek to *forget* our failures, and if we cannot forget, to erase or destroy any object, person, event or memory that disrupts the illusion of perfect harmony between our present self and that with which we desire to identify. In 'Litost', Kundera describes two possible forms of this erasure: if the person who has forced us to experience *litost* is weaker than us, we find a reason to harm him or her; if he or she is stronger than us, 'il ne nous reste plus qu'à choisir une vengeance détournée, une gifle par ricochet, un meurtre par le biais du suicide'/'all we can do is choose circuitous revenge – the indirect blow, a murder by means of suicide'.[76]

Kundera offers various examples of the first response to *litost*, an externalization of internal pain. There is the student who slaps his girlfriend when she proves to be a better swimmer than he; the harassment and eventual arrest of Mirek when he criticizes the Communist Party to which he once belonged; the cruelty of the children who allow Tamina to drown when she fails to exist in harmony with them upon their island. In Kundera's novelistic account of the Czechoslovakian national psyche, however, it is the second response which has dominated: in 1968, when Russian tanks arrived to crush the liberating movement of the Prague Spring, the Czechs were forced to confront their own weakness, and therefore the experience of *litost*. Their response – '*Nous ne voulons pas de compromis, nous voulons la victoire!*'/'*We don't want compromise, we want victory*' – was, the narrator suggests, symptomatic of a revenge against the other translated into the annihilation of the self; the voice of inadequacy saving face by demanding absolute triumph.[77]

But the narrative of *Le Livre* is primarily concerned with a more subtle, but no less devastating, response to the experience of *litost*:

deliberate or inevitable forgetting, enabled by aesthetic forms. Kundera begins *Le Livre* with a powerful example of the form which such a forgetting might take in a political context. In the first pages of the text, the narrator comments upon the experiences of Vladimír Clementis, the high-ranking Communist who was instrumental in organizing the *coup d'état* which led the KSČ to power. Clementis was a key member of the KSČ inner circle, holding the position of Foreign Secretary between 1948 and 1950. But in 1950, Clementis found himself accused as a deviationist; he was evicted from the Party, and in 1952 was hung for treason.

Kundera is principally interested, however, in exploring the ways in which the memory of Clementis has been erased from the history of the KSČ. In 1948, at the peak of his influence, Clementis was photographed standing on a balcony in Prague next to the KSČ leader Klement Gottwald. This photograph, taken just after the successful *coup d'état*, marked the beginning of Communist control in Czechoslovakia, thus documenting a turning point in Czechoslovakian history: the narrator of *Le Livre* comments that '[t]ous les enfants connaissaient cette photographie'/ '[e]very child knew that photograph'.[78] As Hana Pichová suggests, the photograph's prevalence marks it as 'an instrument of coerced remembrance', a cultural artefact designed to commemorate the beauty, glory and, crucially, harmony of the KSČ.[79] But after Clementis's death, the photograph no longer achieves its purpose. Instead of revealing the idyllic values of absolute understanding and identification, it becomes evidence of an *absence* of understanding and identification, proof that there can be no perfect translation between the individual and the collective, between theory and action, between experience and ideology. And this is why, as Kundera reveals, reproductions of the photograph following Clementis's death show Gottwald alone on the balcony: Clementis has been entirely erased from the image. Through this manipulation, the photograph is transformed from a symbol of remembrance into 'an instrument of cultural forgetting', from a glorification of political unity into the means of its sustenance in the face of collapse.[80]

This historical event is uncannily reminiscent of a fictional episode in Orwell's *1984*, published three years before Clementis's death, in which Winston Smith uncovers photographic evidence which proves that forms of historical manipulation are taking place within Big Brother's state. Winston's decision to destroy this evidence is a stark example of the power which photographs can hold as a site of memory, but also the ways in which they can be manipulated to enable forms of forgetting to take place.[81] Kundera's narrative in *Le Livre*, like Orwell's in *1984*, draws our attention to the falsifications which can occur within all our representations of the past. And, as Pichová shows, Kundera's narratives are themselves implicated in historical distortions and alterations. In describing the photograph, the narrator of *Le Livre* claims that Gottwald was hatless and that Clementis took off his own hat and placed it upon Gottwald's head.[82] This claim allows him to end his discussion of the manipulation of the photo with this powerful image: 'De Clementis, il n'est resté que la toque de fourrure sue la tête de Gottwald'/'Nothing remains of Clementis but the fur hat on Gottwald's head'.[83] But, as Pichová reveals, in the original photo, both Gottwald and Clementis are shown to be wearing hats. For Pichová, Kundera's distortion of the photograph in his ekphrastic translation of image into narrative offers us a warning against an unquestioning acceptance of the written word, and highlights the forgetting implicit in our every encounter with aesthetic forms.[84] This warning is, as Steinby notes, problematized by translation: the non-Czech readership for *Le Livre* is unlikely to be familiar with the cultural references required to pick up on this falsification of the image.[85] But this failure of detection, which Steinby suggests is inevitable among a French readership, in fact highlights the erasures, alterations and distortions which pass undetected within all our readings. Several of Kundera's texts explore the ambiguity within aesthetic forms which makes them capable of both liberation and repression, both remembrance and forgetting: artistic and literary works, he suggests, offer us opportunities to rethink our relations to one another and to the world around us, but they can also undermine and overwrite these relations.

In *La Plaisanterie*, for example, the satirical postcard that Ludvik sends to his girlfriend is converted into evidence in a case which sees him accused of political dissidence and sent to work in a mine. In *L'Immortalité*, Kundera explores the power of the political slogan, which he suggests reveals the perfect alliance of aesthetics and politics. Kundera focuses upon a quotation taken from Rimbaud's *Une saison en enfer*: 'Il faut être absolument moderne'.[86] For the protagonist, Paul, this quotation is the symbol of the revolutionary spirit of May 1968. But it only attains this symbolic value through its translation from one historical and formal context into another, namely from Rimbaud's suggestive, sometimes delirious, sometimes disturbing, prose poems of 1873, which meditate on the power and pain of the poetic imagination, to the political slogan scrawled on the walls on Paris in May 1968. This translation, suggests Kundera, is made possible through, and inevitably enacts, a negation of that original moment and form: a betrayal of Rimbaud's verse.[87] In this betrayal, the slogan marks the space where, stripped of the nuances, layers and contexts of its creation, poetry becomes reified into propaganda.

In *L'Insoutenable légèreté de l'être*, Kundera explores another form of aesthetic erasure, which he defines as kitsch. Kitsch is both an attitude and an aesthetics, a way of presenting and interpreting experience which articulates and sustains our innate desire to attain fraternal unity with those around us:

> Le kitsch fait naître coup sur coup deux larmes d'émotion. La première larme dit: Comme c'est beau, des gosses courant sur une pelouse! La deuxième larme dit: Comme c'est beau, d'être ému avec toute l'humanité à la vue de gosses courant sur une pelouse! Seule cette deuxième larme fait que le kitsch est le kitsch. La fraternité de tous les hommes ne pourra être fondée que sur le kitsch.
>
> Kitsch causes two tears to flow in quick succession. The first tear says: How nice to see children running on the grass! The second tear says: How nice to be moved, together with all mankind, by children running on the grass! It is the second tear that makes kitsch kitsch. The brotherhood of man on earth will be possible only on the basis of kitsch.[88]

Kitsch, the narrator suggests, is born of a faith and delight in the power of cliché to evoke and respond to a perceived universal conception of a phrase, event or experience. Throughout *L'Insoutenable légèreté de l'être*, kitsch is represented as a form of aesthetic *mauvaise foi* which fails to engage with the criticism and self-criticism, the particularity, contingency and ambiguity, which Kundera perceives as essential to the potential, if frequently unrealized, ethics of artistic forms. Kitsch represents a form of beauty based upon pre-understanding; a beauty which rejects the unexpected and the surprising in favour of the predictable. This desire for kitsch, Kundera insists, is inescapable: 'nul d'entre nous n'est un surhomme et ne peut échapper entièrement au kitsch. Quel que soit le mépris qu'il nous inspire, le kitsch fait partie de la condition humaine'/'none among us is superman enough to escape kitsch completely. No matter how we scorn it, kitsch is an integral part of the human condition'.[89] Like *litost* then, kitsch is integral to the human soul; indeed, these two responses are part and parcel of the same desire. For while *litost* is an emotion generated by our failure to achieve coherence between our image of reality and reality itself, kitsch is an artistic response which seeks to transcend this failure.

In *Le Livre,* Kundera explores an example of this kitsch erasure and transcendence through his discussion of lyric poetry, an aesthetic form which he suggests reflects a particularly hyperbolic approach to the translation of experience into form. The poetic in Kundera's reading is a mobile term, and Kundera's own aesthetics is formed through a poetic emphasis upon variation, within which the same terms are used again and again but reveal a different tone or overtone in each use. In the next section of this chapter, I discuss the implications of this mobility for Kundera's reading of an ethics of aesthetic form. I explore, through ideas of translation, Kundera's construction of the poetic in *Le Livre*, the relationship he creates between the poetic and the political idyll, and the heuristic opposition he develops between the poetic and the novel form.

An ethics of form

Poetry and lyricism

Throughout *Le Livre*, Kundera develops multiple variations upon the poetic attitude, in both a personal and a political context. In 'Litost', Kundera creates a division between 'une nuit de poésie'/'a night of poetry', the student's romantic interpretation of events, and 'une journée de prose'/'a day of prose', their more banal reality.[90] The ambiguous nature of all Kundera's oppositions should alert us to the fragility of this division: there are illusions, erasures, and clichés within all our narrations, whatever form they take. Nonetheless, this opposition allows Kundera to explore the particular romantic illusions encouraged by what he regards as the hyperbole of the poetic form. For Kundera, lyric poetry exaggerates to create a strong emotional response. In the case of the student, this poetic exaggeration reveals his desire to render all experience lyrical, to translate the concrete and carnal into the gloriously universal and ethereal, a desire which not only affects his narration of his interaction with Christine, but comes to influence his experience of it. The student's desire for lyricism, Kundera suggests, is based upon more than a wish for aesthetic *coherence* in the narrative of his life and loves: in his belief in the 'béatitude' of his encounter with Christine, the student reveals his faith in the possibility of *completion*, which for Kundera is an aesthetically inspired faith in the perfect unity of love as it is experienced and love as it is narrated. Here a heuristic idea of the poetic and its contrast with the prosaic is positioned as the locus of the student's romantic and sexual failure.

The particular dangers Kundera equates with the poetic attitude can be read through the words of the character Pétrarque, who through his name alludes to the Petrarchan standards of ideal love and formal perfection. 'Comprendre c'est se confondre et s'identifier'/'to understand is to merge and to identify with', exclaims Pétrarque, 'C'est ça le mystère de la poésie'/'That is the secret of poetry'.[91] The 'secret' of poetry here is one based upon the faith that understanding produces an absolute identity of two people, and the absolute possession of one by the other, what Steinby describes as 'a dissolving of the boundaries between the self and everything else'.[92] Such a belief is apparent even at the very moment when the student realizes that his poetic attitude is the cause of his romantic failure: 'Il aurait suffi cette nuit d'une seule phrase sensée!'Il aurait suffi d'appeler les choses par leur vrai nom et il pouvait l'avoir'/'Last night, one sensible sentence would have been enough! It would have been enough to call things by their right names, and he could have had her', he wails.[93] The student's interpretation of his failure hinges upon various binary divisions: prose/poetry, sense/nonsense, truth/untruth, possession/non-possession. In recognizing these binaries, the student seems finally to recognize that his relations with Christine have been distorted by his repeated decision to prioritize the poetic over the prosaic, the implicit over the explicit. And yet, ironically, in his faith that 'things' can be called 'by their right names', that one can truly 'have' – possess or understand totally and absolutely – another person, physically, mentally or linguistically, the student reveals, not an awareness of the impossibility of absolute identification with another, but rather a continued faith in its possibility: a faith that a poetics of love will enable him to transcend the differences and discrepancies between two people.

The student is forced to recognize that his poetic conception of romantic experience is woefully misplaced. Yet ironically it is poetry which comes to his rescue, offering him an aesthetic form through which he can evade the experience of *litost* generated by his failure with Christine. Turning full circle, the student re-imagines this story of failure and miscommunication as 'la poésie', a lyrical emblem of thwarted desire, a gloriously perfect aesthetic homage to the tragedy of romantic experience. This poetic homage enables the student to reframe his experience of *litost*, translating his experiences with Christine into a form which corresponds to – as opposed to threatens – his self-perception. In the student's use of poetry to overcome his experience of *litost* we can read the seemingly inevitable return of his attempt to affirm the qualities associated with the perfect translation: the absolutes of identity, unity and understanding. While poetry has often been considered untranslatable – Robert Frost allegedly claimed that 'poetry is what is lost in translation' – Kundera's construction of the poetic in *Le Livre* positions it as an aesthetic form embedded in a belief in the absolute translatability promised by relation, and as a form which can provide the aesthetic illusion of this translatability when it collapses experientially.[94]

Poetry and politics

The dangers Kundera identifies within this lyrical approach to the translation of experience into narrative are not only personal but political, for as he understands only too well himself, there is a connection between poetic absolutism and political absolutism. Between 1950 and 1955 Kundera published two collections of poetry which 'resonate with Communist imagery'; he subsequently sought to erase these collections from his bibliography, refusing to permit their republication or translation.[95] This refusal is perhaps understandable, given the manner of Kundera's subsequent departure from the Party. But, as Woods notes, this erasure through translation has been used as evidence of Kundera's desire to airbrush his past collaboration with the Party.[96] Kundera's decision to erase these texts from his bibliography certainly suggests a collision, and collusion, of fact and fiction through which he seeks to create a coherent narrative of his authorial identity by means of an enforced forgetting of his poetry. As Woods notes, however, Kundera is interested in exploring his poetic experiences: while his poetry has disappeared through a lack of translation, Kundera confronts this forgetting in several texts which explore the motivation to write the very type of ideologically committed poetry which Kundera himself produced.[97] This confrontation is most apparent in *La Vie est ailleurs* (1969), a novel which explores the experiences of a young poet, Jaromil, and his increasingly fanatical Communist beliefs.

Kundera equates Jaromil's poetic desires specifically with youth, and a concomitant naïve adoration of the extremes of emotion existent within both his poetry and his politics. As Jaromil's political ideals shift into Communism, so too does the form and content of his poems: his early fascination with Surrealism develops into 'a poesy of totalitarianism', which depicts the Communist ideals of 'brotherhood, peace, justice, better tomorrows, [...] for comradeship and against isolation, for joy and against gloom, for innocence and against cynicism'.[98] Crucially, while the lyricism of his poetry initially allows Jaromil to map his political beliefs aesthetically, ultimately this lyricism becomes remapped *onto* those beliefs. This leads Jaromil into a tragic betrayal: lyrically faithful to his identification with Communist ideals, he denounces his girlfriend's brother as a political dissident, sacrificing human emotions and loyalty to a fanaticism driven by poetic fantasy. Kundera writes in the novel that '[l] a poésie est un territoire où toute affirmation devient vérité. [...] Le poète n'a besoin de rien prouver; la seule preuve réside dans l'intensité de son émotion'/'Poetry is a domain in which all assertions become true. [...] The poet has no need to prove anything; the only proof lies in the intensity of his emotion'.[99] In the intensity of his lyricism, Jaromil acts as though he can transcend the ambiguity of his particular situation, seeking and even manufacturing poetic idealism not only aesthetically, but personally and politically. Kundera's presentation of the dangers inherent in the lyrical ability to overwrite ambiguity is reminiscent of Plato's decision to expel the poet – 'at third remove from the throne of truth' – from his ideal republic.[100] But while Plato perceived poetry as *destructive* in relation to the realities of the political, Kundera suggests that it is through lyricism, as both an aesthetic and an attitude of absolutism, that totalitarian political power can be *constructed*.

The link Kundera makes here between the poetic and the totalitarian is based upon the fact that both are motivated by the same desire: *se confondre et s'identifier*. In the first of two chapters of *Le Livre* entitled 'Les Anges', Kundera continues his exploration of this connection. The narrator reflects upon his expulsion from the KSČ while he watches groups of people dancing in the streets to celebrate a political anniversary. One of those dancing is the poet Paul Éluard, who, like the fictional Jaromil, embodies the intersection of the political and the poetic. Éluard also features in *L'Immortalité,* where he embodies the alliance of love and the poetic which we saw introduced in the student's story. In *Le Livre,* Éluard's poetry and his politics conjoin through a combination of movement and lyricism; the narrator notes that Éluard 'était en train de danser dans une ronde gigantesque entre Paris, Moscou, Prague, Varsovie, Sofia et la Grèce, entre tous les pays socialistes et tous les partis communistes du monde, et il récitait partout ses beaux vers sur la joie et la fraternité'/'was busy dancing in a gigantic ring between Paris, Moscow, Prague, Warsaw, Sofia, and Greece, between all the socialist countries and all the world's Communist parties, and everywhere he recited his beautiful poems about joy and brotherhood'.[101] In Kundera's depiction of Éluard as part of a 'ronde' we see a balletic and poetic manifestation of a political experience. 'La ronde', in both form and content, embodies the aestheticized lure of unity: it is a formally perfect 'cercle magique' which requires that everyone within it think and act in absolute unity in order that it may sustain its shape and purpose. It is no coincidence that in Kundera's depiction of Éluard and his dancing companions the *content* of the magic circle is political (a celebration of a political anniversary) and its *form* is poetic (built upon rhythm and lyricism).

In an interview with Philip Roth, Kundera comments upon the power of poetic form in relation to the political: 'Nowadays, people all over the world unequivocally reject the idea of gulags, yet they are still willing to let themselves be hypnotized by totalitarian poesy and to march to new gulags to the tune of the same lyrical song'.[102] In equating the poetic with a form of hypnosis, Kundera accords a power to the rhythm and meter of lyric poetry which transcends any actual message it may purport to offer. The very lyricism of this poetry engages the individual in a political moment. Uniting totalitarian forms of political thinking with the poetic, suggests Kundera, enables each to exceed its own boundaries. The lyrical transmits and consolidates the perfection of the totalitarian; the totalitarian affirms and mirrors the perfection of the lyrical. In both 'perfections', it is the fraternal impulse, the human desire to connect interests and find communal meaning, which is at stake. But as Kundera suggests in *Le Livre*, fraternal unity can be constructed upon exclusion as well as inclusion. Translating totalitarian thought into the forms of the poetic is inherently dangerous, not only because it aestheticizes the political, converting individual and disparate experiences into a poetic invocation of unity, harmony and brotherhood, but also because such a translation is reversible, enabling poetic fantasies to be translated into political reality. Exactly in so far as this translation is itself perceived as perfect, as one which can bridge all possible gaps between thought and action, form and content, these poetic-political fantasies prove not only effective but deadly.

'Lorsqu'il n'y a plus moyen d'échapper à la *litost* alors la grâce de la poésie vole à notre secours'/'when [we have] no means of escaping from *litost*, then poetry's charm flies to [our] rescue', writes Kundera.[103] Through this intersection of flight, poetry and *litost*, Kundera explores the dangers of mapping the poetic onto the political. For if *Le Livre* is a book of laughter and forgetting, it is also a book about flights, be those flights of fantasy, flights from the past and the present, or flights of exile and of homecoming. In 'Les Anges', the poetic desire to flee from experiences that are untranslatable into current political narratives – experiences that disrupt the rhetoric of absolute unity and agreement – is represented through a fantasy sequence. As the narrator watches Éluard and his group dancing in the streets, their feet begin to rise from the ground until they are flying above Wenceslaus Square. These rising figures, simultaneously political and poetic, appear untouched by gravity. Are they immune to it, or have they chosen to disregard and transgress the laws of existence?

In Kundera's vision, collective singing and dancing enables the group to rise and to affirm its unifying poetic faith. Yet what appears comic in the student's personal poetic vision becomes dangerous in Kundera's account of Éluard's political one. For as they rise above the streets of Prague, the political poets of *Le Livre* leave below them the mortal relics of Czechoslovakia's political and literary history: 'Au-dessous d'eux [...] dans le crématoire on était en train d'incinérer une députée socialiste et un écrivain surréaliste, la fumée s'élevait vers le ciel comme un heureux présage et j'entendais la voix métallique d'Éluard *«L'amour est au travail il est infatigable.»*'/'below them [...] from the crematorium where they were incinerating a Socialist deputy and a surrealist writer the smoke ascended to the heavens like a good omen, and I heard Éluard's metallic voice: "Love is at work it is tireless."'[104]

The surrealist writer who Kundera refers to in this powerful extract is Záviš Kalandra, a member of the Prague Surrealist group and once a good friend of Éluard's. In 1950 Kalandra was condemned to death for treason by the KSČ: Éluard, called upon to stand up for his friend, refused to say a word against the Party. The fictional betrayal of an individual in the name of a totalitarian poetics, which Kundera describes in *La Vie est ailleurs,* here finds its reality in the death of Kalandra, an individual who Eva Le Grand suggests was convicted for his refusal to match his writing to the dominant political and aesthetic ideal.[105] In *La Vie est ailleurs,* Éluard's betrayal takes form in his ability to distance himself from these events, to soar above them through his faith in the transcendent power of his political beliefs. In *Ordinary Enchantments: Magical Realism and the Remystification of Narrative,* Wendy Faris suggests that the motif of flight in Kundera's work is emblematic of a particular form of escapism which seeks to 'evade questions of mortality and history'.[106] The link Kundera creates between the student's personal experience of love and the political flight of Éluard places dramatic emphasis on the inevitability of such evasions to the human experience. Evading the past, evading what we do not or cannot understand, is a condition of the personal *and* the political. To live in the present, itself a slogan for spontaneity, involves an attempt, successful to varying degrees, to float away from the baggage of the past in all its forms: erasing the past is implicit in the all-absorbing experience of the present, which holds on to fragments of what came before as these are conditioned by our current perception. The flight of the political-poetic dancers takes this evasion a step further. The dancers manage to dissolve gravity entirely, creating a world in which the claims of the smoking crematorium below can be erased, and having been erased, translated seamlessly into present response and present living. Kundera depicts this erasure through a fantasy sequence but, as *Le Livre* attests, he is only too aware that such fantasies have already been realized. Kundera's juxtaposition of the poetic and the political explores the continued and alarming potency of their association.

In *Le Livre*, then, as in *La Vie est ailleurs,* Kundera assigns specific dangers to the poetic. Yet he can only explore these dangers through his own novelistic practice, and this practice has its own poetics which renders the distinction between novel and poetry less rigid than Kundera's rejection of lyric poetry might suggest. Steinby suggests that '[r]enouncing lyrical poetry, or, rather, the lyrical stance, meant for Kundera renouncing an attitude to the world which makes an acceptance of totalitarian ideology possible'.[107] But if lyrical poetry offers a dangerously absolutist approach to the translation of experience into form, can Kundera's novel, built as it is on formal variation, really offer an ethical approach to experience and the aesthetic forms used to understand it?

Poetry and the novel

Literary form as it emerges in Kundera's response to the translation of his texts delineates not just the architecture of a text but the process through which we inhabit our own experiences. In *L'Art du roman* (1986) Kundera writes that 'dans l'art, la forme est toujours plus qu'une forme. Chaque roman, bon gré mal gré, propose une réponse à la question: qu'est-ce que l'existence humaine et où réside sa poésie?'/'in art, the form is always more than a form. Every novel, like it or not, offers some answer to the question: What is human existence, and wherein does its poetry lie?'[108] In this comment, Kundera acknowledges that the novel form is concerned, precisely, with an exploration of the *poetry* of human experience. But the nature of our response to the question Kundera poses above can, he suggests, be read through the aesthetic form in which we choose to respond. Kundera's reading of lyric poetry positions it as a form which responds to this question by prioritizing the idea of an absolute Truth which excludes interrogation and doubt. In *L'Art du roman*, Kundera endows the novel form with a particular ethical power based upon precisely its ability to query preconceived modes of thinking: 'Le monde basé sur une seule Vérité et le monde ambigu et relatif du roman sont pétris chacun d'une manière totalement différente. La Vérité totalitaire exclut la relativité, le doute, l'interrogation et elle ne peut donc jamais se concilier avec ce que j'appellerais l'*esprit du roman.*'/'The world of one single truth and the relative, ambiguous world of the novel are molded of entirely different substances. Totalitarian Truth excludes relativity, doubt, questioning; it can never accommodate what I would call the *spirit of the novel.*'[109] Kundera here emphasizes an ambiguity at the heart of the novel which is opposed to the certainty he associates with lyric poetry. If lyricism is the search for absolute translatability, the novel acknowledges the impossibility of this ambition, focusing instead upon the individual, untranslatable elements which exist within every interaction.

The demarcation Kundera creates here between poetry and prose, and the power he assigns to the novel form to intersect in challenging ways with our understanding of human existence, resonates with Sartre's discussion of engaged literature in 'Qu'est-ce que la littérature?' Like Kundera, Sartre sees the poetic as a response to untranslatability: faced with the challenge of transmitting meaning linguistically, poetry answers by turning language inside out, redeeming the word in and of itself, beyond the (im)possibility of signification. For Sartre, this self-referentiality means that poetry cannot have an impact upon the world, whether positive or negative, for it is concerned with language as object as opposed to mediator of reality. In contrast, prose operates from within language looking out, using words to challenge or confirm our perceptions of reality. For Sartre, this connection with experience enables prose to be committed, demanding that the reader see differently, engage authentically, attempt to change her or his reality.[110] Sartre's separation of prose and poetry enforces conceptions of poetry as inherently untranslatable. For if, in poetry, the word is object, any translation will inevitably alter that object and therefore fail to transmit the essential in and of the poem itself. Sartre's description of prose, on the other hand, hints towards its translatability: unlike poetry, prose is concerned with transmitting meaning. The medium for that transmission may change from language to language, but its essentials, Sartre implies, can be carried across from one to another.

Sartre's dichotomy offers both a model for and a contrast to Kundera's discussions of prose and poetry. On one level, Sartre endows prose with precisely the ambiguity which Kundera suggests is innate within the novel form, an ambiguity which requires the reader to engage freely and authentically in order to create a representation of experience from the words of the author. Yet Sartre differs significantly from Kundera in his insistence that the poetic has no impact upon reality. For Kundera, lyric poetry is in fact deeply engaged, capable of shaping reality dangerously through its formal focus upon unity and perfection, a form designed to soothe and harmonize rather than disturb and discomfort. The difference between Kundera and Sartre in their approach to the possibility of aesthetic engagement reveals that the terms poetic and prosaic are shorthand for a difference of attitude and approach to the relationship between writing and existence which can span either aesthetic arrangement. In fact,

Sartre's investigation of the possibility of commitment in prose invokes precisely the shift away from Surrealism that Jaromil enacts in *La Vie est ailleurs* – a shift from a form which he suggests is concerned only with self-conscious experimentation to one whose purpose is to invoke social change.[111] Yet, as we saw, Jaromil's shift ultimately immerses him further in the illusions which he constructs from his political ideology. Similarly, while Sartre invokes the freedom which can be generated by an authentic engagement with prose, his depiction of the ways in which prose might offer itself to such an engagement sometimes undermines that very freedom by restricting the form that prose can take. It is precisely for this reason that Adorno, in 'Commitment', challenges Sartre's reading of the division between art-for-art's sake and engaged literature. Adorno argues that Sartre deploys form as the servant of an explicit content-based message, a practice which undermines the very freedom and authenticity he (Sartre) ascribes to prose.[112]

Adorno contrasts Sartre's approach with that of Kafka and Beckett, who, he suggests, offer a more productive and challenging engagement with reality through their use of a form which performs the alienation and disturbance other fictional texts only articulate.[113] In *Les Testaments trahis*, Kundera also discusses Kafka as an example of an author who transforms, indeed remakes, the world through the poetry of his novels. Like Adorno, Kundera contrasts Kafka's writing with a work that he believes reveals the failure of an overtly committed literature: Orwell's *1984*. In discussing this contrast, Kundera again divides the poetic from the novelistic, but here he reverses the attributes he assigns to each form: it is Kafka's 'poetry' which brings the reader to an awareness of the complex reality of human freedom; it is Orwell's 'bad novel' which both negates the lucidity of its political message through the ambiguity of the novel form, and destroys the power of that ambiguity through its insistence upon the articulation of those ideas. Orwell's novel, in fact, 'fait lui-même partie de l'esprit totalitaire, de l'esprit de propagande'/'joins in the totalitarian spirit, the spirit of propaganda', by reducing 'une réalité à son aspect purement politique et dans la reduction de ce même aspect á ce qu'il a d'exemplairement négatif [...] le mal totalitaire [...] est précisément la reduction de la vie à la politique et de la politique à la propagande'/'reality to its political dimension alone, and in its reduction of that dimension to what is exemplarily negative about it [...] totalitarian evil [...] is, precisely, the reduction of life to politics and of politics to propaganda'.[114] It is this understanding of the complexity of evil which Kundera suggests Kafka captures and Orwell ignores through the formal properties of their respective texts.

For Kundera, Kafka's *The Castle* is concerned with articulating the disarticulation of K.'s experience, with finding a form for the incomprehensible, fundamentally unpoetic experience he lives through. It is an ambiguous form which matches the impossibility of translating this experience into kitsch or propaganda. But, ironically, translation – at least from the German into French – fails to capture this impossibility: Kundera critiques the ways in which Kafka's French translators have ignored the importance of form within Kafka's novel, rejecting any element which clashes with the conventions of the target language. The changes made by these translators include standardizing sentence and paragraph length; eliminating any repetition of words, regardless of the variance within the source text; and adding punctuation at seemingly appropriate points.[115] Kundera's analysis of this failure of translation, and his own attempt to create a faithful version of an extract of Kafka's text – faithful to the form of the text, rather than a pre-digested content – again reframes the debate between translatability and untranslatability which I have been pursuing in this chapter. Kundera suggests that what fails to be translated of Kafka's texts is precisely their poetic *untranslatability* – their refusal to make peace with the world and reflect that peace in a harmonious aesthetic form.

Kundera's focus upon the poetry of Kafka's texts in *Les Testaments trahis* destabilizes the oppositionary relationship between certainty and ambiguity, poetry and the novel, translatability and untranslatability, which he appears to assert in *Le Livre*. Poetry has traditionally been considered untranslatable because of a link between form and content which is always lost in translation. Roman Jakobson famously claimed that 'poetry is, by definition, untranslatable', while in *Sur la traduction*, Ricœur focuses upon poetry in his exploration of the binary translatable/untranslatable, suggesting that '[l]a poésie offrait en effet la difficulté majeure de l'union inséparable du sens et de la sonorité, du signifié et du signifiant'/'poetry presented the serious difficulty of the inseparable combination of sense and sonority, of the signified and the signifier'.[116] But as Kundera discusses in relation to Kafka, the link between form and content can be as close in prose as it is in poetry. Kundera's reading of the difference between poetry and prose is less concerned with what we call these forms than with how they shape an aesthetic response to our experience. If aesthetic forms seek to create a harmonious, kitsch vision of our relationships and experiences, they respond to the world as if it were inherently translatable. Conversely, if they seek to explore the dissonance between experience and reality, between self and other, between our beliefs and their manifestation, they respond to the ambiguity and the innate untranslatability of our experience.

It is in this sense that for Kundera poetry and prose are not in opposition so much as two sides of the same coin, two ways in which experience and thought are organized aesthetically into a manageable coherence. For we all seek poetry in our narratives, and that poetry can be deployed in a challenging reframing of dissonance, discord and uncertainty. So too, prose has its own lyricism which can produce unilateral effects in its very emphasis on plurality, and the novel can emerge as a tool for propaganda and political agendas. While it would be possible, then, to read Kundera's art-as-ethics as contained within oppositions between poetry and novel, certainty and ambiguity, such oppositions are merely a shorthand which, taken at face value, can narrow rather than expand the ways in which we think about the ethics of aesthetic forms. Indeed, to constrain our thinking to binaries such as these is to deny room for the ethical, for it merely allows us to replace one unilateral understanding of art with another. Kundera's project is to inhabit the borderland between oppositional statements, to push them to their limits until the oppositions collapse and reveal their proximity to one another.

Indeed, despite Kundera's emphasis upon ambiguity in his texts, he is as concerned with the dangers of absolute ambiguity as he is with those of absolute certainty. Kundera explores the proximity of these two dangers by setting up, and then collapsing, another apparent dichotomy within *Le Livre*: an *angelic* attitude to experience, conditioned by a poetic faith in the possibility of certainty and perfect translatability, and a *demonic* one, conditioned by forms of untranslatability and uncertainty. This dichotomy, which Kundera both creates and dissolves in *Le Livre*, further nuances Kundera's ethics of aesthetic forms.

The angels and the Devil

Kundera's decision to position the story of the poetic-political dancers in *Le Livre* under the chapter heading 'Les Anges' connects the poetic to the broader motif of angels, another of the 'mots-thèmes' of *Le Livre*. Angels, the narrator suggests, experience existence as 'ordonné, sagement conçu, bon et plein de sens'/'well ordered, wisely conceived, good, and meaningful' and, as such, are fundamentally opposed to the concept of *litost*, for if *litost* arises from an awareness of the discrepancy between vision and experience, the angels reject that very possibility.[117] Kundera's angels embody the qualities Ricœur associates with the perfect translation, for they seek an absolute identity between their beliefs and the world they create, expressing faith in the fullness of sense in relation to events. Their joy in coherence is expressed by their delighted laughter, 'l'expression de l'être qui se réjouit d'être'/'the expression of being rejoicing in being'.[118] This joy reflects a valorization of the present moment above the hauntings of the past and the possibilities of the future: to rejoice in being is to inhabit a suspended moment 'sans souvenir et sans désir'/'without memory and without desire'.[119] This joy is manifested in ring dancing, in the aestheticized confection of kitsch, in the political idyll: indeed, the narrator of *Le Livre* hears 'le rire effrayant des anges qui couvre de son carillon toutes [ses] paroles'/'the fearsome laughter of the angels [...], drowning all [his] words with its jangle' at the very moment when he falls, or is pushed, from the idyll for political dissidence.[120]

Kundera creates a complement to the world of the angels through his construction of the Devil, 'celui qui refuse au monde divin un sens rationnel'/'the one who refuses to grant any rational meaning to that divinely created world'.[121] The Devil rejects any kitsch agreement with being, insisting that the order of things is not certain, and certainly not perfect. While the angels and the poets rise up *above* the chaos of the world, the Devil, Kundera suggests, tumbles headlong *into* it, laughing, because 'Les choses soudain privées de leur sens supposé, de la place qui leur est assignée dans l'ordre prétendu des choses [...] provoquent chez nous le rire. A l'origine, le rire est donc du domaine du diable'/'Things deprived suddenly of their supposed meaning, of the place assigned to them in the so-called order of things [...] make us laugh. In origin, laughter is the devil's domain'.[122] The angels and the Devil thus exist at opposite ends of the spectrum in relation to the forms which allow them to express their perceptions and their experience of them. The angels see the relation between experience and existence as coherent; the Devil sees this relation as fragmented, distorted, disturbed. If the angels represent a lyrical world where translation is entirely possible, where indeed it is *everything,* and where any elements of individuality and difference must be erased for the sake of unity, the Devil represents a much more ambiguous world where translation is impossible, where it is a *nightmare*, and where endlessly fragmented and mutable meanings prevent any ultimate coherence.

Given Kundera's repeated textual assertions about the dangers of seeking answers as opposed to posing questions, and his emphasis upon the importance of *ambiguity* as an aesthetic quality, could we then read his Devil as the positive converse of the angels, a unique, fragmenting force, capable of liberating us from the dangers of a purely lyrical vision of experience? Could the qualities Kundera assigns to the Devil in *Le Livre* offer a way of accessing the ethical charge Kundera perceives within aesthetic ambiguity and untranslatability? In much of Kundera's theoretical work, the value of the ambiguity which constitutes the novelistic spirit is asserted almost unconditionally. To read the Devil as a positive force would, then, enable a coherent construction of Kundera's aesthetics and his ethics of relation, through which the importance of the ambiguous, the sceptical and the uncertain would be reasserted. For Steinby, the laughter of the Devil is part of Kundera's construction of a responsible alternative to the lyricism of the angels: 'The angels' all-approving laughter is a sign either of an ideological attitude or a childish naïveté, whereas mocking laughter expresses the attitude of a rational human being [...]. For Kundera, skepticism is a sign of maturity and therefore something to strive towards'.[123]

But Kundera's parable is in fact more ambiguous than such a reading would suggest. In his interview with Roth he comments,

> Both kinds of laughter belong among life's pleasures, but when it is carried to extremes it also denotes a dual apocalypse: the enthusiastic laughter of angel-fanatics, who are so convinced of their world's significance that they are ready to hang anyone not sharing their joy. And the other laughter, sounding from the opposite side, which proclaims that everything has become meaningless [...]. Human life is bounded by two chasms: fanaticism on one side, absolute skepticism on the other.[124]

While the majority of *Le Livre* is concerned with the dangers of an angelic fanaticism, in warning of the dangers of 'a dual apocalypse' Kundera is clearly not proclaiming absolute scepticism as the best response to political or aesthetic questions. Indeed, the narrator suggests that 's'il y a dans le monde trop de sens incontestable (le pouvoir des anges), l'homme succombe sous son poids. Si le monde perd tout son sens (le règne des démons), on ne peut pas vivre non plus'/'If there was too much incontestable meaning in the world (the angels' power), man would succumb under its weight. If the world were to lose all its meaning (the devil's reign), we could not live either'.[125] Politically and ethically, a world with only one meaning, an angelic idyll of absolute certainty, crushes any element which is foreign or different; equally, a demonic world with no meaning offers only a nihilistic experience of emptiness. Linguistically and textually, Kundera's focus upon the limitations of either too much sense or absolute nonsense reflects the dangers of both positions. A belief that aesthetic forms can contain absolute semantic stability – the 'translatability' accusation levelled at Kundera by critics of his approach to translation – fails to acknowledge the slipperiness of meaning; at the same time, insisting that aesthetic forms are, because of this slipperiness, inherently untranslatable, undermines their power to challenge and negotiate our social precepts across and between linguistic and cultural boundaries.

How then should we understand Kundera's contrasting representation of the angels and the Devil? The distinction Kundera creates between the angels and the Devil – and, through this, between sense and nonsense, certainty and ambiguity, translatability and untranslatability, lyricism and the novel – is, as with so many of the distinctions in his work, an exploratory and heuristic one. As Steinby argues, Kundera is really interested in the continually changing relation between such oppositions.[126] Kundera's exploration of the proximity of disparate thoughts, feelings and attitudes is exemplified by the origins of laughter of the angels and the Devil, an origin which is grounded in a difference of translation:

> Quand l'ange a entendu pour la première fois le rire du Malin, il en a été frappé de stupeur. [...] L'ange comprenait clairement que ce rire était dirigé contre Dieu et contre la dignité de son œuvre. Il savait qu'il devait réagir vite [...]. Ne pouvant rien inventer lui-même, il a singé son adversaire. Ouvrant la bouche, il émettait des sons entrecoupés, saccadés, [...] mais en leur donnant un sens opposé [...]. Ainsi, l'ange et le diable se faisaient face et, se montrant leur bouche ouverte, émettaient à peu près les mêmes sons, mais chacun exprimait par sa clameur des choses absolument contraires.

> The first time an angel heard the devil's laughter, he was dumbfounded. [...] The angel clearly understood that such laughter was directed against God and against the dignity of his works. He knew that he must react swiftly [...] Unable to come up with anything of his own, he aped his adversary. Opening his mouth he emitted broken, spasmodic sounds [...] but giving them an opposite meaning [...] Thus the angel and the devil faced each other and, mouths wide open, emitted nearly the same sounds, but each one's noise expressed the absolute opposite of the other's.[127]

The laughter of the angels and the laughter of the Devil here have utterly opposed meanings. But these dual meanings, suggests Kundera, take exactly the same form. The difference between the two laughs is thus a difference of translation: the laughter of the Devil is the *original* laughter which reveals the essential absurdity of existence; the laughter of the angels is the *translation* of this original laughter which seeks to impose meaning upon this absurdity. The angels' need for translation arises because they can invent nothing for themselves, positioning translation as a derivative rather than generative force. But the results of this translation offer their own illuminations. Kundera suggests that the certainty of the angels' laughter and the ambiguity of the Devil's are built from the same material. What does this suggest about the relation of absolute uncertainty and absolute certainty, the sceptical and the fanatical, the ambiguous and the lyrical? Are the absolutely untranslatable and the perfectly translatable paradoxically equivalent?

In *Against World Literature* Emily Apter situates her own exploration of the ethics of translation between these two poles. She suggests that the Untranslatable, if conceived as an absolute, inhabits precisely the same territory as the desire for a perfect translation. For to assert the possibility of pure untranslatability is to risk creating 'a fetish of the Other', a fetish which refuses the attempt to understand another, even with the inevitable appropriations this understanding entails.[128] For Apter, 'it would be more accurate to understand the Untranslatable, not as pure difference in opposition to the always translatable [...] but as a linguistic form of creative failure with homeopathic uses.'[129] This creative failure recognizes that untranslatability is a fact, that the attempt at a perfect translation will fail, but that we can only fail because we attempt to succeed. Similarly, the proximity which Kundera creates between the angels and the Devil in *Le Livre* is a recognition of this inevitable desire to convert the untranslatable into the translatable. For this proximity is not the end point of Kundera's argument but rather its beginning. It is the beginning too of his exploration of the affective and historical content of the slipperiness of meaning, and of how such slippages – an inherent part of our response to any world we occupy – can be *manipulated,* politically, textually and personally.

Kundera's exploration of such manipulation hinges upon the way the attitude of the angels and the attitude of the Devil can be conflated. Kundera highlights this potential conflation through his exploration of the original/translated nature of their laughter:

> Un rire ridicule, c'est la débâcle. Pourtant, les anges ont quand même obtenu un résultat. Ils nous ont trompés avec une imposture sémantique. Pour désigner leur imitation du rire et le rire originel (celui du diable) il n'y a qu'un seul mot. Aujourd'hui on ne se rend même plus compte que la même manifestation extérieure recouvre deux attitudes intérieures absolument opposées. Il y a deux rires et nous n'avons pas de mot pour les distinguer.

> Laughable laughter is disastrous. Even so, the angels have gained something from it. They have tricked us with a semantic imposture. Their imitation of laughter and (the devil's) original laughter are both called by the same name. Nowadays we don't even realize that the same external display serves two absolutely opposed internal attitudes. There are two laughters, and we have no word to tell one from the other.[130]

There is an initial linguistic conflation of two different attitudes behind a single word: laughter. As we saw in Derrida's discussion of Plato's use of the word *pharmakon*, it is just this failure to address the slippage of signification which allows us to assert the possibility of stable essences, independent of translation and impervious to it, and convertible into absolutes. Like Ricœur's paradigm of translation, this linguistic conflation has far-reaching ethical implications, its dangers hinging upon the possibility that we might *forget* that there are two different types of laughter, and assert and act out the idea that only *one* exists. When we fail to recognize that there can be two opposed attitudes contained within the same word and the same utterance, we fail to acknowledge both the privilege and the limitations of our own perspective. We see only what we see: as Timothy Mathews suggests, '[o]ptically, a point of view is made in pushing out the others. Affectively, culturally, historically, spontaneously, intimately, publically, in remembering and forgetting, my understanding of you and others still appears to me in my own way of seeing, and in my own blindness'.[131]

As Kundera asserts, this faith in the coherence of our understanding is dangerous: whether we resort to the idyll or to nihilism, place our faith in certainty or scepticism, we fail to acknowledge that these attitudes are part and parcel of the same motivation: a desire to assert our own perspective over that of another. We can never prevent this type of forgetting: our perspective is the only one we know; our laughter is the only one we can express. Nonetheless, we need, Kundera suggests, to find a way to recognize the inevitability of such forgetting; to realize that there can be multiple meanings behind and interpretations of the same laughter; to understand this forgetting even if we cannot thwart it.

In *The Art of Relation*, Mathews asks '[w]hat ethics do we need to understand the repetition of what we do not understand? And what art?'[132] One answer – partial, at best, but all the more pertinent for that partiality – is offered by translation. In multiplying a text into other forms, in repeating it in other languages, in its failures and its attempts to communicate, translation acknowledges the partiality of every perspective, and the impossibility of absolute understanding. In the next section of this chapter, I return to Kundera's discussions of translation in relation to his own work, and suggest that such discussions reveal, not a desire to prevent slippages of meaning – which is itself an impossible task – but a desire to prevent us forgetting that it is these slippages which enable the translation of ambiguity into certainty.

A hospitable translation

Fidelity and betrayal

As I discussed in the introduction to this chapter, critics such as Stanger and Barańczak allege that Kundera writes in a style designed for 'translatability'. Yet the very possibility of attaining such a style is, as I have explored throughout this chapter, one which Kundera repeatedly disputes through narratives which focus upon the inevitable mistranslations which occur in our every attempt to understand another person, or even ourselves. Nonetheless, Kundera is not asserting that translation is an impossibility, that untranslatability is the norm. For even an untranslatable word such as *litost* can be communicated: meaning, though inevitably distorted, can be recreated across linguistic borders through the use of narrative. The reality of translation is that we always find a way through every impasse into some form of communication, however partial and distorted.

In *Sur la traduction*, Ricœur focuses upon this paradox, which he suggests renders the translatable versus untranslatable binary unsustainable as a model for translation theory, as well as in practice. If language were so discrete as to be untranslatable, understanding between languages would be absolutely impossible: 'Il faut alors conclure que la mécompréhension est de droit, que la traduction est théoriquement impossible et que les individus bilingues ne peuvent être que des schizophrènes'/'So we must conclude that misunderstanding is a right, that translation is theoretically impossible and that bilinguals have to be schizophrenics'.[133] A theory and practice of translation which culminates in the conclusion that linguistic diversity is a schizophrenic experience is an infertile path to pursue, and it is disproved by the experiences of bilingual authors such as Atxaga, Kundera and Semprún. The converse posits that because translation does exist there must be some superstructure to language: either an *original* language which we have lost – the utopian possibility of Benjamin's pure language – or an eternal, transcendent linguistic model from which all other languages have grown. This second model is equally unproductive for Ricœur, simply because it *has* been unproductive: 'nul ne peut dire comment on pourrait dériver les langues naturelles, avec toutes les bizarreries qu'on dira plus loin, de la présumée langue parfaite'/'no one can say how the natural languages, with all the peculiarities which we will talk about later, could be derived from the supposed perfect language'.[134] Despite multiple attempts, no empirical sign of linguistic transcendence has been uncovered; as I discussed in Chapter 1, such an idea of perfection involves an absolutist repression of linguistic plurality and the multilingual reality which so many of us inhabit both nationally and transnationally. As in Kundera's discussion of the angels and the Devil, here the weight of either pole in the binary translatable/untranslatable continually supplants the possibility of the other. The empirical diversity of languages is outweighed by the need to accept that some understanding *can* transcend the linguistic separation; the notion of a universal language fails because it has no empirical verification.

This failure of either model to offer a productive approach to the linguistic, social, ethical and political issues of translation enables Ricœur to address a different model: 'fidélité *versus* trahison'/'faithfulness versus betrayal'.[135] Splitting translations according to this dichotomy has allowed theorists and practitioners of translation to valorize translations and translators according to the somewhat indefinite criterion of being *faithful* to the original text or authorial intention. Ricœur's discussion of 'fidélité *versus* trahison' is not concerned, however, with the oppositional nature of these two ideas, but with the space, the border, *between* them. Ricœur's discussion begins with a return to the Babel myth; he is interested in the attitude towards translation of the original builders of the tower of Babel. This attitude, he suggests, was one of *acceptance*: 'La traduction est bien alors une tâche, non au sens d'une obligation contraignante, mais au sens de la *chose à faire* pour que l'action humaine puisse simplement continuer [...]. Ils cessent de bâtir! Façon de dire: c'est ainsi. [...] À partir de cette réalité de la vie, traduisons!'/'Translation is definitely a task, then, not in the sense of a restricting obligation, but in the sense of *the thing to be done* so that human life can continue [...] They left off building the city! That is a way of saying: this is the way things are. [...] Starting from this fact of life, let us translate!'[136] It is the *reality* of translation which Ricœur seeks to understand, its reality as a fact of life which, for Ricœur, offers a paradigm for all our interactions, be they linguistic, political, ethical, social, cultural or affective.

Ricœur's reason for turning to the fidelity/betrayal binary is that, in the space between these two opposites, he believes there exists a productive model for considering this reality of translation. This involves rethinking our understanding of what it means to achieve a *good* translation, a criterion which, he suggests, can never be accurately judged:

> pour qu'un tel critère soit disponible, il faudrait qu'on puisse comparer le texte de départ et le texte d'arrivée à un troisième texte qui serait porteur du sens identique supposé circuler du premier au second. [...] Il n'y a pas [...] de tiers texte entre le texte source et le texte d'arrivée. D'où le paradoxe, avant le dilemme : une bonne traduction ne peut viser qu'à une équivalence présumée, non fondée dans une *identité* de sens démontrable.
>
> for such a criterion to be available, we would have to be able to compare the source and target texts with a third text which would bear the identical meaning that is supposed to be passed from the first to the second [...]. There is no [...] third text between the source text and the target text. Hence the paradox, before the dilemma: a good translation can aim only at a supposed *equivalence* that is not founded on a demonstrable *identity* of meaning.[137]

For Ricœur, this absence of a third text means that we can never determine whether a translation is identical in meaning to the source text. Instead, every translation is caught between fidelity and betrayal, capable of both serving and failing the source text in ways that can never be fully assessed. To perceive a text as translatable or untranslatable fashions translation as a tool which seeks, but often fails, to attain an absolute, perfect identification with an original. But the fidelity/betrayal dichotomy allows us to move beyond this impasse, and approach the mystery and the task of translation as seeking *equivalence* rather than *identicalness*. While identicalness of sense implies a type of absolute correspondence – the poetic uniformity of a political idyll, for example – equivalence, 'the condition of being equal or equivalent in value, worth, function, etc.', enables a working relation with the impossibility of an absolute correspondence.[138] For, whether in translation, politics or our personal lives, we can never truly lose ourselves in another and identify with them completely. Equivalence acknowledges that untranslatable elements are a living reality uncovered in translation, that absolute identicalness can never be measured or attained, and that confronting betrayal as part of fidelity remains the inevitable task of the translator. As Ricœur writes, 'la nature véritable de l'équivalence [...] est plutôt *produite* par la traduction que *présumée* par elle'/'the true nature of equivalence [...] is *produced* by translation rather than *presupposed* by it'.[139]

Throughout Kundera's discussion of the translations of his novels there is a similar focus upon the space between fidelity and betrayal, and a recognition of both the challenges of translation and its ability to illuminate the ethics of our attempts to stabilize meaning, both textually and non-textually. As the title of *Les Testaments trahis* attests, Kundera is fascinated by these concepts of faith and betrayal, understood both as forms of human motivation and as a translational dynamic. He once, somewhat infamously, commented that '[l]a traduction est belle seulement si elle est fidèle'/'a translation is beautiful only if it is faithful', though, as Woods notes, he makes no mention of 'to what the translation should be faithful'.[140] Kundera saves the issue for *Les Testaments trahis*. Here he explores the multiple ways in which art, understood as a testament to the pursuit of freedom and creativity, can be betrayed by its own hermeneutic possibilities, and by the appropriation of these possibilities by the publisher, the reader, the critic and indeed the translator.[141] In this text Kundera elaborates upon the importance of fidelity in translation, stating that '[l]'autorité suprême, pour un traducteur, devrait être le *style personnel* de l'auteur'/'For a translator, the supreme authority should be the author's personal style'.[142] Such a style, suggests Kundera, is often itself transgressive in the source language, working to challenge or reject established grammatical or stylistic modes. Kundera believes that 'tout auteur d'une certaine valeur *transgresse* le «beau style» et c'est dans cette transgression que se trouve l'originalité (et, partant, la raison d'être) de son art. Le premier effort du traducteur devrait être la compréhension de cette transgression'/'every author of some value transgresses against "good style," and in that transgression lies the originality (and hence raison d'être) of his art. The translator's primary effort should be to understand that transgression'.[143] As Woods suggests, Kundera believes that it is this transgression of stylistic norms, itself a powerful aesthetic expression of freedom, that translation runs the risk of betraying.[144]

In *Les Testaments trahis,* Kundera thus nuances the criteria through which a translation can be judged as faithful or a betrayal. Even so, Kundera's claim that '[l]a traduction est belle seulement si elle est fidèle' implies a somewhat circumscribed vision of the role and purpose of translation.[145] But this vision of translation is only limited if the values attributed to fidelity and beauty are stable. In fact, throughout his œuvre Kundera repeatedly questions and challenges those values. In *L'Insoutenable légèreté de l'être*, Kundera explores two different conceptions of beauty:

> En Europe, la beauté a toujours eu un caractère intentionnel. Il y a eu un dessein esthétique et un plan de longue haleine [...]. La beauté de New York a une tout autre origine. C'est une beauté non-intentionnelle. Elle est née sans préméditation de la part de l'homme [...]. Des formes, hideuses en elles-mêmes, se retrouvent par hasard, sans plan aucun, dans d'improbables voisinages où elles brillent tout à coup d'une poésie magique.
>
> Beauty in the European sense has always had a premeditated quality to it. We've always had an aesthetic intention and a long-range plan. [...] The beauty of New York rests on a completely different base. It's unintentional. It arose independently of human design [...] Forms which are in themselves quite ugly turn up fortuitously, without design, in such incredible surroundings that they sparkle with a sudden wondrous poetry.[146]

The difference between the beauty of New York and the beauty of Europe, then, is the difference between the planned and the unexpected, the intentional and the unintentional, between beauty as the preserve of kitsch and the beauty Kundera valorizes in *L'Art du roman*: 'Beauté dans l'art: lumière subitement allumée du jamais-dit'/'Beauty in art: the suddenly kindled light of the never-before-said.'[147] The nuances Kundera finds here echo Kant's separation of the beautiful and the sublime. In Kant's reading, the beautiful delights because it is attractive, pleasant and comprehensible, whereas the sublime challenges, disturbs and overwhelms.[148] A faithful translation, a repetition of a preconceived and prewritten idea, may be beautiful as a European city is beautiful, but it fails to attain the flash of the unforeseen which Kundera here equates with artistic power. Significantly, in an intratextual excerpt from *L'Insoutenable légèreté de l'être* included in *L'Art du roman,* Kundera endows *betrayal* with the potential for such a transgressive flash of originality: 'Trahir, c'est sortir du rang et partir dans l'inconnu'/'betrayal means breaking ranks and going off into the unknown'.[149] To depart into the unknown is itself a form of forgetting the past and, perhaps also the future: it is the triumph of a present that refuses a debt to any previous experience, to any previous text. This is originality, then, but on challenging terms, an originality concerned with the very forms of forgetting which Kundera warns us against in *Le Livre*. But this transgressive originality is also a challenge to the idea of 'le «déjà connu»'/'the already-known', the kitsch and pre-digested expression which, in *L'Art du roman*, Kundera suggests is the very opposite of insight.[150]

So there is a freedom, a beauty, and an insight in betrayal which Kundera suggests does not exist in absolute fidelity, nor in absolute cohesion. Indeed, as Steinby notes, '[i]n Kundera's view, fidelity is an ideal of the sentimental. It is a stubborn insistence on something that has already lost meaning'.[151] Steinby does not connect this vision to Kundera's own comments about the fidelity of translation. But while Kundera argues that a translation is only beautiful if it is faithful, the shifting values he assigns to both these terms suggest that such a 'beautiful' translation is not necessarily the one he would wish for his own novels. Rather, this phrase is part of Kundera's own transgressive challenge to any supposed stability in concepts as subjective as beauty, fidelity and originality.

Indeed, even as he asserts a desire for fidelity Kundera is already undermining it through his own continual rewriting. As Woods notes, 'Kundera has rewritten almost all of his Czech "originals" so that the translations have no original text to be faithful to'.[152] In the same way, his continual revisions of the translations of his texts into French and English render each version temporary and unfinished. The 'definitive' English version of *La Plaisanterie* (published in 1992), for example, is the fifth version of the text. This endless urge to rewrite can be read as a journey towards a perfect translation, a journey which reveals the desire for such perfection to be as inevitable as the desire for kitsch. But this is an urge which can never be satisfied, for perfection – in writing, in translation, in our relations to another – can never be attained. In his 'Author's note' to this edition, Kundera offers 'a promise: there will not be a sixth English-language version of *The Joke*'.[153] Yet the existence of four previous English versions of the text reveals the fragility of this 'promise'.

Kundera's understanding of fidelity in translation, then, is far removed from an absolute replication of the first-written text. Drawing on Philip E. Lewis's essay 'The Measure of Translation Effects', Woods suggests that, because of this continual rewriting, the term 'abusive fidelity' be applied to Kundera's work.[154] Lewis's term suggests that translations can remain abusively faithful to a text by seeking to reproduce its style rather than its content.[155] But I would suggest that the term 'faithful betrayal', which reverses these poles, could also be applied to Kundera's work. Kundera *is* faithful, but that fidelity is reserved for his continual *betrayals* of the certainty and finality of his own aesthetic forms, a faith in the *impossibility* of fidelity.

A faithful betrayal

This 'faithful betrayal' is integral to understanding Kundera's attitude to translation, and particularly his description of the control he maintains over the translation of his novels as 'cette activité sisyphesque'/'this Sisyphean activity'.[156] Sisyphus was condemned to his endless task *because* of his betrayals, his duplicitous manipulation of the secrets of the Gods in an attempt to imprison Death and gain immortality for the human race. The punishment for this betrayal of authority is one of translation – Sisyphus must engage in a never-ending repetition of an original act, displaced each time into a new temporal moment. But while this punishment creates a cause-and-effect relationship between betrayal and translation, it also enables a re-evaluation of betrayal. For if translation is the penalty for transgressing the dictates of the Gods, originality becomes the prize for obeying the dictates of a transcendental authority.

In *Le Mythe de Sisyphe,* Camus suggests that while Sisyphus's repetitive task reveals the futility of our existence, it also illuminates our potential to achieve, through these repetitions, brief and beautiful moments of unexpected individual consciousness and power: 'On retrouve toujours son fardeau. Mais Sisyphe enseigne la fidélité supérieure qui nie les dieux et soulève les rochers'/'One always finds one's burden again. But Sisyphus teaches the higher fidelity that negates the gods and raises rocks'.[157] A faith built upon a betrayal of the Gods; a brief moment of illumination upon a mountain top before an immediate return to the darkness of Hades; a beginning which is also a repetition of the same: in Sisyphus's story we read one of the stories of translation. Sisyphus's endless attempt to lay his rock to rest is an acknowledgement of both the impossibility of finishing the task of translation and the necessity of continuing to try. And, as Camus suggests, the heart of Sisyphus's story is revealed every time he turns from the mountain top to begin his task again. Each repetition Sisyphus completes, each variation of his challenge, offers him an understanding of his experience in ways which one single attempt, an original movement, could not. In Sisyphus's story, nothing is accomplished, but everything is illuminated. For his endless movement assigns significance to the attempt and not the result, to the process of translation and not the final product, in the space between faith and betrayal which is the reality of translation.

This reality of translation, the understanding it reveals through its every attempted repetition of a text, is an integral element of Kundera's novels. In *Le Rideau* Kundera writes that 'la beauté d'un roman est inséparable de son architecture'/'the beauty of the novel is inseparable from its architecture'.[158] While the novel is an attempt to fashion aesthetic coherence from the contingency of experience, the beauty of its architecture, the unique poetry of its form, is contained for Kundera in the powerful affective impact which arises through the novel's ability to bring multiple dialogues, perspectives and genres together. In an interview in 1979, quoted by Woods, Kundera states that 'Je n'ai pas quitté la poésie, je l'ai trahie. Pour moi, la poésie lyrique, ce n'est pas seulement un genre littéraire mais avant tout une conception du monde, une attitude vis-à-vis du monde. J'ai quitté cette attitude comme on quitte une religion.'/ 'I did not leave poetry, I betrayed it. For me, lyrical poetry is not only a literary genre but above all a conception of the world, an attitude vis-à-vis the world. I left this attitude as one leaves a religion'.[159] Through the novel form, then, Kundera seeks to *betray* the values of kitsch and poetic beauty. But how, even in the novel, are we to escape kitsch? Kundera's answer, like Camus's, is that this can be achieved through *repetition*. Just as Sisyphus's task of translation illuminated the shape and form of his human experience, Kundera's use of repetition illuminates the shape and form of his 'faithful betrayal' of the lyrically poetic form.

Repetition and variation

In the final chapter of *Le Livre*, Kundera explores two ways in which we can understand the illuminations made possible by the process of repetition: the first is that repetition can reduce the significance of events, words, relationships; the second is that it can illuminate the permeations within concepts we believe to be stable.[160] 'La Frontière' focuses upon Jan, another Czech émigré, and the absurdity he perceives in attempts to convey our experience through gestures and words. Jan believes that repetition is the key to understanding this innate linguistic and existential absurdity: 'Il suffisait de si peu, de si infiniment peu, pour se retrouver de l'autre côté de la frontière au-delà de laquelle plus rien n'avait de sens: l'amour, les convictions, la foi, l'Histoire. [...] Les choses se répètent et perdent chaque fois une fraction de leur sens'/'It takes so little, so infinitely little, for someone to find himself on the other side of the border, where everything – love, convictions, faith, history – no longer has meaning. [...] When things are repeated, they lose a fraction of their meaning'.[161] The potential for repetition to eliminate sense hinges for Jan upon the idea that repetition fundamentally devalues the original, 'que toute répétition n'est qu'une imitation et que toute imitation est sans valeur [...] vidée de toute signification à force de se répéter au cours des ans'/'all repetition was mere imitation and all imitation was worthless

[...] emptied of all meaning by years of repetition'.[162] Here, standard hierarchies of translation appear to be imposed: like Plato's conception of the simulacrum which I discussed in Chapter 1 through Gilles Deleuze, the copy removes something from the original which prevents it living in another language.[163] This conception of repetition denies the value of imitative action, implicating repetition in the forms of forgetting which, throughout *Le Livre*, Kundera suggests can be translated so dangerously into political absolutism. In this reading, Sisyphus's task would be an action void of meaning, a repetition of the already-said and already-known, destined to be stymied by its lack of originality.

But while repetition can involve a forgetting and a loss of meaning, it can also provide the means through which the inevitability of forgetting and the consequent collapse of signification can be revealed. The narrator of *Le Livre* continues:

> Si Jan définit pour lui-même la frontière comme la dose maximale admissible de répétitions, je suis donc dans l'obligation de le corriger: la frontière n'est pas le résultat de la répétition. La répétition n'est que l'une des manières de rendre la frontière visible. La ligne de la frontière est couverte de poussière et la répétition est comme le geste de la main qui écarte cette poussière.
>
> Since Jan defines the border for himself as the maximum acceptable dose of repetitions, I am obliged to correct him: the border is not a product of repetition. Repetition is only one of the ways of making the border visible. The borderline is covered with dust, and repetition is like a hand whisking away dust.[164]

Here repetition becomes the process of elucidation and illumination which Camus suggests Sisyphus's task reveals. This second conception of repetition moves towards the forms of repetition-with-difference which I explored in Chapter 1 through Deleuze and Atxaga, where repetition gains its own creative value, and the simulacrum offers new ways of thinking about originality.[165] Repetition of the same means that we forget; repetition with difference does not help us remember, but rather allows us to acknowledge the inevitability of our forgetting, the impossibility of transcending our own perspective, the border between meaning and non-meaning which conditions all our interactions.

In *Le Livre*, Kundera's own use of repetition operates in this illuminating way. As Woods notes, Kundera's use of repetition, in dialogue with translation, is at the heart of his particular poetics of the novel: repetition works to emphasise the key words within Kundera's enquiries into the nature of existence and experience.[166] Kundera's use of repetition to explore variations on *litost* operates as such an existential enquiry, enabling Kundera to interrogate the centrality of this emotion, its origins and its repercussions, not only in a personal context but also a collective one, not only romantically but also politically. These variations, which are crucial also to Kundera's exploration of his other key words – laughter, forgetting, the angels, the border – gain their power through the coherence and dissolution of coherence effected by the repetition of the word *litost*. For each variation upon the theme of *litost* – from the student's story, to the story of the Czechoslovakian national soul, to Éluard's poetic transcendence of the death of Kalandra – depends upon an equivalence which connects apparently disparate events without seeking to confuse or merge them, and concentrates upon the border between those events as the location of understanding, which slips even as we try to focus upon it. In this sense, the variations which Kundera enacts through repetition return us to Ricœur's vision of the ethical possibilities of translation, predicated upon equivalence as opposed to identicalness.

Perhaps inevitably, though, translation can also operate to *limit* the understanding that Kundera suggests is enabled by repetition. In an interview with Christian Salmon, Kundera discusses the translation of key words such as *litost*, emphasizing that, '[b]ecause of their categorical character, these words cannot be replaced by synonyms. This always has to be explained over and over again to translators, who, in their concern for "good style", seek to avoid repetition'.[167] As Woods notes, several translators of *Le Livre* have fallen prey to this desire to avoid repetition when translating *litost*: Michael Heim's English translation, for example, adds 'bitterness', 'exasperation', and 'resentment' to the Czech word; Kérel's French translation adds 'cette tristesse particulière'.[168] Kundera's decision to revise and authorize his translations arose precisely from his objection to alterations such as these. For translations which try to avoid repetition of Kundera's 'mots-thèmes' make a fundamental error: by altering the signifier, they seek to invoke an alterity which already exists within the word. Failing to repeat these key words prevents us recognizing the difference which Kundera, like Deleuze, perceives to be inherent within repetition.

But translation also offers an opportunity to illuminate this difference. Kundera has acknowledged that it was only in the process of revising his translations that he became aware of his use of repetition as a formal characteristic and then created a dictionary, 'Quatre-vingt-neuf mots', which explores the nuances he develops within his texts via the repetition of certain key words.[169] In fact, the process of revision via translation also enabled Kundera to extend the importance of repetition within his work. For in the Czech version of *Le Livre*, the chapter headings which correspond to the theme words are organized differently: rather than repeating the title 'Les Anges' across two different sections, the Czech version only uses it once; and while translations of Kundera's French text entitle two chapters 'Les Lettres perdus' – a title which highlights the forgettings of the book's title – the Czech text does not use this title at all. While Kundera has claimed that translation often undermines the form of his texts, his own approach to authorizing the translations of his texts positions it as an opportunity to develop and extend that form, to consolidate the relations between the repetitions he suggests are so crucial to his aesthetic approach.

Repetition reveals to us the precarity of our perspective, the ambiguity at the heart of thinking, and the impossibility of stabilizing it. And yet, as Kundera's experience of translation demonstrates, we always seek stability and hope to convert ambiguity into certainty by choosing one definition over the other. Like the student in *Le Livre*, we choose one side of the border again and again, thereby imposing our perspective on another. Perhaps we can never prevent this imposition, but Kundera suggests that we can, and should, at least acknowledge it. And Kundera's aesthetics of translation – developed through his focus upon the untranslatable word *litost* – is integral to the ways in which he formulates this acknowledgement in *Le Livre*. For, through his attempt and failure to translate this term, Kundera develops a form of linguistic hospitality: a manner of thinking, reading and writing which accepts alternative perspectives but does not purport to transcend its own.

Litost and linguistic hospitality

As an untranslated and 'untranslatable' Czech word within a French text, *litost* makes explicit an implicit, but already present, linguistic collision within both the creation and the reception of *Le Livre*. This collision of Czech and French makes *litost* an example of the type of resistant 'foreignization' which, as I discussed earlier, Lawrence Venuti reads as crucial to an ethics of translation. In *The Scandals of Translation* Venuti suggests that the texts 'that work best, the most powerful in recreating cultural values and the most responsible in accounting for that power, usually engage readers in domestic terms that have been defamiliarized to some extent, made fascinating by a revisionary encounter with a foreign text'.[170] Somewhat ironically, given that Venuti discusses Kundera as an example of an author with a decidedly non-ethical approach to translation, Kundera's use of *litost* within *Le Livre* operates through precisely this type of defamiliarization, reasserting through a linguistic moment of foreignness the specificity of the Czech language, and simultaneously introducing, in the midst of a French text, an emotion Kundera suggests is unique to Czech culture.

As I discussed in the Introduction, Venuti builds his argument about the importance of foreignizing techniques by revisiting a distinction Friedrich Schleiermacher makes in his 1813 essay 'On the Different Methods of Translation'. Schleiermacher considers two options for the translator: 'Either the translator leaves the author in peace as much as possible and moves the reader towards him; or he leaves the reader in peace as much as possible and moves the writer towards him'.[171] Venuti's 'foreignization' shapes the first of these options into a recognition of cultural difference by insisting upon the translated nature of the text being read. Woods suggests that Kundera's use of language loans such as *litost* is designed to engender just such an awareness, forcing the reader into a recognition of the linguistic duality inherent within Kundera's creative process.[172] Language loans problematize the translation process, since the translator must negotiate the deliberate presence of an ostensibly untranslatable word. They also force both translator and reader to become aware of what is foreign and difficult to understand. Reading Kundera's use of language loans as ethical only in this way depends on maintaining another series of divisions: between Czech and French; between domestic and foreign; between reader and writer; between translatability and untranslatability. Yet, as Kundera consistently seeks to emphasize, his texts function in the relation between different identities, languages, literatures and cultures; the relation between the creative processes of reader as well as author; and the relation between visions of absolute translatability and untranslatability.

Is there another way to understand the impact of these language loans? Schleiermacher argues that *either* the reader must come to the author *or* the author to the reader, 'any attempt to combine them being certain to produce a highly unreliable result and to carry with it the danger that writer and reader might miss each other entirely'.[173] Ricœur, on the other hand, suggests that the two methods can be combined: 'Amener le lecteur à l'auteur, amener l'auteur au lecteur, au risque de servir et de trahir deux maîtres, c'est pratiquer ce que j'aime appeler *l'hospitalité langagière*'/'Bringing the reader to the author, bringing the author to the reader, at the risk of serving and of betraying two masters: this is to practise what I like to call *linguistic hospitality*'.[174] In Ricœur's comment the simultaneous action of betrayal and fidelity in translation is again asserted: linguistic hospitality inhabits a borderland between loyalty and disloyalty to the concerns of author and reader. Language loans such as *litost* exist within this hospitable borderland, for they emphasize the relation, rather than an impervious divergence, between the assertions of the author and the interpretations of the reader. In this interpretation, encountering a language loan means encountering the semantic gaps that separate languages, and separating the authorial from the readers' attempts to consolidate a point. Simultaneously, such loans create a hospitable relation between the foreign and the domestic, between the possibility and the impossibility of translation. For these loans have narrative meaning *only* in translation: in a Czech text *litost* is linguistically indigenous and provokes neither reader nor author to acknowledge the presence of the untranslatable.

Yet this is not entirely true, for the question 'What is *litost*?' which is posed in the translations of Kundera's texts is also posed in the Czech 'original', thereby drawing attention to the foreign which already exists within the domestic. As Woods notes,

> Unable to define it even within the Czech language, [Kundera] implied that the word was foreign also in its own language, through its indefinability. By retaining the Czech word in the text and not allowing it to be translated, Kundera was explicitly making his readers aware that what they were reading was a translation, but he concomitantly revealed the foreignness of words in any given language.[175]

The power and unique perspective which *litost* reveals, both thematically and linguistically, forces us to accept 'la différence indépassable du propre et de l'étranger'/'the impassable difference of the peculiar and the foreign', to acknowledge that something is always lacking and lost in translation between our perception and that of another.[176] But this loss is *within* our language as much as *beyond* it; it is an integral element of our inability to transcend our own viewpoint, to see with anything other than our own vision – the very inability, in short, which gives rise to the emotion of *litost* itself.

In this sense, language loans are never simply a form of resistance to the domesticating actions of translation; nor, however, are they encounters with the other designed only to stretch the limits of our own perspective. By its multiple linguistic, semantic, interpersonal and political forms, *litost*, itself spoken in *another* voice, in *another* language – one which Kundera glosses in *Le Livre* but which, in spite of this, remains untranslated – disrupts a narcissistic illusion of unity or absolutism. Yet *litost* also acknowledges the continued dominance of our own perspective, the inevitable narcissism that recognizes the other only in relation to itself. This, as Spivak suggests, is the paradox of translation: 'it is not possible for us as ethical agents to imagine otherness or alterity maximally. We have to turn the other into something like the self in order to be ethical'.[177] Thinking translation ethically, and thinking ethically through translation, means recognizing this appropriative impulse which lies beneath our every attempt at recognition. Negotiating and confronting this impulse requires a hospitable approach which reflects upon its inevitability even as it stakes a claim for the importance of resistance to it. Lying implicit within Kundera's inclusion and use of *litost*, these two elements remain in constant and hospitable tension: *litost* opens the French language to what is foreign to it, even while acknowledging the unavoidable desire to translate that foreign element into domestic terms.

This tension is visible in the ways in which, in the Czech, English and French versions of *Le Livre,* the question of the proper name is approached differently. In Kundera's Czech text the student's lover is called Kristýna.[178] The French translation converts her name to Christine, while both Heim's and Asher's English versions – despite the fact that the former is based on the Czech version and the latter on the French – keep her name as Kristyna, but without the Czech diacritic. In each of these translations Venuti's distinction between domestication and foreignization thus plays out differently. And yet the difference between these versions in fact challenges the stability of Venuti's binary. As Derrida suggests, the proper name always calls out to a double desire: 'traduis-moi, ne me traduis pas'/'translate me, don't translate me'.[179] But in Kundera's work each linguistic version of his text responds to this call differently, the issues of translatability and untranslatability, of the foreign and the domestic, being articulated divergently depending upon which 'authorized' version we read.

This difference between versions is the reality of translation, as Ricœur describes it: a reality in which every translation exists in the tension between appropriation and acknowledgement, impossibility and necessity. Translation is always a task to be dealt with differently, depending on language, audience, time and place. It is to be revised, reconsidered, and rethought in every moment. And this task always involves possible failure. Indeed, even Kundera's authorized translations contain errors of meaning: Asher's authorized English translation of *Le Livre*, for example, mistranslates 's'en vouloir' – to hold against, or resent – as 'to want'.[180] This error is easy to understand when translating from a language in which the verbs for 'to resent' and 'to want' – 's'en vouloir' and 'vouloir' – are so similar. But it also reveals the limits of 'authorization', for every instance of rewriting, whether sanctioned by the author or not, contains the possibility of a misreading or misinterpretation. Perfection in translation is an ideal which can never be fully attained.

For Ricœur, hospitality in translation means acknowledging this fact: 'Travail de traduction [...], travail de deuil aussi, appliqué à renoncer à l'idéal même de la *traduction parfaite'*/'The work of translation [...] the work of mourning too, applied to renouncing the very idea of the *perfect translation*'.[181] Translation thus entails mourning for the loss of utopian and absolute understanding between people and peoples, whether textual, linguistic, romantic or political. But this, Ricœur suggests, is a productive mourning. For in accepting the loss of the perfect translation, we also accept the impossibility of our desire to understand absolutely, identify with, or appropriate another. Through this loss we can build a space of interaction within which what is foreign in another is welcomed as much as erased. It is this that Ricœur defines as *linguistic hospitality:* 'où le plaisir d'habiter la langue de l'autre est compensé par le plaisir de recevoir chez soi, dans sa propre demeure d'accueil, la parole de l'étranger'/'where the pleasure of dwelling in the other's language is balanced by the pleasure of receiving the foreign word at home, in one's own welcoming house'.[182] As Ricœur suggests, drawing upon Antoine Berman's phrase 'l'épreuve de l'étranger', this recognition of the foreign is an ordeal, a challenge to our comfortable assumptions about the stability of our own language and perspective.[183] But it also contains an opportunity for us to connect and to develop our relations both with ourselves and others: 'sans l'épreuve de l'étranger, serions-nous sensibles à l'étrangeté de notre propre langue? Enfin, sans cette épreuve, ne serions-nous pas menacés de nous enfermer dans l'aigreur d'un monologue, seuls avec nos livres? Honneur, donc, à l'hospitalité langagière'/'without the test of the foreign, would we be sensitive to the strangeness of our own language? Finally, without that test, would we not be in danger of shutting ourselves away in the sourness of a monologue, alone with our books? Credit, then, to linguistic hospitality'.[184] Ricœur's conception of linguistic hospitality would see a language open itself up to difference, even as it consumes it: 'L'étranger dans son étrangeté, le lecteur dans son désir d'appropriation'/'The foreigner in his strangeness, the reader in his desire for appropriation': this is the hospitable space of translating and of thinking.[185]

In Kundera's depiction of it, the novel form allows a similar hospitality, in which the existence of the other is announced, yet always annexed. Kundera repeatedly positions ambiguity, uncertainty, variation as the essence of the ethics he reads in the novel. Yet in the quotation I discussed earlier, he also emphasizes the human impulse to translate this ambiguity into certainty:

> L'homme souhaite un monde où le bien et le mal soient nettement discernables car est en lui le désir, inné et indomptable, de juger avant de comprendre. Sur ce désir sont fondées les religions et les idéologies. Elles ne peuvent se concilier avec le roman que si elles traduisent son langage de relativité et d'ambiguïté dans leur discours apodictique et dogmatique. Elles exigent que quelqu'un ait raison.
>
> Man desires a world where good and evil can be clearly distinguished, for he has an innate and irrepressible desire to judge before he understands. Religions and ideologies are founded on this desire. They can cope with the novel only by translating its language and relativity and ambiguity into their own apodictic and dogmatic discourse. They require that someone be right.[186]

This statement reaffirms the idea, raised in Kundera's exploration of the poetic, that a dogmatic politics requires a dogmatic aesthetics to complement it. In confrontation with a more ambiguous aesthetic form such as the novel, dogma seeks to translate its polyphonic language *inhospitably,* appropriating and altering the novel's language so that it too becomes certain. Such a translation is at the heart of the accusation Kundera levels at Orwell's texts in *Les Testaments trahis*. But translation is never a one-way street: if we can translate in one direction, we can always translate in the other. What occurs if we seek to translate dogma into ambiguity? Could the paradigm of linguistic hospitality be applied to this translation, so that we could see the novel as a space which incorporates some dogma into its uncertainty and returns some uncertainty to dogma? Could such a hospitable translation offer an ethically aware mode of reading, writing, thinking and engaging in political questions through the novel form?

In *L'Art du roman,* Kundera comments that 'une fois dans le corps du roman, la méditation change d'essence: une pensée dogmatique devient hypothétique'/'Once it is part of a novel, reflection changes its essence: a dogmatic thought becomes hypothetical'.[187] But this shift from dogma to hypothesis is not a shift from certainty to uncertainty. Rather it is one conditioned by the possibility of repetition, approached as an interaction between these different modes of thought. Through their use of repetition, Kundera's novels recognize the multiplicity of perspective, but also our desire to make sense of this multiplicity within our own perspective. As readers, as critics, as translators, we acknowledge the individual truths of the novel, its variations and repetitions, its untranslatable moments. But we also, always, convert these individual truths into *our* truth, its repetition into themes, those untranslatables into narrative. It is in this sense that the novel is *hospitable*: hospitable to the variance of perspective and the fallibility of our certainties; hospitable to our inability to escape our own perspective. Kundera's novels explore the desire for appropriation and for freedom, for ambiguity and dogma, revealing through repetition and translation the ethics and the aesthetics of the novel to be formed at the location of both forgetting and understanding.

Epilogue: on the border with translation

I began this chapter with the quest for a translation of *litost*; I will end it by acknowledging the failure of this quest, but also the continued desire to complete it. For through this unresolvable quest, through the desire for perfection and the impossibility of attaining it, in the search, the failures, the stories, the diversions and asides, we see the complexity and diversity of our individual memories and interpretations depicted in narrative form. In *Sur la traduction* Ricœur creates a link between the process of creating narrative and the process of translation. He writes that 'de même que dans l'acte de raconter, on peut traduire autrement, sans espoir de combler l'écart entre équivalence et adéquation totale [...]. Il faudra peut-être tout à l'heure faire le deuil du vœu de perfection, pour assumer sans ébriété et en tout sobriété la «tâche du traducteur»/'just as in the act of telling a story, we can translate differently, without hope of filling the gap between equivalence and total adequacy [...] we may soon have to mourn the loss of the wish for perfection in order to take on the "translator's task" without intoxication and in all sobriety.'[188]

In *Le Livre* we can see these tasks of narration and translation as confronting the gap between equivalence and complete adequacy, between the untranslatable and the translatable, between our perspective and that of others, Kundera suggests that this gap – which, as we have seen, can also be conceived as a border – is both almost invisible and ever-present:

> la frontière est constamment avec nous [...] elle est omniprésente, bien qu'elle soit plus ou moins visible selon les circonstances [...].

> Il suffit de si peu, d'une infime courant d'air pour que les choses bougent imperceptiblement, et ce pour quoi on aurait encore donné sa vie une seconde avant apparaît soudain comme un non-sens où il n'y a rien.

> the border is constantly with us [...] it is omnipresent, even though circumstances might make it more or less visible. [...] It takes so little, a tiny puff of air, for things to shift imperceptibly, and whatever it was that a man was ready to lay down his life for a few seconds earlier seems suddenly to be sheer nonsense.[189]

The challenge Kundera levels in *Le Livre* is not to close this gap, but rather to remain alert to our own innate desire to forget that it exists. For we are always on the border between meaning and non-meaning, always in danger of using the instability of language to build our own worlds and then forgetting that they were built upon such loose soil. It is by *forgetting* this border that models, whether of political or literary thought, are sustained. Their strength is predicated on their ability to ignore, to erase, to repress what does not coalesce, to translate ambiguity into certainty, and to convert the sceptical laughter of the Devil into the joyous laughter of the angels.

Translation reveals such forgetting by foregrounding it as an inevitable process within our affective, aesthetic and political relations. Individually and collectively we are constantly erasing, losing and eliding difference through a process of translation between ourselves and others, between our thinking and that of others, between our language and what we believe that language can express and transmit. It is for this reason that translation is both *everything* and a *nightmare*: everything because it reveals our impregnable desire to perfect all our exchanges; a nightmare because it constantly evades the attempt, forcing meaning to slide, to slip, to dissolve as we grasp for it. Translation thus understood is not a rejection of certainty, but rather an acceptance of the impulse to seek it. We can only mourn if we are aware that something has been lost, and in this mourning lies the power of translation to create hospitality from within the desire to appropriate, in the name of whatever utopia. Hospitality means welcoming what is foreign and individual, what is past as well as what is present. By accepting the linguistic untranslatability of *litost*, Kundera's texts invoke hospitality as the site of an interrogation of our relation to each other, and render hospitable the artistic forms through which we evoke and explore that relation.

This hospitality is revealed by the differences between the versions of Kundera's texts in translation which, even when authorized, repeatedly challenge the stability of this authorization, and the relation of the foreign and the domestic. Translation, a form of repetition and reframing, reveals the instability of textual authenticity and authority. In every text, in every moment of writing, Kundera, like all readers, writers and translators, negotiates again and again the border between control and loss of control. As Woods suggests, '[t]hat the ambiguities of language harbour the ambiguities of interpretation should be an entry point for reading Kundera's work, or any work'.[190] The emphatic nature of Kundera's discussion of these translations, his proclamations that only his authority allows their authenticity, is a self-consciously fashioned example of the language on one side of this border, where certainty and an unshakeable confidence in one's own point of view are to be found; on the other side of the border, however, certainty collapses, understanding is to be re-fashioned, and translation is a continual exchange between the twin attractions of fidelity and betrayal.

Notes

1 Milan Kundera, *L'Art du roman* (Paris: Éditions Gallimard, 1986), 144. *The Art of the Novel*, trans. Linda Asher (New York: Grove Press, 1988), 121. All translations of the French text come from this English translation. Page numbers in subsequent references refer to: French text; English text.
2 Milan Kundera and Jordan Elgraby, 'Conversations with Milan Kundera', *Milan Kundera: Fictive Lightness, Fictive Weight: Salmagundi* 73 (1987): 17. http://www.jstor.org/stable/40547912 [Accessed 2 January 2018].
3 Milan Kundera, 'Fourth Congress of the Czechoslovak Writers' Union, 27–29 June 1967', in Dušan Hamšík, *Writers against Rulers*, trans. D. Orpington (London: Hutchison, 1971), 174–5.
4 Milan Kundera, *Les Testaments trahis* (Paris: Gallimard, 1993), 233.
5 Christine Angela Knoop, *Kundera: The Ambiguity of Authorship* (London: Maney for the MHRA, 2011), 13.
6 Milan Kundera, 'Comedy is Everywhere', *Index on Censorship* 6.6 (1977): 6.
7 Tijana Miletic, *European Literary Immigration into the French Language: Readings of Gary, Kristof, Kundera and Semprún* (Amsterdam: Rodopi, 2008), 29.
8 Milan Kundera, *Une rencontre* (Paris: Éditions Gallimard, 2009), 125. *Encounter: Essays*, trans. Linda Asher (New York: HarperCollins, 2010), 104. All translations of the French text come from this English translation. Page numbers in subsequent references refer to: French text; English text.
9 Milan Kundera, 'Un occident kidnappé ou la tragédie de l'Europe Centrale', *Le Débat* 27 (1983): 3–22.
10 Michelle Woods, *Translating Milan Kundera* (Clevedon: Multilingual Matters, 2006), 117.
11 Allison Stanger, 'In Search of *The Joke*: An Open Letter to Milan Kundera', *New England Review* 18 (1997): 96–7.
12 Stanisław Barańczak, *Breathing under Water and Other East European Essays* (Cambridge, MA and London: Harvard University Press, 1990), 236.
13 Søren Frank, *Migration and Literature* (New York: Palgrave Macmillan, 2008), 82.
14 Florence Uniacke, 'Doing it the French Way', *The Spectator*, 21 February 2013. http://blogs.spectator.co.uk/books/2013/02/doing-it-the-french-way/ [Accessed 2 January 2018]
15 Paul Ricœur, *Sur la traduction* (Paris: Bayard, 2004), 18. *On Translation*, trans. Eileen Brennan (London and New York: Routledge, 2006), 9. All translations of the French text come from this English translation. Page numbers in subsequent references refer to: French text; English text.
16 Ricœur, *Sur la traduction*, 17–18; 9.
17 Ricœur, *Sur la traduction*, 18; 9.
18 Emily Apter, *Against World Literature: On the Politics of Untranslatability* (London: Verso, 2013), 3–4.
19 Frank, *Migration*, 82.
20 Milan Kundera, *Le Rideau* (Paris: Éditions Gallimard, 2005), 194–5. *The Curtain*, trans. Linda Asher (New York: HarperCollins, 2006), 166–7. All translations of the French text come from this English translation. Page numbers in subsequent references refer to: French text; English text.
21 Milan Kundera, 'Author's Note', in *Nesmrtelnost* (Brno: Atlantis, 1993), 346. Trans. and quoted in Woods, *Translating Milan Kundera*, 25.
22 See Liisa Steinby, *Kundera and Modernity* (West Lafayette, IN: Purdue University Press, 2013), 3.
23 Milan Kundera, 'Quatre-vingt-neuf mots', *Le Débat* 37.5 (1985): 88.
24 Milan Kundera, *L'Art du roman*, 21; 6–7.
25 Kundera, *L'Art du roman*, 17–18; 7.
26 Steinby, *Kundera and Modernity*, 19.
27 Kundera, *L'Art du roman*, 143–4.
28 Woods, *Translating Milan Kundera*, 41.
29 Woods, *Translating Milan Kundera*, 27–41.
30 Woods, *Translating Milan Kundera*, 42.
31 Knoop, *Kundera*,142.
32 Lawrence Venuti, *The Scandals of Translation: Towards an Ethics of Translation* (New York and London: Routledge, 2002 [1998]), 5–6.

33 Steinby, *Kundera and Modernity*, 3.
34 Milan Kundera, 'Note de l'auteur', in *La Plaisanterie*, trans. Marcel Aymonin and Claude Courtot (Paris: Éditions Gallimard, 1985), 460. All translations from this text are mine.
35 Woods, *Translating Milan Kundera*, 42.
36 Woods, *Translating Milan Kundera*, 21.
37 Milan Kundera, *L'Insoutenable légèreté de l'être*, trans. François Kérel, rev. Milan Kundera (Paris: Éditions Gallimard, 1987), 132. *The Unbearable Lightness of Being*, trans. Michael Henry Heim, rev. Milan Kundera (London: Faber and Faber, 1995 [1984]), 84. All translations of the French text come from this English translation. Page numbers in subsequent references refer to: French text; English text.
38 Ricœur, *Sur la traduction*, 27; 14.
39 Milan Kundera, *L'Immortalité*, trans. Eva Bloch, rev. Milan Kundera (Paris: Gallimard, 1990), 52. *Immortality*, trans. Peter Kussi (London and Boston, MA: Faber and Faber, 1992 [1991]), 40. All translations of the French text come from this English translation. Page numbers in subsequent references refer to: French text; English text.
40 Kundera, *L'Immortalité*, 53; 41.
41 See Steinby, *Kundera and Modernity*, 184 for a further discussion of Kundera's depiction of gesture.
42 Knoop, *Kundera*, 142.
43 My translation.
44 Milan Kundera, *L'Art du roman*, 99–103. See Mikhail Bakhtin, 'Discourse in the Novel', in *The Dialogic Imagination*, trans. Caryl Emerson and Michael Holquist, ed. Michael Holquist (Austin: Texas University Press, 1984) for further discussion of dialogism and polyphony.
45 Kundera, *La Plaisanterie*, 460.
46 Kundera, *La Plaisanterie*, 459.
47 Kundera, *La Plaisanterie*, 462.
48 Rubeš, 'Translation as Condition and Theme in Milan Kundera's novels', in *Contexts, Subtexts and Pretexts: Literary Translation in Eastern Europe and Russia*, ed. Brian James Baer (Amsterdam and Philadelphia, PA: John Benjamins, 2011), 318–19.
49 Rubeš, *Contexts, Subtexts and Pretexts*, 318–19.
50 Fred Misurella, *Understanding Milan Kundera: Public Events, Private Affairs* (Columbia: University of South Carolina Press, 1993), 20.
51 Milan Kundera, 'Conversation in London and Connecticut with Milan Kundera', in *Shop Talk: A Writer and His Colleagues and Their Work*, by Philip Roth (London: Jonathan Cape, 2001), 98.
52 Kundera, in *Shop Talk*, 98.
53 Milan Kundera, *Le Livre du rire et de l'oubli*, trans. François Kérel, rev. Milan Kundera (Paris: Éditions Gallimard, 1985), 102. *The Book of Laughter and Forgetting*, trans. Aaron Asher (London: Faber and Faber, 1996), 87. All translations of the French text come from this English translation. Page numbers in subsequent references refer to: French text; English text.
54 Kundera, *L'Art du roman*, 104; 84.
55 Kundera, *Le Livre*, 186; 166.
56 Kundera, *Le Livre*, 186; 166.
57 Kundera, *Le Livre*, 188; 167.
58 Kundera, *Le Livre*, 186; 166.
59 Kundera, *Le Livre*, 225; 202.
60 Kundera, *Le Livre*, 188; 167–8.
61 Kundera, *Le Livre*, 225– 6; 202.
62 Kundera, *Le Livre*, 227–8; 204. Translation adapted from Asher's version to correct a mistranslation of the phrase 's'en vouloir' as 'to want'. See p. 156 for further discussion of this mistranslation.
63 George Steiner, *After Babel*, 3rd edn (Oxford: Oxford University Press, 1998), 1. 'Preface to Second Edition', in *After Babel*, xii; Kundera, *L'Insoutenable légèreté de l'être*, 132; 84.
64 Ricœur, *Sur la traduction*, 18, 20, 40; 9, 10, 22.
65 Richard Kearney, 'Paul Ricœur and the Hermeneutics of Translation', *Research in Phenomenology* 37 (2007): 147.
66 Kundera, *Le Livre*, 188; 168.
67 Kundera, *Le Livre*, 188; 167.
68 Ricœur, *Sur la traduction*, 17; 9.
69 Kundera, *Le Livre*, 230; 207.
70 Apter, *Against World Literature*, 3–4.

71 Kundera, *Le Livre*, 230–1; 207.
72 Kundera, *Le Livre*, 103–4; 89.
73 Kundera, *Le Livre*, 21–2; 11.
74 Ricœur, *Sur la traduction*, 18–19; 9–10.
75 Kundera, *Le Livre*, 21–2; 11.
76 Kundera, *Le Livre*, 230; 206.
77 Kundera, *Le Livre*, 231; 207
78 Kundera, *Le Livre*, 13–14; 3.
79 Hana Pichová, *Memory in Exile: Vladimir Nabokov & Milan Kundera* (Carbondale and Edwardsville: Southern Illinois University Press, 2002), 90.
80 Pichová, *Memory in Exile*, 90.
81 George Orwell, *1984* (London: Penguin, 2009 [1949]), 88–9.
82 Kundera, *Le Livre*, 13; 3.
83 Kundera, *Le Livre*, 14; 4.
84 Pichová, *Memory in Exile*, 102–3.
85 Steinby, *Kundera and Modernity*, 135.
86 Arthur Rimbaud, *Une saison en enfer* (Brussels: Alliance Typographique, 1873), 52.
87 Kundera, *L'Immortalité*, 212;156.
88 Kundera, *L'Insoutenable légèreté de l'être*, 362; 244.
89 Kundera, *L'Insoutenable légèreté de l'être*, 372; 249.
90 Kundera, *Le Livre*, 227; 204.
91 Kundera, *Le Livre*, 222; 199.
92 Steinby, *Kundera and Modernity*, 30.
93 Kundera, *Le Livre*, 229; 205.
94 Robert Frost, *The Letters of Robert Frost to Louis Untermeyer* (London: Jonathan Cape, 1964), 386.
95 Woods, *Translating Milan Kundera*, 65.
96 Woods, *Translating Milan Kundera*, 89.
97 Woods, *Translating Milan Kundera*, 91.
98 Kundera, in *Shop Talk*, 96.
99 Milan Kundera, *La Vie est ailleurs*, trans. Francois Kérel, rev. Milan Kundera (Paris: Gallimard, 1987 [1973]), 320. *Life is Elsewhere*, trans. Aaron Asher (London: Faber and Faber, 2000), 179–80. All translations of the French text come from this English translation. Page numbers in subsequent references refer to: French text; English text.
100 Plato, 'Theory of Art', in *The Republic*, trans. Desmond Lee, 2nd edn (Harmondsworth: Penguin, 1974), 425.
101 Kundera, *Le Livre*, 109; 93.
102 Kundera, in *Shop Talk*, 97.
103 Kundera, *Le Livre*, 235; 211.
104 Kundera, *Le Livre*, 110; 94–5.
105 Eva Le Grand, *Kundera or The Memory of Desire* trans. Lin Burman (Waterloo, ON: Wilfrid Laurier University Press, 1999), 26.
106 Wendy Faris, *Ordinary Enchantments: Magical Realism and the Remystification of Narrative* (Nashville, TN: Vanderbilt University Press, 2004), 58.
107 Steinby, *Kundera and Modernity*, 11.
108 Kundera, *L'Art du roman*, 190; 161.
109 Kundera, *L'Art du roman*, 25;14.
110 Jean-Paul Sartre, *Situations II: Qu'est-ce que la littérature* (Paris: Gallimard, 1948), 63; 70.
111 Sartre, *Situations*, 225.
112 Theodor Adorno,'Commitment' in *Literature in the Modern World*, trans. Francis McDonagh, ed. Dennis Walder (Oxford: Oxford University Press, 1990), 93.
113 Adorno, 'Commitment', 97.
114 Kundera, *Les Testaments trahis*, 260. from *Testaments Betrayed*, trans. Linda Asher (London and Boston, MA: Faber and Faber, 1995), 223. All translations of the French text come from this English translation. Page numbers in subsequent references refer to: French text; English text.
115 Kundera, *Les Testaments trahis*, 128–36.
116 Roman Jakobson, 'On Linguistic Aspects of Translation', in *The Translation Studies Reader*, ed. Lawrence Venuti, 2nd edn (New York and London: Routledge, 2009 [2004]), 143; Ricœur, *Sur la traduction*, 12; 6.
117 Kundera, *Le Livre*, 102; 84.

118 Kundera, *Le Livre*, 95; 81.
119 Kundera, *Le Livre*, 95; 81.
120 Kundera, *Le Livre*, 122; 106.
121 Kundera, *Le Livre*, 100; 86.
122 Kundera, *Le Livre*, 101; 86.
123 Steinby, *Kundera and Modernity*, 148, 12.
124 Kundera, in *Shop Talk*, 95.
125 Kundera, *Le Livre*, 101; 86.
126 Steinby, *Kundera and Modernity*, 105.
127 Kundera, *Le Livre*, 102; 87.
128 Apter, *Against World Literature*, 20.
129 Apter, *Against World Literature*, 20.
130 Kundera, *Le Livre*, 101–2; 87.
131 Timothy Mathews, *Alberto Giacometti: The Art of Relation* (London and New York: I. B. Tauris, 2014), 229.
132 Mathews, *Alberto Giacometti*, 30.
133 Ricœur, *Sur la traduction*, 29; 15.
134 Ricœur, *Sur la traduction*, 32; 17.
135 Ricœur, *Sur la traduction*, 27; 14.
136 Ricœur, *Sur la traduction*, 36–7; 19–20.
137 Ricœur, *Sur la traduction*, 39–40; 21–2.
138 'Equivalence' in Oxford Dictionaries. http://www.oxforddictionaries.com/definition/english/equivalence [Accessed 30 December 2017]
139 Ricœur, *Sur la traduction*, 63; 35.
140 Kundera, 'Quatre-vingt-neuf mots', 87. My translation. Woods, *Translating Milan Kundera*, 42.
141 Woods, *Translating Milan Kundera*, 42.
142 Kundera, *Les Testaments trahis*, 133; 110.
143 Kundera, *Les Testaments trahis*, 134; 110.
144 Kundera, *Les Testaments trahis*, 132–43; 110–20; see also Woods, *Translating Milan Kundera*, 43–4.
145 Kundera, 'Quatre-vingt-neuf mots', 87.
146 Kundera, *L'Insoutenable légèreté de l'être*, 149; 97–8.
147 Kundera, *L'Art du roman*, 145; 123.
148 Immanuel Kant, *Observations on the Feeling of the Beautiful and Sublime*, trans. John T. Goldthwait, 2nd edn (Oakland: University of California Press, 2004).
149 Kundera, *L'Art du roman*, 177; 123.
150 Kundera, *L'Art du roman*, 168; 130.
151 Steinby, *Kundera and Modernity*, 136.
152 Woods, *Translating Milan Kundera*, 42–43.
153 Milan Kundera, 'Author's Note', in *The Joke*, trans. Aaron Asher (London: Harper Collins, 1992), 323.
154 Woods, *Translating Milan Kundera*, 10.
155 Philip E. Lewis, 'The Measure of Translation Effects', in *Difference in Translation*, ed. Joseph F. Graham (Ithaca, NY and London: Cornell University Press, 1985), 31–62. Quoted in Woods, *Translating Milan Kundera*, 10.
156 Kundera, *La Plaisanterie*, 460.
157 Albert Camus, 'Le Mythe de Sisyphe', in *Œuvres complètes d'Albert Camus* (Paris: Gallimard et Club de l'Honnête Homme, 1983), 238; *The Myth of Sisyphus*, trans. Justin O'Brien (London: Penguin, 1975), 111.
158 Kundera, *Le Rideau*, 187; 180.
159 Normand Biron, 'Entretien avec Milan Kundera', *Liberté* 21.1 (1979), 17. Trans. and quoted in Woods, *Translating Milan Kundera*, 92.
160 Steinby, *Kundera and Modernity*, 138.
161 Kundera, *Le Livre*, 311, 326; 281, 295.
162 Kundera, *Le Livre*, 314; 284.
163 Gilles Deleuze, 'Platon et le simulacre', *Logique du sens* (Les Éditions de Minuit, Paris: 1969), 292–307. For discussion of the types of repetition in Kundera's work, and their relation to Plato and Deleuze, see also Eva Le Grand, 'Voyage dans le temps de l'Europe (ou de l'esthétique romanesque de Milan Kundera)', *L'Infini* 44 (1993): 91.

164 Kundera, *Le Livre*, 328; 298.

165 See Steinby, *Kundera and Modernity*, 138. See also Jørn Boisen, *Une fois ne compte pas: Nihilisme et sens dans L'Insoutenable légèreté de l'être de Milan Kundera* (Copenhagen: Museum Tusculanum Press, 2005), 29–30.

166 Woods, *Translating Milan Kundera*, 44; 102.

167 Milan Kundera, 'The Art of Fiction No. 81', interview by Christian Salmon, in *The Paris Review* 92 (1984). http://www.theparisreview.org/interviews/2977/the-art-of-fiction-no-81-milan-kundera [Accessed 9 January 2018]. (No page references for this text.)

168 Milan Kundera, *The Book of Laughter and Forgetting*, trans. Michael Henry Heim (Harmondsworth: Penguin, 1988 [1980], 122, 123, 121. Milan Kundera, *Le Livre*, 142. As quoted in Woods, *Translating Milan Kundera*, 110.

169 Kundera, 'Quatre-vingt-neuf mots', 87.

170 Venuti, *Translation Studies Reader*, 5.

171 Friedrich Schleiermacher, 'On the Different Methods of Translation', trans. Susan Bernofsky, in *The Translation Studies Reader*, 2nd edn, ed. Lawrence Venuti (London: Routledge, 2002), 49.

172 Woods, *Translating Milan Kundera*, 15.

173 Schleiermacher, 'On the Different Methods', 49.

174 Ricœur, *Sur la traduction*, 42–3; 23.

175 Woods, *Translating Milan Kundera*, 107.

176 Ricœur, *Sur la traduction*, 18; 9.

177 Gayatri Chakravorty Spivak, 'The Politics of Translation', in Venuti, *The Translation Studies Reader*, 372.

178 Milan Kundera, *Kniha smíchu a zapomnění* (1981 Toronto: Sixty-Eight Publishers, 1981), 128.

179 Jacques Derrida, 'Table ronde sur la traduction', in *L'Oreille de l'autre : otobiographies, transferts, traductions*, ed. Claude Lévesque and Christie V. McDonald (Montréal: VLB Éditeur Montréal 1982), 137. 'Roundtable on Translation', in *The Ear of the Other: Otobiography, Transference, Translation*, ed. Christie V. McDonald, trans. Peggy Kamuf (New York: Schocken Books 1985), 102.

180 Kundera, *Le Livre*, 228; 204.

181 Ricœur, *Sur la traduction*, 41–2; 23.

182 Ricœur, *Sur la traduction*, 20; 10.

183 Antoine Berman, *L'Épreuve de l'étranger. Culture et traduction dans l'Allemagne romantique* (Paris: Gallimard, collection 'Tel', 1984).

184 Ricœur, *Sur la traduction*, 52; 29.

185 Ricœur, *Sur la traduction*, 41; 21.

186 Kundera, *L'Art du roman*, 17–18; 7.

187 Kundera, *L'Art du roman*, 98; 79.

188 Ricœur, *Sur la traduction*, 20, 30; 10, 16.

189 Kundera, *Le Livre*, 327–8; 297.

190 Woods, *Translating Milan Kundera*, 174.

Chapter 3
Jorge Semprún's *Quel beau dimanche!*: a 'relevante' translation

Introduction: the struggle of translation

> 'Lutter, écrire, c'est ça ma vie'/'To struggle, to write, that is my life'
> – Jorge Semprún[1]

In the prelude to *Le Langage est ma patrie,* a series of interviews given to the cinematographer Franck Appréderis in 2010, Jorge Semprún summed up his personal moral approach in a French translation of a quotation from F. Scott Fitzgerald's *The Crack-Up*: 'Ainsi, il faudrait comprendre que les choses sont sans espoir et être pourtant décidé de les changer'/'One should, for example, be able to see that things are hopeless and yet be determined to make them otherwise'.[2] This phrase elucidates not only Semprún's moral perspective, but also the texture of the literary and political interrogations through which he develops this perspective in the text I explore predominantly in this chapter, *Quel beau dimanche!* (1980). Semprún's decision to draw upon an intertextual, translated phrase to embody his personal philosophy mirrors his fascination with literature as a site of liberation from the constraints of the monolingual, a fascination which permeates the narrative of *Quel beau dimanche!,* itself a web of intertextual quotations, language loans and translated phrases. Politically, Fitzgerald's comment offers Semprún 'la plus belle définition de la dialectique [...] pour reprendre ce concept déconsidéré, et même ruiné, par l'usage qu'en ont fait les staliniens'/'The most beautiful definition of the dialectic, to re-engage with that concept which was discredited, even ruined, by its Stalinist usage', and it is with the dangers and possibilities of the dialectic, and specifically the Stalinist interpretation of dialectical thinking, that *Quel beau dimanche!* is concerned.[3] Ethically, Fitzgerald's phrase 'sonne comme une morale individuelle de la résistance'/'resonates like an individual ethics of resistance', a resistance which confronts a flawed and hopeless situation, yet nonetheless seeks to interrogate, challenge and ultimately transform those flaws productively.[4] In *Quel beau dimanche!*, this challenge, this interrogation and/as transformation is both textual and political: the text confronts Semprún's painful disillusionment with the Spanish Communist Party (PCE) and with Soviet Communism more generally, and through a narrative which merges fiction and autobiography, the political and the personal, the past and the present, transforms this disillusionment into a powerful call for political responsibility. While Semprún claims that '[l]utter, écrire, c'est ça ma vie', this quotation could then be rephrased: for Semprún, lutter, *c'est* écrire; écrire, *c'est* lutter/to struggle *is* to write; to write *is* to struggle.

In this chapter, I explore Semprún's writing-as-struggle through the multilingual interrogation of personal and political memory and loss he pursues in his texts. The content of this struggle of, for, and with memory is both individual and collective: it is Semprún's struggle to confront and interrogate the losses which permeate his memories of Buchenwald and of Communism, and to critique and challenge the discourses which enabled those losses to be forgotten or erased. Semprún's criticism of the Stalinist use of the dialectic is concerned with the ways in which he believes this use enabled such erasures; he reads the dialectic as a uniquely dangerous rhetorical rewriting of history, which translates the past into new forms according to the demands of the present. But Semprún's narrative is itself a translation – an attempted transfer of past into present, of memory into narrative, of politics into fiction. As Ofelia Ferrán and Gina Herrmann note, 'Semprún continually theorises about the possibility, or impossibility, of translating his life into words'.[5] Like all translations, this exchange reveals ethical dilemmas and ethical opportunities, staging both the erasures and the illuminations inherent within the appropriative impulse to write, and write about, history.

Drawing on Derrida's discussion of what constitutes a 'good' translation in his essay 'Qu'est-ce qu'une traduction "relevante"?', I explore the ethics of translation as an interlingual, intralingual and intersemiotic mode of engaging with, interrogating and rewriting the past. Derrida's essay makes a pertinent comparison between the impulse behind dialectical thinking and the impulse behind translation itself. In this process of comparison, translation is revealed to contain its own dangerous forms of forgetting. But translation also allows us to illuminate the past, as Semprún demonstrates in three different temporal and linguistic translations of the Buchenwald camp motto *Jedem das Seine*, which allow him to interrogate the complexity of the political history through which he lived.

As Ursula Tidd suggests, in Semprún's work, 'ethics becomes co-extensive with aesthetics', and the question which translation raises in Semprún's work is always both an aesthetic and an ethical one.[6] How much responsibility can we take for our inevitable forgetting of the past, and what aesthetic and ethical contribution can writing, thinking and translating make towards helping us recognize this responsibility? In this chapter, I argue that translation involves a transformative engagement with a complex and fragmented past, which in *Quel beau dimanche!* gives a voice to those silenced or erased by the political power of Communism and Nazism.

Semprún: writing between identities

Writing and life

Semprún's biography straddles the political and the literary. Born in Madrid in 1923, Semprún moved to France with his family at the age of 14 to escape possible persecution at the hands of Franco's Nationalist faction during the Spanish Civil War. He joined the French Resistance in 1941, but was captured by the Gestapo while fighting with the *Maquis*, and in September 1943 he was sent to Buchenwald concentration camp, where he remained until April 1945. After liberation, Semprún began working clandestinely for the PCE, using a variety of pseudonyms, until just after the publication of his first work of autobiographical fiction, *Le Grand Voyage*, in 1963. Until the appearance of this text, writing played second fiddle to Semprún's political activities. In *Federico Sánchez vous salue bien* (1993), Semprún explains this decision, commenting that 'J'ai choisi du même élan l'illusion d'un avenir, par le moyen de l'engagement politique, puisque l'engagement dans l'écriture me ramenait à l'enfermement de la mémoire et de la mort'/'I chose the illusion of a future through political commitment, since a commitment to writing enclosed me in memory and death'.[7]

Here, as in his evocatively entitled 1994 text *L'Écriture ou la vie*, Semprún positions the desire to write as the converse rather than the complement of the desire to live. This mutual exclusivity, this writing *or* life, is born of a crucial interaction Semprún perceives between the process of writing and the exploration of memory: writing, he suggests, both requires and enables the writer to engage in a powerful confrontation with his or her memories. For Semprún, this confrontation can be productive and cathartic; equally, however, it can be suffocating, imprisoning the writer in a traumatic and endlessly repeated past.[8] In an interview with *The Paris Review,* he suggests that his initial refusal to attempt a literary reimagining of his memories of Buchenwald hinged upon his fear of being re-incarcerated, through writing, in the camp experience: 'I just knew I could neither relive that experience nor survive it if I worked on the memoir at that time [...]. For me, remembering would have meant death with absolute certainty, suicide that is, and I was very much aware of it.'[9] Semprún's decision to turn to politics rather than literature following his release from the camp arose from his need to survive rather than remember the experience of Buchenwald, a survival which he suggests could only be realized through a separation, and, ultimately substitution, of his political for his authorial identity.

This separation did not dissolve until 16 years after his release, when Semprún finally began writing about his experiences. In *Le Grand Voyage* Semprún confronted the memory of Buchenwald, and through a text which fragments linear chronology and the boundaries of fiction and autobiography, found a way of combining writing *and* life. Writing and politics, however, were not so complementary, for less than a year later, Semprún was expelled from the PCE for anti-political activities. In a detailed discussion of the relationship between translation and memory in Semprún's work, Bella Brodzki suggests that this moment marked the beginning of an enforced segregation of politics and literature, two modes of engaging with the world which had previously been interconnected in Semprún's experience.[10] Yet this segregation ultimately proved liberating, for Semprún had already been experiencing political doubts about the direction of the PCE and the future of Communism more generally. As he comments in 'The Art of Fiction',

> the day came when that contradiction became intolerable, when I refused to perform self-censorship and was thus definitively expelled from the Communist Party. I would put it this way: I didn't choose to become a writer, but I did choose to quit being a man of action. And that opened up the possibility of becoming a writer.[11]

In a reversal of priorities, writing enabled Semprún to survive the fall-out of his political exile: without writing, he suggests, he would have 'disintegrated emotionally' following his expulsion from the Party.[12]

Following this expulsion Semprún began to write prolifically, and by the time of his death in 2011 he had produced more than 30 books, embracing a range of genres from fiction to memoir, screenplays to essays. Semprún's shift from clandestine activist to visible writer was by no means the end of his political engagement, however, for his texts frequently explore political issues: *Autobiografía de Federico Sánchez* (1977) explores the world of the PCE in the post-war period; *Netchaïev est de retour* (1987) turns to the world of extremist left-wing politics, commenting upon the lives and betrayals of a group of ex-anarchists in the 1980s; *Mal et modernité* (1995) is a series of essays interrogating the political history of Europe in the twentieth century. Such texts provide a literary avenue through which Semprún poses increasingly direct questions about the nature of political responsibility, the dangers of political abstraction, and the collective and individual guilt inherent within political decision-making. Simultaneously, Semprún continued to explore the potent memory of Buchenwald which he had begun to negotiate in *Le Grand Voyage* and its 'sequel' *L'Évanouissement* (1967). In *Quel beau dimanche!* (1980), a single Sunday in Buchenwald provides the framework for Semprún to interrogate the historical and political complexity of the camp. *L'Écriture ou la vie* (1994) focuses predominantly on the narrator's life after the liberation of the camp, exploring the narrator's sense that he is still imprisoned, in thought, feeling, and memory, in the camp experiences. It is this affective proximity to Buchenwald which simultaneously hinders the narrator's attempts to recount his camp experiences and compels him to attempt to do so nonetheless. *Le Mort qu'il faut* (2001) returns to the camp in 1944 to explore the 'necessary death' of another man, by means of which the narrator hopes to ensure his own survival. Even those texts which are not set in Buchenwald are infiltrated by its memory: in *La Montagne blanche* (1986), the story of three intellectuals who spend a weekend together in Normandy during the 1980s, the protagonist, Juan Larréa, is an ex-detainee whose memories of the camp haunt both the text and his own present-day life, culminating in his suicide.

Language and identity

Semprún wrote *Le Grand Voyage* in French, his second language, and French remained his literary language of choice. Of the books he published between 1963 and 2011, only three were written in Spanish: *Autobiografía de Federico Sánchez, Federico Sánchez se despide de ustedes* (1993) and *Veinte años y un día* (2003). Semprún's decision to write primarily in French has garnered a great deal of critical attention. Myriam Schleiss focuses upon Semprún's bilingual identity, arguing that his linguistic choices reflect the different elements of his experience: German, his third language, is the language of the camps; Spanish is the language of childhood; while French represents the language of writing, and of adult desire.[13] In a similar vein, Ursula Tidd suggests that Semprún's choice of French reflects a desire for distance from the pain of exile and from the writings of his father, as well as revealing, more simply, the impact of Spanish political censorship.[14] Tijana Miletic suggests that Semprún's choice of language reflects an internal division within both the actual and the affective content of the memories he is seeking to relate. Miletic describes Semprún's political experiences as 'passionate, but nevertheless impersonal', and suggests that it was 'emotionally safe' for him to voice these through his mother tongue. By contrast, she believes that the trauma of his experiences in Buchenwald requires the emotional distance offered by his second language, French.[15] For all three critics, then, the Spanish and French texts can be distinguished not only linguistically but thematically and emotionally, with Semprún's bilingualism reflecting, and indeed enabling, a schism within the textual narration of his past.

To categorize or separate Semprún's texts by language and experience only, however, obscures one of their central elements: the continuous *merging* of experiences, languages and identities. Biographically, Semprún's political persona and his concentration camp experiences are integrally related: his activities for the French Resistance occasioned his imprisonment in Buchenwald, while his experiences at Buchenwald were governed by his membership of the Communist Party, which ran the internal administration within the camp. Semprún's Buchenwald texts, from *Le Grand Voyage* to *Le Mort qu'il faut,* reflect this commingling of political activity and camp experiences: in *Quel beau dimanche!* this relationship is the cornerstone of the text, which segues repeatedly from the narrator's experiences within Buchenwald to his growing political disillusionment after his release. Indeed, the idea that Semprún's political experiences were 'emotionally safe', as Miletic suggests, is profoundly challenged, as the text focuses upon the traumatic effect of the narrator's disenchantment with the PCE.

If the experiences Semprún relates in his texts are not easily segregated, his linguistic choices are no more so. Semprún himself provided multiple reasons – simultaneously pragmatic, personal and political – for his initial decision to write in French, suggesting that it was impelled by his love of the French language, his distance – physical, political and linguistic – from Spain at the time of his capture by the Gestapo, and the censorship imposed by Franco upon the Spanish literary scene until his death in 1975.[16] Semprún's decision to write three texts in Spanish was equally pragmatic: following Franco's death, Semprún was reintegrated into Spain in both a literary and a political sense, becoming

Minister of Culture for the new Socialist government in 1988 and also gaining access to the Spanish readership from which he had previously been isolated. Writing in Spanish thus enabled him to redevelop an element of his linguistic identity which had become segregated from his literary persona:

> I had already published many books in French and was thus in a rather bizarre situation in Spain, where I am considered a Spanish writer who writes in French! The whole thing is either comic, tragic, or just plain silly, depending on your point of view, since technically I am a Spanish writer whose works are translated into Spanish.[17]

This 'technically', however, masks critical questions about the relationship between authorial identity and nationality, between mother tongue and chosen tongue. Is Semprún a Spanish writer simply because he was born in Spain? Is the language he was born with more fundamental to his authorial identity than the language of his texts?

In *L'Écriture ou la vie*, Semprún interrogates the relationship between language and identity, suggesting that his choice of French was in fact more emotional than pragmatic: 'Pour ma part, j'avais choisi le français, langue de l'exil, comme une autre langue maternelle, originaire. Je m'étais choisi de nouvelles origines'/'For my part, I'd chosen French, the language of exile, as another mother tongue. I'd chosen a new nationality for myself'.[18] In this suggestive quotation, national identity becomes fluid, and mother tongue becomes a choice. 'J'avais fait de l'exil une patrie'/'I'd made exile into a homeland' he states, and this contradiction in terms, this homeland-as-exile, explains Semprún's decision to position French, the language which welcomed him following his teenage departure from Spain, as the language of this new and unbounded territory.[19] Yet even this twin mother tongue cannot fully account for the experience of exile, which for Semprún is multiple, formed not only by his initial exile to France, but also by his subsequent exile to a space delimited more by ideological than national boundaries: Buchenwald. Buchenwald is another origin, another homeland, one imposed rather than chosen, but no less fundamental to Semprún's perception of his identity. In *Le Langage est ma patrie,* he relates an anecdote which sums up this perception: 'Et à la question aimable et un peu insolente à la fois [...] «Finalement, tu es quoi, toi? Espagnol? Français? Un homme politique? Un écrivain?» j'ai répondu comme ça, brusquement, sans y réfléchir: «Je suis avant tout un ancien déporté de Buchenwald.»'/'And to the question, amiable and a little insolent at the same time, "Who are you, in fact? Spanish? French? A politician? A writer?", I answered like this, brusquely, without thinking: "I am above all a former detainee of Buchenwald".[20] Such a response, he suggests, was both biographically false and existentially true:

> Je suis évidemment espagnol, français, écrivain et homme politique – et déporté de Buchenwald. Je suis tout cela à la fois. Mais j'ai fait un choix à ce moment-là, pour dire que l'expérience du camp à vingt ans est à la fois politique, existentielle, personnelle, historique, générale, et qu'elle m'a définitivement marqué, [...] je rapporte moi-même tout à mon expérience de déporté. C'est en ce sens que cette expérience est fondatrice.
>
> I am evidently Spanish, French, writer and politician – and a detainee of Buchenwald. I am all these things at once. But I made a choice in that moment to say that the experience of the camp at the age of twenty was political, existential, personal, historical, general, and it marked me definitively [...]. I relate everything to my experience as a detainee. It is in that sense that the experience is fundamental.[21]

For Semprún, Buchenwald represents the centre of meaning, and the centre of meaning's loss, in relation to the disparate strands of his identity – linguistic, national, political, literary: a site where language and understanding were disrupted and brought to coalesce in new forms.[22]

In *Quel beau dimanche!*, the narrator states that '[l]a confusion des langues est l'une des premières expériences de l'exil. La nuit sans sommeil de l'exil est une nuit babélique'/'The confusion of tongues is one of the first experiences of exile. The sleepless night of exile is a night of Babel', and in Buchenwald Semprún experienced this Babelic night, living within a mixture of French, German, English, Russian and Spanish which formed the soundscape of his imprisonment.[23] This linguistic mixture infiltrates Semprún's return to the memory of Buchenwald within his texts: while these narratives are primarily written in French, this second mother tongue is fragmented, and the memories which Semprún relates are frequently generated by the evocative etymological connotations of a single word in Spanish, German or English. It is in this context that Semprún's oft-quoted comment 'ma patrie, c'est Le langage'/'my homeland is language' can be understood.[24] For if Semprún perceives his home to be *Le langage* rather than *une langue,* a global system of communication rather than a specific, nationally determined example of such a system, this home is built, textually, at the interstices of several different languages that are woven into a linguistic patchwork. While this linguistic diversity mirrors the Babelic confusion within the experience of Buchenwald itself, it simultaneously constructs the narrative through which this experience can be narrated.

The losses and gains, destructions and constructions, confusions and elucidations enacted by language are central themes within all Semprún's texts: as Gina Herrmann suggests, 'for Semprún, language is both vehicle and destroyer of hope'.[25] For Semprún, a single word or phrase can spark a painful return to the traumatic memories of Buchenwald. Yet it is also through language and narrative that Semprún submits that these memories can best be explored. In *Quel beau dimanche!*, the narrator demands:

> A-t-on vraiment vécu quelque chose dont on n'arrive pas à faire le récit, à reconstruire significativement la vérité même minime – en la rendant ainsi communicable? [...] Mais peut-on prendre en charge quelque expérience que ce soit sans en maîtriser plus ou moins le langage? C'est-à-dire l'histoire, les histoires, les récits, les mémoires, les témoignages: la vie? Le texte, la texture même, le tissu de la vie?
>
> Has one really experienced something that one is unable to describe, something whose minimum truth one is unable to reconstruct in a meaningful way – and so make communicable? [...] But can one assume any experience without more or less mastering its language? The history – the stories, the narratives, the memories, the eyewitness accounts in which it survives – lives on. The text, the very texture, the tissue of life.[26]

In this powerful assertion of the importance of narrative, the texture and the text of life become integrally connected: one narrates not only to relate a memory but also to relive that memory anew. Whether this connection between writing and living can be achieved, whether memory can be confronted and relived through narrative, or whether it remains continually beyond the grasp of our attempts at aesthetic expression, beyond even our ability to remember what it is we wish to express, is the question at the heart of Semprún's aesthetics.

In positing here that it is through linguistic representation, that is, through artifice and recreation, that his memories of Buchenwald can best be articulated, Semprún diverges from survivor narratives which highlight the impossibility of representing the camp experience in language. E. van Alphen suggests that a failure of the representational possibilities contained within the symbolic order is a crucial part of the difficulty camp survivors find in articulating their experiences.[27] For Romanian author Elie Wiesel, a detainee of both Auschwitz and Buchenwald, only an entirely new language would begin to allow him to narrate his experience of the camps: 'La parole a déserté le sens qu'elle était censée recouvrir. [...] Jamais nous n'exprimerions en paroles cohérentes, intelligibles, notre expérience de la folie absolue. [...] Les mots me paraissaient usagés, bêtes, inadéquats, maquillés, anémiques, je les désirais brûlants. Où dénicher un vocabulaire inédit, un langage premier?'/'The word has deserted the meaning it was intended to convey. [...] We could never express in words, coherent, intelligible words, our experience of madness on an absolute scale. [...] All words seemed inadequate, worn, foolish, lifeless, whereas I wanted them to be searing. Where was I to discover a fresh vocabulary, a primeval language?'[28]

The 'langage premier' sought by Wiesel is not a pre-Babelic utopian language, but a truly original language, one that would be capable of expressing a world rendered incomprehensible by the camps. For Semprún, however, this vocabulary is already present within our existing linguistic structures. The narrator of *L'Écriture ou la vie* asserts that 'L'ineffable dont on nous rebattra les oreilles n'est qu'alibi. Ou signe de paresse. On peut toujours tout dire, le langage contient tout [...] On peut tout dire de cette expérience. Il suffit d'y penser. Et de s'y mettre.'/'The "ineffable" you hear so much about is only an alibi. Or a sign of laziness. You can always say everything: language contains everything. [...] You can tell all about this experience. You have merely to think about it. And set to it.'[29] The somewhat dogmatic tone of the narrator's assertion highlights Semprún's conviction, repeated throughout his texts, that it is *through*, rather than *despite*, narrative and language that he can return to the experience of the camps.

This rejection of the ineffability claim is not, however, an assertion that the traumatic experience of Buchenwald can emerge intact when translated into a narrative form. Rather it is, for Semprún, a recognition that to seek to translate that experience into narrative is part of an endless but ever-changing attempt to negotiate that trauma. As Ursula Tidd has discussed, Semprún's attempted representation of his traumatic experiences is a 'halting journey', one characterized by an attempted repetition of an experience which may always, necessarily, exceed or disturb familiar forms.[30] In a sense, the possibility or impossibility of narrating the experience of Buchenwald is an aside: like every translation, this translation of a traumatic experience into narrative form is always both possible and impossible, always a task to be undertaken in the acknowledgement that it will fail. But it is in the ways in which that imperfect translation occurs, in the attempt to 'tell all' and in the partial nature of that telling, that Semprún reads the value of narrative. The critical point, as the narrator of *L'Écriture ou la vie* suggests, is not whether he can narrate, but the form that narration must take, not *if* but *how*.

The plurality of language within Semprún's texts can be read as part of an attempt to respond to this 'how', through a form of writing permeated with translation. As both Schleiss and Tidd suggest, by narrating and re-narrating, translating and re-translating the same words, sentences and texts, Semprún multiplies the methods of representation available to him for the narration of his memories.[31] Kippur describes how a text by Semprún, ostensibly written in French, will contain whole paragraphs or pages in Spanish, German or English, which Semprún will attempt to translate back into French, glossing and commenting as he does so on the difficulties of the translation in question.[32] This multiple endeavour – writing, translating, glossing, criticism – enables Semprún to account, albeit partially, for the split between lived event and textual representation. By explaining the challenges involved in these particular instances of linguistic translation, Semprún focuses upon the absences, elisions and fragmentations inherent within attempts to render one passage in multiple languages; simultaneously, he confronts the absences, elisions and fragmentations inherent within his attempt to represent, through language, his experience of Buchenwald. For Tidd, this linguistic fragmentation allows Semprún to construct an ethical response to the experience of Buchenwald: 'Bilingualism and intertextuality will be two techniques inter alia deployed by Semprún to write against the disaster by structuring a compassionate relationship to alterity in the re-establishment of culture and civility'.[33] This 'compassionate' poetics, like Kundera's hospitable poetics of the novel, develops through a plurality of voices and languages which piece together the shards of the past until we perceive, between the cracks, the contours of the camp experience.[34]

But are we, as readers, capable of such a perception? The question of reception is, for Semprún, as crucial as that of narration; while the experience of the camps can be expressed in language, it does not follow that it can be understood through language, for the limitations of written memory are those of comprehension as much as of construction. In *L'Écriture ou la vie,* the narrator queries the possibility of exceeding these conceptual limitations: 'Mais peut-on tout entendre, tout imaginer? Le pourra-t-on? En auront-ils la patience, la passion, la compassion, la rigueur nécessaires?'/'But can people hear everything, imagine everything? Will they be able to understand? Will they have the necessary patience, passion, compassion, and fortitude?'[35] The possibility that understanding will not be attained hinges, in part, upon the nature of the experience to be narrated. As Brodzki notes: 'Semprún's point is precisely that although language has the capacity to record, report, or even reimagine what transpired in the crematorium, physical, even temporal proximity will not bring anyone closer to the event, which is experientially untranslatable on any level, from any remove.'[36] But if the events Semprún seeks to narrate are untranslatable, this is due not only to the nature of those events, but also to the inevitable collapse – a failure of translation – which occurs between narration and understanding. This collapse is dramatized by the experiential untranslatability of the camp, but as I discussed in Chapter 2, it also operates, on some level, within every attempted translation between speaking and hearing, writing and reading, creation and reception, and within the very essence of communication itself.

Brodzki describes Semprún as 'an inveterate translator, the ultimate infiltrator', and these designations reveal the integral connection between Semprún's narrative approach and the practice and theory of translation: translation permeates his narratives through his use of language loans and translated intertexts, and it also figures the possibilities and limitations of narrative communication which are at the heart of his aesthetic ethics.[37] As Tidd suggests, 'through this personally formulated language he offers an original approach to the task of Holocaust representation and remembrance in the broader European context'.[38] Yet despite this identification – both aesthetic and ethical – with translation, Semprún only self-translated one of his texts, *Federico Sánchez se despide de ustedes/Federico Sanchez vous salue bien* (1993).[39] Instead, he asked others to recreate his work in French or Spanish as required, although, like Kundera, he has acknowledged the difficulties inherent within this process, suggesting that he always finds it painful to read translations of his texts into Spanish because he knows he would have written the Spanish text differently himself.[40] Given this admission, Semprún's refusal to self-translate seems all the more surprising.

In *The Paris Review*, Semprún offered an explanation for this refusal: describing a conversation he had with the Mexican writer Carlos Fuentes regarding the question, Semprún suggests that 'it would have felt strained, and quite insane in a sense, like writing the same book twice'.[41] Semprún's comment implies rejection of both translation and repetition as valuable literary methods, yet this anecdote is itself a repetition, for Semprún had already narrated this conversation with Fuentes in *L'Écriture ou la vie*. And this version offers a different perspective, one which highlights the role of translation as an integral part of both the writing and the resistance which characterized Semprún's life.

In 1964, *Le Grand Voyage* had just won the Formentor Prize, a literary prize that, at that time, rewarded the winner by having the winning book translated into twelve other languages. Having been presented with eleven translations of his text, Semprún awaits the presentation of the Spanish version. But what arrives is not what he anticipates, for Franco's censors have prohibited the publication of his text in Spain. In order to present the text to the author, a single example of the Spanish version has been created. 'Le format, le cartonnage, le nombre de pages, la jaquette illustrée. […] À un détail près: les pages de mon exemplaire d'aujourd'hui sont blanches, vierges de tout signe d'imprimerie'/'The format, binding, number of pages, jacket illustration […]. Except for one detail: the pages of my presentation copy are blank, without a single printed character'.[42] In this scene, political censorship is enabled by a lack of translation, and a textual simulacrum stands in for an absent text. Symbolically, the missing text is the one written in Spanish; political repression enacts a literal silencing of Semprún's mother tongue. But this silence cannot be absolute precisely because the censored text is a translation, a fragment of a larger text which continues to speak, first in French and then in eleven other languages. It is, paradoxically, the process of translation which both allows for the possibility of such censorship and resists its completion.

It is this resistance to the possibility of textual completion which Fuentes, in Semprún's narration, suggests is the inherent potential of self-translation:

> – D'ailleurs, ajoutait-il, tu aurais dû faire toi-même la version espagnole. Tu n'aurais pas simplement traduit, tu aurais pu te permettre de te trahir. De trahir ton texte originaire pour essayer d'aller plus loin. Du coup, un livre différent aurait surgi, dont tu aurais pu faire une nouvelle version française, un nouveau livre! […] Ainsi […] tu aurais réalisé le rêve de tout écrivain: passer sa vie à écrire un seul livre, sans cesse renouvelé.
>
> Anyway, you should have done the Spanish version yourself. You wouldn't have simply translated, you'd have been able to [betray yourself]. To [betray] your original text, to try to go further with it. This would have created a different book, which you could have turned into a new French version, a whole new book! […] And so […] you will have realized every writer's dream: to spend your life writing a single book, endlessly renewed![43]

Fuentes's comment highlights two of the elements of translation which I discussed in Chapters 1 and 2. As I explored in Chapter 1 through the work of Deleuze and Atxaga, translation can operate as a process of repetition with difference, a form of recreating anew. At the same time, as I discussed in Chapter 2, translation offers a transformative betrayal of textual authority, originality and finality. But Fuentes's comment also elucidates Semprún's unique relationship to translation. For 'un seul livre, sans cesse renouvelé' could be the caption to Semprún's œuvre: while Semprún did not translate *Le Grand Voyage* interlingually, his texts are engaged in a constant intralingual translation, an endless return to and rewriting of the experiences and memories articulated within that first text. In each re-telling, those memories are transformed, not through their translation into another national language, but through their translation across time, re-emerging in each of Semprún's texts in different forms and with different affective and aesthetic resonances. In this temporal translation, Semprún's memories are re-envisioned through a narrative form which confronts the distortions, losses and transformations involved in every attempt to narrate the past.

Through its very absence, the Spanish version of *Le Grand Voyage* thus becomes a symbol for the powerful and endless renewal and growth of Semprún's literary voice: 'De tous les exemplaires du *Grand voyage* que j'avais déjà reçus ce soir-là, que je recevrais encore, l'espagnol était le plus beau. [...] J'en aime l'augure et le symbole: que ce livre soit encore à écrire, que cette tâche soit infinie, cette parole inépuisable'/'Of all the copies of *Le Grand Voyage* that I've been given so far this evening, and that I will yet receive, the Spanish copy is the most beautiful. [...] I love the promise and the symbolism of it: that this book yet remains to be written, that the task is infinite, [this word inexhaustible]'.[44] This infinite task, this inexhaustible language, this endless urge to rewrite, is the texture of Semprún's work. While such rewritings are visible throughout Semprún's texts, in *Quel beau dimanche!* Semprún directly acknowledges the importance of this task, returning to the symbolically blank space of *Le Grand Voyage* with a text which is both a repetition and a translation of that first text; a text which both betrays *Le Grand Voyage* – betrays its certainty, its authority and its finality – and, simultaneously, reveals through forms of writing-as-translation the political betrayal which lies beneath the memories related in its pages.

Quel beau dimanche!: a narrative of loss

Quel beau dimanche! begins with an epigram taken from Milan Kundera's *Le Livre du rire et de l'oubli*: 'La lutte de l'homme contre le pouvoir est la lutte de la mémoire contre l'oubli'/'The struggle of man against power is the struggle of memory against forgetting'; and like *Le Livre*, the text is concerned with questions of memory and forgetting.[45] The novel is ostensibly concerned with describing one Sunday in December in the Buchenwald camp, a Sunday experienced by a narrator who, as always in Semprún's texts, walks the narrow path between fictional and autobiographical characterization. Yet for Semprún, the textual coherence of time and space, like the coherence of genre, is fluid: the narrative of *Quel beau dimanche!* shifts between the narrator's memories of Buchenwald and those of his post-war experiences as a clandestine member of the PCE. While these two experiences are separated spatially, temporally and even politically, they are fundamentally connected on an emotional level, as part of what Brodzki describes as the 'larger narrative of personal and political loss' which characterizes Semprún's work.[46] In *Quel beau dimanche!*, Semprún draws the contours of this loss, moving back and forth in time between the narrator's early, unequivocal faith in Communism and his growing sense of disillusionment with the Party. This disillusionment is prompted by the brutal reality of the Soviet concentration camps, a reality which the narrator is no longer able to ignore or justify through his faith in the overarching aims of Communism. Forced to acknowledge that 'le système politique post-stalinien n'était pas réformable. Le pays du Goulag ne deviendrait jamais celui du socialisme'/'the post-Stalinist political system was not reformable. The country of the Gulag would never become that of socialism', the narrator confronts the collapse of his defining belief-system.[47]

The breakdown of the narrator's allegiance to Communism bridges the gap between fiction and autobiography, mirroring the experience Brodzki refers to as 'emblematic' for Semprún himself: 'Not ideal loss, but the actual loss of an ideal'.[48] In *Quel beau dimanche!* Semprún explores the profound effect of this loss upon the narrator's (and implicitly his own) writing experience, reflecting particularly upon the impact his political disillusionment had upon the validity of the narrative of *Le Grand Voyage*. For despite the lack of overt political discussion within *Le Grand Voyage*, Semprún suggests that this narrative took shape within the framework of his Communist faith; the subsequent collapse of that faith, he submits, fundamentally undermined not only this framework but also the legitimacy of the text itself:

> Toute la vérité de mon témoignage avait pour référence implicite, mais contraignante, l'horizon d'une société désaliénée: une société sans classes où les camps eussent été inconcevables. [...] Mais l'horizon du communisme n'était pas celui de la société sans classes, je veux dire: son horizon réel, historique. L'horizon du

communisme, incontournable, était celui du Goulag. Du coup, toute la vérité de mon livre devenait mensongère.

The very truth of my account had as its implicit but constricting reference the horizon of a disalienated society: a society without classes in which the camps would have been inconceivable. [...] But the horizon of Communism – its real, historical horizon – was not that of a classless society. The horizon of Communism was, inescapably, that of the Gulag. By the same token, the very truth of my book became a lie.[49]

Irrespective of whether he was aware of the existence of the gulags at the time he wrote *Le Grand Voyage*, Semprún perceives himself to have been complicit in a lie or at least an omission of the truth. In an excerpt from a debate he participated in for the socialist movement *Clarté,* quoted in *Quel beau dimanche!,* he argues that one cannot justify anything by claiming ignorance: 'Il y a toujours le moyen de savoir, ou tout au moins de *mettre en question*. [...] Même ignorants, d'ailleurs, réellement ignorants, nous sommes coresponsables, car ce passé est le nôtre et nul ne pourra plus le changer.'/'There are always ways and means of knowing, or at least of *questioning*. [...] Even if we were ignorant, really ignorant, we would still be co-responsible, for that past is our past, and no one can change it.'[50] As Semprún's texts frequently assert, the past is frequently, indeed inevitably, changed by its translation into the present. Indeed, a failure by the Party to address – as opposed to transform – its history is at the heart of the critique Semprún levels at the political uses of dialectical thinking. Yet, on a personal level, Semprún believes that to have written *Le Grand Voyage* while ignorant, intentionally or otherwise, of the existence of the gulags is to be guilty of a failure to take responsibility for the effects of his Communist past.

But how can we assume the effects of a past which we can never grasp absolutely? How, in such circumstances, are we to take responsibility? It is this paradox which Semprún will '*mettre en question*' in *Quel beau dimanche!*, *L'Écriture ou la vie* and beyond. In *Quel beau dimanche!* the narrator suggests that the best form through which to engage in such questioning is a textual one, through which he seeks to 'détruire cette innocence de la mémoire'/'destroy that innocence of the memory': 'Je savais qu'il me faudrait revivre mon expérience de Buchenwald, heure par heure, avec la certitude désespérée de l'existence simultanée des camps russes, du Goulag de Staline. Je savais aussi que la seule façon de revivre cette expérience était de la réécrire, en connaissance de cause, cette fois-ci.'/'I knew that I would have to relive my experience of Buchenwald, hour by hour, with the desperate certainty of the simultaneous existence of the Russian camps, of Stalin's Gulag. I also knew that the only way of reliving that experience was to rewrite it, with full knowledge this time.'[51]

Quel beau dimanche! is the product of this desire to destroy the innocence of memory, a textual reliving of Buchenwald, hour by hour, 'en connaissance de cause'. This developing knowledge, so crucially absent in *Le Grand Voyage*, is highlighted by a chronology which interleaves the hours of this single Sunday with temporal strata from the past and the future; the disturbance enacted by Semprún's realization of the existence of the gulags is reflected by a similarly disrupted retelling of that experience. This distorted chronology is accompanied by what Kippur describes as Semprún's characteristic 'multilingual aesthetics' – his use of language loans, of glossed translations and of a network of translated intertextual quotations – which creates a tissue of languages and texts through which the political, historical and literary losses with which *Quel beau dimanche!* is concerned are explored and interrogated.[52]

Zero hour

Chapitre Zéro begins with the narrator standing in the snow outside the Buchenwald camp, one Sunday in December. Gazing meditatively across the white, empty landscape, he finds his attention drawn to a solitary tree: 'Un arbre, c'est tout, dans sa splendeur immédiate, dans l'immobilité transparente du présent'/'A tree, just that, in its immediate splendour, in the transparent stillness of the present'.[53] Contemplating this instant of natural beauty, frozen – physically and temporally – beneath the snow, the narrator imagines the return of spring, a return as distant and immediate, as impossible and inevitable, as his own death: 'Décembre, combien de mois à attendre? Il serait mort, lui, peut-être. Le bourgeon éclaterait, portant à son terme la vérité profonde de l'hiver. Et il serait mort [...]. Il serait absent, parti en fumée, et le bourgeon éclaterait'/'December; how many more months to wait? He himself might be dead by then. The bud would burst, bringing to an end the profound truth of winter. And he would be dead. [...] He would be absent, gone off in a puff of smoke, and the bud would burst'.[54] Within the beauty of the scene before him, the narrator perceives the shadow of death; beneath the impenetrable snow which surrounds him, he uncovers the promise of new life.[55] Joyous in his recognition of 'cette dialectique élémentaire'/'this crude dialectic', the cycle of birth and death, of presence and absence, of growth and decay, which is life itself, '[i]l riait aux anges, presque béat'/'[h]is face set in an ecstatic, almost beatific smile'.[56]

But this moment of aesthetic and philosophical enlightenment contains the outline of a different, darker experience. The tree which the narrator gazes upon – *un hêtre* in French – is, in German, *Buche*, and it is '[l]a forêt de hêtres sur la colline de l'Ettersberg qui donne son nom au lieudit, Buchenwald'/'The beech forest on the hill known as the Ettersberg [...] which gives its name to the place in question, Buchenwald'.[57] There is etymological and homophonic play here within both the German and the French. *Die Buche* is the German word for 'beech tree' but is also etymologically connected to the German for 'book', *das Buch*; *le hêtre* is the French word for 'beech tree', but is also a homophone of the French verb être, to be. Through this interlinguistic *jeu de mots*, Semprún highlights an intersection of writing and living that is at the heart of his representation of Buchenwald. The presence of the Buchenwald camp is implicit within every element of the narrator's experience, both lived and textual: it is apparent within the beauty of the tree upon which the narrator gazes, just as his death is implicit in the arrival of spring. And, all too soon, the narrator's reverie is brought to an abrupt halt by the intrusion of an SS officer from the camp, pistol aimed at the narrator's back. As the violent reality of Buchenwald disrupts the narrator's solitary contemplation, so too the language of that reality – the abrupt German of the officer's questions and the narrator's responses – disrupts the earlier lyricism of the French narration: '*Was machst Du hier?* demandait-il. Il demandait, le sous-officier, ce qu'il faisait là, lui'/'*Was machst du hier*?' he asked. The warrant officer was asking what he was doing there'.[58] Semprún's translation of the officer's question from German into French, and his subsequent glossing of this translation, together enable him to insert an authorial commentary without interrupting the flow of the narrative. This commentary is less concerned with interrogating the events experienced than with the dynamics of the languages through which that experience is narrated, which takes the form of a perceived tonal and affective difference between German and French:

> *Das Baum,* disait-il finalement, *so ein wunderschönes Baum!* [...] Il était satisfait d'avoir exprimé en allemand, avec une réelle concision, les vrais motifs de sa présence en ce lieu inattendu. L'arbre était, en effet, miraculeux de beauté. En français, toutefois, l'explication aurait eu un tour solennel ou guindé. C'est l'arbre, aurait-il dit en français, un arbre miraculeux de beauté.

> *"Das Baum,"* he said in the end, *"so ein wunderschönes Baum!"*! [...] He was pleased that he had managed to express in German, with real conciseness, the true reasons for his presence in that unexpected place. The tree really was a miracle of beauty. In French, however, the explanation would have had something solemn or affected about it. *"C'est l'arbre,"* he would have said, *"un arbre miraculeux de beauté".*[59]

As French shifts into German and back again, this glossed translation contrasts the apparent truthful brevity of the German with the affected solemnity of the French. This gloss is more than a commentary upon a perceived linguistic difference, however, for it simultaneously emphasizes the contrast between the terse life-or-death reality of the narrator's need to respond to the officer's question and the beauty but irreality of the aesthetic experience which preceded it. Even as the narrator allows himself a moment longer to imagine 'que le sous-officier aurait pour l'arbre les mêmes yeux que lui, [...] ils auraient pu parler ensemble de cette beauté neigeuse'/'that the warrant officer would see the tree as he had [...] they could have talked together about that miracle of beauty', the scene shifts from hypothetical discussion to real danger, the warrant officer pointing his pistol at the narrator's chest and preparing to shout.[60] The proximity of the narrator's death here is no longer a matter of philosophical meditation, but instead an actual and immediate possibility. As the narrator cries out his identification number in German – *'Häftling vier-und-vierzig-tausend-neun-hundert-vier!'* – in order to placate the officer, death, lingering in the smoke from the crematorium, filters onto the scene.[61]

Into this powerful opening Semprún distils the affective tone and aesthetic form of *Quel beau dimanche!* as a whole: the intersection of philosophical contemplation and political violence, the pervasion of death within the camp experience, and the multiplicity of languages and elements of translation that draws out the subtleties of this experience. These meditations are framed by the temporal specificity which the text's title hints at: 'Il est dix heures du matin. C'est dimanche. C'est la fin du mois de décembre'/'It is ten o'clock in the morning. It is Sunday. It is late December', the narrator informs us.[62] Yet even within these opening pages, the narrative exceeds the *cadre* of this single Sunday through Semprún's exploration of the second framework for the text: the space of the camp itself and its proximity to the town of Weimar. It is this proximity that enables Semprún to distort the temporal framework created by the novel's title, as he invokes the echoes of others who, in very different circumstances and at very different times, walked the same landscape as his narrator does now. Semprún focuses particularly upon a figure who is key within the text as a whole: Goethe, who, in the company of Johann Peter Eckermann, walked the space around the Ettersberg Hill at the beginning of the nineteenth century.

Semprún is interested in the symbolic position Goethe inhabits within the space and the history of Buchenwald. The power of Goethe's cultural capital is apparent within the name given to the camp, a fact Semprún highlights by quoting from a letter to Himmler which explains why the camp was not simply named after the Ettersberg Hill upon which it was situated. The letter to Himmler states that this name was impossible, '«car le nom de l'Ettersberg est lié à la vie et à l'œuvre de Goethe»'/'"for the name of the Ettersberg is associated with the life and works of Goethe"'. The narrator elaborates upon this point to explain that, for those in charge of creating the camp, 'son attribution à un camp de rééducation (*Umschulungslager*) où se rassemblerait la lie de la terre ne pouvait que souiller la mémoire du poète'/'invoking his spirit in the name of a re-education camp (*Umschulungslager*), in which the dregs of the earth would be assembled, could only sully the poet's memory'.[63] In this letter, re-situated in the novel, the opposition between Goethe – symbol of German national pride and cultural capital – and those within the camp – the detritus, the dregs of the earth – reveals an enforced separation, created to prevent the contamination of Goethe's memory by its connection with the events unfolding within the camp walls. Semprún's critique throughout the text is directed at the implicit valorization and romanticization of the space of Buchenwald through its connection to Goethe, a romanticization which emphasizes the role aesthetic forms can play in the promotion, as well as the illumination, of political violence.[64]

Goethe also features in *L'Écriture ou la vie*, one of a number of returns and foreshadowings through which Semprún focuses upon an impossible-to-conceive moment *after* Buchenwald. This impossibility is elucidated by the different manifestations of Goethe within these two texts. In *Quel beau dimanche!,* the narrator resurrects Goethe and has him walk beyond the camp walls, in spaces the narrator can only access in fantasy. In *L'Écriture ou la vie*, this imaginary beyond has become an actuality, as the liberated narrator enters Goethe's house, preserved near Weimar, not as a prisoner but as a free man. But the existential impossibility of this *beyond* is the backbone of *L'Écriture ou la vie*, as the narrator explores his sense that he is less a survivor of the camps than someone transformed and transfigured by his experience – 'un revenant', someone returned from the dead.[65] The movement from *Quel beau dimanche!* to *L'Écriture ou la vie*, from this Sunday within the camp to the narrator's liberation from the camp, is thus anything but a linear progression, for as Semprún insists, in the experience of Buchenwald there is no shift from *during* to *after*, *within* to *beyond*, but only 'une contrée immense où ruisselle l'absence'/'this immense land streaming with absence', through which his narrator wanders endlessly.[66] Through this allusion to Goethe, mirrored and doubled across both texts, Semprún asks us to consider where fiction and life, past and present, coalesce and converge. In relation to his experience of Buchenwald, what is imaginary and what is real? Are the ghosts of the past vanished or awaiting resurrection? And what role does writing, and particularly writing which incorporates an aesthetics of translation, play in enabling or repressing this 'revenant' past?

In both texts, these questions of textual memory are dramatized not only by the 'visitation' of Goethe but also by the echo of Léon Blum, the French socialist minister and three-time prime minister, who was imprisoned by the Nazis in a house next to Buchenwald at the same time that Semprún was incarcerated in the camp. Separated by more than a hundred years, Goethe and Blum collide not only within the space of Buchenwald but also, translated in time, through a process of textual re-imagination. For in 1901 Blum wrote a text named *Nouvelles conversations de Goethe avec Eckermann*, in which he too imagined an immortal Goethe living in the late nineteenth century. *Nouvelles conversations* is an intertextual blueprint for *Quel beau dimanche!*, and Semprún terminates Chapitre Zéro with an excerpt from it: ' «*3 juillet 1898*, «Dîné chez Goethe qui me cite un mot singulier de Racine. Quand il eut achevé le plan de *Phèdre*, il dit à un ami: Ma pièce est finie. Il ne me reste plus que les vers à écrire.»'/'"*July 3 1898*, "Dined at Goethe's. He told me an interesting story about Racine. When he had finished planning *Phèdre*, he said to a friend: '"My play is finished. All that remains is to write the lines."'[67]

This quintuple intertextual sequence – Semprún's rewriting of Blum's reimagining of Eckermann's paraphrasing of Goethe's citation of Racine's discussion of writing – opens the narrative of *Quel beau dimanche!* and reveals the texture of the text: its translation of different voices – some literary, some political, some fictional, some real – into a dialogic framework through which Semprún negotiates his experiences of loss. The narrator's response to this excerpt – simply, 'Écrivons'/'Let us write', – concludes Chapitre Zéro.[68] By ending this textual 'zero hour' – the hour when, in military terms, decisions are made and attacks begin – with a collective call to write, Semprún positions it also as a collective call to struggle: *écrire, c'est lutter*; *écrivons, c'est luttons*. But here, to recall Barthes, 'écrire' is an intransitive verb: there is no object to be written, and the subject, while collective, is ambiguous.[69] Who is the 'we' addressed here? And against what or whom, or *for* what or whom, are 'we' to struggle through writing?

This powerful call to write is followed immediately, at the start of Chapter 1, by the words which make up the novel's title: 'Les gars, quel beau dimanche!'[70] The speaker is Fernand Barizon, the narrator's counterpoint and companion: standing in the camp courtyard in the early hours of this December Sunday, he cries out these words which, in the context of the camp experience, appear incomprehensible to the narrator: 'il n'a pas dit merde. Il a dit quel beau dimanche, les gars! en français'/'he had not said "*merde*!"'. He had said, "*Quel beau dimanche, les gars*!" in French'.[71] This unlikely utterance offers Semprún another opportunity to interrogate the differences between French and German, and between the values he assigns to each: 'S'il avait voulu dire merde, d'ailleurs, il aurait dit *Scheisse,* car les mots importants ne sont pas français [...] On dit *Scheisse, Arbeit, Brot,* tous les autres mots importants, en allemand. Pain, travail, merde: tous les vrais mots'/'In any case, if he had wanted to say "*merde*!"' he would have said "*Scheisse*", because the important words were not French. [...] He said "*Scheisse*", "*Arbeit*", "*Brot*", all the important words, in German. Shit, work, bread: all the real words'.[72] As in the episode with the tree, Semprún creates a distinction between a language capable of truthfully representing the camp experience – German – and a language concerned with articulating the aesthetic – here written quite literally in the French word 'beau'.

How are we to understand this dichotomy? The narrator's interpretation of Barizon's call conceives it as integrally connected to a past memorialized through its aesthetic pleasures, and through the contrast between this remembered beauty and the present camp reality:

> Un souvenir, sans doute, des beaux dimanches d'autrefois venu le saisir au moment où il allait plonger dans les tourbillons de neige. [...] Il a peut-être eu le sentiment de la sottise inacceptable de ce monde où il y a les dimanches sur la Marne – ailleurs, avant, loin, de l'autre côté, dehors – et puis cette neige floconneuse, obstinée, de l'Ettersberg.
>
> It must have been the memory of other beautiful Sundays, at home, on the banks of the Marne, which suddenly invaded him as he was about to dash into the swirling snow [...]. Perhaps he felt the unacceptable stupidity of a world in which there are Sundays on the Marne – elsewhere, long ago, far away, on the other side, outside – and then this obstinate fleecy snow of the Ettersberg.[73]

The irony within Barizon's call, the disjunction between these memories and his experience, between the beauty of the Marne and the reality of the camp, exists in a constant tension, a tension which highlights the innate injustice of the camp experience. To adapt Keats, beauty is not truth, truth beauty; rather, the truth of the camp experience exists precisely in its inability to be aestheticized and romanticized, in the impossible and inevitable gap between this Sunday and the Sundays of a long-ago freedom, an experiential gap emphasized by the linguistic disjunction Semprún creates when translating between the German and the French. The Sunday at Marne is dramatically elsewhere, beyond, before, outside, and untranslatable into the possibility of the camp.

Yet these time and space markers – 'ailleurs, avant, loin' – reveal not only an experiential disjunction but also a conceptual one, emphasized by the insurmountable temporal gap between the Sunday *now* and the Sunday *then*. For all memory is in debt to a past it cannot fully redeem: the Sunday at Marne is 'loin' not only because it is empirically and affectively such a different experience from the Sunday at the camp, but also because every attempt to remember in the present is an impossibility which pushes the past further and further into oblivion. When we translate the past into the present, we confront that past but we also seek to move away from it: the 'living-on' which Benjamin evokes as the movement of translation is a movement of survival but also of forgetting.[74] This loss not only *of* memory but *as* memory is staged in *Quel beau dimanche!* by the appropriations and misinterpretations which run through the narrator's attempt to translate Barizon's memories into his own narrative. For, as the final pages of *Quel beau dimanche!* reveal, the narrator's interpretation of Barizon's call is comically misplaced:

> Dis donc, ce matin, quand t'es parti en criant: «Les gars, quel beau dimanche!», tu pensais à quoi? [...] Ce matin? dit Barizon, je ne m'en souviens pas. [...] A ce putain de dimanche, je suppose, dit Barizon [...] Tu ne pensais pas à la Marne, par hasard? [...] Quelle Marne? dit-il. La bataille de la Marne? [...] J'éclate de rire.
>
> By the way, this morning, when you came out shouting, "*Les gars, quel beau dimanche!*", what were you thinking about?" [...] "This morning," said Barizon, "I don't remember". [...] About this shitty Sunday, I suppose," [...] ["You weren't thinking about the Marne, by any chance?" [...] "What Marne?", he said, "the Battle of the Marne?" [...] I burst out laughing'].[75]

Sheridan's English translation of this section of the text ends with the words 'I suppose', a decision which emphasizes the ways in which the 'living-on' of translation always allows a re-envisioning of an existing text. But it also reveals the ways in which the inevitably transformative impulse of translation can become an appropriation, one which disrupts a text's interpretative possibilities and disturbs its affective content, for this elision fundamentally shifts the focus of the extract, in fact erasing the very appropriation with which Semprún is concerned. For the narrator's annexation of Barizon's thoughts dramatizes the same process of appropriation at play within the narrative impulse as that which characterizes the student's story in Kundera's *Le Livre*. But this annexation also reveals the power of narrative to create memory: the narrator finally realizes 'd'où vient cette Marne qui m'a hanté, ce matin, que j'ai imagine dans la mémoire de Barizon. Elle me vient de Giraudoux, bien sûr'/'from where that Marne came which haunted me, this morning, that I imagined in Barizon's memory. It came from Giraudoux, of course'.[76] In *Quel beau dimanche!*, as well as in several of Semprún's other texts, the narrator often reflects upon the words of Jean Giraudoux when remembering his time as a member of the *Maquis* or his incarceration in Buchenwald. Here, the intrusion of Giraudoux into the narrator's narrative reveals memory to be a tissue of elements forgotten, elements imagined, elements translated from other texts, other voices, other authors, which enable us to construct the past as we want, indeed as we expect, to see it.

Semprún's retelling of a Sunday within the camp raises questions as much about the impulse to narrate and to understand as about the nature of the experience to be narrated and understood. Semprún forces us to consider where this Sunday lies – in memory, in imagination, in expectation, in text, in the past, in the present? And, just as importantly, we must consider *whose* memory (imagination, expectation, text, past or present) is being invoked. In positioning Barizon's words 'quel beau dimanche' – the title of the text itself – as the first moment of writing following the imperative and collective 'écrivons', Semprún provides the subject matter for his call for a collective form of writing. What is to be written is this Sunday, which slips from the narrator's grasp even as he narrates it, even as Semprún writes it, even as we read it, for it is already being translated elsewhere into another's memory, voice, text and time. In this sense, *Quel beau dimanche!* is a question as much as an exclamation, revealing Semprún's fascination with the relationship between agency, temporality, and memory as evoked within aesthetic forms. What beauty can there be within the camp experience and within the memory of that experience? How can such an experience be translated into an aesthetic form without betraying or silencing the voices and echoes of those who also experienced it, or without being complicit in an erasure of precisely the past moment which it seeks to grasp? What form, indeed what language, is capable of such a narration? As his intralingual translation of *Le Grand Voyage* as *Quel beau dimanche!* suggests, Semprún insists that our relation to the past is never static but always altered by the present; reminiscence is a pendulum which swings repeatedly between significance and irrelevance, nostalgia and amnesia. The account of Buchenwald which Semprún offered in *Le Grand Voyage* is 'mensongère', not only because he wrote the text before he was aware of the existence of the gulags, but also because every attempt to translate memory into an aesthetic form inevitably erases, overwrites and distorts the past which it seeks to recover. 'Écrivons' states the narrator of *Quel beau dimanche!*, but this writing, its possibility and impossibility, as staged by translation, is not the end of the text but its beginning, not its answer but its question.

Memory and memorialization

Semprún's concern with the difficulties of translating his memories of Buchenwald into an aesthetic form commensurate with their complexity is paralleled by another attempt to memorialize this traumatic past: the Buchenwald memorial, created by Fritz Cremer in 1958. Memorials dramatize the innate problems within all attempts to translate memory into an aesthetic form. As Peter Rosenbaum notes in 'The Buchenwald Memorial and its *Différend*', 'memorials always signify a forgetting. [...] Memorials remind us of our forgetfulness and reinforce this forgetting by containing and sealing off the potentially dangerous forgetting that emanates from the past'.[77] In seeking to mark and commemorate the past, memorials allow us to forget that we are incapable of remembering an original event, purporting to frame and contain what is an unframeable, uncontainable past. The dangers of this approach to memory are illustrated by the form of the Buchenwald memorial, which Semprún, through the voice of his narrator, subjects to a vehement critique:

> C'était dégueulasse. Une tour, des groupes de sculptures, du marbre, une allée bordée de murs couverts de bas-reliefs, des escaliers monumentaux. [...] Je me suis borné, timidement, à [...] raconter mon vieux rêve: qu'on abandonne le camp au lent travail de la nature, de la forêt, des racines, de la pluie, de l'érosion éclatante des saisons. Un jour, on redécouvrirait les bâtiments de l'ancien camp envahis par le foisonnement irrésistible des arbres. [...] Mais non;

un mémorial, quelque chose qui avait un sens éducatif, politique, voilà ce qu'ils avaient construit.

> It was disgusting. A tower, groups of marble sculptures, an avenue bordered with walls covered with bas-reliefs, monumental steps. [...] Shyly, I just told [...] my old dream: that the camp should be left to the slow work of nature, to the forest, to the roots, to the rain, to the irreversible erosion of the seasons. One day, people would rediscover the buildings of the old camp overgrown by the irresistible profusion of trees. [...] But no, a memorial, something educational, political, that's what they had built.[78]

The contrast Semprún evokes between the 'lent', 'éclatante' and 'irrésistible' invasion of nature the narrator desires and the 'construit', 'monumentaux' 'murs' of the memorial that exists emphasizes the memorial's reification of an intangible past in a concrete form. The narrator imagines a memorial which could reflect the transience of memory: one capable of changing, growing, dying and being reborn in different forms. Instead, he finds an artistic construction which seeks to profit – politically, educationally, affectively – from the deaths that it purports to commemorate.

In *The Buchenwald Child: Truth, Fiction and Propaganda*, William John Niven comments upon the form of this profit, suggesting that the human figures which make up this memorial statue are depicted in a way which elides the violence and trauma of the experience of Buchenwald:

> Far from looking emaciated, they are characterized by muscularity, and the shirts, coats, or robes with which they have been fitted out are anything but ragged. [...] The whole memorial complex, in fact, stresses the success of the prisoners' struggle against death and fascism. The prisoners are to be understood as men who threw off their yoke to become shapers of their own destiny. [...] The victimhood of those who were butchered and starved by the SS as a matter of course [...] is given little attention in the final memorial.[79]

Niven's commentary focuses upon a memorial conceived not to remember the deaths at Buchenwald but to assert the possibility of transcending those deaths – indeed, death itself – by rendering them meaningful within the context of a broader, justifiable struggle: the struggle through which Communism triumphed over Fascism. In tension with the dialectical celebration of life and death which opens *Quel beau dimanche!,* this *absence* of death within the memorial becomes particularly pertinent. Death is no longer part of the memory of Buchenwald, and the lives which continue beyond it, but is rather an element to be repressed – just as nature has been repressed – in the creation of a sculptural narrative of fraternal triumph and resistance.

The dangers of this triumphant narrative are twofold. Firstly, the memorial elides what is, for Semprún, 'l'essentiel' of the camp experience: the collective living-through-death which reveals not only the absolute evil of the camp but also its fraternal impulse. For Semprún, death cannot be vanquished by the fraternal but is instead the *experience* of the fraternal as lived within Buchenwald: death – its promise, proximity, inevitability – is the experience shared by all those imprisoned within the camp.[80] At the same time, this collective experience of death only occurs because of the existence of absolute evil, as manifested by the creation of the camps. In this sense, Buchenwald is the embodiment of the quotation from André Malraux's *Le Miroir des limbes* which provides the epigram to *L'Écriture ou la vie*: 'la région cruciale de l'âme où le Mal absolu s'oppose à la fraternité'/'the crucial region of the soul where absolute Evil and fraternity [confront one another]'.[81] For to experience Buchenwald is to experience both the absolute evil and the fraternity of death, manifested within a space where survival and sacrifice, individualism and collectivism, destruction and cooperation, exist in constant tension.

Semprún's reading of Malraux is indebted to Kant's conception of radical evil in *Religion within the Limits of Reason Alone*, a French translation of which the narrator of *L'Écriture ou la vie* reads just prior to his incarceration in Buchenwald.[82] The temporal intersection of the narrator's arrest – the moment which led, ineluctably, to Buchenwald – with a reading of this translation of Kant's text positions the text as the beginning of Buchenwald in two senses: not only does this reading precede the narrator's experience of the camps, but the subject matter foreshadows the nature of that experience. Kant emphasizes that our choice of whether to be good or evil is not a choice between the human and the inhuman, but rather between two equal and possible outcomes of our freedom *as* humans.[83] Responding to Kant's claim, the narrator of *L'Écriture ou la vie* insists that '[i]l est [...] dérisoire de s'opposer au Mal, d'en prendre ses distances, par une simple référence à l'humain, à l'espèce humaine... Le Mal est l'un des projets possibles de la liberté constitutive de l'humanité de l'homme'/'it's ridiculous to oppose Evil, to distance oneself from it, through a simple reference to what is human, to mankind... Evil is one of the possible designs of the freedom essential to the humanity of man – the freedom from which spring both the humanity and the inhumanity of man'.[84] For Semprún, it is only by acknowledging that the camps are at all times a possible result of our humanity that any real understanding of the camp experience can be attained.

A failure to acknowledge the inevitable possibility of the camps is the second danger contained within the narrative of triumph evoked by the Buchenwald memorial. In *L'Écriture ou la vie*, Semprún suggests that the memorial sets up a symbolic, but false, conflict between the oppression of the prisoners under Nazi control and their liberation in the name of Communism.[85] As Siobhan Kattago suggests, the Socialist Unity Party saw the creation of the memorial as an opportunity to glorify the Communist resistance to Fascism within Buchenwald, and thereby legitimize their claims to power within the German Democratic Republic.[86] Semprún argues that this symbolic glorification is misleading, in part because it hinges upon an opposition between Communism and Fascism which is as illusory as that between fraternity and evil. In *L'Écriture ou la vie*, Semprún acknowledges his naivety in this regard: the narrator of the text reveals his faith that when Nazism came to an end, there would be no need for camps such as Buchenwald.[87] But, as the gulags reveal, the existence of the camps extends beyond the specificity of the Nazi ideology into the ideology Semprún had believed would negate their very possibility: that of Communism.

It is this illusory opposition which is at the heart of the fallacies Semprún perceives within *Le Grand Voyage*, and which he seeks to shatter in *Quel beau dimanche!* Despite the ideological differences between Fascism and Communism, the narrator insists that they share a common essence, embodied within their reliance upon the use of concentration camps such as Buchenwald. 'Faire travailler et corriger, rééduquer par le travail forcé, n'est-ce pas là que se trouve l'identité profonde, quelles que soient les différences dues aux circonstances historiques, ou même géographiques, entre les deux systèmes?'/'To put to work and to correct, to re-educate by forced labor, is that not where the profound identity is to be found, whatever the differences due to the historical or even geographical circumstances between the two systems?', he asks.[88]

When *Quel beau dimanche!* was written, Semprún was unaware that there was, in fact, a geographic relation between these two systems embodied within Buchenwald itself. For Buchenwald is a translated site: between 1945 and 1950, the site of the Nazi concentration camp in which Semprún spent eighteen months was converted into the Soviet internment camp NKVD 2. Buchenwald is thus representative, not only of Nazi atrocities, but also of Soviet ones, mirroring spatially the conflicted political history which Semprún, as an ex-detainee of the Nazi camp and an ex-Communist, is seeking to come to terms with in the pages of *Quel beau dimanche!* As Bella Brodzki notes, the question for Semprún is '[h]ow to memorialize, even contain, these two pasts, without relativizing or equating them, in the same symbolic and physical landscape? What constitutes appropriate, respectful, responsible commemoration of the history of each regime, without confusing or conflating their respective crimes?'[89]

As Couze Venn discusses in relation to Auschwitz and Hiroshima, very different experiences of trauma can resonate with each other in illuminating ways. Yet we must always respect the particularity of these experiences. Via Derrida, Venn reads this simultaneous connection and particularity in relation to the question of the proper name:

> the proper name [...] makes a requirement both of untranslatability and translatability, that is, it requires, on the one hand, that one respects the irreducible specificity and singularity associated with the proper name [...] which exceeds representation and would lose meaning in translation. Yet, on the other hand, the proper name, because it stands in testimony to a debt, summons one to attempt to translate the experience into a common idiom, as a response to suffering and fragility and a sign of solidarity.[90]

As Derrida discusses, the proper name always calls for both translatability and untranslatability; 'traduis-moi'/'translate me' into understanding and connection; 'ne me traduis pas'/'do not translate me', for I am unique, and can never be adequately represented or narrated.[91] Buchenwald and NKVD 2, two proper names situated within one space, exist within this tension between connection and separation, calling for an approach which can understand their relation without overwriting their specificity. The possibility of this overwriting is always present in any attempt to translate the traumatic experiences embodied by one proper name into another. The relationship between the memorialization of Buchenwald and that of Auschwitz reveals one way in which such an overwriting can occur. As Rosenbaum describes, the Buchenwald memorial was in fact designed to memorialize Auschwitz *via* Buchenwald, to translate the specificity of these two camps into one narrative of the concentration camp experience. On one level, the memorialization of both camps within one space allows the atrocities committed in both to stand together, as Venn suggests, in solidarity and 'testimony to a debt'. But this combined testimony ultimately erases the other camp also connected to Buchenwald: NKVD 2. For as Rosenbaum describes, in seeking to connect

Buchenwald to Auschwitz, the memorial programme at Buchenwald specifically erased the history of NKVD 2 in order to create a meaningful and cohesive narrative of the horrors of the Nazi camp programme.[92]

Semprún's concern throughout *Quel beau dimanche!* is how to bring this translatable/untranslatable binary into dialogue, how to find an aesthetic form capable of acknowledging the parallels between different experiences of totalitarianism without absorbing these differences into a homogeneity which ultimately erases as much as it remembers. Semprún's own experiences of translation offered one answer to these questions. For it was, he suggests, only after *Quel beau dimanche!* was translated into German that he became aware of the double history contained within the space of Buchenwald camp itself. In *L'Écriture ou la vie,* Semprún discusses this discovery, describing the moment when, following a discussion of the German translation of *Quel beau dimanche!*, a reader approached him and told him the story of NKVD 2.[93] As Semprún narrates it, then, translation quite literally illuminated the connection between Buchenwald and NKVD 2 which was masked in the official memorial.

But the connection between the two different totalitarian regimes is also part of Semprún's own experiences as both a Communist and a detainee of the Nazis. For Semprún, it is by translating these experiences into narrative form that he can begin to understand them in ways that connect but do not conflate these two traumatic histories. In *Quel beau dimanche!*, this understanding requires the narrator to address his failure to see or accept the parallels between Buchenwald and the gulags during his time as a member of the PCE. Alongside his struggle to find an appropriate aesthetic form to narrate the traumatic experience of Buchenwald and the loss of his political faith, Semprún is thus also concerned with understanding the sleight of thought or memory which enabled him to continue as a Communist despite his growing awareness of the flaws and failings within the Communist dream: indeed, the question '[p]ourquoi sommes-nous toujours communistes?'/'Why are we still Communists?' is posed three times, and provides the concluding question to the text as a whole.[94] In *Written in Red*, Gina Herrmann suggests that the answer to this question hinges upon the ideological polarization of Europe at that period; to reject Communism, she suggests, was an implicit valorization of Fascism.[95] But Semprún's own response in *Quel beau dimanche!* suggests that his continued Communist faith rested on an illusion about Communism which he maintained even in the face of all evidence to the contrary: 'L'illusion de maintenir et de faire progresser les valeurs du Communisme, malgré le parti communiste ou même contre lui'/'the illusion of maintaining and of fostering the values of Communism, despite the Communist Party or even against it'.[96] The narrator's ability to maintain this illusion hinges upon a refusal to confront the contradictions between those 'valeurs' and the reality of their implementation.

How can we take responsibility for the past if we do not acknowledge its complexity and contradictions? How can we acknowledge its losses if we insist upon focusing only upon its triumphs? These questions are at the heart of *Quel beau dimanche!,* taking particular form in Semprún's focus upon the role played by the dialectic, a process of thinking which, he suggests, enabled him to ignore, indeed, forget, the existence of these contradictions, and even to profit from them just as the memorial profits from death and the contradictions of Buchenwald's past. From the opening pages of *Quel beau dimanche!,* when the narrator experiences the 'dialectique élémentaire' of life and death, Semprún foregrounds the power of dialectical argumentation and its important role in both human thought and human experience. But the positivity of this initial moment of dialectical thinking is contrasted with Semprún's depiction of the Party's – and the narrator's own – use of the dialectic as a form of historical and political justification to support a series of fundamentally flawed ideological, ontological and ethical premises. In *Quel beau dimanche!,* Semprún's aesthetics of translation elucidates not only the flaws he perceives within Stalinist dialectical argumentation, but also the power and prevalence of the impulse which draws us towards such forms of thinking.

The dialectic

Dialectical forgettings

The dialectic as a model of political and philosophical thinking has a long and potent intellectual history. For Plato, the dialectic was a Socratic method which perceived the internal contradictions in every argument, and ultimately overcame these in order to uncover the truth of concepts such as justice, love or piety. The Hegelian dialectic contains a similar desire to overcome, as embodied within the formula 'abstract, negative, concrete'.[97] Every abstraction, Hegel suggests, contains its own negation; this negation, however, can be resolved through *Aufhebung,* an 'untranslatable' German word which represents the sublation of the abstract and the negative into a concrete force of progression and change which produces a higher form of consciousness.[98] It is this concept of progress which is integral to the

Marxist-Leninist version of the dialectic. Here the formula of Hegel's thinking is reversed: dialectical materialism seeks to address the materiality of social change rather than to overcome that materiality itself.[99] In both the Hegelian and the Marxist forms however, the same crucial formulation is asserted: the dialectic operates as a movement of progression *through* the contradictory.

Semprún's critique of the dialectic in *Quel beau dimanche!* is not aimed at this formulation itself, but rather at its manipulation by Stalin's Communist Party; under Soviet Communism the dialectical alliance of progress and contradiction was reified and hardened into a myth that was then read backwards to embrace Marxism itself:

> Si j'en crois les textes qui se réclament aujourd'hui du marxisme [...], le marxisme semble être [...] une activité idéologique dont la fonction essentielle consisterait à produire des concepts capables d'occulter la réalité, de mythifier l'histoire, d'escamoter le grossier impact des faits historiques. Le marxisme semble réduit à n'être plus que l'art et la manière de justifier le cours des choses.
>
> If the writings that claim to be Marxist today are to be believed [...] Marxism [...] seems to be an ideological activity whose essential function is to produce concepts capable of obscuring reality, or mystifying history, of concealing the crude impact of historical facts. Marxism seems reduced to being no more than the art of justifying the way things turn out.[100]

This interrogation of Marxism by Semprún is part of a more general critique in *Quel beau dimanche!* of the appropriations of Marxist thinking by Stalinist Communism, a critique which Derrida also explores in *Spectres de Marx*.[101] While Derrida seeks to deconstruct the connection which has been created between Marx and the gulags, however, Semprún is interested in exploring precisely how this connection was created through a misinterpretation of Marx's approach to the dialectic.

The vision of the dialectic as a process enabling an endless justification of the present is apparent in Stalin's 1938 text, *Dialectical and Historical Materialism*:

> dialectics holds that internal contradictions are inherent in all things and phenomena of nature [...] the struggle between these opposites, the struggle between the old and the new, between that which is dying away and that which is being born, between that

> which is disappearing and that which is developing, constitutes the internal content of the process of development […]. Everything depends on the conditions, time and place.[102]

Here, the dialectic emphasizes the relativity of all structures and experiences, indeed the relativity of history itself. But in Stalin's interpretation this relativity is simultaneously a justification, for it enables all past systems and structures to become meaningful as part of a continuous social evolution: 'only such an approach saves the science of history from becoming a jumble of accidents and an agglomeration of most absurd mistakes', he writes.[103] The Stalinist dialectic is concerned with the construction of meaning through an engagement with history which seeks to overcome the contradictions within that history, an unethical translation of the contingencies of the past into a coherent historical narrative.

In *Quel beau dimanche!,* Semprún challenges the wisdom of such historical justifications, suggesting that the coherence required by such a dialectical narrative prevents a productive engagement with the past on its own terms: 'C'est l'art et la manière de toujours retomber sur ses pattes'/'It's the art of always falling on your feet'.[104] Semprún's battle with the dialectic is not only concerned with the ways in which dialectical thinking operates to justify the events of the past, but also with its apparent inevitability as an intellectual procedure, and the consequences of that inevitability. Throughout *Quel beau dimanche!* Semprún interrogates this 'art' of the dialectic. He describes how the Stalinist formulation of the dialectic involved a rejection of any form of thought considered 'trop peu dialectique, puisqu'elle ne parvenait pas à justifier pleinement la réalité, puisqu'elle prétendait l'expliquer dans ses contradictions et non pas la glorifier dans la solution ou le dépassement (l'*Aufhebung,* camarades, l'*Aufhebung*!) desdites contradictions'/'insufficiently dialectical, because it failed to justify reality completely, because it claimed to explain it in its contradictions and not to glorify it in the resolution or supersession (*Aufhebung*, comrades, *Aufhebung*!) of the afore-mentioned contradictions'.[105]

In Semprún's discussion here, a failure to engage with the past becomes a failure to engage with the present. Semprún is only too aware, however, of the attractions of such forms of thinking, and of the innate human urge to translate the past according to our own needs and desires. Indeed, the narrator of *Quel beau dimanche!* justifies his own somewhat unpalatable actions through just such a dialectical formulation. Presented with evidence of the innocence of Hungarian

Communist László Rajk, condemned to death as a capitalist spy during one of Stalin's show trials, the narrator retreats from this threat to the coherence of his ideological beliefs by calling upon the transformative power of the dialectic:

> Car, même si Rajk était innocent, il ne fallait pas quitter le parti pour autant. [...] Nous avions une phrase pour justifier dialectiquement cette attitude. Mais oui, dialectiquement. Nous disions qu'il valait mieux se tromper avec le parti que d'avoir raison en dehors de lui ou contre lui. Car le parti incarnait la vérité globale, la raison historique. Une erreur du parti ne pouvait être que partielle et passagère. Le cours même de l'histoire la corrigerait. Une vérité contre le parti ne pouvait être, elle non plus, que partielle et passagère. Stérile, donc, et néfaste, puisqu'elle risquait d'obnubiler, d'obscurcir, d'oblitérer la vérité globale de notre raison historique. L'arbre qui vous cachait la forêt, la vérité qui vous cachait la Vérité et qui en devenait mensongère.

> For even if Rajk were innocent, one should still not leave the Party [...]. We had a phrase to justify this attitude, dialectically. We said that it was better to be wrong with the Party than to be right outside it or against it. For the Party embodied overall truth, historical reason. An error on the part of the Party could only be partial and temporary. The very course of history would correct it. A truth against the Party, by the same token, could only be partial and temporary. Sterile, therefore, and pernicious, since it ran the risk of obscuring, obliterating, the overall truth of our historical reason. The tree that kept you from seeing a forest, the truth that hid the Truth and thus became a lie.[106]

As innocence turns to guilt and wrong to right, individual moments of truth become tools in the service of an overarching Truth. In this critical moment of ideological confusion, the narrator reveals his understanding of the Party's dialectic as a power which confronts, synthesizes and transcends the elements of the past which contradict its vision of the present and the future. Semprún, like Kundera in *Le Livre du rire et de l'oubli*, represents the narrator's rhetorical transcendence of the material contradictions of the past through the metaphor of flight: 'Je me trouvais archangélique. Je battais doucement des ailes sur le trottoir du boulevard Saint-Germain, je m'envolais vers le ciel vif-argent du bolchévisme'/'I felt like the Archangel Michael. I gently beat my wings on the sidewalk of the Boulevard Saint-Germain and flew up toward the bright silver sky of

Bolshevism'.[107] As in *Le Livre,* this metaphor of flight emphasizes a desired evasion of the unforeseen and uncontrollable elements of the past. Unlike Walter Benjamin's angel of history whose 'face is turned toward the past' as he wrestles with a storm which 'irresistibly propels him into the future to which his back is turned', the angelic here turns its back upon the past, irresistibly propelling itself, through the justifications of the dialectic, into a future which is already mapped out.[108] 'Hence' as Stalin himself wrote, 'in order not to err in policy, one must look forward, not backward'.[109]

Translation and the dialectic

By narrating this episode, Semprún positions narrative as a way to '*mettre en question*' his own Communist past and to challenge the dialectical justifications which he suggests sustained it: écrire, c'est lutter. But in his exploration of the dangers of the dialectic in the pages of *Quel beau dimanche!* Semprún also stages the ways in which all forms of writing, and particularly those which employ translated intertexts, are motivated and governed by the same impulses towards angelic flight which the dialectic promotes. For narrative can itself be dialectical, weaving fictions around the past and re-ordering history into new forms. As Flynn and Judovitz suggest, '[n]arrative, after all, is usually processful, temporalizing, and totalizing, as is Hegelian dialectic [...] Given that narrative is often multilevel and, when required, can be self-critical as well, the similarity of its argument to that of dialectic may be very strong'.[110]

Semprún's approach to writing exemplifies several of these elements: his manipulation of chronology, the self-criticism displayed by his continual desire to rewrite, and the dynamics he creates between apparently opposing ideas reveal a constant staging of the dialectic between his past and his present, his ideological faith and his growing doubt. In *Written in Red*, Gina Herrmann suggests that memoirs of Communism – including *Quel beau dimanche!* – are frequently permeated by a rhetoric which reveals a continued faith in the ideals of Communism: 'the recourse to Communist rhetorical patterns within the autobiographical narratives signals in and of itself the depth of the political commitment enacted by these authors in the exposition of their conversion'.[111] For Herrmann, these rhetorical tropes are apparent even in texts such as *Quel beau dimanche!* which were written substantially after Semprún's exit from the Party and which ostensibly mark his growing rejection of that rhetoric: she refers to what she calls the 'residue of Stalinist language' which permeates his work.[112] The narrative qualities Herrmann reads in Semprún's work – self-righteous and inquisitorial, yet self-repressed – may indeed reflect this continuing residue, for his rewriting of his Communist past presents it as entrenched within the very rhetoric he seeks to evade. The close connections between Semprún's narrative approach and the dialectical approach he condemns in *Quel beau dimanche!* reveal the vulnerability of that condemnation, staging the difficulty, perhaps the impossibility, of escaping our innate attraction to dialectical constructions.

This connection is particularly pertinent in relation to Semprún's use of translated intertexts. For intertexts can be deployed to construct the narrative we wish to see, particularly when translated into our own language. Indeed, the narrator of *Quel beau dimanche!* creates his own justifications through such translations. As he attempts to justify the flaws within Communism following his discovery of Rajk's innocence, he weaves multiple quotations into his dialectical reasoning:

> J'aurais pu jeter à la figure de cet importun quelques vers de Maïakovski. Ou quelques vers d'Aragon. Ou encore [...] je lui aurais lancé à la figure les phrases de Bertholt Brecht: «Celui qui lutte pour le communisme – doit savoir se battre et ne pas se battre – dire la vérité et ne pas la dire – rendre service et refuser ses services – tenir ses promesses et ne pas les tenir – s'exposer au danger et fuir le danger – se faire reconnaître et rester invisible – Celui qui lutte pour le communisme – ne possède, de toutes les vertus, qu'une seule – celle de lutter pour le communisme.»
>
> I would have thrown in my critic's face a few lines from Mayakovsky. Or a few lines from Aragon. Or [...] I would have thrown in my critic's face Bertholt Brecht's words: 'He who struggles for Communism/must know how to fight and how not to fight/to tell the truth and not tell it/to serve and to refuse his services/to keep his promises and not to keep them/to expose himself to danger and to flee danger/to be recognized and to remain invisible/He who fights for Communism/possesses, of all the virtues, only one/that of fighting for Communism.'[113]

The stream of possible textual justifications to which the narrator appeals desperately and ironically in an attempt to salvage his faith in the Party reveals Semprún's ultra-intimate means of highlighting the lure of justification. This excerpt is reminiscent of Mme Raphael's intransitive urge to belong in *Le Livre*. Here, however, the narrator has found the direct object for that urge – Communism – and now seeks a textual form through which to complement it. Like the dialectic, then, such quotations enable the continuation and consolidation of a threatened individual and ideological coherence. While, as I discussed in Chapters 1 and 2, translated intertextual excerpts can enable ethical and hospitable forms of textual inclusivity, by challenging chronicity and authority such texts can also enable motivated narratives of the past to be repeatedly recreated.

This dialectical recreation is particularly pertinent to translations, which inevitably involve the distortion of historical order, pulling a text from its original context and transforming it into a new form to appease the demands – linguistic, formal and content-based – of the present moment. Indeed, as Peter Fawcett discusses in 'Ideology and Translation', Marxist-oriented translation theory perceived the essence of translation to be, precisely, dialectical: 'As in all good dialectical practice', he writes, 'the thesis (source language) and the antithesis (target language) are resolved in the synthesis of translation'.[114] Implicit within Fawcett's description of this Marxist conception of 'good' dialectical practice is the question I have been pursuing of how we might define a 'good' translation, whether that translation be between languages or between memory and narrative. The relationship Fawcett describes between translation and synthesis reveals both the ethical possibilities and the limitations of translation. In every narrative – thought, remembered, spoken, written, lived – we attempt this translation-as-synthesis of the contradictory in order to construct a coherent path from past to present to future. As Timothy Mathews comments, 'We read what we read, in our own imaginings, translating and synthesising in the present of our reading and living'.[115] Can we ever avoid this synthesis of past in present, other voices into our own, which takes place in translation?

Perhaps we cannot escape our desire to dialectically synthesize the past into narrative. But we can at least acknowledge this desire. Key to this acknowledgement is the proximity between translation and dialectical thinking, a proximity which gives translation a uniquely powerful vision of the illusions within dialectical thinking itself. In *Quel beau dimanche!*, this proximity is emphasized by Semprún's focus upon the German language loan *Aufhebung* as the embodiment of both the possibilities and the flaws within dialectical thinking.

Translating the dialectic: *aufheben* as *relever*

For the narrator, the irreality of the dialectic is embodied by the 'untranslatable' Hegelian term *Aufhebung*. 'C'est la maudite *Aufhebung* qui fout en l'air la dialectique hégélienne, qui la rend irréelle à force de perfection'/'It's [the] damned *Aufhebung* that explodes the Hegelian dialectic, makes it unreal because of its striving after perfection'.[116] Like Ricœur's discussion of the impossibility of the perfect translation which I explored in Chapter 2, the narrator's emphasis upon the perfection of *Aufhebung* highlights the illusions this desire for perfection involves. Throughout *Quel beau dimanche!,* the noun *Aufhebung* and the verb *aufheben,* which means both 'to raise up' and 'to preserve', become the root of Semprún's broader critique of the dialectic, the grammar of an endless attempt to synthesize the contradictions of the past and the present into a perfect dialectical narrative. For Derrida, in his essay 'De l'économie restreinte à l'économie générale', Hegel's *Aufhebung* is precisely the mark of a discourse which seeks to understand negativity only insofar as it offers a progression towards a higher ideal:

> elle signifie *l'affairement* d'un discours s'essoufflant à se réapproprier toute négativité, à élaborer la mise en jeu en *investissement,* à *amortir* la dépense absolue, à donner un sens à la mort, à se rendre du même coup aveugle au sans-fond du non-sens dans lequel se puise et s'épuise le fond du sens.

> it signifies the busying of a discourse losing its breath as it reappropriates all negativity for itself, as it works the "putting at stake" into an investment, as it amortizes absolute expenditure; and as it gives meaning to death, thereby simultaneously blinding itself to the baselessness of the nonmeaning from which the basis of meaning is drawn, and in which this basis of meaning is exhausted.[117]

In this evocative quotation *Aufhebung* is seen as the textual figure of a desire to absorb meaninglessness into sense, find a significance for death, and resolve all conflicts and complexities into a coherent discourse. Derrida's reading of *Aufhebung* is particularly relevant in relation to the two sorts of forgetting which I discussed earlier: the memorial at Buchenwald, and the narrator's unabated justification of his Communist faith. For Semprún's discussion of these two failures of memory connects them to precisely this desire to progress beyond the incomprehensible elements of the past by sublimating them in the name of a greater cause: the triumphant configuration of the memorial statue which, in order to assert the triumph of Communist resistance, masks the victimhood of those who died at Buchenwald, and the narrator's dialectical justifications which, to maintain the broader Truth of the Party, erase the reality of the Communist experience. In *Quel beau dimanche!, Aufhebung* is the textual figure for a power constructed upon contradictions which, though never fully reconciled, are still nevertheless masked, a power built upon an attempted transcendence of death through the triumphant memorialization of the dead. Semprún's struggle with his past in *Quel beau dimanche!* is, then, a struggle against *Aufhebung*: a power created through a rhetorical forgetting of any element of reality or history which contradicts the premises upon which that power is constructed.

If *lutter, c'est écrire*, can this struggle against *Aufhebung* be achieved through writing? In *L'Écriture et la différence*, Derrida reveals the flaws within Hegel's dialectical argumentation, precisely by focusing upon the impossibility of transcending the textuality of that argument, a textuality embodied by the untranslatability of *Aufhebung*. As Philippe Büttgen notes, writing in Barbara Cassin's *Dictionnaire des intraduisibles*,

> Aufheben *et* Aufhebung *sont révérés comme des fétiches de l'intraduisible. Le «double sens» (pour reprendre les termes de Hegel) d'un verbe,* aufheben, *qui signifie à la fois «maintenir, conserver» et «faire cesser, mettre fin» est non seulement connu des exégètes de Hegel et des spécialistes de philosophie allemande, mais appartient tout simplement à la culture philosophique d'aujourd'hui.*
>
> *Aufheben* and *Aufhebung* have been revered as fetishes of the untranslatable. The "double meaning" (to adopt Hegel's term) of a verb, *aufheben*, that means both "maintain, preserve" and "halt, end" has not only been recognised by Hegel's interpreters and specialists in German philosophy but has become simply part of today's philosophical culture.[118]

This 'fetishization' of the untranslatability of *aufheben*, provoked by its double meaning, is apparent in the philosophical weight which Hegel gives to the word. For it is through, and not despite, the contradictions inherent within the meaning of the verb *aufheben* – the fact that, in German, the term means simultaneously to raise up and to negate – that Hegel develops his approach to the dialectic. In *Science of Logic*, Hegel suggests that it is the untranslatability of *aufheben* which makes it the perfect example of the overcoming through contradiction which he perceives as the essence of the dialectical process towards full consciousness. Derrida quotes Hegel's text as follows:

> Lexicologiquement, ces deux déterminations de *l'Aufheben* peuvent être considérées comme deux significations du mot. Il

> est remarquable qu'une langue en soit venue à employer un seul et même mot pour deux significations contraires. La pensée spéculative *se réjouit* de trouver [nous soulignons] dans la langue des mots qui ont par eux-mêmes un sens spéculatif, et la langue allemande en possède plusieurs.
>
> Lexicologically, these two determinations of the Aufheben may be considered as two meanings of the word. It is remarkable that a language comes to use one and the same word to express two opposed meanings. Speculative thought is *delighted* [*my italics*] to find in language words which by themselves have a speculative sense; the German language possesses several of these.[119]

By emphasizing Hegel's *delight* in finding these two significations within one word, Derrida highlights the inherent, and fortuitous, untranslatability of *aufheben*. It is this good fortune which enables Hegel to represent the process of profit through negation that he perceives as fundamental to the dialectic itself. Hegel thus profits from the contradictions within *aufheben* himself, using the ambivalence of this term to produce an affirmative philosophical concept.

For Derrida, however, translation reveals that the profit Hegel reads in *Aufhebung* is fundamentally unobtainable. Hegel's formulation of the dialectic, he suggests, is itself constructed upon a contradiction which cannot be synthesized: the need to perceive *Aufhebung* as simultaneously translatable and untranslatable, as both able to exceed the written form of its expression and only comprehensible through that form. Derrida's comment returns us to the relationship between translatability and untranslatability that I explored in Chapter 2. For Derrida, as for Ricœur, there is a proximity between translatability and untranslatability, and it is by acknowledging this proximity that Derrida confronts the flaws within Hegel's formulation. For, in order to embody the philosophical process of overcoming through contradiction which Hegel suggests underpins certain universal categories of existence – being, identity, cause, effect – *Aufhebung* must be untranslatable. But unless this process applies only to a specifically German experience of existence, *Aufhebung* must also be translatable, capable of representing and transcending its own contradictions not only in German but in every language. Only through this translatability can *Aufhebung* mark the universality of Hegel's dialectical thinking. Hegel's exploration of *Aufhebung* thus hinges upon an inherent paradox: on the one hand, Hegel acknowledges, welcomes, indeed requires, the lack of semantic stability within this term; on the other, he represses this lack, reproducing his thinking from within a discourse which depends upon precisely the semantic stability which *Aufhebung* as a word has already dissolved.

Translation forces an acknowledgement that it is impossible to overcome the contradictions of *Aufhebung* or the traces they leave. In *Marges de la philosophie,* Derrida returns to *Aufhebung* and disrupts Hegel's claim that 'la langue allemande détient le privilège intraduisible'/'the [...] untranslatable privilege is wielded by the German language' by translating the verb form of this noun, *aufheben*, into French.[120] The word Derrida finds to translate *aufheben* is 'relever', a verb which, like the German, contains multiple meanings: '*Aufheben,* c'est relever, au sens où "relever" veut dire à la fois déplacer, élever, remplacer et promouvoir dans un seul et même mouvement'/'*Aufheben* is relever, in the sense in which *relever* can combine to relieve, to displace, to elevate, to replace and to promote, in one and the same movement'.[121] While Hegel's exploration of *aufheben* requires it to be simultaneously untranslatable *between* languages and translatable *beyond* the language of its articulation, Derrida's translation of *aufheben* as *relever* reverses this paradox: *aufheben,* he suggests, can never be translated *beyond* language but only *between* languages, via the use of words such as *relever* which themselves contain the traces of other meanings which can never be synthesized or overcome.

Through translation Derrida thus multiplies *aufheben*, forcing it to write itself as other: 'On plie l'*Aufhebung* – la relève – à s'écrire autrement. Peut-être, tout simplement, à s'écrire. Mieux, à tenir compte de sa consommation d'écriture'/'The *Aufhebung* – *la relève* – is constrained into writing itself otherwise. Or perhaps simply into writing itself. Or better, into taking account of its consumption in writing'.[122] Translating *aufheben* as *relever* encapsulates this folding and consumption within writing, for *relever* is both the double of *aufheben* and the textual mark of its *différance*: an understanding that every articulation involves a combination of spatial, temporal and semantic difference and deferral. Just as Derrida's term requires writing to reveal its variance from the word 'différence', so too the *différance* within *aufheben* can only be articulated through a writing which reveals the simultaneous translatability and untranslatability of the term. For while *relever* reveals that *aufheben* can be translated, the subtle but endless differences of signification between the French and the German words reveal the inevitable imperfection of that translation, the gaps and elisions between languages which prevent the possibility of any absolute identity of meaning. By first unmasking and then reversing the paradox of translatability/untranslatability which Hegel both demands of and assigns to *Aufhebung*, Derrida throws into relief the semantic instability of *Aufhebung* which Hegel's discourse conceals.

In Derrida's reading it is translation which forces *Aufhebung* 'à s'écrire autrement', because, in its essence, translation *is* writing-as-other: an endless doubling and folding which consumes and regurgitates texts and words without seeking to exceed the textuality of its own process. In acknowledging its own textuality, translation forces the dialogues and narratives it confronts – whether literary or political – to acknowledge their own textuality, the fictional constructions, the masked interpretations, which are integral to all narratives, whatever their purpose or form. The 'relevance' of bringing translation into an exploration of these forms of thinking is not to suggest that we can evade these constructions, but to shift the emphasis so that we can become aware that all our translations between past and present, between theory and action, between experience and memory, are subject to an interpretative impulse which is then masked.

Translating translation: *relever* as the essence of translation

How can we avoid the fantasy which enables us to forget that we forget? Or is it only in fantasy that we can create and sustain the illusion that we have not forgotten? In 'Qu'est-ce qu'une traduction "relevante"?', Derrida extends the dynamic between translation and *Aufhebung* further by employing the same verb – relever – to translate the essence of translation itself. 'Ce mot "relevant", ce participe présent en situation d'attribut, il se voit ici confier une tâche exorbitante. Non pas la tâche du traducteur, mais la tâche de définir, rien de moins, l'essence de la traduction.'/'This word "relevant," this present participle that functions as a predicate, is here entrusted with an exorbitant task. Not the task of the translator, but the task of defining – nothing less – the essence of translation.'[123] In translating both *aufheben* and the action of translation as *relever*, Derrida positions translation not only as the process through which *Aufhebung* is forced to confront its own limitations, but also as a mode of thought and engagement with others which limits the dialectical forgetting of the past enacted by *Aufhebung* itself. He writes:

> Ce que démontrerait cette traduction par le mot "relevante", ce serait aussi, exemplairement, que toute traduction devrait être par vocation relevante. Elle assurerait ainsi la survie du corps de l'original (survie au double sens que lui donne Benjamin dans *La Tâche du traducteur*, *fortleben* et überleben: vie prolongée, vie

> continuée, *living on*, mais aussi vie par-delà la mort). N'est-ce pas ce que fait une traduction? Est-ce qu'elle n'assure pas ces deux survies en perdant la chair au cours d'une opération de change? En élevant le signifiant vers son sens ou sa valeur, mais tout en gardant la mémoire endeuillée et endettée du corps singulier, du corps premier, du corps unique qu'elle élève et sauve et relève ainsi.
>
> What the translation with the word "relevant" also demonstrates, in an exemplary fashion, is that every translation should be relevant by vocation. It would thus guarantee the *survival* of the body of the original (*survival* in the double sense Benjamin gives it in "The Task of the Translator," *fortleben* and überleben: prolonged life, continuous life, *living on*, but also life after death). Isn't this what a translation does? Doesn't it guarantee these *two* survivals by losing the flesh during a process of conversion *[change]*? By elevating the signifier to its meaning or value, all the while preserving the mournful and debt-laden memory of the singular body, the first body, the unique body that the translation thus elevates, preserves, and negates *[relève]*?[124]

Translation, when 'relevante', is a form of writing imbued with an unsynthesizable movement between death and life, part of an endless and ultimately impossible recognition of the debt to the past, to the voices of others, which are silenced by the progression towards perfection embodied in the aspirations of *Aufhebung*. Rather than seeking to mimic dialectical forms of synthesis and erasure, a 'relevante' translation of memory into narrative, past into present, acknowledges this impulse towards synthesis and, through this acknowledgement, stages a potential resistance to it, creating a space where those memories are elevated, transformed and thrown into relief through their translation into different aesthetic forms.

In the final section of this chapter, I explore Semprún's writing as a 'relevante' translation, one which, by translating his experiences into a textual form, seeks to throw light on the losses of his past without ever accounting for them or totalizing them. In this textual commemoration, the dialectical forgettings with which the text is concerned are confronted, and *Aufhebung* is redeemed from the erasures enacted by the impulse – political, literary, human – towards synthesis and transcendence, to become instead the textual representation of this translational movement between, but never beyond, life and death. In this resolutely textual redemption, *Aufhebung* is itself 'relevantly' translated, and the human impulse towards synthesis is revealed, emphasized, even transformed, but never overcome.

A 'relevante' translation

Translating *Jedem das Seine*: Goethe and Blum

What would a 'relevante' translation look like? In 'Qu'est-ce qu'une traduction "relevante"?', Derrida contrasts 'relevance' with a traditional European conception of a 'good' translation: 'il faut que, hors de toute paraphrase, explication, explicitation, analyse, etc., la traduction soit quantitativement équivalente à l'original'/'the translation must be *quantitatively* equivalent to the original, apart from any paraphrase, explication, explicitation, analysis, and the like'.[125] Translation is here positioned as a form of absolute equality which presupposes a universality within language through which signifieds can be transferred intact between different languages. While Ricœur's use of the term 'equivalence' in translation emphasizes a relation but not an identity of value, Derrida's use of the term suggests that the traditional conception of a good translation depends upon the possibility of achieving absolute parity between the source and target text. While such a translation may be *skilfully* good, however, it cannot be conceived as *ethically* good, for it fails to account for the differences between languages themselves, thereby determining an ethics of exchange which seeks to raze and synthesize difference in order to create an illusory notion of universality.

Derrida suggests that this 'good' conception of translation is disrupted by forms which emphasize, through the use of glossing, the semantic remainder which persists even within an attempted linguistic synthesis. Glossing threatens the univocity of the word by insisting upon what is hidden within language and challenging the 'loi économique du mot, qui définit l'essence de la traduction au sens strict'/'economic law of the word, which defines the essence of translation in the strict sense'.[126] Translations which include glosses mark and comment upon every inevitable failure to attain absolute equivalence with an original. In this sense, they become 'relevante' insofar as they are concerned with the proliferation of semantic meaning revealed by translation, rather than its limitation.

Semprún's own use of glossing can be read as part of an attempt to disrupt any supposed universality on a linguistic level by repeatedly exceeding the norms of translatability and expanding and elaborating upon the (un)translatability of the expressions on which his attention is fixed. In *Quel beau dimanche!* Semprún focuses upon one particular example of a manipulated language loan, the German phrase and camp motto *Jedem das Seine*, 'to each his (or her) own'. Fixed, to this day, in iron upon the main gate of the camp, *Jedem das Seine* is a slogan with a long history. A translation of the Latin *suum cuique*, made famous in Cicero's philosophical dialogue as an exemplum of the fairness of the justice system, it remains the official Latin motto of the German military police, and appeared – in its German translation – in works by Martin Luther and Johann Sebastian Bach, before being appropriated by the Nazis at Buchenwald as a textual justification for the creation of the camp. As Semprún noted in a speech which he gave in 2010, sixty-five years after the liberation of Buchenwald, this appropriation reflects a deeply cynical and arrogant conception of equality: 'Une sentence référant à l'égalité entre les êtres humains à l'entrée d'un camp de concentration, au seuil d'un endroit mortifère, un lieu consacré à l'injustice la plus arbitraire et la plus brutale, où il n'existait pour les déportés que l'égalité face à la mort!'/'A sentence referring to equality amongst human beings at the entrance to a concentration camp, on the threshold of a space of death, a place consecrated to the most arbitrary and brutal injustice, where for the detainees there only existed equality before death!'[127]

It is the cynicism inherent in the choice of *Jedem das Seine,* a phrase which purports to speak of the equality of all men, as the motto for a camp built upon a tremendous and destructive inequality, which motivates Semprún's exploration of this phrase. In *Tradition, Translation, Trauma,* Susan Bassnett suggests that the injustice and violence represented by *Jedem das Seine* is a form of translation of 'what is inscribed in the gates of Dante's Hell, composed in Italian eight hundred years ago, although serving a completely different purpose and emanating from a totally different ethics'.[128] But through his interlingual and intralingual translations of *Jedem das Seine,* Semprún queries how different this purpose and ethics can be, for as he reveals, *Jedem das Seine* is always repeated, always repeatable, and always marks the edge between the living and the dead, the deserving and the punished, the evil and the fraternal, 'au seuil d'un endroit mortifère'.[129]

'Qu'aurait dit Goethe', the narrator asks, 's'il avait remarqué l'inscription forgée dans le fer de la grille monumentale du camp *Jedem das Seine*?'/'what [would] Goethe [...] have to say about this inscription over the Buchenwald gate, TO EACH HIS DUE?'[130] Semprún's question invokes not only the echoes of Goethe which permeate the space of the Buchenwald camp, but also the philosophical proximity which Semprún discovers between Goethe's thinking on liberty and the cynicism of the camp motto. Interleaving extracts from Goethe's actual texts with imagined conversations between Goethe and Eckermann, Semprún suggests that Goethe, had he truly been immortal, would have perceived the inscription over the gates of Buchenwald as the embodiment of an ideal form of freedom:

> je trouve très significatif et très encourageant qu'une inscription semblable orne la porte d'entrée d'un lieu de privation de liberté, de rééducation par la contrainte de travail. Car enfin, qu'est-ce que cela signifie, «à chacun son dû»? N'est-ce pas là une excellente définition d'une société organisée pour défendre la liberté de tous, celle de l'ensemble de la société, au détriment s'il le faut d'une liberté individuelle exagérée et néfaste? [...] À chacun son dû, en effet, à chacun la place qui lui est due, par la naissance, le talent, dans la hiérarchie des libertés et des contraintes individuelles qui font la liberté de tous.
>
> I find it most significant and encouraging that such an inscription should decorate the gates of a place where freedom has been withdrawn, a place of re-education through forced labor. For, after all, what does it mean, 'to each his due'? Is it not an excellent motto for a society organized to defend the freedom of all, to the detriment, if necessary, of an excessive, harmful individual freedom? [...] To each his due, indeed, to each the place that is due to him, through birth or talent, in the hierarchy of individual freedom and constraints that make up the liberty of us all.[131]

It might seem paradoxical that Semprún's imagined Goethe is inspired to this vision of collective liberty by the words marked upon the iron gates of Buchenwald, gates which deny the liberty of those within. And yet it is precisely this paradox which explains the particular cynicism that Semprún reads in *Jedem das Seine*, for in Goethe's imagined reaction the motto comes to define a hierarchical form of collective liberty built at the expense of the freedom of the individual. Through this reading *Jedem das Seine* becomes, ironically, the *most* appropriate epigram for the Buchenwald camp. For Buchenwald is the culmination of a conception of freedom which depends upon repressing the individual, upon rejecting the 'untranslatable' which I explored in Chapter 2: it is a site which embodies the Nazi insistence upon the existence of a superior race, and the legitimization this provided them to humiliate, torture and murder those they conceived as inferior.

The imagined Goethe's understanding of *Jedem das Seine* brings us to the collision of radical evil and fraternity with which Semprún is concerned in *L'Écriture ou la vie*. Here the fraternal, prioritized above the individual, becomes a means of repression; the search for equality is converted into the experience of radical evil embodied in Buchenwald. In 'Mal et modernité', Semprún comments upon this contamination, implicating Goethe in a form of humanism which, in its abstraction, fails to acknowledge the structures of human existence:

> Il semble bien que Goethe [...] [n'ait] pas vraiment saisi le sens reél et profound des thèses kantiennes. [...] le mal est radical parce qu'[...] il s'enracine dans l'être même de l'homme, dans l'être-homme, indépendamment de toute détermination historique ou sociale; [...] comme source et suite de la liberté constituante de l'être-homme.
>
> It seems that Goethe [...] did not really grasp the real and profound meaning of Kant's theories [...] Evil is radical because [...] it is rooted in the very being of man, in being human, independent of any historical or social determinism; [...] as both the source and the consequence of the essential freedom of all human beings.[132]

The imagined Goethe's abstract musings on the nature of human liberty and equality miss the radical reality of evil which, for Semprún, exists precisely *in*, and not in opposition to, these expressions of liberty and equality.

This omission is particularly pertinent because of the symbolic power of Goethe within cultural memory. The memory of Goethe, Semprún suggests, has been deployed to enable a subsequent forgetting of the reality of the camp experience. It is this potent cultural heritage to which the narrator himself appeals later in the text, defending himself to the SS officer against the potential repercussions of his decision to leave the designated route of the camp, by claiming that he wanted to look at 'Goethe's tree', the tree beneath which Goethe and Eckermann are believed to have conversed: 'Il a l'air très intéressé. – Goethe! S'exclame-t-il. Vous connaissez l'œuvre de Goethe? J'incline la tête modestement. Il m'a dit «vous», peut-être sans s'en rendre compte. Le fait que je connaisse l'œuvre de Goethe l'a fait changer de ton, instantanément. C'est beau, la culture, quand même.'/'He looks very interested. "Goethe!" he exclaims. "So you know the works of Goethe?" A distinct change of tone. *Kultur* has its uses. I nod modestly'.[133]

In the black comedy of this collision of the literary and the political, Goethe's name becomes symbolic of a form of cultural capital which can engender respect even for those within the camp. The nub of Semprún's critique here is directed at the implicit valorization and romanticization of the space of Buchenwald through its connection to Goethe. The narrator's comment following his interrogation by the SS officer reveals the dangers of such cultural valorizations; the exclamation 'C'est beau, la culture' is as ironic as the exclamation 'Quel beau dimanche!' after which the text itself is named. The exploitation of Weimar's literary past to mask its political reality is embodied by the relationship between Goethe and the Buchenwald camp, by this interplay of the literary and the political which transgresses temporal and conceptual boundaries; it is this mask which Semprún seeks to confront and expose through his own interplay of the literary and the political, enabled by intertextuality and by his translation of *Jedem das Seine* into the voice of Goethe.

Semprún explores a supposedly ethical alternative to Goethe's prioritization of collective liberty through another glossed translation of *Jedem das Seine*, provided this time in the voice of Léon Blum. While in *L'Écriture ou la vie,* these two literary figures are brought together through their occupation of the same space at different times, in *Quel beau dimanche!* this temporal disjunction is annulled with comic results: the imaginary Goethe, fascinated by Blum's audacity in ventriloquizing his voice in *Nouvelles conversations de Goethe avec Eckermann*, attempts to uncover the location of Blum's incarceration near Buchenwald, much to the chagrin of Semprún's imagined Eckermann, who is put out by Blum's appropriation of his role as Goethe's interrogator. Semprún quotes liberally from Blum's 'Notes d'Allemagne', which Blum began writing a few days after his incarceration by the Nazis in a house near Buchenwald. In these notes, Blum offers a 'revolutionary' conception of equality, which he has translated from Plato: *'l'égalité équité, qui accepte le "matériau" humain tel qu'il est, qui reconnaît comme un fait premier la diversité, la variété, et par conséquent l'inégalité intrinsèque des données humaines et qui se traduit, non par l'uniformité numérique, mais par la juste proportion maintenue entre les données humains inégales.'*/'equality-equity, which accepts the human "raw material" as it is, which recognizes as a premise the diversity, variety, and consequently intrinsic inequality of the human givens, and which is expressed, not in numerical uniformity, but in the maintenance of a just proportion between the unequal human givens.'[134] In this 'égalité équité', absolute identification is renounced in favour of an equality formed through variety and diversity, one which recognizes rather than represses differences, whether linguistic, social, ontological or ideological. Blum suggests that this vision of equality has a radical power: '*Ce concept de l'égalité est pleinement révolutionnaire*'/'This concept of equality is fully revolutionary', he writes in 'Notes d'Allemagne'.[135]

The importance of acknowledging difference, here evoked by Blum, is at the heart of the ethical conception of translation which I read through Deleuze and Ricœur in Chapters 1 and 2. In his discussion of a 'relevante' as opposed to 'good' translation, Derrida similarly emphasizes the value of recognizing diversity and variety: glossed translations, such as those employed by Semprún, challenge the idea(l) of absolute identity of meaning between two different languages and recognize rather than repress the inevitable differences which are revealed by translation. For all three theorists, then, an ethics of translation emerges in the ways that translation allows us to acknowledge diversity, the same type of acknowledgement which Blum offers as his revolutionary conception of equality. But Semprún's exploration of Blum's thinking ultimately destabilizes this ethical and positive dynamic, for the intertextual insertion by Blum upon which Semprún focuses culmiates, ironically, in Blum writing the very phrase which, unbeknownst to him, is written on the gates of the camp next to his own lodge: '*J'ai toujours considéré que l'égalité était le respect exact de la variété et, par conséquent, de l'inégalité naturelle. Les formules de l'égalité sont, non pas* Tous à la toise *ou* Tous dans le même sac, *mais* Chacun à sa place *et* À chacun son dû.'/'I have always considered that equality was the scrupulous respect of variety and, consequently, of natural inequality. The formulas of equality, consequently, are, not THE SAME STANDARD FOR ALL, but EACH HAS HIS PLACE and TO EACH HIS DUE.'[136] Semprún's exploration of Blum's words returns us, through the French translation, to *Jedem das Seine*. And this return – the culmination of Blum's theoretical desire to prioritize variety above uniformity – undermines the ethical potential of this dimension of Blum's work. For as the inscription of *Jedem das Seine* is translated from the gates of Buchenwald onto the pages of Blum's work and back again, from German to French, and back to German, the abstract gap between *tous* and *chacun*, between an equality built through identification and an equality built through difference is diminished: *Jedem das Seine,* the pinnacle of Blum's 'revolutionary' exploration of that equality through difference, is simultaneously the motto of the Nazi repression of that difference.

The parallel Semprún shows between Blum's theoretical discussion of *Jedem das Seine* and the words which appear on the camp gates highlights one of Semprún's most troubling thoughts: that the ethical conception of equality and liberty embodied by *Jedem das Seine* translates only too easily into a repressive and destructive reality. *Jedem das Seine* may be distorted in its translation from philosophy to action, from Latin to German, from the pages of a book to the gates of Buchenwald. But the possibility of this translation emphasizes Semprún's overriding argument regarding the reality of the camp experience: that the experience of radical evil is not inhuman but is contained in the very possibilities and philosophies to which humans accord the greatest ethical value. Through the use of glossed translations, Semprún emphasizes the ways in which translation questions our ability to respect difference rather than affirming or confirming our ability to do so.

Mistranslating *Jedem das Seine*: Chalamov and Semprún

The ease with which even the most ostensibly ethical phrases can be converted into repression is behind the third of Semprún's explorations of *Jedem das Seine*: a misremembering of the term which the narrator suggests appears in the French translation of Varlam Chalamov's *Kolyma Tales,* a series of short stories which Chalamov, who spent seventeen years in Soviet labour camps, wrote about the Kolyma gulag. Semprún quotes from one story in *Récits de Kolyma,* in which Chalamov refers to the motto above the gates of Buchenwald:

> Chalamov écrit: «On dit qu'au-dessus des camps de concentration allemands figurait une citation de Nietzsche: chacun pour soi». Et dans les récits sans doute colportés par des Russes qui auraient évoqué, dans un baraquement de Kolyma, leur expérience de Buchenwald, *Jedem das Seine* avait fini par devenir *Jeder für Sich*: «À chacun son dû» était devenu «Chacun pour soi».
>
> Shalamov writes: 'It is said that over the German concentration camps there appeared a quotation from Nietzsche: "Everyone for himself". And in the accounts that must have been brought back by Russians talking, in some hut in Kolyma, of their experience in Buchenwald, *Jedem das Seine* ended up as *Jeder für Sich*: TO EACH HIS DUE had become EVERYONE FOR HIMSELF'.[137]

In showing this slippage from 'à chacun son dû' to 'chacun pour soi', Semprún highlights the damaging impact of a political transformation. For this phrase only reappears in Chalamov's book about the Kolyma gulag because some of the Russians who were interned in Buchenwald for contravening the Nazi ideals were, ironically, later interned in the Soviet Gulags, repressed by the Communist ideology they had fought so long to establish. In their transfer to the Gulags they also transferred the words written upon the gate of Buchenwald, 'et comme souvent, presque inévitablement, dans les récits transmis de bouche à oreille, le sens de l'inscription initial s'était peu à peu transformé'/'And, as happens so often, almost inevitably, in accounts transmitted by word of mouth, the meaning of the original inscription had gradually become transformed'.[138] But this is not a transformation of the beliefs of those imprisoned in both Buchenwald and Kolyma; rather it is a transformation of Communism itself, so that those who were once part of this programme have become excluded by it.

Through his exploration of Chalamov's discussion of *Jedem das Seine*, Semprún highlights the ideological connections between Buchenwald and Kolyma: the misremembering of *Jedem das Seine*, created by its oral transmission from Buchenwald to Kolyma, occurs because of an inherent identity between these two camp experiences, which enables the same individuals to be incarcerated for transgressing two different political movements. This common essence between the camps transcends historical and geographical specificity, but it also transcends ideological specificity, for it reveals the human impulse expressed by *Jedem das Seine*: the impulse to assign to others what we believe to be their due and to find an ideological mirror which best reflects what we believe we should receive.

The breadth of this human impulse is dramatized by the ideological duality of the camp experience at Buchenwald: translated across time and ideology, *Jedem das Seine* marks the gates of both the Nazi camp and the Soviet NKVD 2. And, as the motto for two ostensibly opposed ideologies, *Jedem das Seine* illuminates the role played by intertextuality in enabling the translation of ideal into ideology, impulse into slogan. Slogans such as *Jedem das Seine* are powerful, not because they reflect a unique ideological moment, but because they reveal the general human impulse to give symbolic meaning to the contingent and the everyday. The slogan represents this impulse translated into soundbite, painted upon walls, branded upon placards, wrought in iron upon gates, engraved upon memorials; it is 'mythic' in the sense Barthes gives this word in *Mythologies*, seeking to naturalize the implicitly historical into an eternal image through which universal values can be asserted.[139]

Even as Semprún engages with literature's potential to map the contours of an ethics of communication and representation based on difference, though, he again acknowledges the role literature plays in distorting that ethics, in reifying those questions into motivated answers. Indeed, Semprún's narration of Chalamov's discussion of *Jedem das Seine* reveals this process of mistranslation – and consequent appropriation – to be at play even within his own use of quotation. For the 2003 French translation of *Récits de Kolyma* does not, in fact, contain the misremembering to which the narrator of *Quel beau dimanche!* refers, but accurately cites the phrase as '*À chacun son dû*'.[140] According to *this* translation then, Chalamov's text quotes and translates *Jedem das Seine* correctly; it is Semprún's own text, *Quel beau dimanche!*, which contains and creates the misremembering to which he alludes.

This 2003 translation is based in part upon Katherine Fournier's 1980 translation of the text, the text which Soledad Fox suggests Semprún read.[141] Yet both this text and *Quel beau dimanche!* were published in the same year, and in the text itself the narrator states that he read *Récits de Kolyma* in 1969. For this reason, Ursula Tidd suggests that Semprún probably read a collection of Chalamov's tales published by Maurice Nadeau in 1969.[142] However, this edition of the text only contains a selection of Chalamov's stories, and does not include the story 'Rations de campagne' upon which Semprún draws for his exploration of *Jedem das Seine*. Given that Semprún does not reference the translation of Chalamov upon which he draws, it is impossible to know for certain the origins of his slippage: whether it originated from a mistranslated, and subsequently corrected, French translation which Semprún read; whether Semprún himself misread, misremembered or misquoted it; or whether, if it was a misquotation, this was accidental or deliberate. In fact, Semprún's misquotation of Chalamov's phrase is not the first time he has been implicated in such a misremembering: as Fox notes, Semprún also misquoted the phrase on the gates at Buchenwald in *Le Grand Voyage*, replacing it with *Arbeit macht frei* – 'work sets you free' – the slogan which actually appeared on the gates at Auschwitz. Fox suggests that this misquotation is deliberate, part of an attempt by Semprún to align his first text with existing literature concerned with narrating the concentration camp experience, within which Auschwitz frequently appears as the symbol of the Holocaust.[143] This particular instance of miswriting is, then, implicated in precisely the types of forgetting which Semprún critiques in relation to the Buchenwald memorial: in attempting to create resonances between the experiences of Auschwitz and Buchenwald, Semprún ultimately overwrites some of the specific realities of Buchenwald itself.

Taken individually and together, these two instances of misappropriation or forgetting reveal an obstacle to thinking of writing through translation as an inherently ethical act, an act capable of challenging discourses which appropriate, mask and overwrite other voices and other pasts. For translation inevitably contains its own non-ethical element: the element which appropriates without any real reference, which synthesizes and erases the trace of the text from which it originated. While any intertextual quotation, removed from its original context, can betray just as much as call to mind the text from which it originated, translated quotations enact this betrayal on multiple levels, for in translation it is not only the context which is altered but the language of the original quotation which is distilled and, inevitably, distorted in the voice of another. Can writing-as-translation, a form of writing which incorporates an aesthetics of translation, transcend the ethical dilemmas of its own form, and resist the appropriations it enables? Or is all translation a betrayal, not only of an original text, but of the voices of the past to which it bears witness?

A 'relevante' translation of *Jedem das Seine*

Taken together, these complexities return us to the question I have been pursuing through Semprún and Derrida, and in this book more generally: what is a *good* translation? This question asks us to consider not only what qualities within a translation we would consider to be 'good', but also what criteria we would use to define 'good' itself. Effective, high-quality and proficient? Or virtuous, noble and respectable? Is a *good* translation a question of skill or of ethics? In Semprún's translation of his memories into a textual form, would a good translation seek to achieve the impossible task of replicating the past exactly as it was? Or, given that the past is always shifting and altering in its own translation into memory, is there a virtue in distortion, in misappropriation and mistranslation?

For Derrida, 'la traduction la plus relevante (celle qui se présente comme le transport du signifié intact dans un signifiant véhiculaire indifférent) est la moins relevante qui soit'/'the most relevant translation (that which presents itself as the transfer of an intact signified through the inconsequential vehicle of any signifier whatsoever) is the least relevant possible'.[144] 'Relevante', Derrida suggests, operates at the intersection of the English word 'relevant' – appropriate, pertinent, significant – and the French verb *relever* – to raise up, to emphasize, to throw into relief, to displace or change ('la relève de la garde'/'the relief [*relève*] of the guard').[145] The essence of 'une traduction "relevante"' is revealed by the difference of meaning between the English and French words. For Derrida, the most 'relevante' translation does not involve the perfect (and impossible) transmission of the meaning of a signifier – the signified – from one language into another. Rather, a 'relevante' translation involves a confrontation between the two languages in question, a confrontation which enacts a 'relève' – a substitution, an elevation, perhaps even a transformation – upon that signified which reveals its meaning only in the ways that that meaning is always being displaced and deferred elsewhere.

This displacement is at play within the slippage from *Jedem das Seine* to *Chacun pour soi* in Semprún's discussion of Chalamov's text. The narrator of *Quel beau dimanche!* comments that *Chacun pour soi* 'n'a strictement aucun rapport, nul besoin d'en faire la démonstration'/'of course, is not at all the same thing'.[146] And yet there *is* a relation between these two phrases. For, in the political context Semprún is exploring, the context which enables both Buchenwald and Kolyma to exist, 'each to their own' *inevitably* morphs into 'everyone for themselves'. This phrase expresses the desire for the collective with which one identifies – whether that be an ideological or national group – to be the best it can – even, perhaps especially, at the cost of the repression or erasure of those excluded from this collective. But not only this: as Semprún's narratives of life within Buchenwald attest, *Chacun pour soi* is not only the essence of the Nazi and Communist ideologies which run the camps, but also a condition of survival within the camps themselves, for behind every survival lies the possible triumph of one individual at the expense of another, or, conversely, the sacrifice of one person's life for another. Here, in this mistranslation, the clash of the fraternal and of radical evil is manifested on a linguistic level: *Jedem das Seine* and *Chacun pour soi* are two sides of the same coin, of the experience of what it means to be human, distilled and catalysed within the camp experience. The substitution of names on a list of those to be sent to the forced labour camp Mittelbau-Dora; the decision to steal another inmate's food, or to share one's own; even, as *Le Mort qu'il faut* describes, the possibility of achieving one's own survival through the death of another – these narratives explore, through the intensity of the camp experience, the ethical dilemmas and possibilities which constitute our human desire for survival. While *Chacun pour soi* is not a 'good' translation of *Jedem das Seine* – it fails to transfer, intact, one signified into another signifier – it is, nonetheless, a 'relevante' translation, expressing, through its own linguistic slippage, the human impulse towards fraternity *and* evil which erupts at both Buchenwald and Kolyma.

In Semprún's engagement with translation, a value is thus assigned to the 'relevante' failure to translate perfectly, a failure which stages the slippages and distortions involved in the translation of memory into narrative. In this regard, the three translations of *Jedem das Seine* which Semprún explores through the voices of Blum, Goethe and Chalamov, are themselves 'relevante': in their relation to each other, they dramatize the distortions and mistranslations at play in any interaction of the aesthetic and the political, whether that interaction occurs in a memorial, a slogan, or a narrative. Paradoxically, then, the ethics of writing-as-translation is implicit within those aspects of its practice which appear to reveal the lack of ethics in any writing: by appropriating, synthesizing and mistranslating other voices, other texts, other narratives and other memories, writing-as-translation illuminates the losses and appropriations involved in all memory, all narrative, all experience.

But this translation of voices from *beyond* the camp – spatially, temporally and conceptually – also highlights crucial elements *within* the nature of the camp experience that are explored by Semprún in *Quel beau dimanche!,* and *L'Écriture ou la vie*. Semprún's intertextual exploration of the shift from *Jedem das Seine* to *Chacun pour soi* is a journey from Goethe and Eckermann – who exist before the time, before the very conception of the camp, only inhabiting the same temporal plane as the camp within the narrator's imagination – to Chalamov, whose words reveal the continuation of the impulses and ideas upon which the camp was founded. Clearly, this journey far exceeds the boundary of the Sunday at Buchenwald which Semprún describes; it is a journey from the inconceivable to the conceivable; from a moment *before* or *beyond* the conception of the camps to a moment when *before* and *beyond* themselves seem inconceivable. Semprún's most troubling thoughts are concerned with the possibility that it is not only within memory that the camps continue to exist, but within human thought, impulse and society. For if, as Semprún's intertextual exploration of Goethe and Blum suggests, thinking equality and liberty culminates in thinking *Jedem das Seine,* and *Jedem das Seine* culminates in Buchenwald and Kolyma, can there be any thinking without the possibility of thinking the camps, and any thinking the camps without the possibility of creating the camps?

In *Dialectic of Enlightenment,* Adorno and Horkheimer suggest that Enlightenment thinking, with its valorization of enlightened reason, brings us ineluctably to the type of totalitarianism revealed by the existence of the camps. To insist that we can, through reason, understand and master all aspects of existence leads, they suggest, to Nazism and the tragedy of the Holocaust, for it allows the dominance of singular versions of reality in which '[t]he mere existence of the other is a provocation'.[147] Similarly, Giorgio Agamben suggests that the concentration camp is the culmination of precisely the modern, democratic validation of the rights of the individual which promised a liberation from such forms of tyranny. Ultimately, Agamben posits, this liberation inscribes politics into the individual life, ironically embedding the individual more firmly into a state apparatus which regulates every aspect of our lives. In this regulation, those who fail to conform are excluded, entering a 'state of exception' for which the camps become the inevitable receptacle.[148]

How can we respond to this seemingly ineluctable movement from the ostensibly enlightened, democratic and liberal to the existence of the camps? Adorno and Horkheimer speak of 'the necessity for enlightenment to reflect upon itself if humanity is not to be betrayed'.[149] One possible form for this reflection is to redeem the mimetic action, which they suggest has been over-regulated and denigrated by enlightenment rationality. For Agamben, too, art can offer an avenue to explore the inevitability of the camp experience. But this testimony must acknowledge its limitations: bearing witness, he suggests, can only occur in relation to the *remnants* of an experience always caught between loss and redemption.[150] Semprún's response in *Quel beau dimanche!* speaks to both of these ethical attempts to respond to the challenge of narrating the realities of Buchenwald. His writing is always concerned with the possibility of copying reality through art, with bearing witness to his past in narrative form. But, as his three different intertextual translations of *Jedem das Seine* reveal, that testimony is always fragmented, disrupted and situated *in between* voices, perspectives and temporal moments in a way which refuses to combine these remnants into a single narrative. As Tidd suggests, in writing, translating, quoting and imagining Goethe and Blum, Semprún 'forces both the ideological vision of German Enlightenment humanism incarnated by Goethe and the failures of proletarian internationalism and social democracy, represented by Blum, to face the reality of Buchenwald's existence'.[151] And this reality, always complex, always permeated with misrememberings, with the history of NKVD 2 as well as Buchenwald, with both Nazi and Communist repression, can only be narrated in intertextual and translated fragments which contradict and challenge one another in the very ways in which they connect.

As Susan Bassnett notes, '[t]ranslation [...] always involves a relationship that spans time and space. [...] That relationship reminds us that all texts are in a way connected, that the world we live in is a vast network of connecting threads, so many of which began to be spun aeons ago.'[152] Paradoxically, then, Semprún's focus upon the words which marked the gates of his own incarceration opens rather than closes the frame of his text: translating this phrase linguistically from German to French allows him simultaneously to translate it temporally, carrying us on an intertextual journey away from the gates of Buchenwald into an exploration of the other echoes and voices which constitute the memory, the legacy, and the very possibility of the camp. As Bassnett goes on to write, translation always involves crossing a 'threshold from one world into another'.[153] In repeating *Jedem das Seine* within the pages of *Quel beau dimanche!* Semprún draws the reader across this threshold, exploring the space between the living and dead, between the past and present, between man's humanity and man's inhumanity, which for him, constitutes the essential truth of Buchenwald.

In *Le Masque et le masqué,* María Semilla Durán suggests that the multiplicity of memory, conceived through the figures of Blum and Goethe, operates as 'une sorte d'absolutisation de l'écho, de la trace, comme si l'espace pourrait garder et contenir un précipité du temps, un semblant d'éternité'/'a sort of absoluteness of the echo of the trace, as if the space could hold and contain a rushing of time, a semblance of eternity'.[154] But the echoes Semprún offers here are never absolute; rather, they disrupt any attempted synthesis of the conflicted memories of his past and of the space of the Buchenwald camp. By fragmenting the temporal and ideological unity of the space which the Buchenwald memorial represents as one of spatial wholeness, writing-as-translation inscribes an ethical alterity into Semprún's representation of Buchenwald and into his discussion of *Jedem das Seine*. In so doing, it throws into relief the contradictions, both theoretical and historical, in which it is implicated, forcing Buchenwald – like *Aufhebung* – to write itself as other, to write itself in memory of the echoes of the dead.

Intertextuality: translating the voices of the dead

In her monograph on Semprún's work, *Jorge Semprún: Writing the European Other*, Ursula Tidd focuses upon the role of intertextuality within Semprún's attempt to write the trauma of his experiences. Intertextuality, she suggests, enacts the 'narrator's repeated disappearance from the testimonial text [...]. The narrator seeks other words and the words of others to communicate his exile and Buchenwald experience, as if the multiplication of linguistic and cultural resources might ultimately succeed in expressing his Holocaust experience'. This multiplication writes otherness into Semprún's narration, enabling 'the self to encounter and exist in relationship to its own alterity as well as the alterity of others'.[155] In Tidd's reading, Semprún reflects Levinas's discussion of the necessity of hearing the voice of the Other in its irreducible alterity. In this account, Semprún's deployment of intertextuality is a response which seeks to 'keep' faith with this irreducibility, to listen to the Other in the words, language and voice of that alterity.[156]

This relationship to alterity is, however, always negotiated and shaped by the self: the intertextual excerpts which appear within *Quel beau dimanche!* are selected by Semprún, and they are discussed and framed by the narratorial voice in the text who shapes the reader's understanding of them. In this sense, Semprún's extensive quotation from Goethe, Blum and Chalamov hints, in each reading and rewriting, at a memory in translation *between* Semprún's voice and the voices of others, and at a textual illumination of a past which is always sinking into oblivion, nostalgia or glorification, through every attempt to address and witness it. These quotations and translations are integral, not only to Semprún's writing of memory in *Quel beau dimanche!*, but to the continuously altered formation of those memories themselves. The narrator suggests that his rejection of Communism as a viable ideological model was compelled by literature, specifically his reading of the French translation of Solzhenitsyn's *One Day in the Life of Ivan Denisovich* in 1963: 'En une nuit, ces quelques dizaines de pages avaient réussi à me faire voir ce que des années d'expérience, depuis 1956, des dizaines d'heures de discussion et de lectures n'étaient pas parvenus à éclaircir pour moi de manière définitive'/'In one night, those few dozen pages had managed to make me see what years of experience, from 1956 onwards, had failed to elucidate for me definitively'.[157] This definitive illumination, prompted by Solzhenitsyn's narration of the brutality of the Soviet concentration camps, forces the narrator to acknowledge that the failures of Communism can no longer be redeemed through dialectical and intertextual justifications.

His subsequent reading of Chalamov's *Récits de Kolyma* consolidates this realization; the narrator finds his memory layered by the words of this text, his camp experiences multiplied and expressed through the mouth of another: 'J'avais l'impression que [...] je flottais comme un fantôme dans la mémoire de quelqu'un d'autre. Ou alors c'était Chalamov qui flottait dans ma mémoire à moi comme un fantôme. C'était la même mémoire, en tout cas, dédoublée'/'I felt like a ghost floating in someone else's memory. Or was it Shalamov floating in my memory like a ghost? It was the same memory in any case, [doubled and] divided in two'.[158] The camp the narrator remembers here is one he has visited only through literature. And yet it is this *textual* memory which infiltrates the narrator's experience in a form that is, at times, more powerful and tenacious than the memory of his lived experience of Buchenwald.

This phantom memory offers both illumination and oblivion: ghosts can appear in many guises, but they can also fade or be obscured. In this intertextual excerpt, however, oblivion is briefly held at bay, as Semprún writes the dead into the dual memory of the two camps:

> Les têtes coupées des paysans russes, raconte Chalamov, s'alignaient devant la baraque de la *kommandantura,* à Kolyma. Yeux ouverts sur la mort. Yeux fous, d'un bleu pale, d'un gris glacial: petits lacs où s'était reflétée l'ardeur subite et mortelle du printemps. Yeux fous de la folie russe. La même folie qu'à Buchenwald. La même folie de vivre des paysans russes dans les camps de Hitler et les camps de Staline. Il n'y a plus de mémoire innocente, plus pour moi.
>
> The heads of the Russian peasants, Shalamov tells us, were lined up in front of the *kommandantura* at Kolyma. Eyes open on death. Mad eyes, pale-blue, icy-gray: tiny lakes in which was reflected the sudden, lethal ardor of spring. [The same madness as at Buchenwald. The mad desire for life within] the Russian peasants in Hitler's camps and in Stalin's. There is no such thing as innocent memory. Not for me any more.[159]

The memory of the dead is doubled and re-inscribed through a narrative itself formed through a doubling and a re-inscription of Chalamov's text. In this doubling, those deaths are translated, temporally, geographically and linguistically, from their original context – Chalamov's tales of Kolyma, written in Russian between 1954 and 1973 – into a new one – Semprún's narrative of Buchenwald, written in French in 1980. But unlike the decontextualized translation of quotation into dialectical justification, this out-of-context translation reveals the forms of its own concealment. For the innocence of memory which Semprún seeks to disrupt in *Quel beau dimanche!* is born of a faith *in* context, a faith that even the most horrific events, such as those that took place at Buchenwald or Kolyma, can be contained, and understood, within their context; as Alan Bennett wrote in *The History Boys,* 'to put something in context is a step towards saying it can be understood and that it can be explained. And if it can be explained then it can be explained away'.[160] By revealing, through intertextuality, that these two different but parallel experiences of torture and death exceed the context of their happening, Semprún's narrative refuses the explanations and understandings to which Bennett alerts his readers. In his English translation, Sheridan omits this reference to Buchenwald. But this omission ignores the critical connection between these two traumas: the experiences of death at Buchenwald and at Kolyma cannot be erased, synthesized or overcome, but only written, over and over, in different forms.

Throughout *Quel beau dimanche!* Semprún uses intertextuality to insist upon the impossibility of moving beyond the losses and the memories of this traumatic past; the narrator, and the reader, are continually returned to that past, even in the midst of seemingly unrelated experiences. In one powerful section, Chalamov's text intrudes quite literally into the flow of the narrator's memories of Buchenwald and of his time in the PCE: 'J'étais à Londres, je lisais les *Récits de Kolyma,* de Varlam Chalamov. C'était à la fin du printemps, en 1969'; 'Mais j'étais à Londres et je lisais les *Récits de Kolyma,* de Varlam Chalamov'; 'J'étais à Londres, je lisais dans les *Récits de Kolyma*'; 'Je lisais les *Récits de Kolyma,* à Londres, la gorge serrée'/'I was in London, reading Varlam Shalamov's *Kolyma Tales*. It was in the late spring on 1969'; 'But I was in London, reading Varlam Shalamov's *Kolyma Tales*'; 'I was in London, reading in *Kolyma Tales*'; 'I was reading *Kolyma Tales* in London, my heart in my mouth'.[161] Here, in the constant return of the text's title, the memories articulated in and created by Chalamov's text become uncrushable, repeatedly rising to the surface of the narrator's memories of other times and other experiences. But this is *imperfect* memory, in both tense and form: the repetition of this past action, this reading of Chalamov's text in a present narrative, shifts in each repetition, the first reading erased by the second, the second distorted by the third, and so on, endlessly. This, then, is a textual erasure of memory as much as a return, for memory re-read and re-written is also memory altered, tracing its own forgetting.

This textual circling without progress which moves between the losses of the past and the losses of that past in the present has an ethical value, giving the fragments and ruins of the past their own momentum which is not dialectically subsumed beneath the thrust of the future. In this circling, Benjamin's angel of history beats its wings against the force of the future; it cannot move backwards, into the past, but it can, perhaps, achieve an equilibrium, a moment of suspension in the present through which past and present can be illuminated, even while they remain vulnerable to further erasure and loss. It is in the present that history has meaning for Benjamin. As Mathews discusses in *Tradition, Translation, Trauma,* Benjamin draws history with a Janus-face: even as we look backwards into the past, we simultaneously look forward; these two viewpoints are synthesized in the present, which is the only temporal plane which can be *seen* as opposed to simply faced.[162] Benjamin's vision of history is dialectical, but his history is not a synthesis of past and present which enables a progression into a new, implicitly better, future; rather, it is a synthesis of a past and a future in a present which, like the narrative of *Quel beau dimanche!,* is troubled and disrupted by echoes and foreshadowings which can never be fully or clearly perceived.

Benjamin articulates powerfully the difference between a cause-and-effect attitude to history, and one in which fragments of the past are allowed to leap out of sequence and illuminate moments of the present:

> Historicism contents itself with establishing a causal connection between various moments in history. But no fact that is a cause is for that very reason historical. It became historical posthumously, as it were, through events that may be separated from it by thousands of years. A historian who takes this as his point of departure stops telling the sequence of events like the beads of a rosary. Instead, he grasps the constellation which his own has formed with a definite earlier one.[163]

Benjamin's concept of the constellation highlights the way in which the past and the present come together in an expansive yet connected array of fragmentary moments which interact tangentially rather than causally. For Benjamin, these historical constellations appear in writing through the process of translation and quotation: 'To write history thus means to *cite* history. It belongs to the concept of citation, however, that the historical object in each case is torn from its context'.[164] As I have discussed, the dangers of this tearing from context are implicit in translation and in quotation, manifested within the slogan and within the dialectic as a mode of thought. But if this process is to be acknowledged as much as masked, quotation must become a doubling, indeed a multiplying, of different voices and of different pasts, as in Semprún's quotation from Chalamov. In this sense, quotation offers a 'relevante' translation – a transformation and a displacement – which reveals the constellations and connections between those voices and pasts.

This 'relevante' translation of past into present, this constellation of different moments pulled from linearity to reveal their indefinite relation to each other, is at the heart of the chronological fragmentation within *Quel beau dimanche!* As the narrator comments, his life and writing are not a flow towards an end point but a continuous repetition and back-and-forth: 'Ma vie est constamment défaite, perpétuellement en train de se défaire, de s'estomper, de partir en fumée. Elle est une suite hasardeuse d'immobilités, d'instantanés, une succession discontinue de moments fugaces, d'images qui scintillent passagèrement dans une nuit infinie.'/'My life is constantly being undone, perpetually undoing itself, growing blurred, going up in smoke. It is a random succession of arrested moments, of snapshots, a discontinuous succession of fleeting instants, of images that flicker momentarily in an endless night.'[165] The ethical value Semprún perceives within this continual ebb and flow of life and death is revealed in the final pages of *Quel beau dimanche!*. The narrator returns to the moment with which *Quel beau dimanche!* began – a snowy Sunday, the perfect tree, the crude dialectic revealed by the tree and the snow. But this time this experience is distilled through the narrator's own memory, and through his conversation with another – a Jehovah's Witness also imprisoned in the camp, whom the narrator refers to simply as Jehovah.

> Tout à l'heure [...] Jehovah m'avait demandé si j'avais passé un bon dimanche. J'avais pensé à cet arbre. [...] J'avais eu l'impression fugitive de découvrir une vérité essentielle: la vérité de cet arbre, de tous les arbres autour, toute la forêt, toutes les forêts, le monde qui n'avait nul besoin de mon regard. [...] Pendant un bref instant d'éternité, j'avais contemplé cet arbre avec le regard d'au-delà de ma mort, avec les yeux de ma propre mort. Et l'arbre était toujours aussi beau. Ma mort ne mutilait pas la beauté de cet arbre. [...] Oui, dis-je à Jehovah, un très bon dimanche.

> Just now [...] Jehovah asked me if I'd had a good Sunday. I thought of that beech tree. [...] For a brief moment, I thought I had discovered some fundamental truth: the truth of that tree, of all the trees around, the whole forest, every forest, the word, which had no need of my gaze. [...] For a brief moment of eternity, I looked at that tree with a gaze from beyond my death, with the eyes of my own death. And the tree was still as beautiful. My death did not diminish its beauty. [...] 'Yes', I say to Jehovah, 'a very good Sunday'.[166]

Here, in the substitution of 'bon' for 'beau', the *impossibility* of an aesthetically beautiful translation of the reality of the camp experience into narrative is replaced by the *possibility* of a good translation, understood in the sense of Derrida's 'relevante' translation: one which recognizes the inevitable and unsubsumable presence of death beneath the experience to be narrated.[167] In her discussion of this extract, Ursula Tidd argues that the narrator realizes that 'the Other in the form of life will always transcend the egoic perceiving subject'.[168] Yet this transcendence is always temporary and imperfect: the narrator can only experience this redemption through memory and narrative: by reflecting upon and rewriting the 'beau dimanche' of the past as a 'bon dimanche' in the present. And, as Semprún suggests throughout his discussion of the dialectic, life and beauty cannot ultimately transcend death, or the limitations of our own subjective perspective, but only remain in 'relevante' dialogue with them.

In these final pages of *Quel beau dimanche!*, the different forgettings which I have discussed in this chapter are brought together by their 'relevante' translation into a narrative which elevates, transforms, but never entirely redeems them. Here the memory of the dead and the power of nature, erased by the memorial, are returned to the memory of Buchenwald. Here too, the formula with which the narrator revealed his own dialectical justifications earlier in the text is reversed: 'L'arbre qui vous cachait la forêt, la vérité qui vous cachait la Vérité et qui en devenait mensongère'/'The tree that kept you from seeing a forest, the truth that hid the Truth and thus became a lie' is transformed into 'cet arbre' and 'une vérité essentielle', one of many different, individual, truths which the narrator realizes cannot be synthesized into a single vision, whether personal, historical or political.[169] And finally, the text returns us to the elementary dialectic of life and death, spring and winter, with which it began. Through this return, Semprún's narrative enacts a 'relevante' translation of the dialectic itself, highlighting, displacing and transforming this form of thinking to reveal its power, beyond its political incarnations, to narrate the experience in which Semprún is immersed. At the start of *Quel beau dimanche!,* the narrator reflects that 'ce bourgeon fragile, encore impalpable, cette verte moiteur végétale dans le ventre enneigé du temps, ne serait pas seulement la négation mais aussi l'accomplissement de l'hiver. Le vieux Hegel avait raison'/'that delicate, still-impalpable bud, that green vegetal dampness in the snow-covered belly of time, would be not only the negation, but also the fulfillment of winter. Old Hegel was right'.[170] In the final lines of *Quel beau dimanche!* this 'raison' is elucidated: Hegel's own *Aufhebung* is transformed into the written articulation of a constant and continuous movement between life and death, past and future, nature and man, which can never be transcended.

This dialectical circulation of life and death is the 'vérité essentielle' which is the heart of *Quel beau dimanche!,* and which remained unwritten in *Le Grand Voyage*. And this recognition of the inevitable, endless presence of death and loss characterized by Semprún's return, over and over again, to the losses within his past, produces its own form of textual memorial to that past. Unlike the camp memorial which converts the memory of the dead into a triumph of resistance, the narrative Semprún creates in *Quel beau dimanche!* acknowledges the permeation of death, in multiple forms, throughout all the experiences told and retold. For Semilla, Semprún's use of textual repetition lends to his experiences precisely this more fluid form of memorial, one in which each book adds to the construction of a textual monument to Semprún's experience of trauma, loss and pain. But, as Semilla insists, this is not a fixed or closed memorial, concerned with endorsing or profiting from the deaths it commemorates.[171] Rather, this textual memorial is always in a process of movement and flux, for narrative, as Semprún's texts repeatedly attest, is a never-finished transcription of the experience of a death continually being relived.[172]

This continual re-beginning, generated by an insurmountable debt to the voices of the past, is the essence of both translation and the narration of *Quel beau dimanche!*. It is the essence, indeed, of all Semprún's texts. For *Quel beau dimanche!* is another unfinished text, another attempt to translate memory into narrative, which in its inevitable failure carries that memory beyond its own pages into other beginnings, other texts, into *L'Écriture ou la vie* and beyond it. In this sense, the commemorative space Semprún creates in *Quel beau dimanche!* is one of renewal and change, a living and breathing memorial which embodies its loss even as it seeks to salvage scraps from it, not so much a site of memory as a site of translation.

This site of translation is inevitably disjointed and unfinished, since translation does not render memory perfectly, but only in fragments. As Derrida comments, 'peut-être une traduction est-elle vouée à la ruine, à cette forme de mémoire ou de commémoration qu'on appelle une ruine; la ruine est peut-être sa vocation et un destin qu'elle accepte dès l'origine'/'but perhaps a translation is devoted to ruin, to that form of memory or commemoration that is called a ruin; ruin is perhaps its vocation and a destiny that it accepts from the very outset'.[173] To struggle against forgetting through translation is not, then, to remember *what* we have forgotten but simply *that* we have forgotten. Perhaps this is what makes it an ethical space, enabling Semprún to confront the losses and elisions within his political past. For a struggle is a continuous motion, a never-finished action, destined, like translation itself, to be repeated again and again, in recognition of 'la mémoire endeuillée et endettée du corps singulier'/'the mournful and debt-laden memory of the singular body'.[174] In the process of translation, the debt to the past is never redeemed but endlessly deferred; never overcome but only partially salvaged. Semilla posits the recognition of this debt as the momentum behind the narrative of *Quel beau dimanche!*: a debt towards the dead and towards the survivors which takes form in a resistance to the ideologically governed histories which Semprún explores through a narrative of translation and rewriting.[175] For to resist is to re-inscribe and re-lose that past over and over again, in different forms and different spaces.

Epilogue: *luttons, écrivons, traduisons*

Quel beau dimanche! develops the relationship – integral to all Semprún's work – between *luttons* and *écrivons*. In this text, both the subject and the object of Semprún's writing coalesce in an attempted resistance to the erasure of the losses which have permeated his past. For, in a sense, the subject and object of *écrivons* are one and the same: as Brodzki suggests, to articulate truthfully the experience of loss which is anyone's, we need to speak of the dead, in the voices of the dead which are never ours.[176] This ventriloquism contains its own dangers: for the narrator, 'rien ne m'autorisera jamais à parler au nom des morts, l'idée même de m'attribuer ce rôle me remplit d'horreur'/'nothing will ever give me the right to speak for the dead, and the very idea of assuming that role fills me with horror'.[177] This horror can be understood as a fear of betraying those who are unable to narrate for themselves in the translation, and potential appropriation, of their voices, even into an aesthetic form designed to allow those voices to speak. As Semprún repeatedly acknowledges within the pages of *Quel beau dimanche!*, this appropriative impulse cannot be evaded: our personal and our political thinking, our individual and our collective actions, are governed by this dialectical desire to synthesize the past into a comprehensible form.

But insofar as this appropriation can be acknowledged and written, the erasure of the past against which Semprún struggles in *Quel beau dimanche!* can, at the very least, be subjected to a 'relevante' translation into narrative. This 'relevante' translation simultaneously displaces, elevates and transforms the voices of the dead, creating a tissue of different, translated, intertextual voices of those who are gone – Goethe, Blum, Solzhenitsyn, Chalamov – through which Semprún transcribes his experiences. The ending of *Quel beau dimanche!* in French emphasizes the importance of these voices to the affective force of Semprún's narrative. In the company of Barizon, the narrator begins to recite an extract from a Giraudoux text; Barizon interrupts him, and the narration turns to the narrator's discussion with the Jehovah's witness and his recognition of his 'bon dimanche'. It is at this moment that Sheridan ends his English translation of *Quel beau dimanche!*, choosing not to translate the final lines of Semprún's text. In so doing, Sheridan alters the ending of the text: for an English reader, the Sunday which Semprún describes in his novel ends with the narrator's affirmation that he has had a 'good' day. But the very final lines of the French version of *Quel beau dimanche!* continue the narrative away from this emphasis upon what is good to return again to what is 'relevante': these voices from the past, formed of other texts and other memories, which can never be fully interrupted, never fully silenced, never fully understood, for they always return, translated again and again into new forms and new texts: 'je préfère Giraudoux', states the narrator, 'C'est avec lui que j'ai envie de finir ce dimanche'/'I prefer Giraudoux. It's with him that I want to finish this Sunday'.[178] This is the 'we' of the *écrivons* with which the text began, the voices and memories of other texts, other authors, other languages. 'Écrivons': let us speak with the dead, in their multiple and fragmented voices, but not in their name.

Notes

1 Jorge Semprún and Franck Appréderis, *Le Langage est ma patrie* (Paris: Libella-Maren Sell Editions, 2013), 16. All translations from this text are mine.
2 Semprún and Appréderis, *Le Langage*, 15–16; F. Scott Fitzgerald, *The Crack-up* (New York: New Directions, 1945), 69.
3 Semprún and Appréderis, *Le Langage* ,16.
4 Semprún and Appréderis, *Le Langage* ,16.
5 Ofelia Ferrán and Gina Herrmann, 'Introduction', in *A Critical Companion to Jorge Semprún: Buchenwald, Before and After*, ed. Ofelia Ferrán and Gina Herrmann (New York: Palgrave Macmillan, 2014), 3.
6 Ursula Tidd, *Jorge Semprún: Writing the European Other* (London: Legenda, 2014), 75.
7 Jorge Semprún, *Federico Sanchez vous salue bien* (Paris: Éditions Grasset & Fasquelle, 1993), 27. My translation.
8 See Ofelia Ferrán in *Working Through Memory: Writing and Remembrance in Contemporary Spanish Narrative* (Cranbury, NJ: Associated University Presses, 2007).
9 Jorge Semprún, interview with Lila Azam Zanganeh, 'The Art of Fiction No. 192', trans. Sara Sugihara, in *The Paris Review* 180 (2007). http://www.theparisreview.org/interviews/5740/the-art-of-fiction-no-192-jorge-semprun [Accessed 3 January 2018]. (No page references for this text.)
10 Bella Brodzki, *Can These Bones Live?: Translation, Survival and Cultural Memory* (Stanford, CA: Stanford University Press, 2007), 176.
11 Semprún, 'The Art of Fiction No. 192'.
12 Semprún, 'The Art of Fiction No. 192'.
13 Myriam Schleiss, *Le Bilinguisme comme atout de l'écrivain: Représentations du bilinguisme et fonctions stylistiques des marques transcodiques dans l'œuvre de Jorge Semprun* (Saarbrücken, Germany: Editions universitaires européennes, 2011), 51–68.
14 Tidd, *Jorge Semprún*, 23.
15 Tijana Miletic, *European Literary Immigration into the French Language: Readings of Gary, Kristof, Kundera and Semprun* (Amsterdam: Rodopi, 2008), 32.
16 Semprún and Appréderis, *Le Langage*, 29.
17 Semprún, 'The Art of Fiction No. 192'.
18 Jorge Semprún, *L'Écriture ou la vie* (Paris: Gallimard, 1994), 284. *Literature or Life*, trans. Linda Coverdale (New York: Penguin, 1997), 275. All translations of the French text come from this English translation. Page numbers in subsequent references refer to: French text; English text.
19 Semprún, *L'Écriture ou la vie*, 284; 275.
20 Semprún and Appréderis, *Le Langage*, 74.
21 Semprún and Appréderis, *Le Langage*, 74.
22 Tidd, *Jorge Semprún*, 99.
23 Semprún, *Quel beau dimanche!*, (Paris: Éditions Grasset, 2003 [1980]), 120. *What a Beautiful Sunday!*, trans. Alan Sheridan (London: Abacus, 1984 [1982]), 72. Unless stated otherwise, all translations of the French text come from this English translation. Page numbers in subsequent references refer to: French text; English text.
24 Jorge Semprún, '...vous avez une tombe aux creux des nuages...', in *Mal et modernité: Suivi de «... vous avez une tombe au creux des nuages ...»* (Castelnau-le-Lez: Climats, 1995), 102. All translations from this text are mine.
25 Gina Herrmann, *Written in Red: The Communist Memoir in Spain* (Urbana and Chicago: University of Illinois Press, 2010), 177.
26 Semprún, *Quel beau dimanche!*, 71; 39.
27 E. van Alphen, 'Symptoms of Discursivity: Experience, Memory, and Trauma', in *Acts of Memory: Cultural Recall in the Present*, ed. Mieke Bal, Jonathan Crewe and Leo Spitzer (Hanover, NH: University Press of New England, 1999), 27.
28 Elie Wiesel, 'Pourquoi j'écris' in *Paroles d'étranger* (Paris: Seuil, 1982), 8. 'Why I Write', trans. Rosette C. Lamont, in *Confronting the Holocaust: The Impact of Elie Wiesel*, ed. Alvin H. Rosenfeld and Irving Greenberg (Bloomington and London: Indiana University Press, 1978), 201.
29 Semprún, *L'Écriture ou la vie*, 23; 13–14.

30 Ursula Tidd, 'Exile, Language, and Trauma in Recent Autobiographical Writing by Jorge Semprun', *The Modern Language Review* 103.3 (July 2008): 701.
31 See Schleiss, *Le Bilinguisme*, 36; Tidd, *Jorge Semprún*, 100.
32 Sara Kippur, 'Translating Semprun', *Michigan Quarterly Review, The Translation Issue: Within and Beyond the Metropole,* 52.2 (2013). http://hdl.handle.net/2027/spo.act2080.0052.207 [Accessed 3 January 2018]. (No page references for this text.)
33 Tidd, *Jorge Semprún*, 79.
34 Tidd, *Jorge Semprún*, 100; 108.
35 Semprún, *L'Écriture ou la vie*, 24; 14.
36 Brodzki, *Can These Bones Live*, 163–4.
37 Brodzki, *Can These Bones Live*, 182–3.
38 Tidd, *Jorge Semprún*, 73.
39 Ferrán and Herrmann, *Critical Companion*, 35.
40 Semprún, 'The Art of Fiction No. 192'.
41 Semprún, 'The Art of Fiction No. 192'.
42 Semprún, *L'Écriture ou la vie*, 281; 272.
43 Semprún, *L'Écriture ou la vie*, 285; 275–6. Translation modified to reflect Semprún's use of the term 'trahir' – 'to betray' – which Linda Coverdale renders as 'transform', thus losing some of the more troubling connotations of Semprún's narrative.
44 Semprún, *L'Écriture ou la vie*, 282–3, 285; 273, 276. My modification highlights Semprún's particular focus upon the role of language within his attempt to translate his experiences in Buchenwald into narrative.
45 Milan Kundera, *Le Livre du rire et de l'oubli*, trans. François Kérel, rev. Milan Kundera (Paris: Gallimard, 1985), 14. *The Book of Laughter and Forgetting*, trans. Aaron Asher (London: Faber and Faber, 1996), 2.
46 Brodzki, *Can These Bones Live*, 173.
47 Semprún, *Quel beau dimanche!*, 431; 274.
48 Brodzki, *Can These Bones Live*, 178.
49 Semprún, *Quel beau dimanche!*, 433; 276.
50 Semprún, *Quel beau dimanche!*, 428; 272.
51 Semprún, *Quel beau dimanche!*, 433; 275–6.
52 Kippur, 'Translating Semprun'.
53 Semprún, *Quel beau dimanche!*, 16; 2.
54 Semprún, *Quel beau dimanche!*, 17; 2.
55 See also Carol L. Bernstein, 'Semprun, Philosophy and the Texture of Literature', in *A Critical Companion to Jorge Semprún: Buchenwald, Before and After*, ed. Ofelia Ferrán and Gina Herrmann (New York: Palgrave Macmillan, 2014), 114.
56 Semprún, *Quel beau dimanche!*, 17; 2
57 Semprún, *Quel beau dimanche!*, 21; 5.
58 Semprún, *Quel beau dimanche!*, 18; 3.
59 Semprún, *Quel beau dimanche!*, 18; 3.
60 Semprún, *Quel beau dimanche!*, 18; 3.
61 Semprún, *Quel beau dimanche!*, 20; 4.
62 Semprún, *Quel beau dimanche!*, 20; 5.
63 Semprun, *Quel beau dimanche!*, 28; 9–10.
64 See *Why Weimar?: Questioning the Legacy of Weimar from Goethe to 1999*, ed. Peter M. Daly, Hans Walter Frischkopf, Trudis E. Goldsmith-Reber and Horst Richter (New York: Peter Lang, 2003).
65 Semprún, *L'Écriture ou la vie*, 24; 15.
66 Semprún, *L'Écriture ou la vie*, 24; 15.
67 Semprún, *Quel beau dimanche!*, 29; 10. For the original quotation, see Léon Blum, *Nouvelles Conversations de Goethe avec Eckermann* (Paris: Gallimard, 1937), 86.
68 Semprún, *Quel beau dimanche!*, 29; 10.
69 Roland Barthes, *Essais critiques* (Paris: Éditions de Seuil, 1964), 89.
70 Semprún, *Quel beau dimanche!*, 32; 12. This sentence appears untranslated in French in Sheridan's text.
71 Semprún, *Quel beau dimanche!*, 31; 11.
72 Semprún, *Quel beau dimanche!*, 31; 11.
73 Semprún, *Quel beau dimanche!*, 32; 12.

74 Walter Benjamin, 'The Task of the Translator', in *One-way Street and Other Writings*, trans. J. A. Underwood (London: Penguin, 2009), 31.
75 Semprún, *Quel beau dimanche!*, 435; 277. Square brackets indicate my translation.
76 Semprún, *Quel beau dimanche!*, 435. My translation.
77 Peter Rosenbaum, 'The Buchenwald Memorial and its *Différend*', in *Why Weimar?*, ed. Daly et al., 224.
78 Semprún, *Quel beau dimanche!*, 47; 22.
79 William John Niven, *The Buchenwald Child: Truth, Fiction and Propaganda* (New York: Camden House, 2007), 60–1.
80 Semprún, *L'Écriture ou la vie*, 121; 89.
81 Semprún, *L'Écriture ou la vie*, 78; 55. Translation modified from Coverdales, which translated 's'oppose' as 'hang in the balance', which loses the element of confrontation I read in Semprún's words. See André Malraux, *Le Miroir des limbes II: La corde et les souris* (Paris: Gallimard, 1976).
82 Semprún, *L'Écriture ou la vie*, 216; 163–4.
83 Immanuel Kant, *Religion within the Limits of Reason Alone*, trans. Theodore M. Greene and Hoyt H. Hudson (New York: Harper and Row, 2008 [1960]).
84 Semprún, *L'Écriture ou la vie*, 99; 88.
85 Semprún, *L'Écriture ou la vie*, 315; 306.
86 Siobhan Kattago, *Ambiguous Memory: The Nazi Past and German National Identity* (Westport, CT: Praeger, 2001).
87 Semprún, *L'Écriture ou la vie*, 71–2; 62.
88 Semprún, *Quel beau dimanche!*, 161– 2; 98.
89 Brodzki, *Can These Bones Live*, 174.
90 Couze Venn, *The Postcolonial Challenge: Towards Alternative Worlds* (London and New Delhi: Sage Publications, 2006), 162.
91 Jacques Derrida, 'Table ronde sur la traduction', in *L'Oreille de l'autre: otobiographies, transferts, traductions*, ed. Claude Lévesque and Christie V. McDonald (Montréal: VLB Éditeur Montréal 1982), 137. 'Roundtable on Translation', in *The Ear of the Other: Otobiography, Transference, Translation*, ed. Christie V. McDonald, trans. Peggy Kamuf (New York: Schocken Books, 1985), 102.
92 Rosenbaum, 'The Buchenwald Memorial', 227.
93 Semprún, *L'Écriture ou la vie*, 314–5; 305.
94 Semprún, *Quel beau dimanche!*, 426; 271.
95 Herrmann, *Written in Red*, 82.
96 Semprún, *Quel beau dimanche!*, 428; 272.
97 See Thomas R. Flynn and Dalia Judovitz, 'Introduction', in *Dialectic and Narrative*, ed. Thomas R. Flynn and Dalia Judovitz (Albany: State University of New York Press, 1993), xi.
98 G. W. Friedrich Hegel, *Science de la logique*, 1, trans. Pierre-Jean Labarrière and Gwendoline Jarczyk (Paris: Aubier, 1972 [1812]).
99 Karl Marx, 'Afterword to the Second German Edition', in *Capital*, vol. 1, ed. Friedrich Engels, trans. Samuel Moore and Edward Aveling (London: S. Sonnenschein, Lowery & Co., 1887 [1873]), included in *Marx-Engels Reader*, ed. Robert C. Tucker, 2nd edn (New York: W.W. Norton & Company, Inc., 1978 [1972]), 301.
100 Semprún, *Quel beau dimanche!*, 356; 227.
101 Jacques Derrida, *Spectres de Marx: L'État de la dette, le travail du deuil, et la nouvelle Internationale* (Paris: Éditions Galilée, 1993).
102 Joseph Stalin, *Dialectical and Historical Materialism* (Moscow: Foreign Languages Publishing House, 1949), 7–9.
103 Stalin, *Dialectical and Historical Materialism*, 9.
104 Semprún, *Quel beau dimanche!*, 113–14; 68.
105 Semprún, *Quel beau dimanche!*, 116; 70.
106 Semprún, *Quel beau dimanche!*, 89; 51.
107 Semprún, *Quel beau dimanche!*, 87; 50.
108 Walter Benjamin, 'Theses on the Philosophy of History', in *Illuminations*, trans. Harry Zohn (London: Jonathan Cape, 1973), 259.
109 Stalin, *Dialectical and Historical Materialism*, 10.
110 Flynn and Judovitz, *Dialectic and Narrative*, xii.
111 Herrmann, *Written in Red*, 83.
112 Herrmann, *Written in Red*, n.10, 217.

113 Semprún, *Quel beau dimanche!*, 87; 50.

114 Peter Fawcett, 'Ideology and Translation', in *Routledge Encyclopedia of Translation Studies*, ed. Mona Baker (London: Routledge, 2006), 110. Fawcett is here referring to Givi R. Gachechiladze's formulation that translation resolves 'contradiction through a creative synthesis of the two national systems, the original and the translation, of the two creative individualities, the author and the translator. This is also dialectics of translation'. Givi R. Gachechiladze, 'Realism and Dialectics in the Art of Translation', *Babel* 13.2 (1967): 91.

115 Timothy Mathews, 'Reading the Invisible with Cees Nooteboom, Walter Benjamin and Alberto Giacometti', in *Translation, Tradition, Trauma*, ed. Jan Parker and Timothy Mathews (Oxford: Oxford University Press, 2011), 319.

116 Semprún, *Quel beau dimanche!*, 257; 162.

117 Jacques Derrida, *L'Écriture et la différence* (Paris: Seuil, 1967), 377–8. All translations from this text come from *Writing and Difference*, trans. Alan Bass (London: Routledge Classics, 2001 [1978]), 324–5.

118 Philippe Büttgen, 'Aufheben' in *Vocabulaire européen des philosophies: Dictionnaire des intraduisibles* ed. Barbara Cassin (Paris: Éditions du Seuil, 2004), 152. *Dictionary of Untranslatables: A Philosophical Lexicon*, ed. Barbara Cassin, ed. and trans. Emily Apter, Jacques Lezra and Michael Wood (Princeton, NJ: Princeton University Press, 2014), 71.

119 As quoted in Derrida, *L'Écriture et la différence*, 168; 142. For the original quote, see Hegel, *Science de la logique*, 93–4.

120 Derrida, *L'Écriture et la différence*, 377; 324.

121 Jacques Derrida, *Marges de la philosophie* (Paris: Les Éditions de Minuit, 1972), 143. *Margins of Philosophy*, trans. Alan Bass (Chicago: University of Chicago Press, 1982), 121.

122 Derrida, *Marges de la philosophie*, 21; *Margins of Philosophy*, 19.

123 Derrida, 'Qu'est-ce qu'une traduction "relevante"?', in *Quinzièmes assises de la traduction littéraire: Arles 1998* (Arles: Actes Sud, 1999), 29. 'What is a "Relevant" Translation?', trans. Lawrence Venuti, *Critical Inquiry*, 27.2 (2001):182. All translations of the French text come from this English translation. Page numbers in subsequent references refer to: French text; English text.

124 Derrida, 'Qu'est-ce qu'une traduction "relevante"?', 46–7; 199.

125 Derrida, 'Qu'est-ce qu'une traduction "relevante"?', 27–8; 180–1.

126 Derrida, 'Qu'est-ce qu'une traduction "relevante"?', 28; 181.

127 Semprún and Appréderis, *Le Langage*, 38.

128 Susan Bassnett, 'Prologue', in *Translation, Tradition, Trauma*, ed. Parker and Mathews, 7.

129 Semprún and Appréderis, *Le Langage*, 38.

130 Semprún, *Quel beau dimanche!*, 152; 93.

131 Semprún, *Quel beau dimanche!*, 324; 207–8.

132 Jorge Semprún, 'Mal et modernité', in *Mal et modernité*, 32.

133 Semprún, *Quel beau dimanche!*, 206–7; 201.

134 Semprún, *Quel beau dimanche!*, 331; 210. For the original quotation, see Léon Blum, 'Notes d'Allemagne', in *L'Œuvre de Léon Blum*, V, 1940–1945 (Paris: Éditions Albin Michel, 1955), 504.

135 Semprún, *Quel beau dimanche!*, 331; 211.

136 Semprún, *Quel beau dimanche!*, 331; 211.

137 Semprún, *Quel beau dimanche!* 153; 93.

138 Semprún, *Quel beau dimanche!*, 152–3; 93.

139 Roland Barthes, *Mythologies* (Paris: Éditions du Seuil, 1957).

140 Varlam Chalamov, 'Rations de campagne', in *Récits de la Kolyma*, trans. Catherine Fournier, Sophie Benech and Luba Jurgenson (Lagrasse: Verdier, 2003), 73.

141 Soledad Fox Maura, *Ida y vuelta. La vida de Jorge Semprún* (Barcelona: Debate, 2016), 105.

142 Tidd, *Jorge Semprún*, n. 90, 111. Varlam Chalamov, *Récits de Kolyma*, trans. Olivier Simon and Katia Kerel (Paris: Denoël, Les Lettres nouvelles, 1969).

143 Fox, *Ida y vuelta*, 107.

144 Derrida, 'Qu'est-ce qu'une traduction "relevante"?', 42; 194–5.

145 Derrida, 'Qu'est-ce qu'une traduction "relevante"?', 44; 196.

146 Semprún, *Quel beau dimanche!*, 134; 93.

147 Max Horkheimer and Theodor W. Adorno, 'Preface (1944 and 1947)', in *Dialectic of Enlightenment: Philosophical Fragments*, ed. Gunzelin Schmid Noerr, trans. Edmund Jephcott (Stanford, CA: Stanford University Press, 2002 [1969]), xiv.

148 Giorgio Agamben, *Homo Sacer: Sovereign Power and Bare Life*, trans. Daniel Heller-Roazen (Stanford, CA: Stanford University Press, 1995), 122–3.
149 Horkheimer and Adorno, *Dialectic*, xvii
150 Giorgio Agamben, *Remnants of Auschwitz*, trans. Daniel Heller-Roazen (New York: Zone Books, 1999), 162.
151 Tidd, *Jorge Semprún*, 153. As Tidd discusses, a similar confrontation is at stake in Semprún's play *Le Retour de Carola Neher* (Paris: Gallimard, 1998), in which a fictional encounter is staged between Neher, who was imprisoned in a Soviet gulag after fleeing Germany as a Communist, and Goethe and Blum.
152 Bassnett, 'Prologue', in *Tradition, Translation, Trauma*, ed. Parker and Mathews, 8.
153 Bassnett, 'Prologue', 6–7.
154 María Angélica Semilla Durán, *Le Masque et le masqué: Jorge Semprun et les abîmes de mémoire* (Toulouse: Presses Universitaires du Mirail, 2005), 97. All translations from this text are mine.
155 Tidd, *Jorge Semprún*, 100.
156 Tidd, *Jorge Semprún*, 141. See Emmanuel Levinas, *Totalité et infini: essai sur l'extériorité* (The Hague, Boston and London: Martinus Nijhoff Publishers, 1980 [1961]), 10–13.
157 Semprún, *Quel beau dimanche!*, 431; 274.
158 Semprún, *Quel beau dimanche!*, 136; 83. Square brackets indicate my translation.
159 Semprún, *Quel beau dimanche!*, 136; 83. Square brackets indicate my translation.
160 Alan Bennett, *The History Boys* (Faber and Faber: London, 2004), 74.
161 Semprún, *Quel beau dimanche!*, 136,141,148, 151; 83, 86, 90, 91.
162 Timothy Mathews, 'Conclusion: Can Anyone Look in Both Directions at Once?' in *Translation, Tradition, Trauma*, ed. Parker and Mathews, 336–7.
163 Walter Benjamin, 'Theses on the Philosophy of History', 265.
164 Walter Benjamin, *The Arcades Project*, trans. Howard Eiland and Kevin McLaughlin (Cambridge, MA: Harvard University Press, 1999 [1982]), 476.
165 Semprún, *Quel beau dimanche!*, 367; 234.
166 Semprún, *Quel beau dimanche!*, 436; 277.
167 See Carol L. Bernstein, 'Semprun, Philosophy, and the Texture of Literature', 114–15.
168 Tidd, *Jorge Semprún*, 142.
169 Semprún, *Quel beau dimanche!*, 89; 51.
170 Semprún, *Quel beau dimanche!*, 17; 2.
171 Semilla, *Le Masque*, 103.
172 Semprún, *L'Écriture ou la vie*, 282; 273.
173 Derrida, 'Qu'est-ce qu'une traduction "relevante"?', 28; 181.
174 Derrida, 'Qu'est-ce qu'une traduction "relevante"?', 47; 199.
175 Semilla, *Le Masque*, 102.
176 Brodzki, *Can These Bones Live*, 185.
177 Semprún, *Quel beau dimanche!*, 244; 153.
178 Semprún, *Quel beau dimanche!*, 437; My translation.

Epilogue
On violence and vision: translation and Europe

Translation deterritorializes the rigidity of our national, linguistic and historical positions. Translation reveals the possibility of approaching otherness in the spirit of recognition rather than appropriation. And translation allows us to confront the impulse to synthesize the complexity of the past into a uniform narrative in the present. The three journeys of translation which I have pursued in this book open onto aesthetic and ethical landscapes which take form through a shift from singularity to plurality. One voice becomes multiple voices, drawn from the past as well as the present, each offering divergent perspectives. One language becomes many languages, offering an interlinguistic network which challenges monolingual boundaries, not only across texts, but within them as well. One text in one language becomes many texts in many languages, each a 'becoming' of that first text, connected tangentially one to another.

This shift from the single to the plural resonates, in the work of each author I have discussed, with a somewhat idealized vision of Europe as a multilingual, democratic and open community in which unity is always inscribed with difference. Atxaga's writing of his Obaban village into a broader European framework through intertextuality positions this framework as an ethical alternative to the isolation of the Basque linguistic and literary scene. Indeed, in an interview, Atxaga suggests that European multilingualism offers an implicit resistance to the type of nationalist linguistic politics with which the Basque Country has struggled:

> Un buen porcentaje de europeos son bilingües e incluso trilingües. [...] creo que la idea de una única lengua, sea el inglés o sea cualquier otra, es inviable. A los veinte años de establecerse esa única lengua empezarían a aparecer dialectos, dialectos que acabarían convirtiéndose en lenguas. [...] Y si no ocurriera tal cosa, aún peor, porque sería la señal de que un Gobierno totalitario estaría controlando todo, hasta la lengua doméstica.

> A good percentage of Europeans are bilingual and even trilingual. […] I think the idea of a single language, be it English or any other, is impossible. Within twenty years of establishing such a language, dialects would appear, and these dialects would themselves eventually become languages. […] And it would be even worse if such a thing did not happen, because it would signal that a totalitarian government could control everything, even domestic languages.[1]

Atxaga here emphasizes a form of political freedom he suggests is inherent within multilingualism, the embodiment of a democratic community able to resist cultural domination. This multilingual reality is, as Gabilondo suggests, always caught up in questions of repression and colonialism, as well as freedom and democracy.[2] But it is a reality Atxaga suggests must be addressed if we are to perceive and confront, rather than consolidate, the illusions of linguistic essentialism.

Kundera's conception of the novel as an innately ethical aesthetic form is also integrated into questions of European identity. As Steinby discusses in *Kundera and Modernity*, Kundera suggests that the 'spirit' of the novel is fundamentally connected to that of Europe: 'a spirit of quest, adventure, questioning and challenge, a spirit of the relativity of truth'.[3] For Steinby, the shared values Kundera assigns to European authors are undermined by the fact that 'an author's instrument, his or her language, represents a fundamental restriction on such unity'.[4] But as Kundera asserts repeatedly and diversely, in his texts and in his responses to the translations of those texts, when we approach the language of another we always seek to translate it into our own style and idiom. Kundera's 'European' novels, positioned in an *ailleurs* between Czech and French, explore and acknowledge the inevitability of the appropriative impulse at stake within translation from one language into another. Yet this inevitability has its own ethical value: Kundera suggests that what makes his novels European, rather than Czech or French, is precisely that they are not constrained to one language; rather, moving between and across languages, they are always caught up in the questions of translation. And these questions require us both to recognize the limitations of openness and understanding between different languages and cultures and to continue to seek this openness by challenging the dominance of single perspectives, languages, and national identities.

For Semprún, the existence of a European politics is the best response to *Jedem das Seine*: our inability to escape the claims of 'to each their own' is transformed, he suggests, by a European conception of unity though difference. In his interview with Franck Apprédéris, Semprún suggests that the network of thought and language created by the incarceration of political prisoners in the Buchenwald camp represents the epitome of the European future he desires: 'la pensée de l'Europe est née dans cette communauté'/'European thought was born in that community', he claims.[5] In Semprún's reading, Buchenwald, a space born of a desire to assert the dominance of one nation and one language over others, becomes a space through which such dominance can be contested through the community built there, upon non-national and non-linguistic boundaries. For Semprún, this community is defined by its openness: 'L'identité européenne [...] c'est précisément l'ouverture à l'altérité; la curiosité inlassable, rationnelle des différences; le goût de la découverte, de ses aventures voyageuses'/'European identity [...] is precisely openness to otherness; a relentless, rational curiosity towards difference; the taste of discovery, of its nomadic adventures'.[6] In invoking its welcoming of alterity, its desire for difference, Semprún positions Europe as the political and spatial manifestation of the ethical potential of translation itself.

A weak utopia, or a potential community?

Semprún's comment about the openness of the European community was written in 2005. Thirteen years later, his depiction of Europe as the site of this unity through difference remains utopian. Just as the destiny of translation is never to keep its promise, so too European democracy does not always speak for the many but often for the few. Europe contains the promise of an open, diverse yet harmonious community; yet, like translation, that openness has limitations. In this sense, we might agree with Lawrence Venuti that translation opens on to a possible community which is always both ideologically inscribed and idealistically resistant to that inscription:

> Translation is always ideological because it releases a domestic remainder, an inscription of values, beliefs, and representations linked to historical moments and social positions in the receiving culture. [...] Yet translating is also utopian. The domestic inscription is made with the very intention to communicate the foreign text, and so it is filled with the anticipation that a community will be created around that text – although in translation. [...] A translation projects a utopian community that is not yet realized.[7]

Translation repeatedly and diversely negotiates the poles of communication and appropriation, community and individualism. Thinking translation, and thinking its ethics, means thinking about the best translation we can, the best community we can, and the best ways we can formulate our relations to one another. This 'best' is always unobtainable: what we read as a good translation depends on the context and the criteria we bring with us as we attempt to define its terms. Yet in our attempts to articulate, to find the shape of, a good translation, we begin to understand what Derrida describes as the 'promise' of translation:

> Cette promesse fait signe vers un royaume à la fois «promis et interdit où les langues se réconcilieront et s'accompliront». [...] Ce royaume n'est jamais atteint, touché, foulé par la traduction. Il y a de l'intouchable et en ce sens la réconciliation est seulement promise. Mais une promesse n'est pas rien, elle n'est pas seulement marquée par ce qui lui manque pour s'accomplir. [...] Qu'il soit ou non honoré n'empêche pas l'engagement d'avoir lieu et de léguer son archive. Une traduction qui arrive, qui arrive à promettre la réconciliation, à en parler, à la désirer ou faire désirer, une telle traduction est un événement rare et considérable.
>
> This promise signals a kingdom which is at once "promised and forbidden where the languages will be reconciled and fulfilled." [...] This kingdom is never reached, touched, trodden by translation. There is something untouchable, and in this sense the reconciliation is only promised. But a promise is not nothing, it is not simply marked by what it lacks to be fulfilled. As a promise, translation is already an event, and the decisive signature of a contract. Whether or not it be honored does not prevent the commitment from taking place and from bequeathing its record. A translation that manages, that manages to promise reconciliation, to talk about it, to desire it or make it desirable – such a translation is a rare and notable event.[8]

Derrida offers us translation as a promise and as a prohibition. For him, translation contains the possibility of a desired understanding between and across diverse languages, texts, and sites of authorship. Yet he also recognizes that this is an understanding which can never be fully realized.

Both Venuti and Derrida position translation as an action able to reveal the shape of a utopian community, one in which difference can be acknowledged but also traversed, to enable forms of reconciliation and understanding. For both thinkers, this utopia is, by its very nature, unobtainable: nonetheless, translation can hint towards it in ways which allow us to think differently about our relationships and our communities. For Jacques Lezra, however, these utopian ideas of translation are inherently unhelpful, condemning us to an abstraction which ends up saying nothing at all:

> Globalization has taken our tongues from us – local, autochthonous, idiomatic, ancestral tongues. Its clamorous internationalism hangs critics on a mute peg, with no common voice or general vocabulary on which to string alternative inter- or transnational forms of work, thought, and organization. [...] We ask in this context what might be the genealogy of the recent turn to "translation," of its "new" characterization as a communication of singularities, of its deployment as a weak-utopian concept on which a critique of economic and cultural globalization can be mounted.[9]

Lezra's strongly worded critique of this 'weak' utopia calls attention to the dangers as well as the possibilities of an ethics of translation. According to Lezra, invoking a European community founded upon the vision of diversity revealed by translation, as Atxaga, Kundera and Semprún all do to varying degrees, cannot combat the violent reality of the conflicts which confront us – territorial, national, political. Nor can acknowledging translation as the voice of singularity offer resistance to the homogeneity of globalization.

But, precisely *in* the ways that this utopian vision fails to materialize, thinking about European identity through questions of translation elucidates the challenges confronting that identity. Any utopian conception of Europe will falter from the start unless it acknowledges the repression Europe has enacted both beyond and within its own borders. And, as Cheyfitz discusses in *Poetics of Imperialism*, this repression is fundamentally bound up with questions of translation: he suggests that 'our imperialism historically has functioned (and continues to function) by substituting for the difficult politics of translation another politics of translation that represses these difficulties'.[10] This substitution allows a reading of the translation of European values into other cultures, the heart of the European colonial project, as neutral or even positive, rather than conditioned by forms of erasure and oppression. To truly understand Europe, in its past and present incarnations, involves understanding the reality of translation and the role it has played within the creation, consolidation and collapse of these incarnations.

The universal and the particular

Translation resonates with our understanding of European identity because both are constrained by the tension between the universal and the particular. As Giesen and Eder suggest, European identity is caught between a need to define itself as a transnational or post-national project, operating outside the borders of national or ethnic identity, and the desire to impose itself as the embodiment of a democratic and pluralistic approach which, ironically, always constructs itself in opposition to those who do not embody these values.[11] The borders of Europe take shape in relation to this dynamic: within those borders, the struggles of nationalism challenge ideas of homogeneous European values; outside them, the need to protect the apparent homogeneity of those values becomes a reason to refuse entry to those who live by different ideals. In much the same way, translation always highlights the tension between the national and the transnational. As Apter suggests, translation 'breaks the isomorphic fit between the name of the nation and the name of a language'; reading in translation opens onto 'language worlds characterized by linguistic multiplicity and phantom internations'.[12] Yet, as Venn discusses, this opening up can also lead to a universalism which, in its very claims that global understanding is possible, 'leads to the tyranny of the common idiom'.[13] It is this dilemma which Derrida addresses in relation to the tower of Babel. For if Babel reveals a dissolution of understanding, the birth of linguistic confusion, it also stages that dissolution as a response to the desire to impose a single idiom – the name of its builders, the family of Shem – upon the world.[14]

How can we understand difference without losing our own identity? How can we welcome that difference without seeking to erase it? These questions are negotiated again and again in the bilingual approaches to writing which Atxaga, Kundera and Semprún pursue in their texts. Hokenson and Munson describe the bilingual writer as a 'citizen of no language or perhaps traitor to two': either positioned in a no-man's-land, or in two places at once, the identity of a bilingual author is always mediated by questions of belonging and betrayal, singularity and plurality. This identity, formed across the constraints of language and nation, represents a continual challenge to those constraints. In their texts, Atxaga, Kundera and Semprún suggest that this challenge is essential if we are to negotiate and disrupt the violence enacted in the name of nation and language. But this disruption is not without its own challenges: the collapse of the nation, as Hannah Arendt suggests, also entails a loss of rights, an expulsion from a space which protects us as much as it imprisons or excludes, an exile which is linguistic but also cultural, political, social and affective.[15]

The ways in which Atxaga, Kundera and Semprún write about Europe in their work speak to this dichotomy. For, even as all three suggest that Europe embodies the possibility of a democratic and pluralistic community, the Europe they describe in their texts, through an aesthetics of translation, emerges as a space of repression as much as of liberation. This aesthetics of translation raises the spectres of nationalism, of colonization, of war and of exile, of the Nazi camps and the Gulag. But it cannot lay these to rest, for Europe is founded upon them: they are the history of Europe, both written from inside its borders and seen from outside them. Indeed, the utopian vision of a multilingual Europe which all three authors invoke, based around a welcoming of otherness, a curiosity towards difference, a fragmenting of linguistic essentialism and an unassailable relativity, is an illusion which collapses repeatedly in relation to the historical and political moments Atxaga, Kundera and Semprún describe in their work. In *Obabakoak*, Atxaga depicts the challenge and loss involved in multilingualism: the movements towards other languages and cultures described in the text are always accompanied by loss, even as the decision to reject those other languages and cultures offers only isolation and silencing. In Kundera's *Le Livre*, the relationship between untranslatability and translatability reveals that plurality is always waiting to be translated into univocity, the democratic into the totalitarian, the ambiguous into the certain. And Semprún's discussion of a European identity built around a multilingual understanding of alterity situates this understanding in Buchenwald, the site of an absolute repression and attempted erasure of that alterity.

In fact, even as Atxaga, Kundera and Semprún use their writing to invoke Europe as a space open to a plurality of voices, their texts sometimes limit that plurality or shape it in reductive ways. As Ursula Tidd discusses in *Writing the European Other*, Semprún rarely includes the voices of women in his writing of otherness into his ideal European community.[16] Similarly, Gabilondo suggests that Atxaga sometimes erases gender, racial and sexual differences in his desire to create a paradigmatic allegory of Basque difference, a move which Gabilondo suggests makes his texts 'indifferent' to the complexity of Basque identities.[17] And, as O'Brien notes, Kundera's texts often seem to enforce a misogynistic conception of women, writing the female body through a male gaze which repeatedly defines his female characters in relation to stereotyped and divisive gender binaries.[18] The attempt by each author to articulate otherness through the incorporation of an aesthetics of translation thus silences some voices in the very ways in which it makes others speak. The silencing of these voices undermines the ethical potential of the authors' work. But it also acknowledges the challenges of realizing this potential. For even as we invoke an ethics of difference and particularity, we risk overwriting that ethics by failing to acknowledge the partiality of all our attempts at communication, the ease with which speaking to and with others can be translated into speaking for or over them.

In *Poetics of Imperialism*, Cheyfitz suggests that this risk is inherent to those of us who operate from within a Western European patriarchal model. Terrified of what we do not understand, even as we claim to desire this understanding, '[w]e talk to ourselves about ourselves, believing in a grand hallucination that we are talking with others'.[19] Cheyfitz's comment seems particularly perceptive in the current political climate, as we negotiate the challenges of social media echo chambers in which the only voices we hear are those who already concur with us. In this bubble we believe translation to be unnecessary, for – as in Kundera's idyll – we all think the same; and, if we encounter someone who does not agree with us, we seek to diminish or discredit their perspective, to exclude them from our utopia of harmony and consensus, even as we describe that utopia as a pluralistic and tolerant one. Perhaps, as Agamben suggests, democracy – at least in its current incarnation – is not always so different from totalitarianism after all. For, as he describes in *Homo Sacer*, in giving priority to our personal politics and seeking to free the individual from the regulations of state apparatus, that apparatus becomes part of our individual life: we sustain the shape of our democratic perspective by rejecting what does not conform to it – a move that echoes the totalitarian control which it purports to reject.[20]

Indeed, the risk that we may make a claim about the importance of diversity in ways which fundamentally undermine that diversity is always a possibility within any community which attempts to create consensus through difference. In *L'Autre cap*, Derrida suggests that 'Les projets européens les mieux intentionnés, apparemment et expressément pluralistes, démocratiques et tolérants, peuvent tenter [...] d'imposer l'homogénéité d'un médium, de normes de discussion, de modèles discursifs'/'The best intentioned of European projects, those that are quite apparently and explicitly pluralistic, democratic, and tolerant, may try [...] to impose the homogeneity of a medium, of discursive norms and models'.[21] As Derrida suggests here, projects which seek to create a universal ethics based around a recognition of singularity and tolerance can often do so in reductive ways, thereby dictating the ways that difference can be understood, or at least failing to address it in all its possible permutations. In doing so, such an ethics may turn those differences into an easily comprehensible narrative of ethical responses to alterity, a narrative which can flatten out or overwrite those differences in its quest to acknowledge their parity of value.

The task of translation

Kundera describes his ideal Europe as 'Le maximum de diversité dans le minimum d'espace'/'maximum diversity in minimum space'.[22] Yet this diversity is not an answer to the issues of European identity, but always a question: how can we *respond* to the ethical promise of diversity, without either erasing it in the name of universalism or converting it into nationalism? In *L'Autre cap*, Derrida links this problematic question to issues both of translation and of European identity: 'Quelle philosophie de la traduction dominera en Europe? Dans une Europe qui devrait désormais éviter aussi bien les crispations nationaliste de la différence linguistique que l'homogénéisation violente des langues à travers la neutralité d'un médium traducteur, prétendument transparent, métalinguistique, universel?'/'What philosophy of translation will dominate in Europe? In a Europe that from now on should avoid both the nationalistic tensions of linguistic difference and the violent homogenization of languages through the neutrality of a translating medium that would claim to be transparent, metalinguistic, and universal?'[23] Derrida's question dramatizes the ways in which thinking translation can help us think about the ever-shifting shape of a possible European community, even as that thinking always risks sliding into forms of essentialism itself. For his call to translation here does not position it as an action concerned with asserting the singular above the collective, but rather as a task always concerned with negotiating the claims of that singularity in relation to the pull of the universal.

The link Derrida identifies between translation and an understanding of European identity is one in which the possibility of reconciliation always confronts its dissolution into potential violence. Thinking translation and thinking Europe does not mean seeking refuge in utopian solutions, but rather understanding that the tension between the universal and the particular inherent in both presents us with a task to be approached again and again, without the possibility of resolution: 'Le *même devoir* dicte de respecter la différence, l'idiome, la minorité, la singularité, mais aussi l'universalité du droit formel, le désir de traduction, l'accord et l'univocité, la loi de la majorité, l'opposition au racisme, au nationalisme, à la xénophobie'/'The *same duty* dictates respecting differences, idioms, minorities, singularities, but also the universality of formal law, the desire for translation, agreement and univocity, the law of the majority, opposition to racism, nationalism, and xenophobia'.[24] This double duty towards the claims of particularity and universality, the untranslatable and the translatable, is the task of translation and the task of understanding European identity in its difference as well as its similarity.

This task is not easy; the desire to construct coherent narratives about Europe is as difficult to avoid as the desire to construct coherent narratives about translation. Indeed, it is tempting to take Derrida's comment as a reflection upon the issues facing Europe as a whole. But Derrida's discussion of the double duty confronting Europe is implicitly situated within the context of French Republican universalism, a universalism governed by the maxim *liberté, égalité, fraternité*. And, like the fictionalized Goethe's response to *Jedem das Seine* in *Quel beau dimanche!*, in which *Jedem das Seine* symbolizes a collective liberty dependent upon the constraint of individual freedoms, *liberté, égalité, fraternité* also invokes an equality in which individual freedoms may be subsumed in the name of the collective good. But not all European projects are caught up in the same contradictions between the universal and the singular: equality is not a prescribed virtue everywhere we look; tolerance takes a multitude of forms; and the battle to prevent pluralism ending in essentialism is playing out differently across the continent. The European projects Derrida discusses in *L'Autre cap* reveal one way to conceive the challenges facing the European community more generally. But is this how Europe looks from the Basque Country? Is it how it appears in the Czech Republic? How is Europe shaped for and by those who feel their identity to be shared between nations, languages and identities? Thinking about these differences means trying not to dissolve Europe itself – its problems and its successes – into a homogeneous whole. If we want to avoid the 'grand hallucination' of which Cheyfitz speaks, we need to recognize that, while the borders between nations within Europe have become increasingly permeable, at least for those with the right passports, the languages we speak, both interlingually and intralingually, remain as diverse as ever.

This recognition fails as often as it succeeds. But this failure is itself essential. If we formulate our ethics, whether in regard to the ways in which we translate or the ways in which we relate as communities, only in relation to the ways that we manage to achieve comprehension and communication – in relation to the ideal of a perfect translation – we ignore the insights which arise from mistranslation and misunderstanding. If we seek always to translate our failings into success then we maintain an illusion of understanding which limits our ability to confront the reality of our experiences. We will be like those on Atxaga's island of Euskera who insist that the island is sufficient in and of itself; like Kundera's student writing poetry to reframe his romantic failures; like Semprún's narrator calling upon the dialectic to erase the contradictions in his past. The insistence that failures of understanding and connection can be transcended erases the vision which translation offers us through those failures. For translation is ethical precisely because it can never transcend its limitations: the pure language which Benjamin invokes as the utopian ideal of translation can never be attained: instead, each individual language calls to others in its particularity, seeking through them to move towards a universal completeness and understanding which is always subject to its own retranslations, always just out of reach.[25]

As Cheyfitz notes, 'Benjamin's notion of supplementarity, with its suggestion of a community of languages with mutual needs, resists the mastery of one language by another'.[26] But it also calls to this mastery, acknowledging our desire for universality even while drawing attention to the impossibility of attaining it without diminishing the claims of the particular. In the translation of one text into multiple languages, the universal and the particular meet in a relationship of connection which can never be finally resolved: every translation is a fragment of a perfect translation into a universal language, in its fragmentary nature both hinting towards that perfection and resisting it. As Richard Kearney, responding to Ricœur's thinking on translation, suggests: 'The creative tension between the universal and the plural ensures that the task of translation is an endless one, a work of tireless memory and mourning, of appropriation and disappropriation, of taking up and letting go, of expressing oneself and welcoming others'.[27] This creative tension is ethical precisely in the ways in which it cannot be resolved. For the reality is that translation is not a utopia, whether weak or strong. It is at the heart of our constant struggle to find meaning and transmit that meaning in ways that are appreciative but not appropriative. And this struggle needs to be acknowledged when we are thinking about how we might formulate a European identity; the failures of Europe must be recognized as much – if not more – than its successes. By approaching the shape of a European community through an awareness that this community can never be a utopia but only a battle to respond continually to the demands of the universal and the particular, the challenges of recognizing differences and the desire for common understanding can be brought into a productive confrontation.

A philosophy of translation and a philosophy of life

I began this book with a quotation from Anne Michaels's *Fugitive Pieces*, in which it was suggested that choosing a philosophy of translation might give an indication about our philosophy of life. But can the ways in which we translate really help us think about the ways in which we live? As Lezra suggests, translation does not provide answers to the challenges of an increasingly violent global community. But it does at least raise the questions which are crucial to any engagement with these challenges. When does clamour become silence? When do too many voices mean that there is no one left to hear? These dilemmas are at the heart of translation. For Babel incarnates the problematic dichotomies of silence versus speech; of listening versus deafness; of renouncing understanding versus a never-ending attempt to understand, in the face of failure. We all speak different languages, whether interlingually or intralingually. We can choose to respond to this difference through silence, abandoning our attempt to construct, giving up on our desire to understand. Or we can choose to build from *within* that difference, acknowledging the inevitable miscommunications and misrepresentations we will make, that understanding will crumble even as we try to formulate it. Translation reveals to us both the possibility and the failure of communication; both the form and the absence of connection; both the shape and the formlessness of our understanding of community. The territories of language, nation, historical moment and individual perspective can never be fully exceeded: our lines of flight always return us somewhere; as some borders collapse, others are constructed, imprisoning us once again within our monolingual universe. We forget the past in the ways we remember it. But this failure offers, perhaps, its own measure of success. By failing to attain the utopian ideal of perfect communication through translation we confront the mistranslations and untranslatables within all our relations.

Indeed, the ethical value of translation derives from its ability to reveal that our openness to other perspectives finds its limit in our inability to see through any eyes but our own, confronting us with our ignorance as much as our insight. The value of translation is thus contained in both its violence and its vision: in its aggressive annexations of the spectres of the past – original text, language, author and moment of publication – and its ability to represent these annexations. Bermann and Wood describe 'the ethical double bind in any act of translation – the impossibility of fully rendering another's voice or meaning, and yet the necessity of making the attempt'.[28] Impossibility and necessity: this is perhaps the best way to understand translation. Neither the impossibility nor the necessity of translation is a matter of choosing between the binary opposites of translatable and untranslatable; relevant and irrelevant; foreign and domestic; fluent and resistant; visible and invisible. Translation is always a space *between*, an encounter and a confrontation, a negotiation and an appropriation. In the encounters it enables – between languages, between texts, between reader and writer – translation invites us to confront the instability of textual authority, to lose our confidence in the possibility of stable meanings and universal truths.

Losing truth means acknowledging that there are no answers to the ethical challenges raised by translation. But in its simultaneous impossibility and necessity, translation reveals its *reality*, its *lived* space, where communication and silence, remembrance and forgetting, confront each other repeatedly and diversely. The questions raised through translation by Atxaga, Kundera and Semprún explore the specific historical and geographical moments in which their texts were conceived, written, published, translated and read. But through translation, those moments are also fragmented, deterritorialized, brought into hospitable contact with others. The violence of translation shows us *our* violence: the appropriations and aggressions we enact upon the other languages and perspectives which surround us, the elements we forget even as we seek to remember. In illuminating the space of our struggle to understand without annexation, translation offers us a space to begin this understanding. There is no end to this task, as there is no end to translation. But there is value in the attempt. In trying and failing to translate ethically, we do, perhaps, begin to see differently, to perceive the impossibility and the necessity of our attempts at ethical forms of understanding.

Notes

1 Bernardo Atxaga, 'Interview – Howl'. https://www.atxaga.eus/testuak-textos/interview-howl [Accessed 3 January 2018]. My translation.
2 Joseba Gabilondo, *Remnants of the Nation: Prolegomena to a Postnational History of Contemporary Basque Literature* (Bilbao: University of the Basque Country Press, 2006) (in Basque). Translation in English under contract with Tamesis. Introduction and first chapter available at: https://www.academia.edu/5129880/Remnants_of_the_Nation_Prolegomena_to_a_Postnational_History_of_Contemporary_Basque_Literature._Bilbao_University_of_the_Basque_Country_Press_2006._in_Basque_._Translation_in_English_under_contract_with_Tamesis._Introduction_and_first_chapter_available_here [Accessed 29 December 2017], 6.
3 Liisa Steinby, *Kundera and Modernity* (West Lafayette, IN: Purdue University Press, 2013), 14.
4 Steinby, *Kundera and Modernity*, 2.
5 Jorge Semprún and Franck Appréderis, *Le Langage est ma patrie* (Paris: Libella-Maren Sell Editions, 2013), 89.
6 Jorge Semprún, *L'Homme européen* (Paris: Plon, 2005), 45. My translation.
7 Lawrence Venuti, 'Translation, Community, Utopia', in *The Translation Studies Reader*, ed. Lawrence Venuti, 2nd edn, 498–9 (London: Routledge, 2002).
8 Jacques Derrida, 'Des tours de Babel', in *Difference in Translation*, ed. Joseph F. Graham. (Ithaca, NY and London: Cornell University Press, 1985), 228; 'Des Tours de Babel', trans. Joseph F. Graham, in *Difference in Translation*, ed. Graham, 191.
9 Jacques Lezra, '*Nationum Origo*', in *Nation, Language and the Ethics of Translation*, ed. Sandra Bermann and Michael Wood (Oxford and Princeton, NJ: Princeton University Press, 2005), 203–4.
10 Eric Cheyfitz, *The Poetics of Imperialism: Translation and Colonization from The Tempest to Tarzan* (Oxford and New York: Oxford University Press, 1991), 104.
11 Bernhard Giesen and Klaus Eder, 'European Citizenship: An Avenue for the Social Integration of Europe' in *European Citizenship between National Legacies and Postnational Projects*, ed. Klaus Eder and Bernhard Giesen (Oxford: Oxford University Press, 2001), 2–3.
12 Emily Apter, *Against World Literature: On the Politics of Untranslatability* (London: Verso, 2013), 411.
13 Couze Venn, *The Postcolonial Challenge: Towards Alternative Worlds* (London, Thousand Oaks and New Delhi: Sage Publications, 2006), 163.
14 Jacques Derrida, *L'Oreille de l'autre: otobiographies, transferts, traductions*, ed. Claude Lévesque and Christie V. McDonald (Montréal: VLB Éditeur, 1982), 100–1. *The Ear of the Other: Otobiography, Transference, Translation*, ed. Christie V. McDonald, trans. Peggy Kamuf (Schocken Books, New York, 1985), 100–1.
15 Hannah Arendt, 'The Decline of the Nation-State and the End of the Rights of Man', in *The Origins of Totalitarianism* (New York: Harcourt, Brace and Co., 1951), 299.
16 Ursula Tidd, *Jorge Semprún: Writing the European Other* (London: Legenda, 2014), 161–2.
17 Joseba Gabilondo, 'Indifference as Terror: On State Politics and Basque Literature in Globalization', *Oihenart* 25 (2010): 231.
18 John O'Brien, *Kundera and Feminist Criticism: Dangerous Intersections* (New York: St Martin's Press, 1995), 5.
19 Cheyfitz, *Poetics of Imperialism*, xv.
20 Giorgio Agamben, *Homo Sacer: Sovereign Power and Bare Life*, trans. Daniel Heller-Roazen (Stanford, CA: Stanford University Press, 1995), 121.
21 Derrida, *L'Autre cap, suivi de la démocratie ajournée* (Paris: Les Éditions de minuit, 1991), 54; *The Other Heading: Reflections on Today's Europe* (Bloomington and Indianapolis: Indiana University Press, 1992), 54.
22 Milan Kundera, *Le Rideau*, (Paris: Éditions Gallimard, 2005), 45; *The Curtain*, trans. Linda Asher (New York: HarperCollins, 2006), 31.
23 Derrida, *L'Autre cap*, 58; *The Other Heading*, 58.
24 Derrida, *L'Autre cap*, 76–7; *The Other Heading*, 78.
25 Walter Benjamin, 'The Task of the Translator', in *One-way Street and Other Writings*, trans. J. A. Underwood (London: Penguin, 2009), 29–45.
26 Cheyfitz, *Poetics of Imperialism*, 135.
27 Richard Kearney, 'Introduction: Ricoeur's Philosophy of Translation', in *On Translation*, trans. Eileen Brennan (London and New York: Routledge, 2006), xx.
28 Sandra Bermann and Michael Wood, 'The Ethics of Translation', in *Nation, Language and the Ethics of Translation*, 89.

Bibliography

Primary texts

Atxaga, Bernardo. *The Accordionist's Son*, translated by Margaret Jull Costa. London: Vintage, 2008 [2007].

Atxaga, Bernardo. *Dos hermanos: El cuarto canto*, translated by Bernardo Atxaga. Madrid: Ollero & Ramos, 1995.

Atxaga, Bernardo. 'Escribo en una lengua extraña', in *Nueva Etiopía: Canciones, conversaciones y poemas*. Madrid: El Europeo, 1996, 17–18.

Atxaga, Bernardo. *Esos cielos*, translated by Bernardo Atxaga. Madrid: Ediciones B, 1996.

Atxaga, Bernardo. *El hijo del acordeonista*, translated by Asun Garikano and Bernardo Atxaga. Madrid: Punto de lectura, 2006 [2003].

Atxaga, Bernardo. *El hombre solo*, translated by Bernardo Atxaga. Madrid: Ediciones B, 1994.

Atxaga, Bernardo. 'Interview – Howl'. https://www.atxaga.eus/testuak-textos/interview-howl [Accessed 3 January 2018]. My translation.

Atxaga, Bernardo. *Lista de locos et otros alfabetos*. Madrid: Ediciones Siruela, 1998.

Atxaga, Bernardo. 'Mesa redonda', *Vasos comunicantes* 4 (1994): 53–64.

Atxaga, Bernardo. 'Mi primera lengua', in *Um lugar llamado Obaba*. Madrid: Alfaguera, 2013, 15–24.

Atxaga, Bernardo. 'My First Language', in *The Threepenny Review* 108 (2007), translated by Margaret Jull Costa, no page references. http://www.threepennyreview.com/samples/atxaga_w07.html [Accessed 8 August 2015].

Atxaga, Bernardo. *Obabakoak*. Donostia: Erein, 1988.

Atxaga, Bernardo. *Obabakoak*, translated by Bernardo Atxaga. Madrid: Punto de Lectura, 2008 [1989].

Atxaga, Bernardo. *Obabakoak*, translated by Margaret Jull Costa. London: Vintage, 2007 [1992].

Atxaga, Bernardo. *Obabakoak: Ein literarisches Puzzle*, translated by Gió Waeckerlin Induni. Hannover: Schönbach, 1991.

Atxaga, Bernardo. *Obabakoak: A Novel*, translated by Margaret Jull Costa. New York: Pantheon Press, 1993.

Atxaga, Bernardo. *Obabakoak of het ganzenbord*, translated by Johanna Vuyk-Bosdriesz. Amsterdam: Nijgh en van Ditmar, 1992.

Atxaga, Bernardo. *Obabakoak: Stories from a Village*, translated by Margaret Jull Costa. Minneapolis: Greywolf Press, 2010.

Atxaga, Bernardo. *Obabakoak: Um Lugar Chamado Obaba*, translated by Ibon Sarasola and Egito Gonçalves. Lisbon: Quetzal Editores, 1992.

Atxaga, Bernardo. 'Preguntas desde Japón', 2004. https://www.atxaga.eus/es/testuak-textos/preguntas-desde-japon [Accessed 29 December 2017].

Atxaga, Bernardo. *Siete casas en Francia*, translated by Asun Gorikano and Bernardo Atxaga. Madrid: Alfaguera, 2009.

Atxaga, Bernardo. *Soinujolearen semea*. Pamplona: Pamiela, 2003.

Atxaga, Bernardo. 'Superficies de la literatura vasca', in *Um lugar llamado Obaba*. Madrid: Alfaguera, 2013, 25–46.

Atxaga, Bernardo. *Two Brothers*, translated by Margaret Jull Costa. London: Harvill Press, 2001.

Atxaga, Bernardo and Hasier Etxeberria, 'Bernardo Atxaga', translated by Koldo Biguri, in Etxeberria, *Cinco escritores vascos: entrevistas de Hasier Etxeberria*. Irun: Alberdania, 2002.

Kundera, Milan. *L'Art du roman*. Paris: Éditions Gallimard, 1986.

Kundera, Milan. *The Art of the Novel*, translated by Linda Asher. New York: Grove Press, 1988.

Kundera, Milan. *The Book of Laughter and Forgetting*, translated by Michael Henry Heim. Harmondsworth: Penguin, 1988 [1980].

Kundera, Milan. *The Book of Laughter and Forgetting*, translated by Aaron Asher. London: Faber and Faber, 1996.

Kundera, Milan. 'Comedy is Everywhere', *Index on Censorship* 6.6 (1977): 4–7.

Kundera, Milan. *The Curtain*, translated by Linda Asher. New York: HarperCollins, 2006.

Kundera, Milan. *Encounter: Essays*, translated by Linda Asher. New York: HarperCollins, 2010.

Kundera, Milan. 'Fourth Congress of the Czechoslovak Writers' Union, 27–9 June 1967', in *Writers against Rulers*, by Dušan Hamšík, translated by D. Orpington. London: Hutchison, 1971, 167–77.

Kundera, Milan. *L'Immortalité*, translated by Eva Bloch, revised by Milan Kundera. Paris: Gallimard, 1990.

Kundera, Milan. *Immortality*, translated by Peter Kussi. London and Boston, MA: Faber and Faber, 1992 [1991].

Kundera, Milan. *L'Insoutenable légèreté de l'être*, translated by François Kérel, rev. Milan Kundera. Paris: Gallimard, 1987.

Kundera, Milan. *The Joke*, translated by Aaron Asher. London: Harper Collins, 1992.

Kundera, Milan. *Kniha smíchu a zapomnění*. Toronto: Sixty-Eight Publishers, 1981.

Kundera, Milan. *Life is Elsewhere*, translated by Aaron Asher. London: Faber and Faber, 2000.

Kundera, Milan. *Le Livre du rire et de l'oubli*, translated by François Kérel. Paris: Gallimard, 1979.

Kundera, Milan. *Le Livre du rire et de l'oubli*, translated by François Kérel, revised by Milan Kundera. Paris: Éditions Gallimard, 1985.

Kundera, Milan. *Nesmrtelnost.* Brno: Atlantis, 1993.

Kundera, Milan.'Un occident kidnappé ou la tragédie de l'Europe Centrale', *Le débat* 27 (1983): 3–22.

Kundera, Milan. *La Plaisanterie*, translated by Marcel Aymonin and Claude Courtot. Paris: Gallimard, 1985.

Kundera, Milan. 'Quatre-vingt-neuf mots', *Le débat* 37.5 (1985): 87–118.

Kundera, Milan. *Une rencontre*. Paris: Gallimard, 2009.

Kundera, Milan. *Le Rideau*. Paris: Gallimard, 2005.

Kundera, Milan. *Testaments Betrayed,* translated by Linda Asher. London and Boston, MA: Faber and Faber, 1995.

Kundera, Milan. *Les Testaments trahis.* Paris: Gallimard, 1993.

Kundera, Milan. *The Unbearable Lightness of Being*, translated by Michael Henry Heim, revised by Milan Kundera. London: Faber and Faber, 1995 [1984].

Kundera, Milan. *La Vie est ailleurs*, translated by Francois Kérel. Paris: Gallimard, 1987 [1973].

Kundera, Milan and Jordan Elgraby, 'Conversations with Milan Kundera', *Milan Kundera: Fictive Lightness, Fictive Weight: Salmagundi* 73 1987: 3–24. http://www.jstor.org/stable/40547912 [Accessed 2 January 2018].

Kundera, Milan and Philip Roth, 'Conversation in London and Connecticut with Milan Kundera', in *Shop Talk: A Writer and His Colleagues and Their Work*, by Philip Roth. London: Jonathan Cape, 2001, 90–100.

Kundera, Milan and Christian Salmon, 'The Art of Fiction No. 81', *The Paris Review* 92 (1984). http://www.theparisreview.org/interviews/2977/the-art-of-fiction-no-81-milan-kundera [Accessed 2 September 2015]. No page references for this text.

Semprún, Jorge. *Autobiografía de Federico Sánchez* Barcelona: Planeta, 1977.

Semprún, Jorge. *L'Écriture ou la vie*. Paris: Gallimard, 1994.

Semprún, Jorge. *L'Évanouissement*. Paris: Gallimard, 1967.

Semprún, Jorge. *Federico Sánchez se despide de ustedes.* Barcelona: Tusquets, 1993.

Semprún, Jorge. *Federico Sanchez vous salue bien*. Paris: Éditions Grasset & Fasquelle, 1993.

Semprún, Jorge. *Le Grand Voyage*. Paris: Gallimard, 1972 [1963].
Semprún, Jorge. *L'Homme européen.* Paris: Plon, 2005.
Semprún, Jorge. *Literature or Life,* translated by Linda Coverdale. New York: Penguin, 1997.
Semprún, Jorge. 'Mal et modernité', in *Mal et modernité: Suivi de «... vous avez une tombe au creux des nuages ...».* Castelnau-le-Lez: Climats, 1995, 1–88.
Semprún, Jorge. *La Montagne blanche*. Paris: Gallimard, 1986.
Semprún, Jorge. *Le Mort qu'il faut*. Paris: Gallimard, 2001.
Semprún, Jorge. *Netchaïev est de retour*. Paris: Lattés, 1987.
Semprún, Jorge. *Quel beau dimanche!* Paris: Éditions Grasset, 2003 [1980].
Semprún, Jorge. *Le Retour de Carola Neher*. Paris: Gallimard, 1998.
Semprún, Jorge. *Veinte años y un día.* Barcelona: Tusquets Editores, 2003.
Semprún, Jorge. '...vous avez une tombe aux creux des nuages...', in *Mal et modernité: Suivi de «... vous avez une tombe au creux des nuages ...».* Castelnau-le-Lez: Climats, 1995, 89–123.
Semprún, Jorge. *What a Beautiful Sunday!*, translated by Alan Sheridan. London: Abacus, 1984 [1982].
Semprún, Jorge and Franck Appréderis. *Le Langage est ma patrie.* Paris: Libella-Maren Sell Editions, 2013.
Semprún, Jorge and Lila Azam Zanganeh. 'The Art of Fiction No. 192', translated by Sara Sugihara, in *The Paris Review* 180 (2007). http://www.theparisreview.org/interviews/5740/the-art-of-fiction-no-192-jorge-semprun [Accessed 9 January 2018].

Secondary texts on Bernardo Atxaga

Apalategui, Ur. *La Naissance de l'écrivain Basque: l'Évolution de la problématique littéraire de Bernardo Atxaga.* Paris: L'Harmattan, 2000.
Ascunce Arrieta, José Angel. *Bernardo Atxaga: Los demonios personales de un escritor.* San Sebastián: Saturrarán, 2000.
Axular, Pedro. *Despues, Gero*, bilingual text, translated by Luis Villasante. Oñati: Jakin, 1976.
Clark, Robert P. *The Basques, the Franco Years and Beyond.* Reno: University of Nevada Press, 1979.
Domínguez, César. 'Historiography and the Geo-literary Imaginary', in *A Comparative History of Literatures in the Iberian Peninsula*, edited by Fernando Cabo Aseguinolaza, Anxo Abuín Gonzalez and César Domínguez. Amsterdam: John Benjamins, 2010, 102–116.

Faber, Sebastiaan. 'El mundo está en todas partes: la subversión fantástica de Jorge Luis Borges y Bernardo Atxaga', *Revista Canadiense de Estudios Hispánicos* 28.3 (2004): 519–39.

Gabilondo, Joseba. 'Indifference as Terror: On State Politics and Basque Literature in Globalization', *Oihenart* 25 (2010): 217–40.

Gabilondo, Joseba. *Remnants of the Nation: Prolegomena to a Postnational History of Contemporary Basque Literature.* Bilbao: University of the Basque Country Press, 2006 (in Basque). Translation in English under contract with Tamesis. Introduction and first chapter available at: https://www.academia.edu/5129880/Remnants_of_the_Nation_Prolegomena_to_a_Postnational_History_of_Contemporary_Basque_Literature._Bilbao_University_of_the_Basque_Country_Press_2006._in_Basque_._Translation_in_English_under_contract_with_Tamesis._Introduction_and_first_chapter_available_here [Accessed 29 December 2017].

Gil-Oslé, Juan Pablo. 'Bernardo Atxaga: canon, plagio y euskera literario', *Bulletin of Spanish Studies* XCI.6 (2014): 869–87.

Hulme, Harriet. 'Creating Anew, Again: Deserted Islands and Textual Inhabitations in Bernardo Atxaga's *Obabakoak*', *Comparative Critical Studies* 11.2–3 (2014): 265–280.

Hulme, Harriet. 'A Politics of Form: Fantasy and Storytelling as Modes of Resistance in the Work of Atxaga and Kundera', in *Fear and Fantasy in a Global World*, edited by Susana Araujo and Marta Pinto. Amsterdam: Rodopi, 2015, 211–38.

Hulme, Harriet. 'Self-Translating Between Minor and Major Languages: A Hospitable Approach in Bernardo Atxaga's *Obabakoak*', in *Self-Translation and Power: Negotiating Identities in Multilingual European Contexts*, edited by Olga Castro, Svetlana Page and Sergi Mainer. Basingstoke: Palgrave Macmillan, 2017, 165–88.

Jull Costa, Margaret. Email to Harriet Hulme, 9 March 2014.

Jull Costa, Margaret. 'Translating Bernardo Atxaga's *Obabakoak*', *Salzburg Studies in English Literature, Poetic Drama and Poetic Theory* 204 (1998): 279–83.

Jull Costa, Margaret. 'Translation and Reading', in *Between the Lines*, conversation with Timothy Mathews, 11 September 2013. http://www.ucl.ac.uk/multidisciplinary-and-intercultural-inquiry/between-the-lines/between-the-lines-podcasts-publication/margaret-jull-costa-translation [Accessed 3 January 2018].

Kurlansky, Mark. *The Basque History of the World*. London: Vintage, 1999.

Lasagabaster, Jesús María. 'Introducción a la narrativa vasca actual', in *Antología de la narrative vasca actual*, edited by Jesús María Lasagabaster. Barcelona: Ediciones del Mall, 1986, 11–43.

Lasagabaster, Jesús María. 'Introduction: Basque Literary History', in *Basque Literary History*, edited by Mari Jose Olaziregi, translated by Amaia Gabantxo. Reno: University of Nevada Press, 2013, 13–21.

Manterola Agirrezabalaga, Elizabete. 'La autotraduccíon en la literature vasca', in *Aproximaciones a la autotraducción*, edited by Xosé Manuel Dasilva and Helena Tanquiero. Vigo: Editorial Aademia del Hispanismo, 2011, 111–40.

Manterola Agirrezabalaga, Elizabete. 'Collaborative Self-Translation in a Minority Language: Power Implications in the Process, the Actors and the Literary Systems Involved', in *Self-Translation and Power: Negotiating Identities in Multilingual European Contexts*, edited by Olga Castro, Svetlana Page and Sergi Mainer. Basingstoke: Palgrave Macmillan, 2017, 191–215.

Manterola Agirrezabalaga, Elizabete. *Literatura vasca traducida*. Bern: Peter Lang, 2014.

Manterola Agirrezabalaga, Elizabete. 'Paratextual Analysis of the Work by Bernardo Atxaga', in *Translation Peripheries: Paratextual Elements in Translation*, edited by Anna Gil-Bardají, Pilar Orero and Sara Rovira-Esteva. Bern: Peter Lang, 2012, 83–100.

Manterola Agirrezabalaga, Elizabete. 'La traducción de la literatura vasca a otras lenguas', *mTm: minor Translating major – major Translating minor – minor Translating minor* 3 (2011): 58–79.

Martín, Annabel. 'Modulations of the Basque Voice: An Interview with Bernardo Atxaga', *Journal of Spanish Cultural Studies* 1.2 (2000): 193–204.

Nair, Parvati. *Configuring Community: Theories, Narratives, and Practices of Community Identities in Contemporary Spain*. London: MHRA, 2004.

Olaziregi, Mari Jose. *Waking the Hedgehog: the Literary Universe of Bernardo Atxaga*, translated by Amaia Gabantxo. Reno: University of Nevada Press, 2005.

Olaziregi, Mari Jose. 'Worlds of Fiction: An Introduction to Basque Narrative', in *Basque Literary History*, edited by Mari Jose Olaziregi, translated by Amaia Gabantxo. Reno: University of Nevada Press, 2013, 137–200.

Perret, Sally. 'In the Name of the Nation? The National Award in Narrative Literature, and the Democratization of Art in Spain (1977–2013)', *Journal of Spanish Cultural Studies* 16.1 (2015): 77–93.

Rodríguez, Enma. 'Bernardo Atxaga: me gusta la sobriedad', in *El Mundo*, 26 November 1989.

Santana, Mario. 'On Visible and Invisible Languages: Bernardo Atxaga's *Soinujolearen semea* in Translation', in *Writers in Between Languages: Minority Literatures in the Global Scene*, edited by Mari Jose Olaziregi. Reno: Center for Basque Studies, University of Nevada, 2009, 213–29.

Secondary texts on Milan Kundera

Barańczak, Stanisław. *Breathing under Water and Other East European essays*. Cambridge, MA and London: Harvard University Press, 1990.

Biron, Normand. 'Entretien avec Milan Kundera', *Liberté* 21.1 (1979): 17–33.

Boisen, Jørn. *Une fois ne compte pas: Nihilisme et sens dans L'insoutenable légèreté de l'être de Milan Kundera*. Copenhagen: Museum Tusculanum Press, 2005.

Faris, Wendy. *Ordinary Enchantments: Magical Realism and the Remystification of Narrative*. Nashville, TN: Vanderbilt University Press, 2004.

Frank, Søren. *Migration and Literature*. New York: Palgrave Macmillan, 2008.

Knoop, Christine Angela. *Kundera: The Ambiguity of Authorship*. London: Maney for the MHRA, 2011.

Le Grand, Eva. *Kundera or The Memory of Desire*, translated by Lin Burman. Waterloo, ON: Wilfrid Laurier University Press, 1999.

Le Grand, Eva. 'Voyage dans le temps de l'Europe (ou de l'esthétique romanesque de Milan Kundera)', *L'Infini* 44 (1993): 73–97.

Miletic, Tijana. *European Literary Immigration into the French Language: Readings of Gary, Kristof, Kundera and Semprun*. Amsterdam: Rodopi, 2008.

Misurella, Fred. *Understanding Milan Kundera: Public Events, Private Affairs*. Columbia: University of South Carolina Press, 1993.

O'Brien, John. *Kundera and Feminist Criticism: Dangerous Intersections*. New York: St Martin's Press, 1995.

Pichová, Hana. *Memory in Exile: Vladimir Nabokov & Milan Kundera*. Carbondale and Edwardsville: Southern Illinois University Press, 2002.

Rubeš, Jan. 'Translation as Condition and Theme in Milan Kundera's novels', in *Contexts, Subtexts and Pretexts: Literary Translation in Eastern Europe and Russia*, edited by Brian James Baer. Amsterdam and Philadelphia, PA: John Benjamins, 2011, 317–22.

Stanger, Allison. 'In Search of *The Joke*: An Open Letter to Milan Kundera', *New England Review* 18 (1997): 93–100.

Steinby, Liisa. *Kundera and Modernity*. West Lafayette, IN: Purdue University Press, 2013.

Woods, Michelle. *Translating Milan Kundera*. Clevedon: Multilingual Matters, 2006.

Secondary texts on Jorge Semprún

Bernstein, Carol L. 'Semprun, Philosophy and the Texture of Literature', in *A Critical Companion to Jorge Semprún: Buchenwald, Before and After*, edited by Ofelia Ferrán and Gina Herrmann. New York: Palgrave Macmillan, 2014, 107–24.

Brodzki, Bella. *Can These Bones Live?: Translation, Survival, and Cultural Memory*. Stanford, CA: Stanford University Press, 2007.

Céspedes, Jaime. 'Jorge Semprún, Brecht and Theater', in *A Critical Companion to Jorge Semprún: Buchenwald, Before and After*, edited by Ofelia Ferrán and Gina Herrmann. New York: Palgrave Macmillan, 2014, 251–70.

Ferrán, Ofelia. *Working Through Memory: Writing and Remembrance in Contemporary Spanish Narrative*. Cranbury, NJ: Associated University Presses, 2007.

Ferrán, Ofelia and Gina Herrmann, 'Introduction', in *A Critical Companion to Jorge Semprún: Buchenwald, Before and After*, edited by Ofelia Ferrán and Gina Herrmann. New York: Palgrave Macmillan, 2014, 1–36.

Fox Maura, Soledad. *Ida y vuelta. La vida de Jorge Semprún*. Barcelona: Debate, 2016.

Herrmann, Gina. *Written in Red: The Communist Memoir in Spain*. Urbana and Chicago: University of Illinois Press, 2010.

Kippur, Sara. 'Translating Semprun', *Michigan Quarterly Review, The Translation Issue: Within and Beyond the Metropole* 52.2 (2013). http://hdl.handle.net/2027/spo.act2080.0052.207 [Accessed 3 January 2018].

Schleiss, Myriam. *Le Bilinguisme comme atout de l'écrivain: Représentations du bilinguisme et fonctions stylistiques des marques transcodiques dans l'œuvre de Jorge Semprun*. Saarbrücken, Germany: Editions universitaires européennes, 2011.

Semilla Durán, María Angélica. *Le Masque et le masqué: Jorge Semprun et les abîmes de mémoire*. Toulouse: Presses Universitaires du Mirail, 2005.

Tidd, Ursula. 'Exile, Language, and Trauma in Recent Autobiographical Writing by Jorge Semprun', *The Modern Language Review* 103.3 (July 2008): 697–714.

Tidd, Ursula. *Jorge Semprún: Writing the European Other*. London: Legenda, 2014.

Other critical and related texts

Adorno, Theodor. 'Commitment', in *Literature in the Modern World*, edited by Dennis Walder, translated by Francis McDonagh. Oxford: Oxford University Press, 1990, 89–99.

Agamben, Giorgio. *Homo Sacer: Sovereign Power and Bare Life*, translated by Daniel Heller-Roazen. Stanford, CA: Stanford, University Press, 1995.

Agamben, Giorgio. *Means Without End: Notes on Politics*, translated by Cesare Casarino and Vincenzo Binetti. Minneapolis: University of Minnesota Press, 2000.

Agamben, Giorgio. *Remnants of Auschwitz*, translated by Daniel Heller-Roazen. New York: Zone Books, 1999.

Alighieri, Dante. *The Divine Comedy*, translated by C. H. Sisson. Oxford: Oxford University Press, 2008.

Apter, Emily. *Against World Literature: On the Politics of Untranslatability*. London: Verso, 2013.

Apter, Emily. *The Translation Zone: A New Comparative Literature*. Princeton, NJ and Oxford: Princeton University Press, 2006.

Arendt, Hannah. *The Origins of Totalitarianism*. New York: Harcourt, Brace and Co., 1951.

Bakhtin, Mikael. *The Dialogic Imagination*, edited by Michael Holquist, translated by Caryl Emerson and Michael Holquist. Austin: Texas University Press, 1984.

Barth, John. *Literature of Exhaustion: Literature of Replenishment*. Lord John Press, 1982.

Barthes, Roland. 'De l'œuvre au texte', *Revue d'esthétique* 24 (1971): 225–32.

Barthes, Roland. *Essais critiques*. Paris: Éditions de Seuil, 1964.

Barthes, Roland. 'From Work to Text', in *Image, Music, Text*, translated by Stephen Heath. London: Fontana Press, 1977, 155–64.

Barthes, Roland. 'La Mort de l'auteur', in *Le Bruissement de la langue*, Paris: Seuil, 1984 [1968], 63–9.

Barthes, Roland. *Mythologies*. Paris: Éditions du Seuil, 1957.

Bassnett, Susan. 'Prologue', in *Tradition, Translation, Trauma: The Classic and the Modern*, edited by Jan Parker and Timothy Mathews. Oxford: Oxford University Press, 2011, 1–10.

Bassnett, Susan and André Lefevere. 'General Editors' Preface', in *Translation/History/Culture: A Sourcebook*, edited by André Lefevere. London: Routledge, 1992.

Benjamin, Walter. *The Arcades Project*, translated by Howard Eiland and Kevin McLaughlin. Cambridge, MA: Harvard University Press, 1999 [1982].

Benjamin, Walter. 'The Task of the Translator', in *One-way Street and Other Writings*, translated by J. A. Underwood. London: Penguin, 2009, 29–45.

Benjamin, Walter. 'Theses on the Philosophy of History', in *Illuminations*, translated by Harry Zohn. London: Jonathan Cape, 1973, 255–66.

Bennett, Alan. *The History Boys*. Faber and Faber: London, 2004.

Berman, Antoine. *L'Épreuve de l'étranger. Culture et traduction dans l'Allemagne romantique*. Paris: Gallimard, collection 'Tel', 1984.

Berman, Antoine. *The Experience of the Foreign: Culture and Translation in Romantic Germany*, translated by S. Heyvaert. Albany: State University of New York Press, 1992.

Bermann, Sandra. 'Introduction', in *Nation, Language and the Ethics of Translation*, edited by Sandra Bermann and Michael Wood. Oxford and Princeton, NJ: Princeton University Press, 2005, 1–10.

Bermann, Sandra and Michael Wood. 'The Ethics of Translation', in *Nation, Language and the Ethics of Translation*, edited by Sandra Bermann and Michael Wood. Oxford and Princeton: Princeton University Press, 2005, 89–91.

Bhabha, Homi. *The Location of Culture*. New York: Routledge, 1994.

Blum, Léon. 'Notes d'Allemagne', in *L'Œuvre de Léon Blum, V, 1940–1945*. Paris: Éditions Albin Michel, 1955, 500–14.

Blum, Léon. *Nouvelles conversations de Goethe avec Eckermann*. Paris: Gallimard, 1937.

Borges, Jorge Luis. 'La biblioteca de Babel', in *Ficciones*. Madrid: Alianza Editorial, 1997 [1974], 89–100.

Borges, Jorge Luis. 'Pierre Menard, autor del Quijote', in *Ficciones*. Madrid: Alianza Editorial, 1997 [1974].

Büttgen, Philippe. 'Aufheben', in *Vocabulaire européen des philosophies: Dictionnaire des intraduisibles*, edited by Barbara Cassin. Paris: Éditions du Seuil, 2004, 152–6.

Büttgen, Philippe. 'Aufheben', in *Dictionary of Untranslatables: A Philosophical Lexicon*, edited and translated by Emily Apter, Jacques Lezra and Michael Wood. Princeton, NJ: Princeton University Press, 2014, 71–6.

Calvino, Italo. *If on a Winter's Night a Traveller*, translated by William Weaver. London: Vintage, 1998 [1981].

Calvino, Italo. 'Tradurre è il vero modo di leggere un testo', *Saggi 1945–1985*, vol. 2, ed. Mario Barenghi. II Milan: Mondori (1995): 1825–31.

Camus, Albert. 'Le Mythe de Sisyphe', in *Œuvres complètes d'Albert Camus*. Paris: Gallimard et Club de l'Honnête Homme, 1983.

Camus, Albert. *The Myth of Sisyphus*, translated by Justin O'Brien. London: Penguin, 1975.

Chalamov, Varlam. *Kolyma: Récits de la vie des campes*. Paris: Francios Maspero, 1980.

Chalamov, Varlam. 'Rations de campagne', in *Récits de la Kolyma*, translated by Catherine Fournier, Sophie Benech and Luba Jurgenson. Lagrasse: Verdier, 2003, 63–80.

Chalamov, Varlam. *Récits de Kolyma*, translated by Olivier Simon and Katia Kerel. Paris: Denoël, Les Lettres nouvelles, 1969.

Cheyfitz, Eric. *The Poetics of Imperialism: Translation and Colonization from The Tempest to Tarzan*. Oxford and New York: Oxford University Press, 1991.

Copeland, Rita. *The Poetics of Imperialism: Translation and Colonization from The Tempest to Tarzan*. Oxford and New York: Oxford University Press, 1991.

Corngold, Stanley. 'Comparative Literature: the Delay in Translation', in *Nation, Language and the Ethics of Translation*, edited by Sandra Bermann and Michael Wood. Oxford and Princeton, NJ: Princeton University Press, 2005, 139–45.

Cortázar, Julio. 'Las babas del Diablo', in *Las armas secretas*. Madrid: Cátedra, 1990, 123–39.

Cronin, Michael. *Translating Ireland*. Cork: Cork University Press, 1996.

D'Ablancourt, Nicolas. 'Prefaces to Tacitus and Lucian' (1640 and 1654), translated by Lawrence Venuti, in *The Translation Studies Reader*, edited by Lawrence Venuti. New York and London: Routledge, 2009 [2004], 31–7.

Daly, Peter M, Frischkopf, Hans Walter, Goldsmith-Reber, Trudis E. and Richter, Horst (eds). *Why Weimar?: Questioning the Legacy of Weimar from Goethe to 1999*. New York: Peter Lang, 2003.

Davis, Kathleen. *Deconstruction and Translation*. London and New York: Routledge, 2014 [2001].

Defoe, Daniel. *Robinson Crusoe*. Oxford: Oxford University Press, 1983 [1719].

Deleuze, Gilles. 'Causes et raisons des îles désertes', in *L'île déserte et autres textes (1953–1974),* edited by David Lapoujade. Paris: Éditions de Minuit, 2002, 11–17.

Deleuze, Gilles. 'Desert Islands', in *Desert Islands and Other Texts 1953–1974*, translated by Michael Taormina. Paris: Semiotexte, 2004, 9–14.

Deleuze, Gilles. *Différence et répétition*. Paris: Presses Universitaires de France, 1993 [1968].

Deleuze, Gilles. *Difference and Repetition*, translated by Paul Patton. London and New York: Continuum, 2001 [1994].

Deleuze, Gilles. 'Plato and the Simulacrum', translated by Rosalind Krauss, *The MIT Press* 27 (1983): 45–56.

Deleuze, Gilles. 'Platon et le simulacre', in *Logique du sens*. Les Éditions de Minuit, Paris: 1969, 292–307.

Deleuze, Gilles and Félix Guattari. *Kafka: Pour une littérature mineure*. Paris: Les Éditions de Minuit, 1975.

Deleuze, Gilles and Félix Guattari. *Kafka: Toward a Minor Literature*, translated by Dana Polan. Minneapolis: University of Minnesota Press, 1986.

Deleuze, Gilles and Félix Guattari. *Mille plateaux*. Paris: Les Éditions de Minuit, 1980.

Deleuze, Gilles and Félix Guattari. *A Thousand Plateaus: Capitalism and Schizophrenia*, translated by Brian Massumi. London and New York: Continuum, 2004 [1987].

Deleuze, Gilles and Claire Parnet. *Dialogues*. Paris: Flammarion, 1977.

Deleuze, Gilles and Claire Parnet. *Dialogues II*, translated by Hugh Tomlinson and Barbara Habberjam. New York: Columbia University Press, 2007 [1987].

Derrida, Jacques. *L'Autre cap, suivi de la démocratie ajournée.* Paris: Les Éditions de minuit, 1991.

Derrida, Jacques. *The Ear of the Other: Otobiography, Transference, Translation*, edited by Christie V. McDonald, translated by Peggy Kamuf. New York: Schocken Books, 1985.

Derrida, Jacques. *L'Écriture et la différence*. Paris, Seuil, 1967.

Derrida, Jacques. *Marges de la philosophie*. Paris: Les Éditions de Minuit, 1972.

Derrida, Jacques. *Margins of Philosophy*, translated by Alan Bass. Chicago: University of Chicago Press, 1982.

Derrida, Jacques. *Le Monolinguisme de l'autre ou la prothèse de l'origine*. Paris: Éditions Galilée, 1996.

Derrida, Jacques. *Monolingualism of the Other, or the Prosthesis of Origin*, translated by Patrick Mensah. Stanford, CA: Stanford University Press, 1998.

Derrida, Jacques. *L'oreille de l'autre: otobiographies, transferts, traductions*, edited by Claude Lévesque and Christie V. McDonald. Montréal: VLB Éditeur, 1982.

Derrida, Jacques. *The Other Heading: Reflections on Today's Europe*. Bloomington and Indianapolis: Indiana University Press, 1992.

Derrida, Jacques. 'La Pharmacie de Platon', in *La Dissémination*. Paris: Seuil, 1972, 77–214.

Derrida, Jacques. 'Plato's Pharmacy', in *Dissemination*, translated by Barbara Johnson. London: The Athlone Press, 1981, 61–171.

Derrida, Jacques. 'Qu'est-ce qu'une traduction "relevante"?', in *Quinzièmes assises de la traduction littéraire: Arles 1998*. Arles: Actes Sud, 1999, 21–48.

Derrida, Jacques. *Spectres de Marx: L'État de la dette, le travail du deuil, et la nouvelle Internationale*. Paris: Éditions Galilée, 1993.

Derrida, Jacques. 'Des Tours de Babel', in *Difference in Translation*, edited by Joseph F. Graham. Ithaca, NY and London: Cornell University Press, 1985, 209–48.

Derrida, Jacques. 'Des Tours de Babel', translated by Joseph F. Graham, in *Difference in Translation*, edited by Joseph F. Graham. Ithaca, NY and London: Cornell University Press, 1985, 165–207.

Derrida, Jacques. 'What is a "Relevant" Translation?', translated by Lawrence Venuti, *Critical Inquiry* 27.2 (2001): 174–200.

Derrida, Jacques. *Writing and Difference*, translated by Alan Bass. London: Routledge Classics, 2001 [1978].

De Swaan, Abram. *Words of the World: The Global Language System*. Cambridge: Polity Press, 2002.

Eliot, T. S. *The Sacred Wood: Essays On Poetry and Criticism*. London: Methuen & Company Ltd, 1921.

Even-Zohar, Itamar. 'Interference in Dependent Literary Polysytems', *Poetics Today* 11.1 (1990): 121–30.

Fawcett, Peter. 'Ideology and Translation', in *Routledge Encyclopedia of Translation Studies*, edited by Mona Baker. London: Routledge, 2006, 106–11.

Fitzgerald, F. Scott. *The Crack-up*. New York: New Directions, 1945.

Flynn, Thomas R. and Dalia Judovitz. 'Introduction', in *Dialectic and Narrative*, edited by Thomas R. Flynn and Dalia Judovitz. Albany State University of New York Press, 1993.

Frost, Robert. *The Letters of Robert Frost to Louis Untermeyer*. London: Jonathan Cape, 1964.

Gachechiladze, Givi R. 'Realism and Dialectics in the Art of Translation', *Babel* 13.2 (1967): 87–91.

Genette, Gérard. *Paratexts: Thresholds of Interpretation*, translated by Jane E. Lewin. Cambridge: Cambridge University Press, 1997.

Genette, Gérard. *Seuils*. Paris: Éditions du Seuil, 1987.

Giesen, Bernhard and Klaus Eder. 'European Citizenship: An Avenue for the Social Integration of Europe', in *European Citizenship between National Legacies and Postnational Projects*, edited by Klaus Eder and Bernhard Giesen. Oxford: Oxford University Press, 2001, 1–13.

Giraudoux, Jean. *Suzanne et le Pacifique*. Paris: Livre de Poche, 1997 [1921].

Godard, Barbara. 'Deleuze and Translation', *Parallax* 6.1 (2000): 56–81.

Godard, Barbara. 'L'Éthique du traduire: Antoine Berman et le «virage éthique» en traduction', *TTR: traduction, terminologie, rédaction*, 14.2 (2001): 49–82.

Goodchild, Philip. *Deleuze and Guattari: An Introduction to the Politics of Desire*. London: SAGE, 1996.

Grutman, Rainier. 'Self-translation', in *The Routledge Encyclopedia of Translation Studies*, edited by Mona Baker and Gabriela Saldanha. London: Routledge, 2009, 257–60.

Hegel, G. W. Friedrich. *Science de la logique*, 1, translated by Pierre-Jean Labarrière and Gwendoline Jarczyk. Paris: Aubier, 1972 [1812].

Heidegger, Martin. *Hölderlin's Hymn 'The Ister'*, translated by William McNeill and Julia Davis. Bloomington and Indianapolis: Indiana University Press, 1996 [1984].

Hokenson, Jan Walsh and Marcella Munson. *The Bilingual Text: History and Theory of Literary Self-Translation*. London: Routledge, 2014.

Hooper, John. *The New Spaniards*. Harmondsworth: Penguin, 1995.

Hooper, Kirsty. *Writing Galicia Into the World: New Cartographies, New Poetics*. Liverpool: Liverpool University Press, 2011.

Horkheimer, Max and Theodor W. Adorno. *Dialectic of Enlightenment: Philosophical Fragments*, edited by Gunzelin Schmid Noerr, translated by Edmund Jephcott. Stanford, CA: Stanford University Press, 2002 [1969].

Jakobson, Roman. 'On Linguistic Aspects of Translation', in *The Translation Studies Reader*, edited by Lawrence Venuti. New York and London: Routledge, 2009 [2004], 138–43.

Jerome, 'Letter to Pammachius', translated by Kathleen Davis, in *The Translation Studies Reader*, edited by Lawrence Venuti. London: Routledge, 2002, 21–30.

Kafka, Franz. *The Metamorphosis*, translated by David Wyllie. Classix Press, 2009.

Kant, Immanuel. *Observations on the Feeling of the Beautiful and Sublime*, translated by John T. Goldthwait. Oakland: University of California Press, 2004.

Kant, Immanuel. *Religion within the Limits of Reason Alone*, translated by Theodore M. Greene and Hoyt H. Hudson. New York: Harper and Row, 2008 [1960].

Kattago, Siobhan. *Ambiguous Memory: The Nazi Past and German National Identity*. Westport, CT: Praeger, 2001.

Kearney, Richard. 'Introduction: Ricoeur's Philosophy of Translation', in *On Translation*, translated by Eileen Brennan. London and New York: Routledge, 2006, vii–xx.

Kearney, Richard. 'Paul Ricœur and the Hermeneutics of Translation', *Research in Phenomenology* 37 (2007): 147–59.

Lejeune, Philippe. *Le Pacte autobiographique*. Paris: Seuil, 1975.

LeVan, Michael. 'Aesthetics of Encounter: Variations on Translation in Deleuze', *International Journal of Translation* 19.2 (2007): 51–66.

Levinas, Emmanuel. *Totalité et infini: essai sur l'extériorité*. The Hague, Boston, London: Martinus Nijhoff Publishers, 1980 [1961].

Lewis, Philip E. 'The Measure of Translation Effects', in *Difference in Translation*, edited by Joseph F. Graham. Ithaca, NY and London: Cornell University Press, 1985, 31–62.

Lezra, Jacques. '*Nationum Origo*', in *Nation, Language and the Ethics of Translation*, edited by Sandra Bermann and Michael Wood. Oxford and Princeton, NJ: Princeton University Press, 2005, 203–28.

Malraux, André. *Le Miroir des limbes II: La corde et les souris*. Paris: Gallimard, 1976.

Marks, John. 'Franz Kafka', in *The Deleuze Dictionary*, edited by Adrian Parr, revised edition. Edinburgh: Edinburgh University Press, 2010, 137–9.

Marx, Karl. 'Afterword to the Second German Edition', in *Capital*, vol. 1, edited by Friedrich Engels, translated by Samuel Moore and Edward Aveling, 1873; London: S. Sonnenschein, Lowery & Co., 1887, included in *Marx–Engels Reader*, edited by Robert C. Tucker. New York: W.W. Norton & Company, Inc., 1978 [1972], 299–302.

Mathews, Harry. 'The Dialect of the Tribe', in *Country Cooking and Other Stories*. Providence, RI: Burning Deck, 1980.

Mathews, Timothy. *Alberto Giacometti: The Art of Relation*. London: I. B. Tauris, 2013.

Mathews, Timothy. 'Conclusion: Can Anyone Look in Both Directions at Once?', in *Translation, Tradition, Trauma: The Classic and the Modern*, edited by Jan Parker and Timothy Mathews. Oxford: Oxford University Press, 2011, 333–46.

Mathews, Timothy. 'Reading the Invisible with Cees Nooteboom, Walter Benjamin and Alberto Giacometti', in *Translation, Tradition, Trauma: The Classic and the Modern*, edited by Jan Parker and Timothy Mathews. Oxford: Oxford University Press, 2011, 317–32.

Michaels, Anne. *Fugitive Pieces*. London: Bloomsbury, 1998 [1996].

Murdoch, Iris. *Under the Net*. London: Penguin, 1960 [1954].

Niven, William John. *The Buchenwald Child: Truth, Fiction and Propaganda*. New York: Camden House, 2007.

Orwell, George. *1984*. London: Penguin, 2009 [1949].

Parr, Adrian. 'Deterritorialisation/Reterritorialisation', in *The Deleuze Dictionary*, edited by Adrian Parr, revised edition. Edinburgh: Edinburgh University Press, 2010, 69–72.

Parr, Adrian. 'Repetition', in *The Deleuze Dictionary*, edited by Adrian Parr, revised edition. Edinburgh: Edinburgh University Press, 2010, 225–6.

Pilar Totoricaguena, Gloria. *Basque Diaspora: Migration and Transnational Identity*. Reno: University of Nevada Press, 2005.

Plato. 'Phaedrus', in *The Dialogues of Plato*, translated by B. Jowett. Oxford: Oxford University Press, 1953, 107–89.

Plato. *The Republic*, translated by Desmond Lee. Harmondsworth: Penguin, 1974.

Pym, Anthony. *On Translator Ethics: Principles for Mediation between Cultures*, translated by Heike Walker. John Benjamins: Amsterdam, 2012, 21–2. This English text is a version of Anthony Pym, *Pour une éthique du traducteur*. Arras: Artois Presses Université 1997.

Pym, Anthony. 'Schleiermacher and the Problem of Blendlinge', *Translation and Literature* 4.1 (1995): 5–30.

Randall, Marilyn. *Pragmatic Plagiarism: Authorship, Profit, and Power*. Toronto: University of Toronto Press, 2001.

Reinhard, Kenneth. 'Kant with Sade, Lacan with Levinas', *Modern Language Notes* 110.4 (1995): 785–808.

Ricœur, Paul. *On Translation*, translated by Eileen Brennan. London: Routledge, 2006.

Ricœur, Paul. *Sur la traduction*. Paris: Bayard, 2004.

Rimbaud, Arthur. *Une saison en enfer*. Brussels: Alliance Typographique, 1873.

Rosenbaum, Peter. 'The Buchenwald Memorial and its *Différend*', in *Why Weimar?: Questioning the Legacy of Weimar from Goethe to

1999, edited by Peter M. Daly , Hans Walter Frischkopf, Trudis E. Goldsmith-Reber and Horst Richter. New York: Peter Lang, 2003, 223–36.

Said, Edward. *Orientalism*. New York: Pantheon, 1978.

Sartre, Jean-Paul. *Situations II: Qu'est-ce que la littérature*. Paris: Gallimard, 1948.

Schleiermacher, Friedrich. 'On the Different Methods of Translating' (1813), translated by Susan Bernofksy, in *The Translation Studies Reader*, edited by Lawrence Venuti. London: Routledge, 2002, 43–63.

Spivak, Gayatri Chakravorty. 'The Politics of Translation', in *The Translation Studies Reader*, edited by Lawrence Venuti. London: Routledge, 2002, 369–88.

Stagoll, Cliff. 'Becoming', in *The Deleuze Dictionary*, edited by Adrian Parr. Edinburgh: Edinburgh University Press, 2010, 25–7.

Stalin, Joseph. *Dialectical and Historical Materialism*. Moscow: Foreign Languages Publishing House, 1949.

Steiner, George. *After Babel*. Oxford: Oxford University Press, 1998.

Steiner, George. *ERRATA: An Examined Life*. New Haven, CT: Yale University Press 1999 [1997].

Still, Judith and Michael Worton. *Intertextuality: Theories and Practices*. Manchester: Manchester University Press, 1991.

Thomas, Dylan. *Fern Hill: A Poem*. Markham, ON: Red Deer College Press, 1997.

Toscano, Alberto. 'Capture', in *The Deleuze Dictionary*, edited by Adrian Parr. Edinburgh: Edinburgh University Press, 2010, 44–6.

Toury, Gideon. *Descriptive Translation Studies and Beyond*. Amsterdam and Philadelphia, PA: John Benjamins, 1995.

Turner, Victor W. *The Ritual Process: Structure and Anti-Structure*. Harmondsworth: Penguin, 1969.

Uniacke, Florence. 'Doing it the French Way', *The Spectator* 21 February 2013. http://blogs.spectator.co.uk/books/2013/02/doing-it-the-french-way/[Accessed 2 January 2018].

van Alphen, E. 'Symptoms of Discursivity: Experience, Memory, and Trauma', in *Acts of Memory: Cultural Recall in the Present*, edited by Mieke Bal, Jonathan Crewe and Leo Spitzer. Hanover, NH: University Press of New England, 1999, 24–38

Venn, Couze. *The Postcolonial Challenge: Towards Alternative Worlds*. London, Thousand Oaks and New Delhi: Sage Publications, 2006.

Venuti, Lawrence. 'Introduction', in *Rethinking Translation: Discourse, Subjectivity, Ideology*, edited by Lawrence Venuti. London: Routledge, 1992, 3–17.

Venuti, Lawrence. *The Scandals of Translation: Towards an Ethics of Difference*. London: Routledge, 2002 [1998].

Venuti, Lawrence. 'Translation, Community, Utopia', in *The Translation Studies Reader*, edited by Lawrence Venuti. London: Routledge, 2002, 482–502.

Venuti, Lawrence. *The Translator's Invisibility. A History of Translation*. London: Routledge, 2008.

Villiers de l'Isle-Adam, Auguste. *La Torture par espérance*. Bayonne: les Germes, 1994.

Whitfield, Teresa. *Endgame for ETA: Elusive Peace in the Basque Country*. London: Hurst, 2014.

Wiesel, Elie. 'Pourquoi j'écris', in *Paroles d'étranger*. Paris: Seuil, 1982, 7–14.

Wiesel, Elie. 'Why I Write', translated by Rosette C. Lamont, in *Confronting the Holocaust: The Impact of Elie Wiesel*, edited by Alvin H. Rosenfeld and Irving Greenberg. Bloomington and London: Indiana University Press, 1978, 200–6.

Williams, Stewart. 'Virtually Impossible: Deleuze and Derrida on the Political Problem of Islands and Island Studies', *Island Studies Journal* 7.2 (2012): 215–34.

Wilson, W. Daniel. 'Culture and the Authoritarian State in Classical Weimar', in *Why Weimar?: Questioning the Legacy of Weimar from Goethe to 1999*, edited by Peter M. Daly , Hans Walter Frischkopf, Trudis E. Goldsmith-Reber and Horst Richter. New York: Peter Lang, 2003, 3–19.

Woodward, Keith and John Paul Jones III. 'On the Border with Deleuze and Guattari', in *B/ordering Space*, edited by Henk van Houtum, Olivier Kramsch and Wolfgang Zierhofer. Aldershot: Ashgate, 2005, 235–48.

Other sources

'Equivalence', in *Oxford Dictionaries*. http://www.oxforddictionaries.com/definition/english/equivalence [Accessed 30 December 2017].

Index

www.ingramcontent.com/pod-product-compliance
Lightning Source LLC
LaVergne TN
LVHW050023250826
846302LV00004B/19